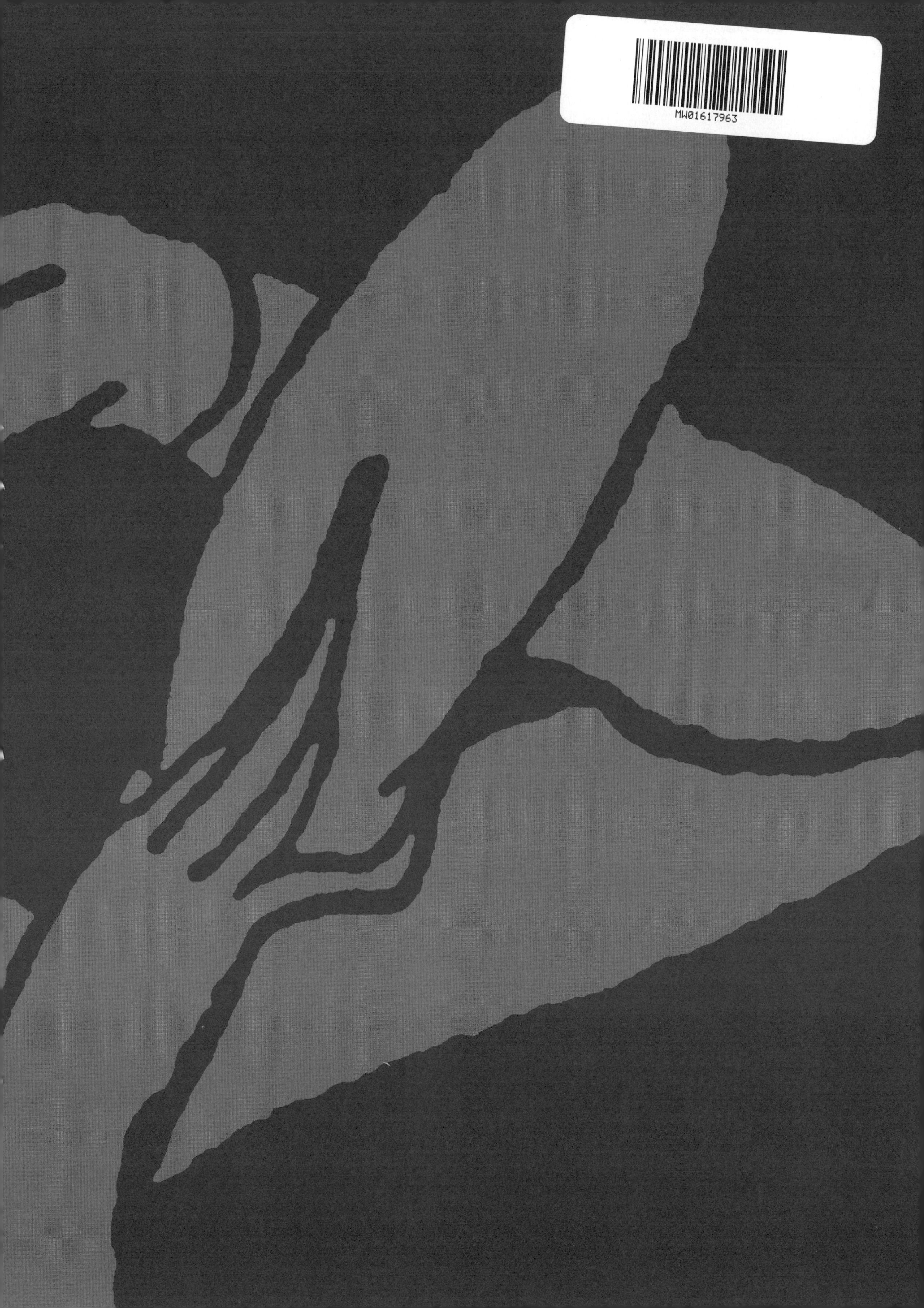

MW01617963

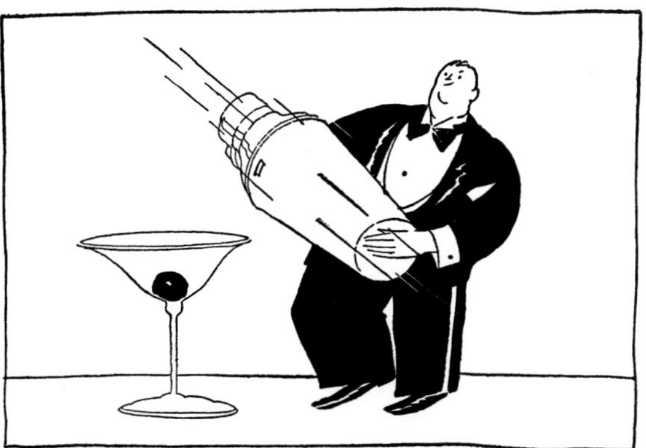

Preparing for the Journey.

RUSSELL PATTERSON

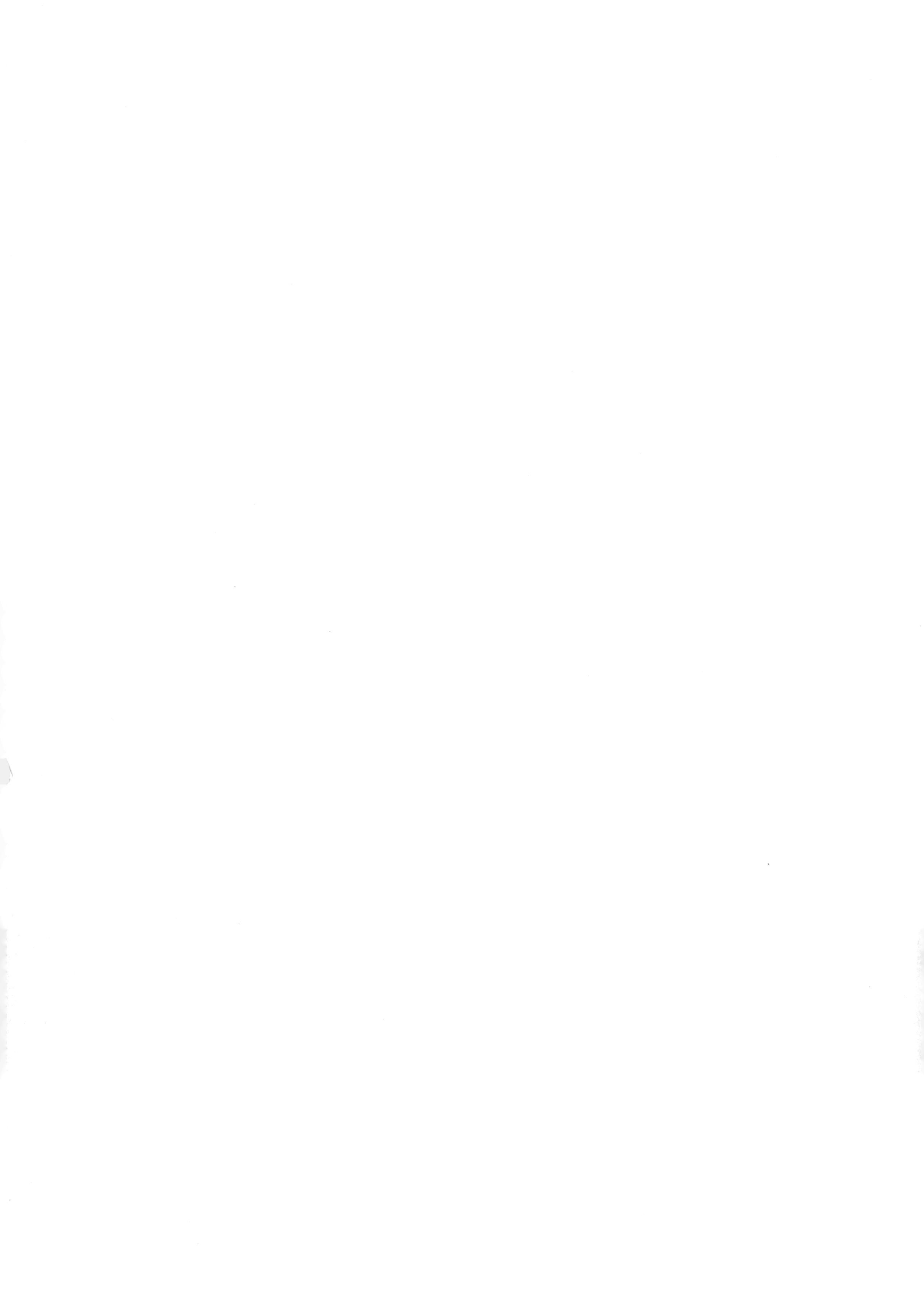

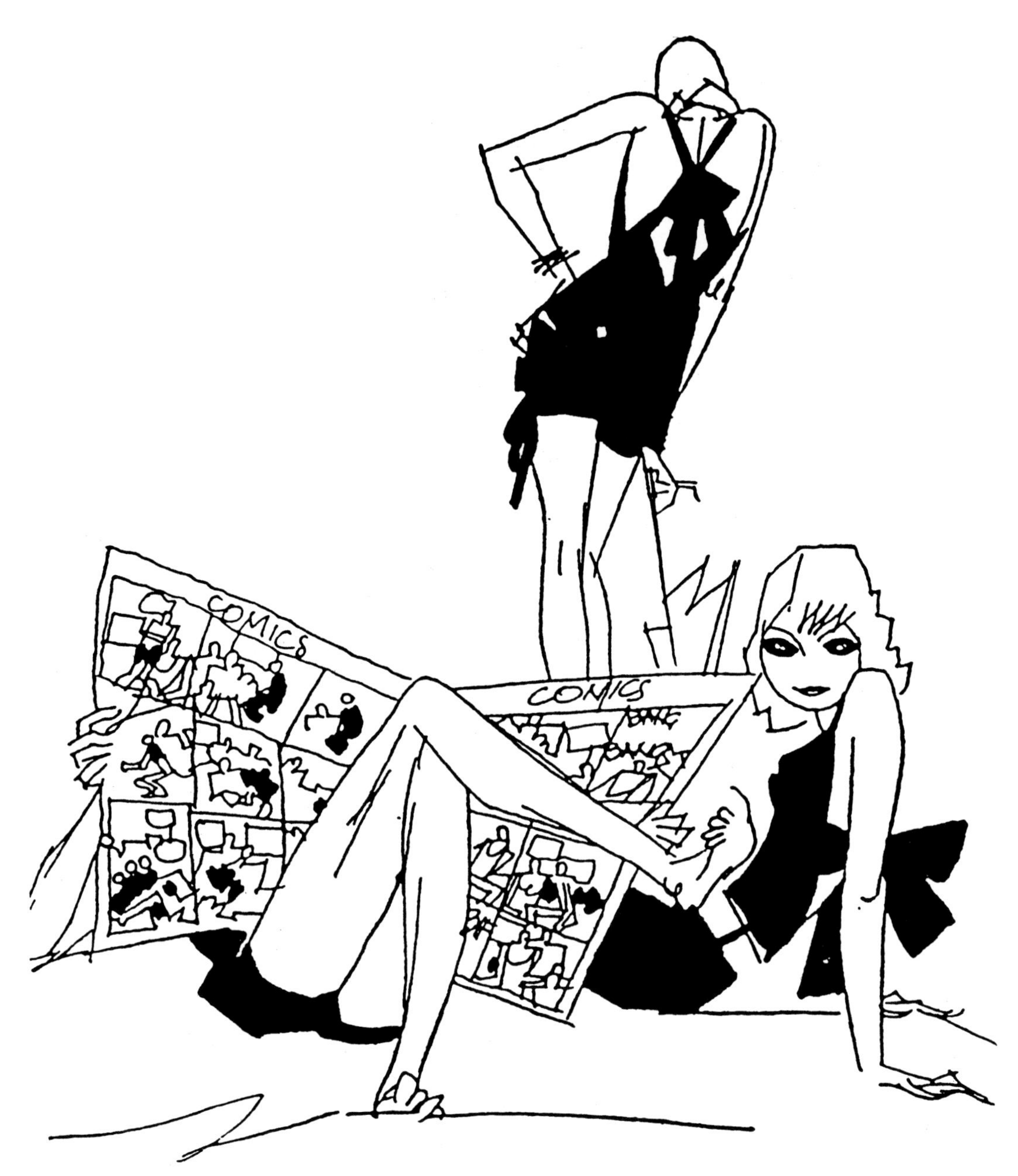

EDITED BY SHANE GLINES AND ALEX CHUN

TOP HATS AND FLAPPERS

THE ART OF RUSSELL PATTERSON

ART DIRECTOR: JACOB COVEY
COPY EDITOR: GREG SADOWSKI
PROMOTION: ERIC REYNOLDS
PRODUCTION ASSISTANT: ANGELA STORK
PUBLISHED BY GARY GROTH & KIM THOMPSON

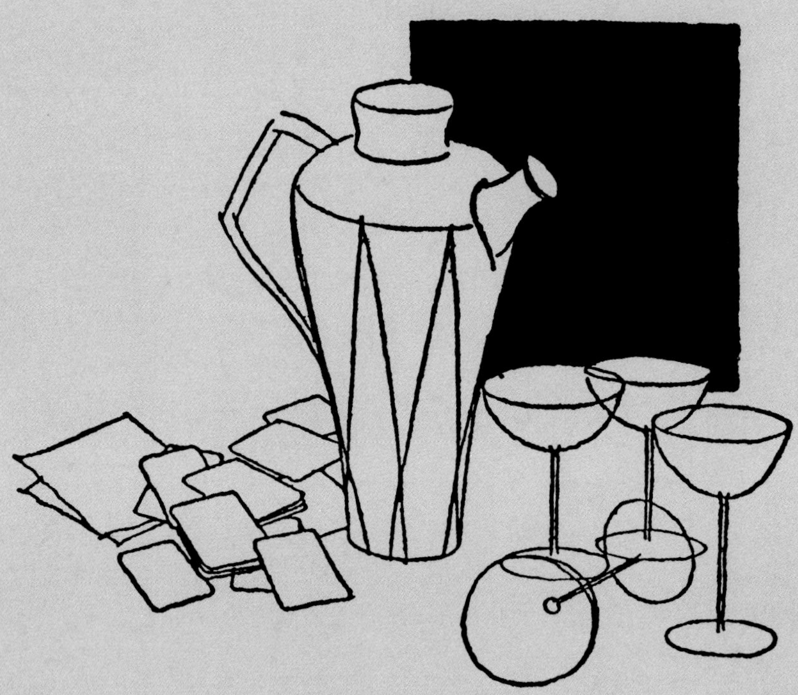

ACKNOWLEDGEMENTS: A special thanks goes out to Howard Chaykin, Stuart Ng of Stuart Ng Books, Joakim Gunnarsson and Glen Murakami, who generously donated their expertise and research material; Gary Groth and Kim Thompson for their continued support; Jacob Covey, Greg Sadowski and the rest of the Fantagraphics crew.

TOP HATS & FLAPPERS: THE ART OF RUSSELL PATTERSON is copyright © 2006 Fantagraphics Books. Introduction copyright © 2006 Armando Mendez. All rights reserved. Permission to quote or reproduce material for reviews must be obtained from the publisher.

To receive our free catalogue of fine comics and books, please dial 1-800-657-1100 or visit our website at Fantagraphics.com. First Fantagraphics Books edition: June, 2006. ISBN 1-56097-737-X. Printed in China.

Distributed in the U.S. by W.W. Norton and Company, Inc. (1-212-354-5500). Distributed in Canada by Raincoast Books (1-800-663-5714). Distributed in the UK by Turnaround Distribution (1-208-829-3009).
000

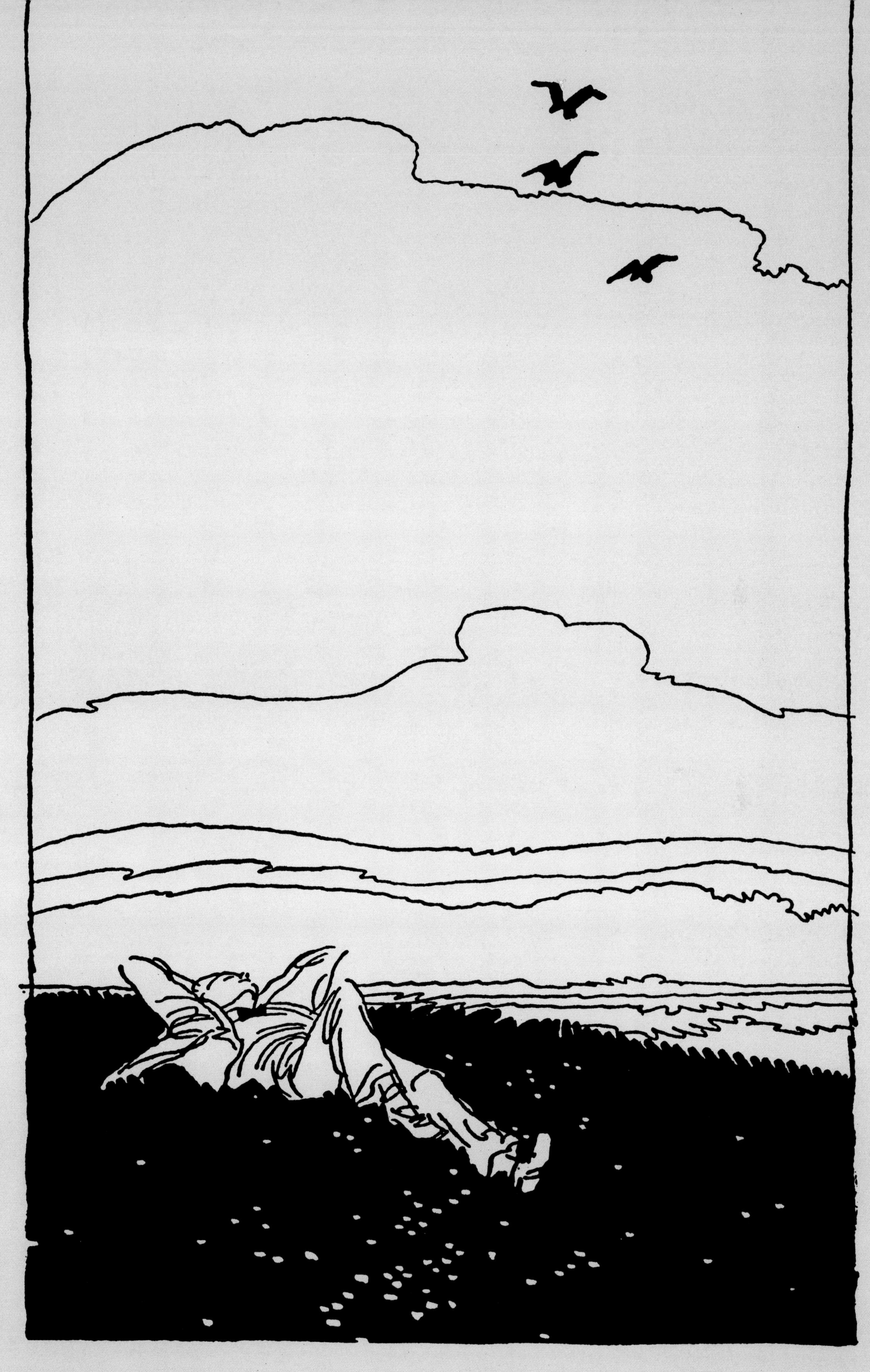

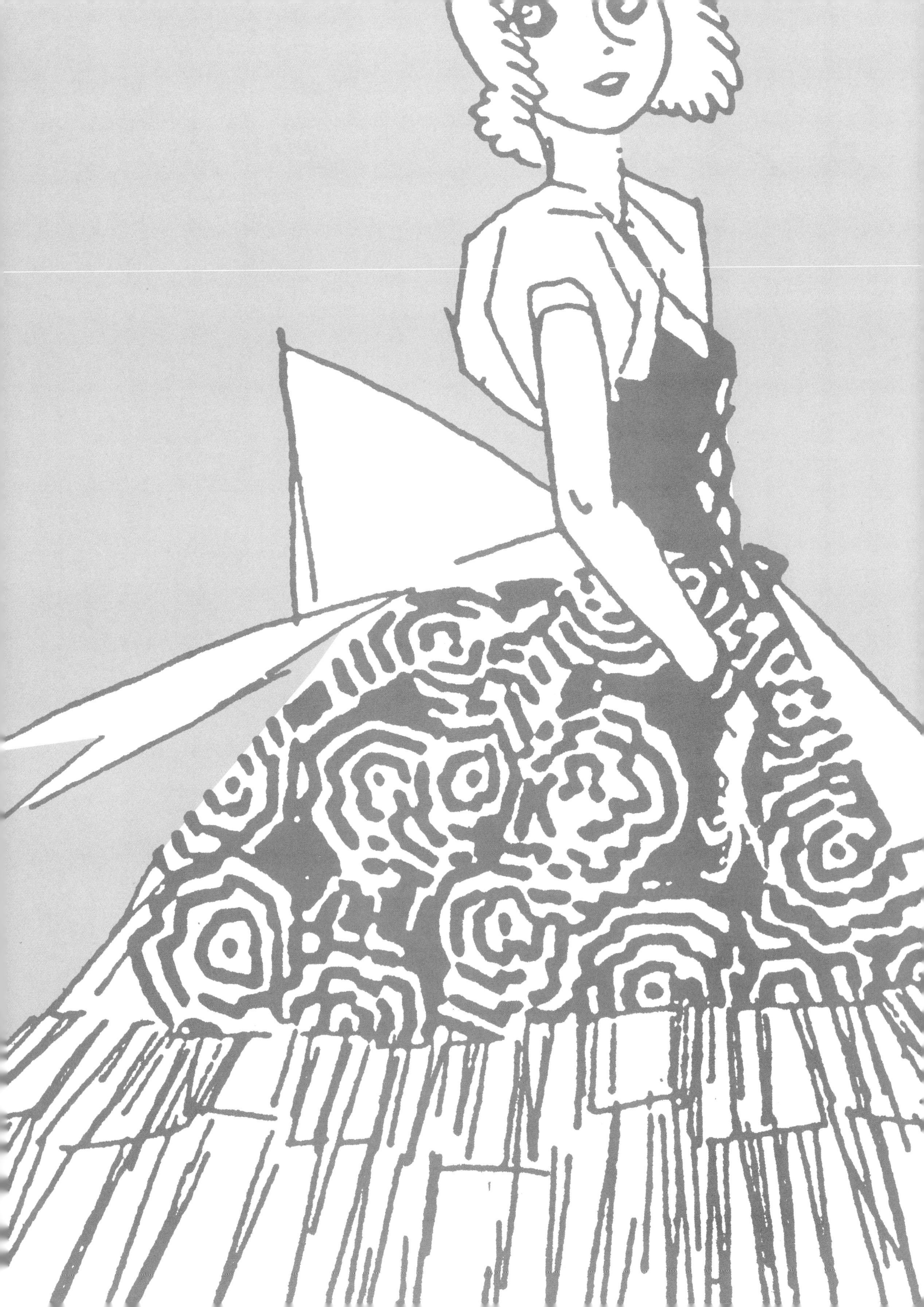

NYMPH ERRANT

THE LIFE AND LEGACY OF RUSSELL PATTERSON

by

ARMANDO MENDEZ

It makes for a great story. Perhaps it's the great American story.

A young talented artist stands at a crossroads. His name is Russell Patterson, and at the age of 30, he's wondering once again: when will his big break happen?

The road so far, a trek from Omaha through Montreal and then to Chicago, has been difficult. Defying his family's wish to pursue a traditional career, he's been through a lot to become an artist, including an aborted college education, short stints as an undistinguished newspaper cartoonist and World War I service (where he learned to fly but never left his surrogate country). In 1923 Chicago, his current residence, he's found anonymous and unsatisfying work rendering furniture and interiors for department-store catalogs.

Then, like so many other artists of his generation, he travels to Paris and for a time realizes his dream: attending life-drawing classes, painting, having long, abstract, passionate discussions with other like-minded artists about art and life. It didn't matter that his money soon ran out, forcing him to sleep on cold hard floors, or that it took the considerable help of his salesman brother to pay for his return passage.

Back to mobster-controlled prohibition Chicago and a cold splash of reality. Though he returns from Paris with 40 paintings and the experience of a lifetime, he also comes back to a large debt, and even worse, back to hacking out catalog interiors and still-lifes, another faceless drone trapped in the web of advertising.

In the spring of 1924, he takes another shot at artistic fulfillment. He travels West and arranges an exhibition in hopes of selling old canvasses and creating new ones. It is a disaster. He finds the Southwestern vistas too magnificent for his skill and gallery patrons mostly indifferent to his paintings. On the trip back to Chicago (a "horror" he later recalled) behind the wheel of a jalopy that spends more time in the shop than on the road, he has plenty of time to think. On one side of Paradise he sees the nationally known illustrators Charles Dana Gibson, James Montgomery Flagg, and J.C. Leyendecker, all of whom Patterson idolized. On the other side he sees the young irreverent cartoonists John Held, Jr.

and Ralph Barton, rapidly gaining popularity in the emerging humor magazines with their depictions of the white-hot girls of the roaring '20s.

Patterson's mind wanders back to Paris and to the life-drawing classes where he practiced nudes. He remembers one girl in particular, a dark brunette with a taste for ribbons and a shy yet teasing manner as she undressed and dressed for each session.

Fast-forward to Christmas Day 1925, just over a year removed from his humbling trip West. He arrives in New York City as a regular cover artist, along with Held and Nell Brinkley, for *College Humor* and *Judge*. Within months, he's making New York-sized money, $2,000 dollars a week, and the society columns are abuzz with the new "Fair-Haired Boy of the Arts." O. O. McIntyre, in the morning *American Home Journal*, proclaims that Patterson's "girl paintings have changed the picture of the country," and that he "has a studio on top of the Heckschler Building, rides to and from there in a chauffeur-driven Rolls Royce and when he's tired, he rests on his black sixty-five foot schooner."

And when the stock market crashed in October of 1929, Patterson says he lost "only" $60,000 and "had a hell of a time spending all the rest."

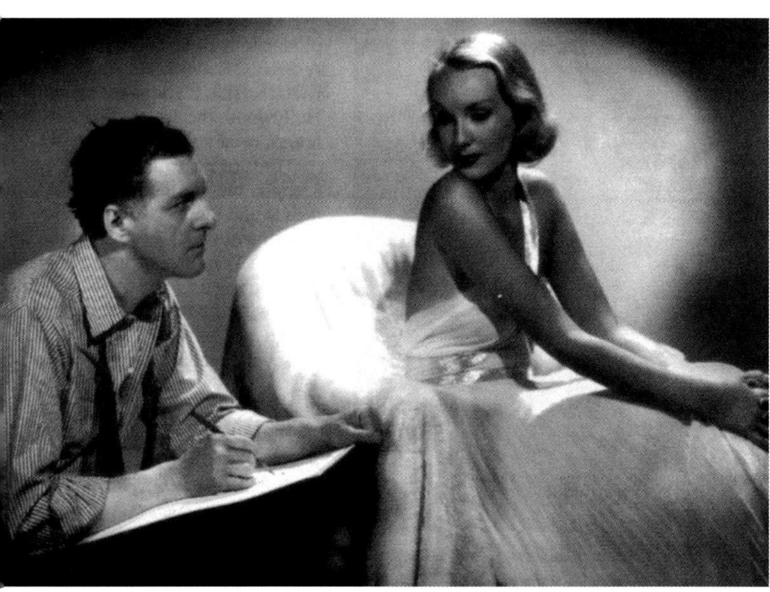

Patterson was often photographed in the 1920s and 1930s sketching models, actresses and beauty contestants. A publicity still from 1937.

Why Russell Patterson? What made him stand apart?

Imagine America in the 1920s, the last stand of the Golden Age of Illustration and a time of tremendous social change. While traditional illustrators portrayed the times with a polished and fully rendered romanticism, the cartoonists' energetic and combustible pen-and-ink strokes more fittingly captured the era's verve and excitement, whether in a downtown speakeasy or uptown at The Stork Club, hot jazz bands or windy jump seats, slinky gowns set against top hats and tails.

As documented by the usual histories, Patterson wasn't the first, the best known, the highest paid or the most closely identified artist of the period. He is, however, the artist with the longest legacy, which continues to reach out to next month's *Playboy* magazine. Unlike most of his contemporaries, Patterson didn't vanish after the crash of the Great Depression. Instead, he found new ways to adapt his style for a public hungry for sexy, light entertainment—in newspaper strips and magazine covers, Hollywood and Broadway posters, costumes and set designs, even amusement parks and WAC uniforms—maintaining his foothold all the way to the Cold War and beyond.

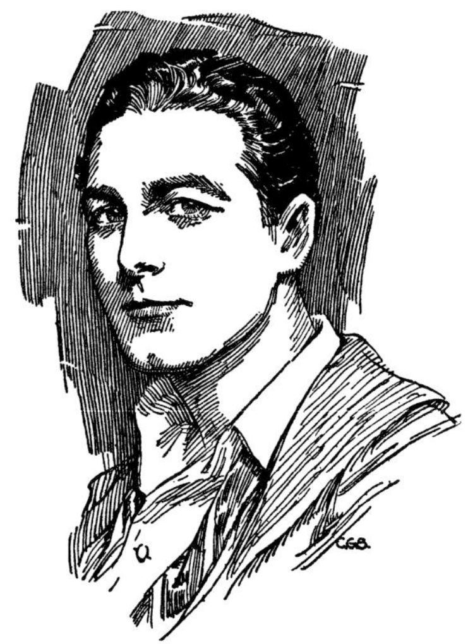

Patterson owed it all to that long trip east back to Chicago. Somewhere along that bumpy road he decided to do his own version of the modern woman—simultaneously brazen and innocent—a concept he first conceived during the cold days between November and May, warming himself in a Latin Quarter garret.

WHAT COLLEGE DID TO ME

Patterson died in the spring of 1977, just as the Delaware Art Museum and its director Rowland Eliza began mounting the artist's first major retrospective. "An Exhibition of the Art of Russell Patterson" ran for just a month in the summer of 1977, but it became the de facto celebration of his life and career.

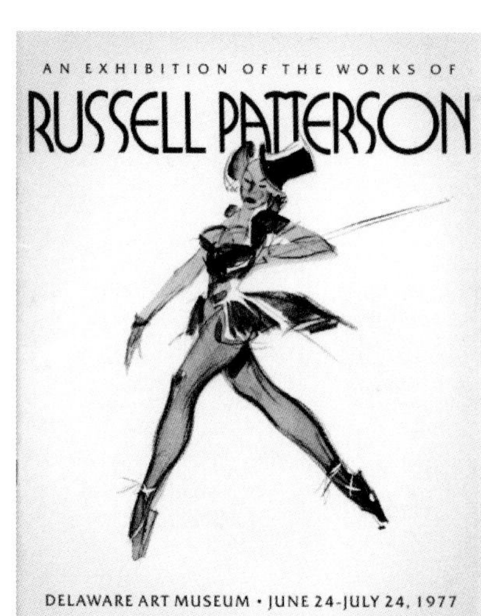

Eliza's biography on Patterson for the exhibition booklet, along with the short pieces that Patterson wrote for the National Cartoonists Society in preparation of his planned memoirs, provide much of the current biographical data on Patterson and offer a glimpse into the life of an artist who, according to legendary cartoonist Milton Caniff, held a "king-pin place among illustrators."

Russell Patterson was born in Omaha, Nebraska, on December 26, 1893, the second son of an austere railroad lawyer who moved his family along train routes

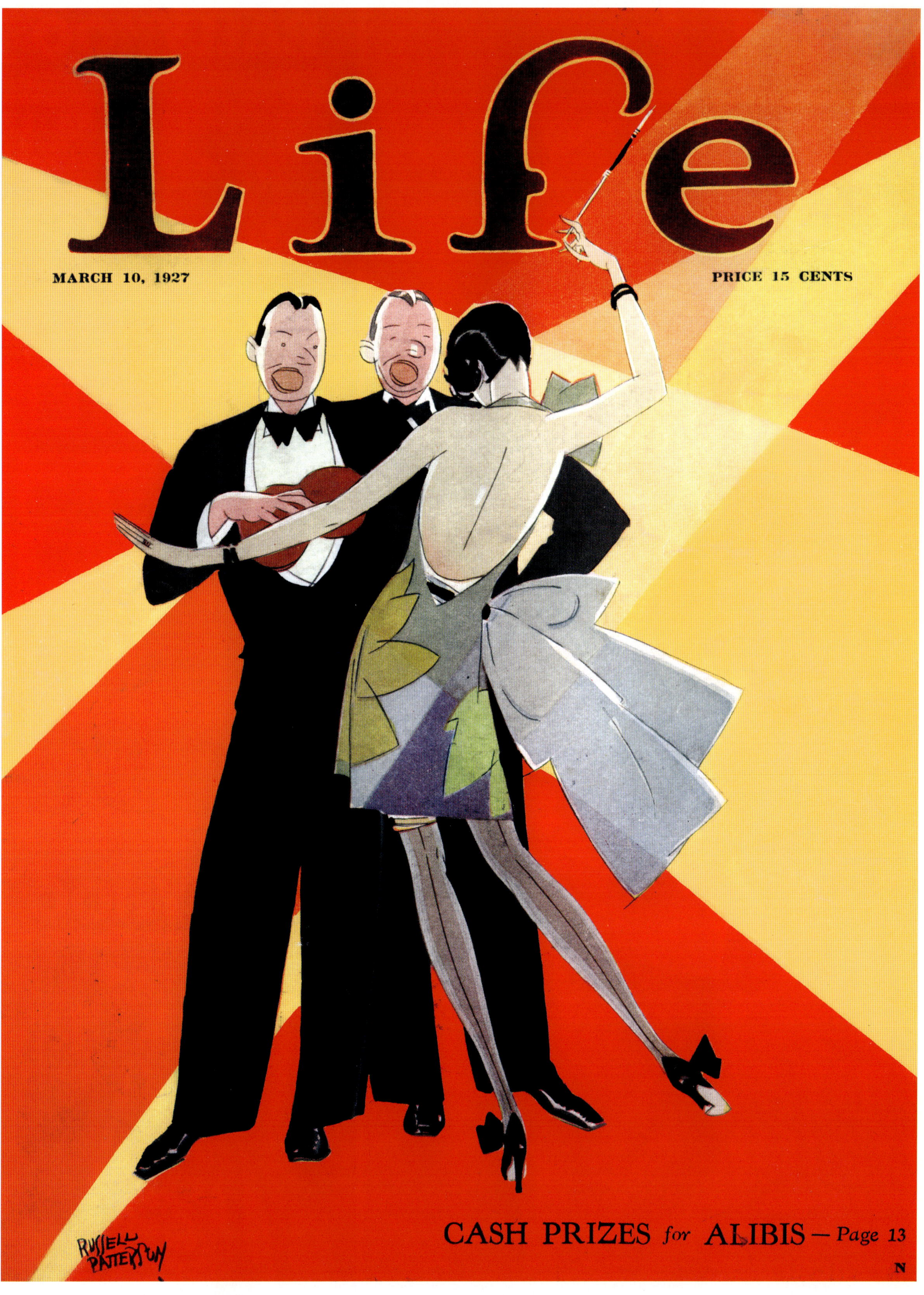
Life
MARCH 10, 1927
PRICE 15 CENTS
CASH PRIZES for ALIBIS — Page 13
N
RUSSELL PATTERSON

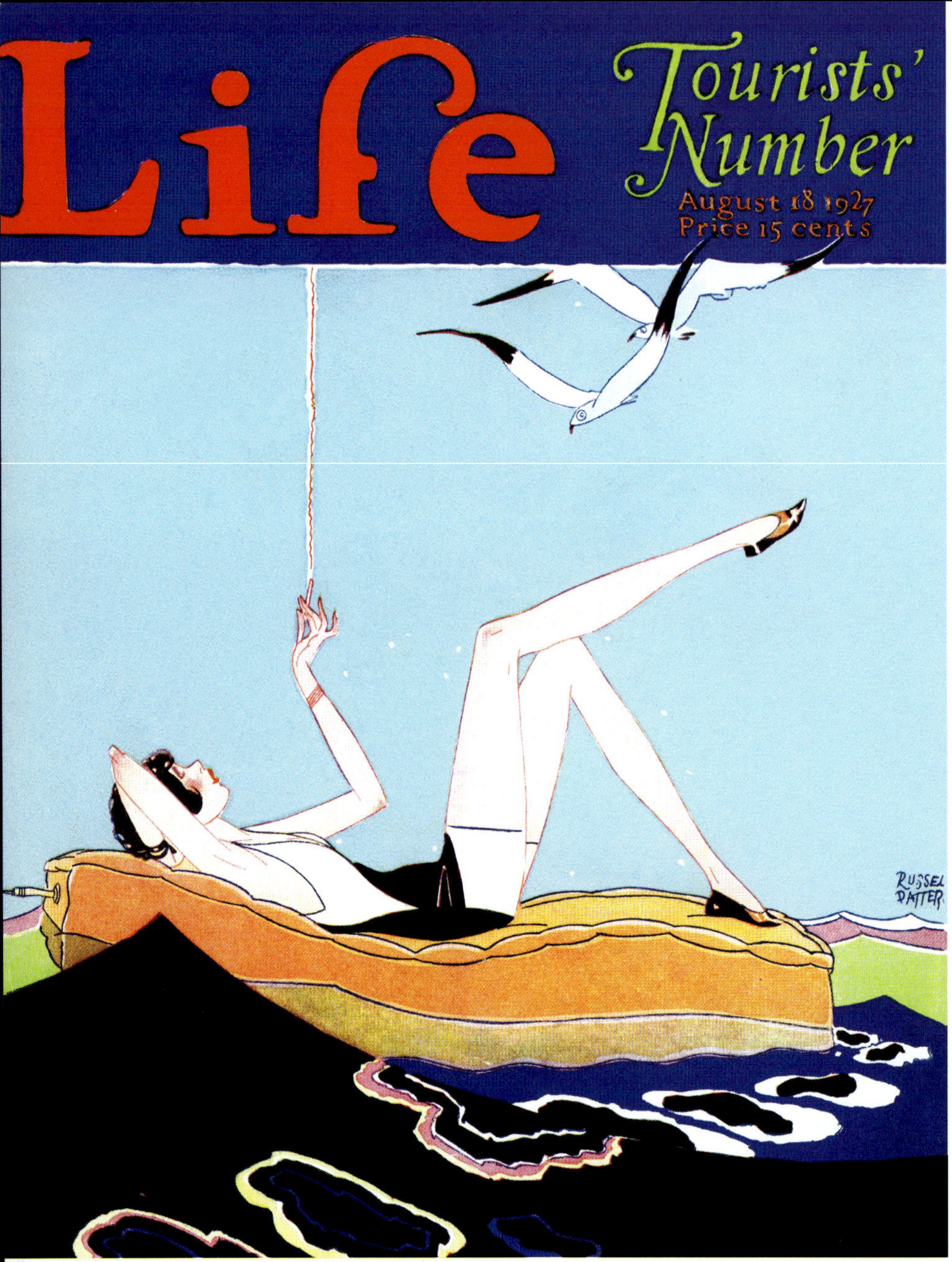

Life
Tourists' Number
August 18 1927
Price 15 cents
RUSSEL PATTER

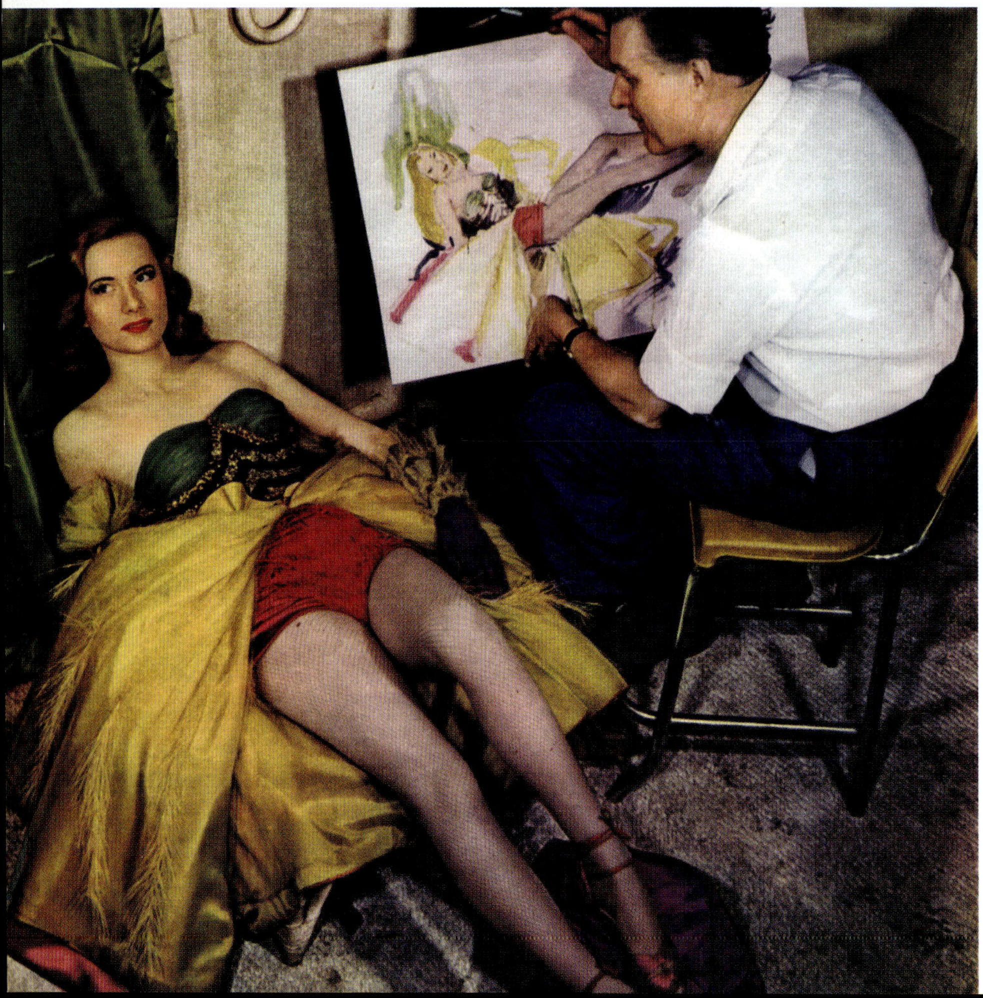

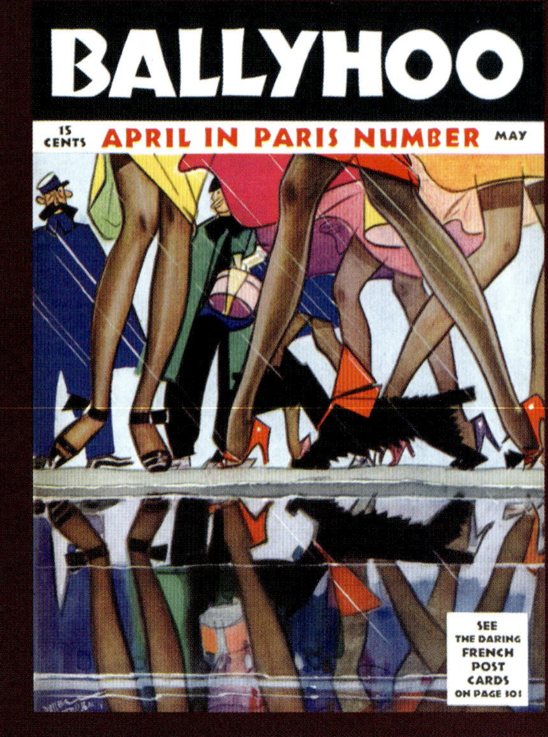

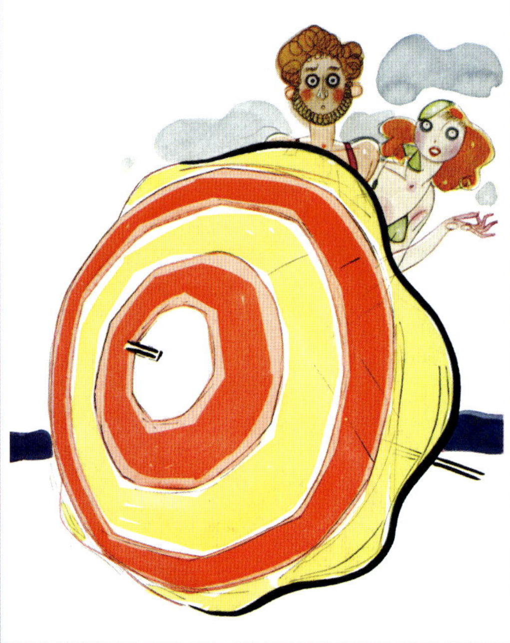

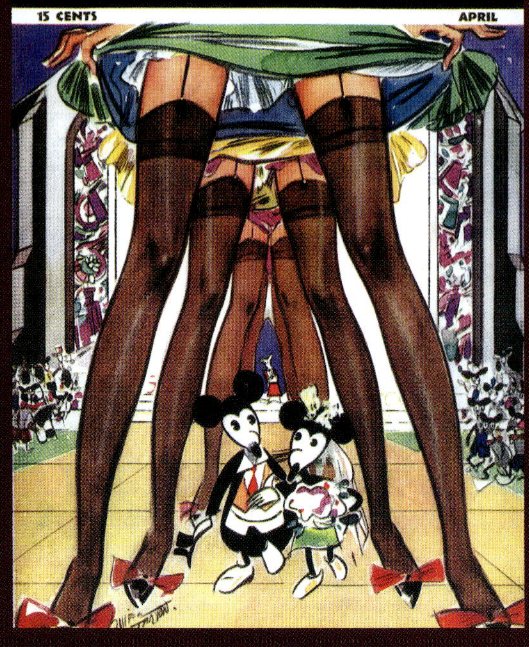

BALLYHOO

SPORTING EDITION!

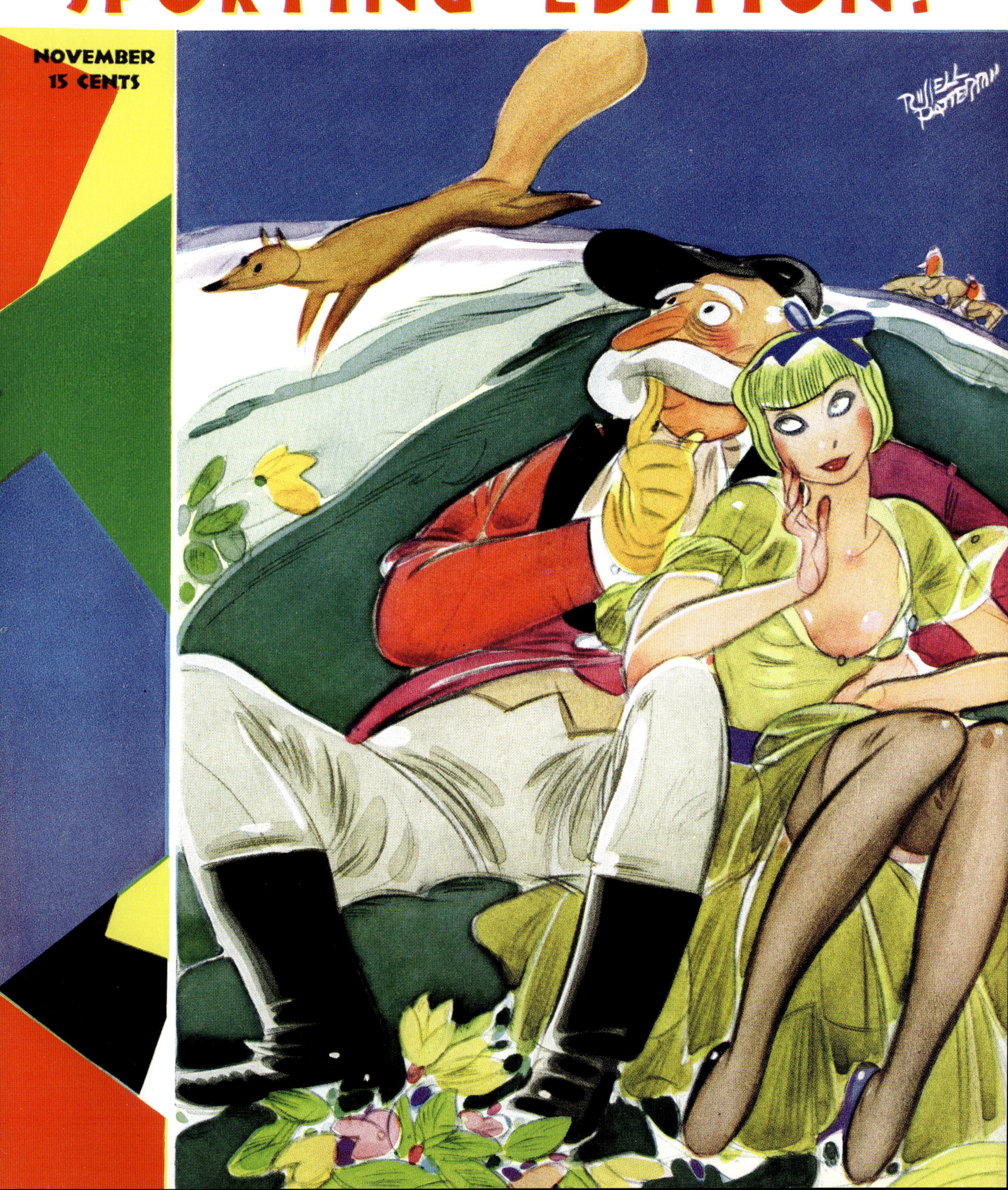

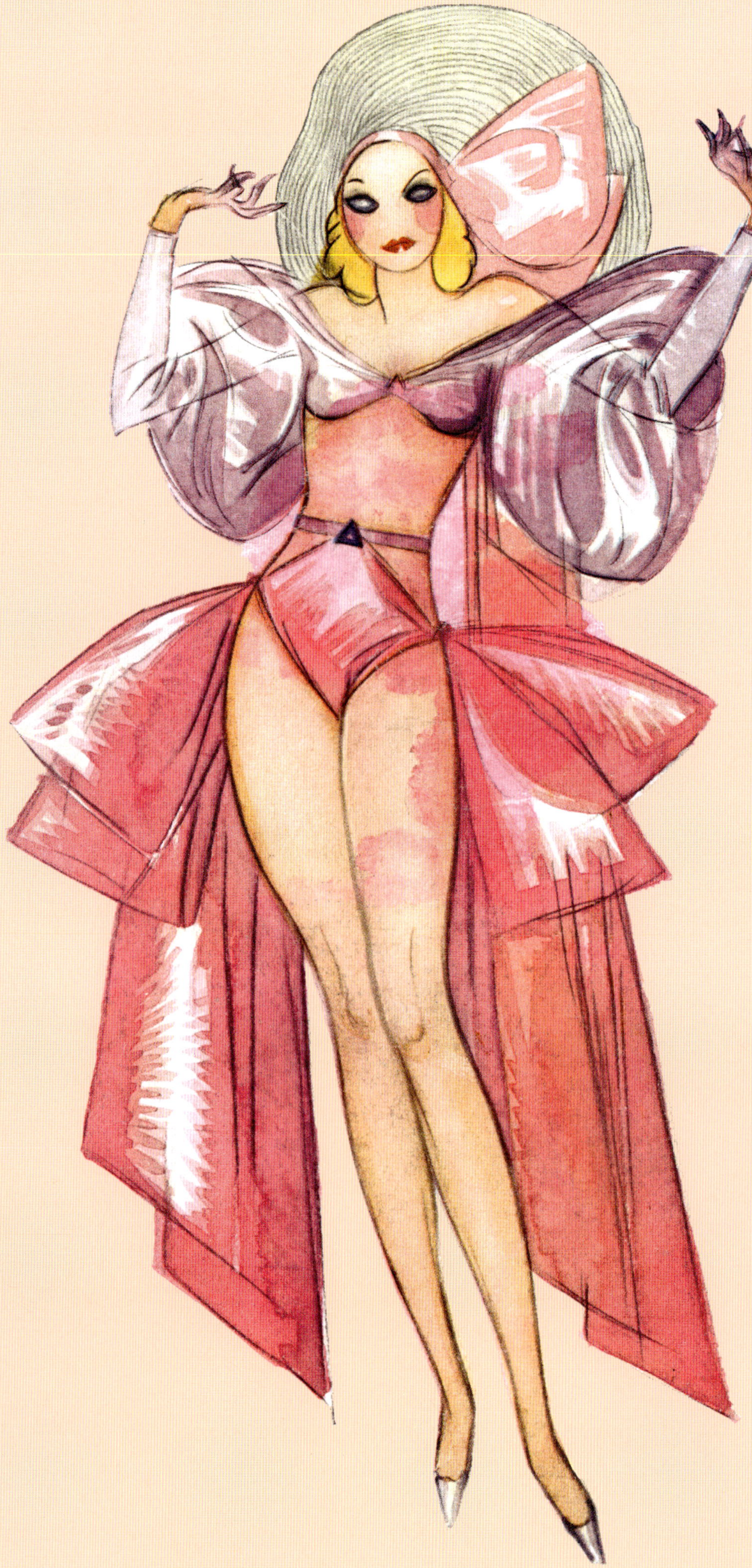

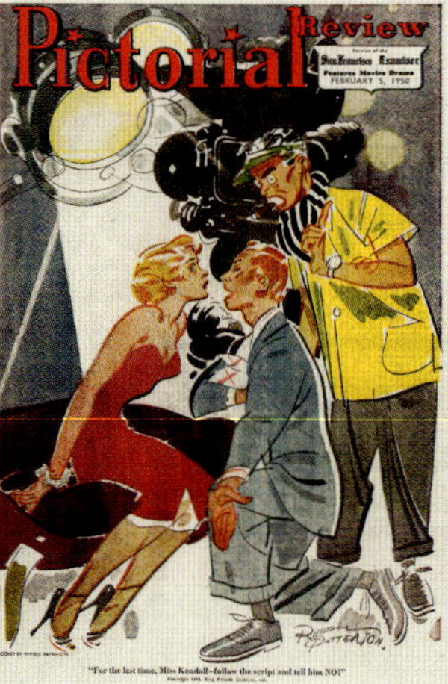

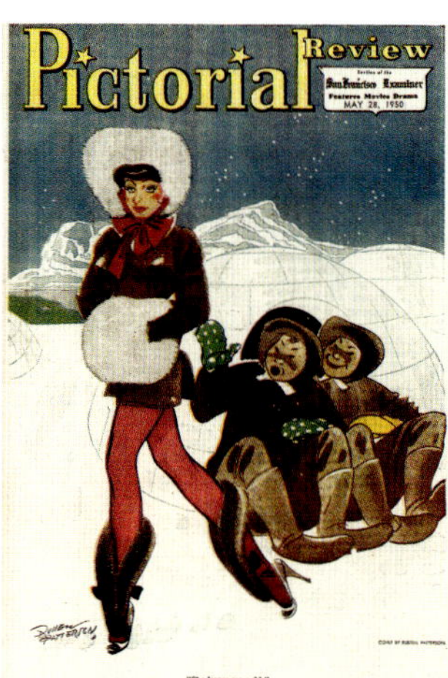

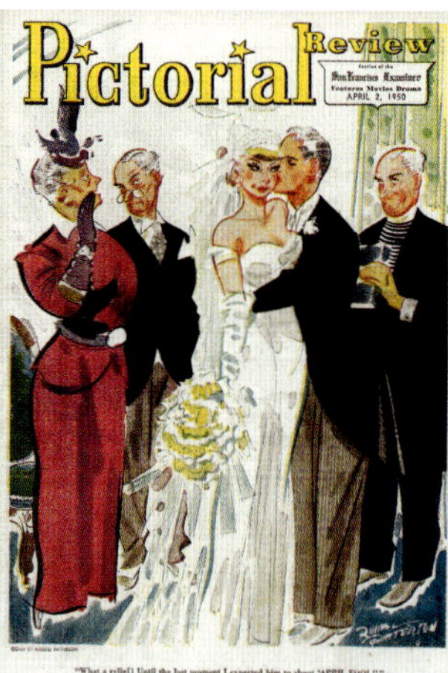

Patterson's color work appeared mostly on magazine, newspaper and book covers. But he also did elaborate color studies for Hollywood, as in this costume design for 1934. Later, Patterson would be the regular cover artist for Hearst's *American Weekly* throughout the Second World War.

Overleaf:
Ad featuring puppets from the late 1930s. Patterson designed every element of the sets, down to the clothes, jewelry and floral arrangements.

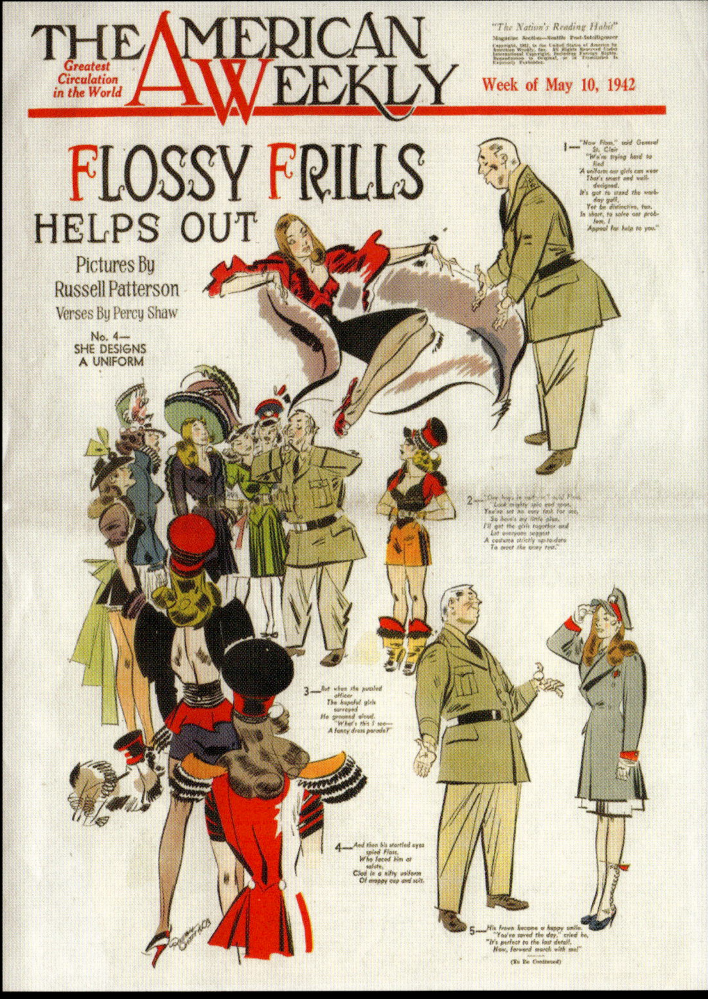
THE AMERICAN WEEKLY
Greatest Circulation in the World
"The Nation's Reading Habit"
Week of May 10, 1942
FLOSSY FRILLS
HELPS OUT
Pictures By
Russell Patterson
Verses By Percy Shaw
No. 4—
SHE DESIGNS
A UNIFORM
3—But when the puzzled officer
The hopeful girls surveyed
He groaned aloud,
"What's this I see—
A fancy dress parade?"
4—And then his startled eyes spied Floss,
Who faced him at salute,
Clad in a nifty uniform
Of snappy cap and suit.
5—His frown became a happy smile.
"You've saved the day," cried he,
"It's perfect to the last detail.
Now, forward march with me!"
(To Be Continued)

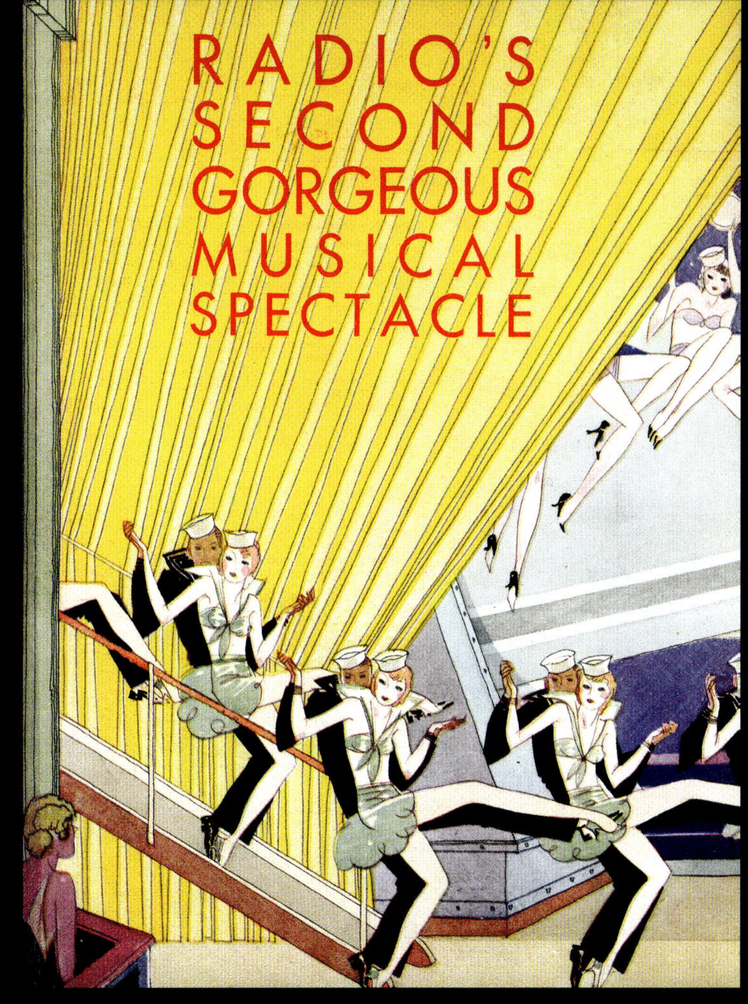
RADIO'S
SECOND
GORGEOUS
MUSICAL
SPECTACLE

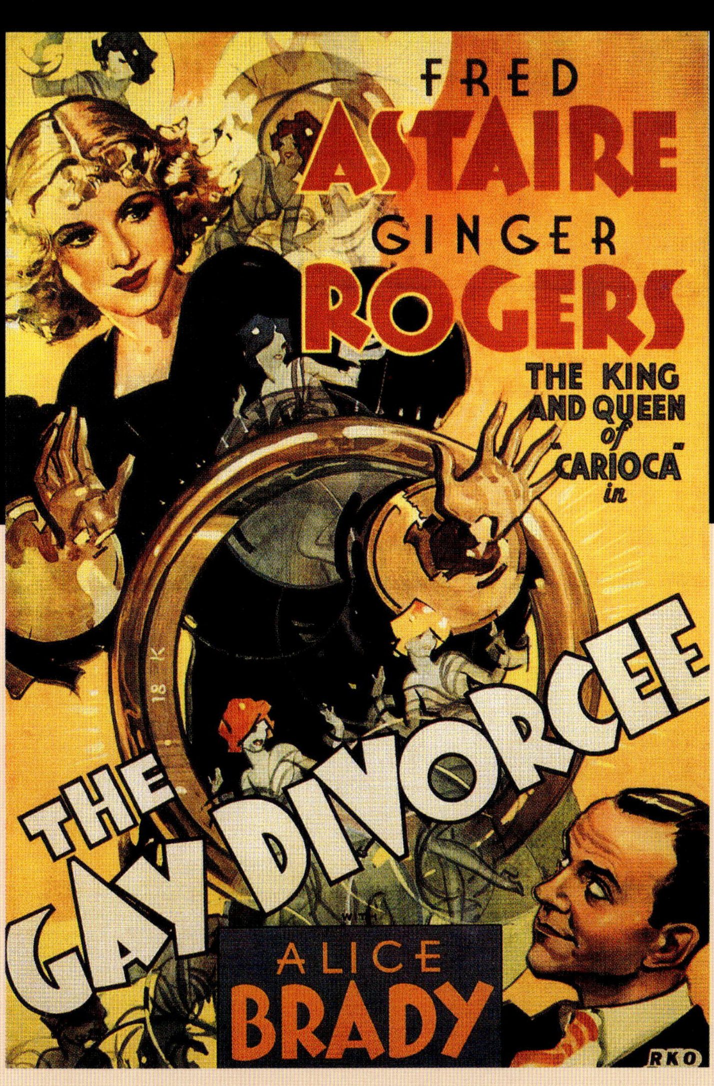
FRED
ASTAIRE
GINGER
ROGERS
THE KING
AND QUEEN
of
"CARIOCA"
in
THE
GAY DIVORCEE
ALICE
BRADY
RKO

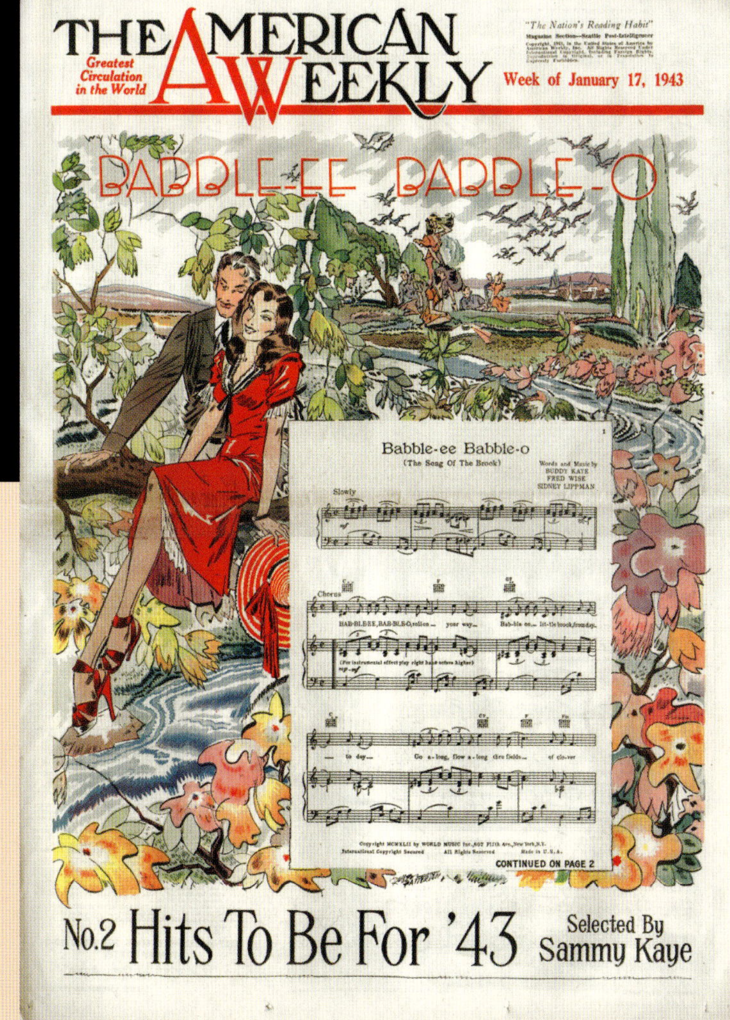
THE AMERICAN WEEKLY
Greatest Circulation in the World
"The Nation's Reading Habit"
Week of January 17, 1943
BABBLE-EE BABBLE-O
Babble-ee Babble-o
(The Song Of The Brook)
Words and Music by
BUDDY KAYE
FRED WISE
SIDNEY LIPPMAN
Slowly
Chorus
CONTINUED ON PAGE 2
No.2 Hits To Be For '43
Selected By
Sammy Kaye

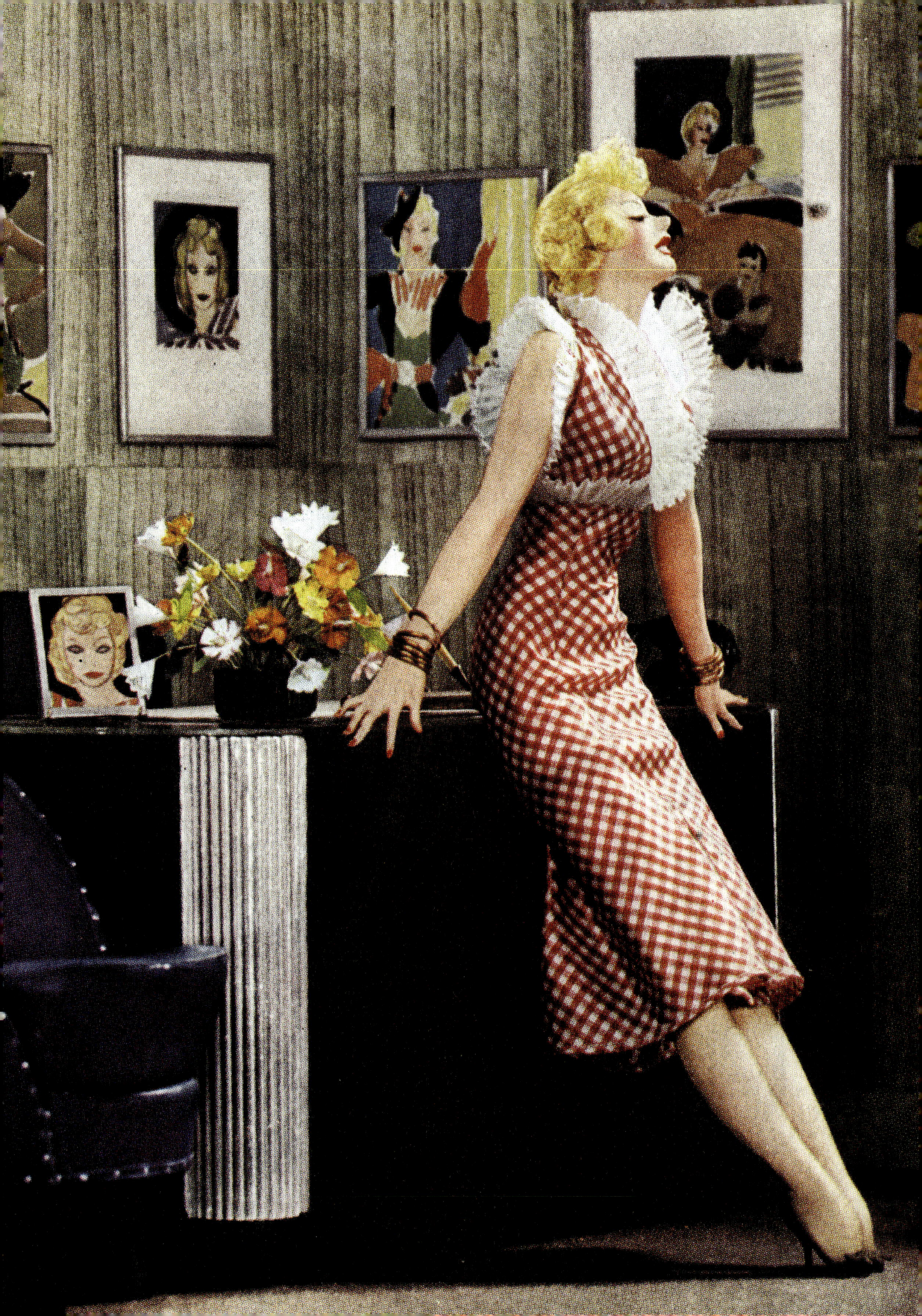

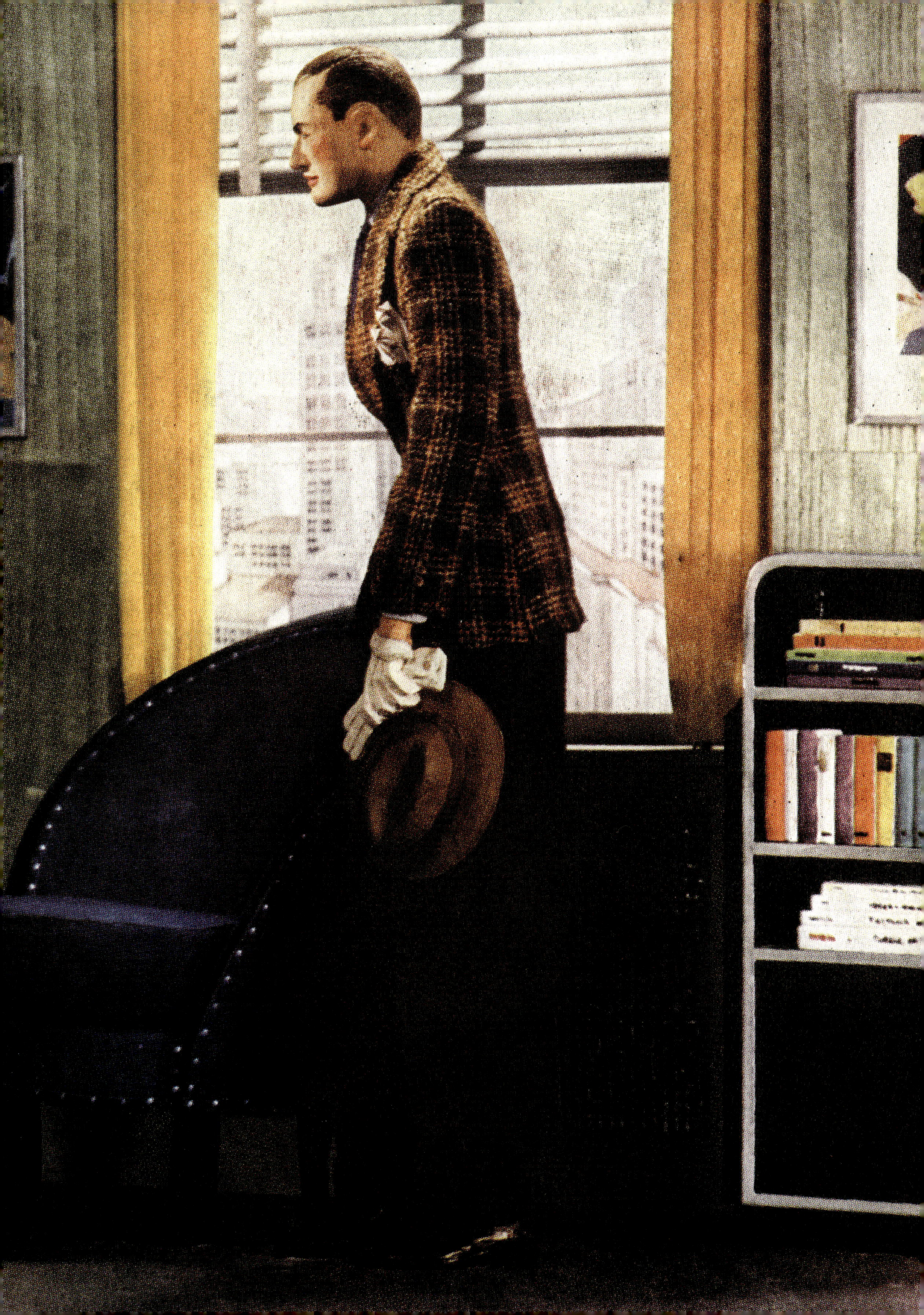

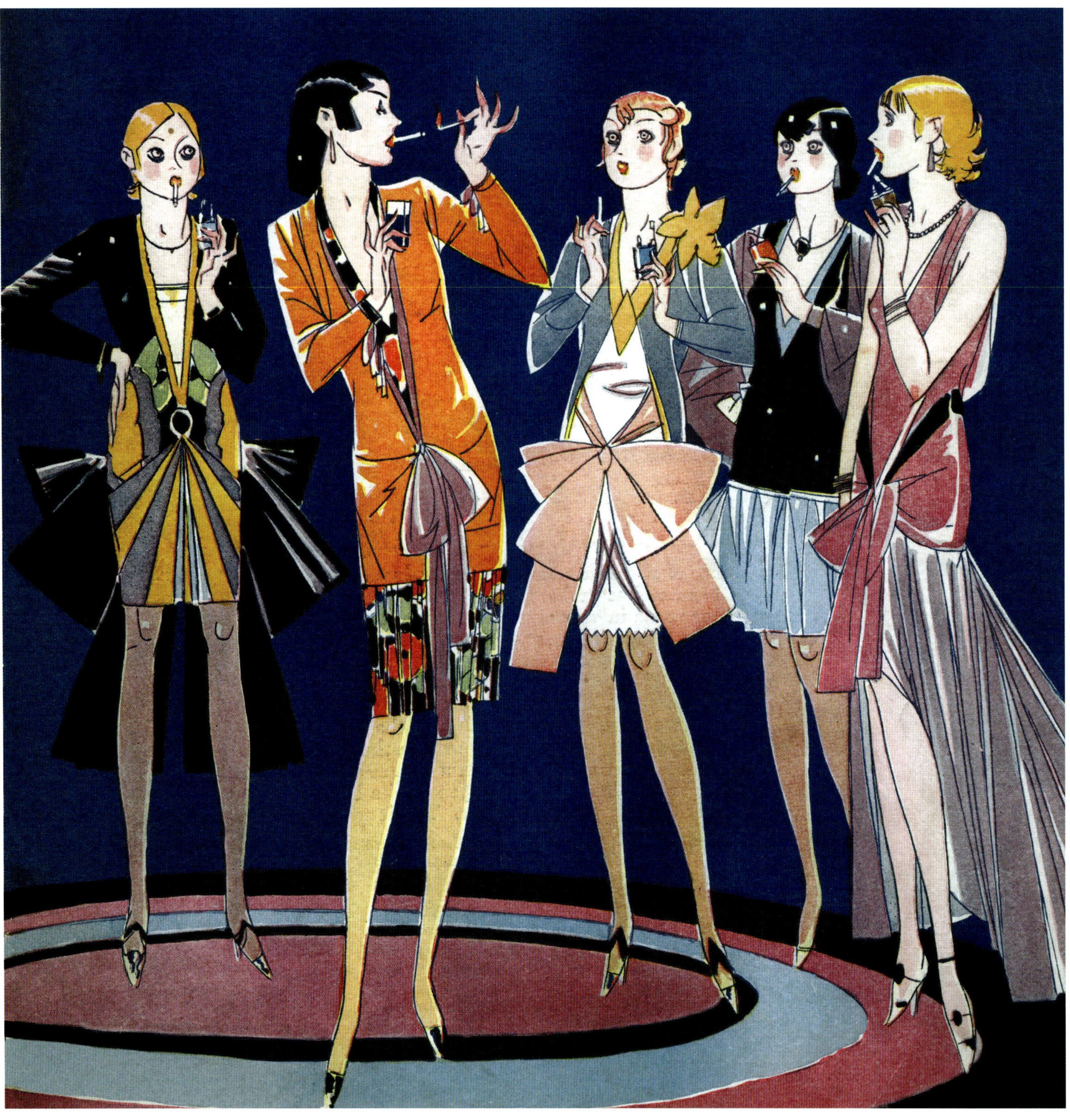

like a river pilot navigates a river. While Patterson was still a young boy, his family followed the Canadian-Pacific line west from Newfoundland to Toronto before settling in Montreal. Patterson never delved too deeply into these early years, other than to remark that he could not remember a time when he could not draw. Even as a child he deftly copied the leading illustrators of the day, including Gibson and Flagg. He was known as a neighborhood prodigy, and used his father's upstairs home office as his first studio, where his nearly exact copies proudly adorned its four walls.

Patterson's first artistic epiphany occurred at the age of 17, shortly after his high-school graduation. As he noted in his unfinished memoirs:

The picture is very clear in my mind. I was sitting alone in the new library at St. Patrick's School in Montreal. It wasn't very popular, for the boys couldn't get used to it. It was a cold room, simply furnished, shelves only on one wall with very few books and a long table of long chairs. I found the room the ideal place to study. I was preparing for my examinations at McGill [University]. How many times the question would rise, "Study for what?" My father, a real student, wanted me to be some sort of an engineer but somehow this sort of thing didn't appeal to me.

On the table were a few dated magazines. I picked up the one on top, Collier's. *On the cover was a drawing by Joseph Leyendecker. I had seen many of his drawings before. His work was very popular.*

This picture was a side view of a man walking a collie. He was the college man of the day. He had the Leyendecker turned up nose and the strong chin. He was smoking a large meerschaum pipe and was wearing a red skullcap, a heavy white broad women's turtle neck sweater, gray peg top trousers, knobtoed shoes and tan gloves. The collie's coloring matched, brown, tan and white.

I studied the cover for a long time and decided then and there, I wanted to be a cover artist. That night when I got home, I took my father aside and proudly said, 'I want to be an artist.' All hell broke loose.

Patterson's father eventually backed off—but only slightly—from his high academic expectations. He gave his son a chance to become a creative professional by allowing him to study architecture at McGill University (Patterson also counted another Montreal school, Monumente Nationale, in his academic credits, which he presumably attended concurrently). Patterson only lasted a year at McGill, however, when a fire at his family-owned hotel cut short his formal schooling.

Patterson's professional career began at the *Montreal Star*, where he processed orders for ads over the counter. He was then taken under the wing of the staff cartoonist at the *Evening Standard*, who thrilled Patterson when he noted that the young artist had picked up a "beautiful pen line." His time at that paper and a series of others was brief, a combination of Patterson's restlessness and ill-fitting assignments. Finally, he received a job as a cartoonist for another French language Montreal newspaper, *La Patrie*, drawing and writing a strip titled "Pierrorette y Pierrot." After a year he was fired again, admitting later that he failed to do the assignments as required, either turning in pieces too late or conniving to get his pen-and-ink cartoons published throughout the paper behind the back of his exasperated editor.

Having worn out his welcome at the local papers, Patterson turned to other outlets. In his unfinished autobiography he wrote, "A friend of mine had a Chicago man visiting him by the name of Jake Calvert, head of the Remick Music Company. He told me if I ever came to Chicago, he'd give me work. A few months later, I packed up and went to Chicago where I landed with $8.00 so I looked him up fast. He gave me the song covers to do, $15 apiece..."

Tapping into his architectural training, Patterson produced commercial drawings for department stores such as Carson, Pirie and Scott and Marshall Field, and interiors for the John M. Symthe Furniture Co. during the early part of the 1910s (Patterson noted that he was rarely allowed to draw figures).

From 1916 to 1919, he intermittently attended the Art Institute of Chicago, and sometime during WWI, most likely before America's entry in 1917, Patterson returned to Canada and enlisted in the Royal Canadian air corps. Yet he never left the country, as once his graphic talents were revealed he spent the duration of his service as an artist. After the War, he returned to drawing interiors in Chicago, and in 1918, married his first wife, Constance Burke, a union that 10 years later produced a daughter, Elinor.

FROM THIS MOMENT ON

This is a new age in which we live, an age of restless activity—a vibrant age, an age of snap, pep, vim—an age of new thought, of new dress, of new standards, of new codes, and side by side with this new order of things has grown a new expression of the artistic, both in the form of our music and of our art...This NEW ART is the last word in Humorous Illustration—a departure from the purely theoretical, traditional, academic viewpoint, in allowing a certain freedom of line, that gives snap, vivacity, and sprightliness to the figure—crisply depicting the spirit of the times.

—Sales brochure,
The Russell Patterson Course, 1927

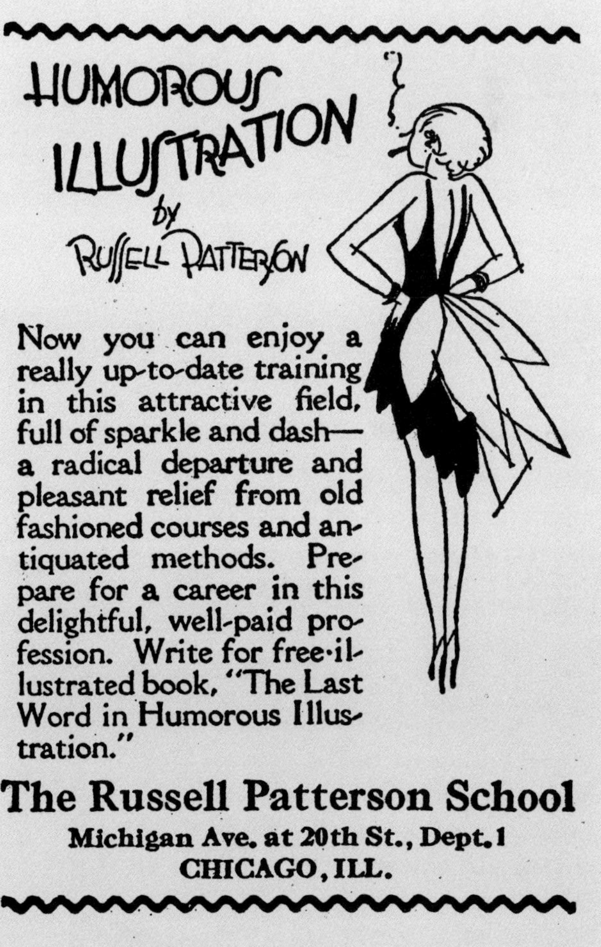

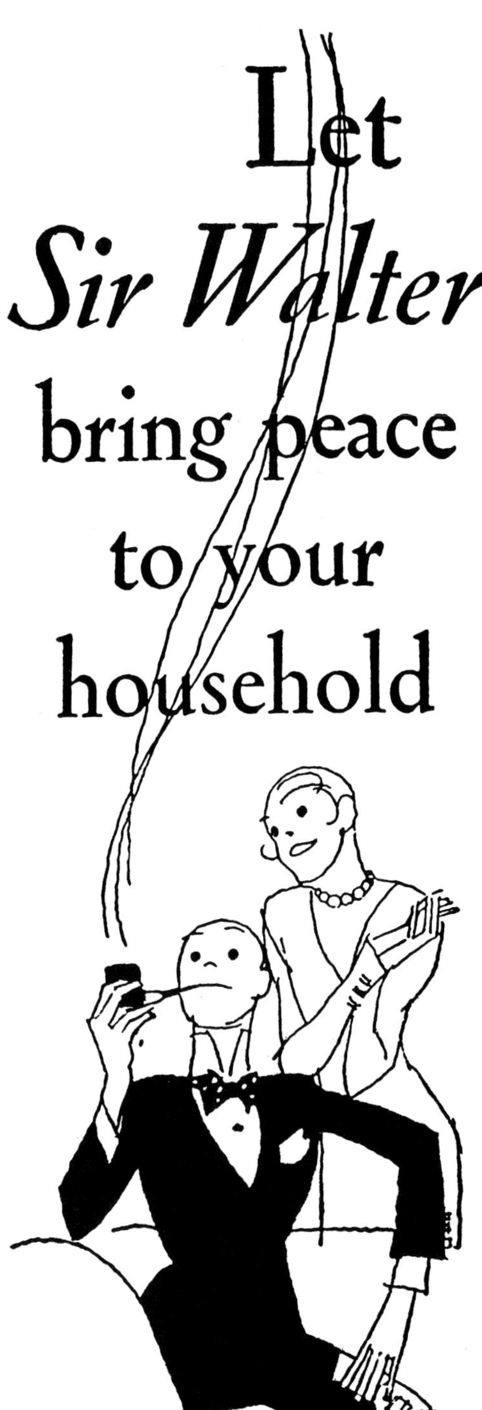

YOUR pipe is in right with friend wife the moment she gets that new and milder fragrance of Sir Walter's favorite mixture. A welcome blend of choice, mild tobaccos, kept fresh in a heavy gold foil wrap. Be fair to yourselves, men, and fair to the fair sex. Let Sir Walter make your pipe a pipe of peace.

LIMITED OFFER
(for the United States only)
If your favorite tobacconist does not carry Sir Walter Raleigh, send us his name and address. In return for this courtesy, we'll be delighted to send *you* without charge a full-size tin of this *milder* pipe mixture.
Dept. X, Brown & Williamson Tobacco Corp.
Winston-Salem, N. C.

When Patterson returned to Chicago in 1924 after his disastrous trip to California and armed with the vision of his comely Parisian brunette, he began to insert her into his work and the effect was immediate. He lost all his old assignments but it didn't matter. The seed was there, and it was the right direction. Slowly he started to gain momentum and found a new muse, "a beautiful little figure model who had never even read about a flapper but she did look like one." Eventually, mostly through the efforts of his resourceful brother Tom, he started to work in a bright and brazen style heavily influenced by his stay in Paris. He introduced the raccoon coat and the floppy galoshes that gave flappers their name, styles he remembered as popular during his college days in Canada. Then, one day, Patterson answered a knock on his studio door, and it was opportunity itself in the form of Pete Martin and Julian Brazelton, the editor and art director, respectively, for *College Humor*.

In just a little over two years, Patterson went from being relatively unknown to becoming one of the country's most admired and highly paid illustrators during an age when top illustrators were treated as celebrities. By the end of the decade, his illustrations appeared in all the leading magazines including *The Saturday Evening Post*, *Vogue*, *Vanity Fair*, *Cosmopolitan*, *Redbook*, *Photoplay*, *College Humor*, *Judge* and *Ballyhoo*. His "Patterson Girl" appeared in ads for clothes, soap, furs, cars, furniture, cement, hosiery, mattresses, and vacuums. She soon became a novelty in her own right, featured on jigsaw puzzles and paper dolls, and headlined weekly comic strips distributed in Hearst's *American Home Journal*. Patterson also designed men's and women's clothing, wrote columns, judged beauty contests, and decorated window displays.

AN AMERICAN IN PARIS

What Patterson brought to Chicago and then to New York was more than just self-confidence. He contributed his own utterly alluring version of the "new woman," a distinctly American personification of a feminist movement that had been developing for years in Europe.

Earlier in the century, when sweeping changes were occurring in the European fashion and art worlds, Paul Poiret (the self-proclaimed "Sultan of Fashion" and "Pasha of Paris") engaged illustrator Paul Iribe in 1908 to embellish his designs in a limited-edition publication called *Les Robes de Paul Poiret*. The publication proved such a tremendous success that couturier Poiret followed it three years later with another volume, this time with illustrations by Georges Lepape, that became an even greater success. The second volume spawned the publication of *La Gazette du Bon Ton* (*The Magazine of Good Breeding*),

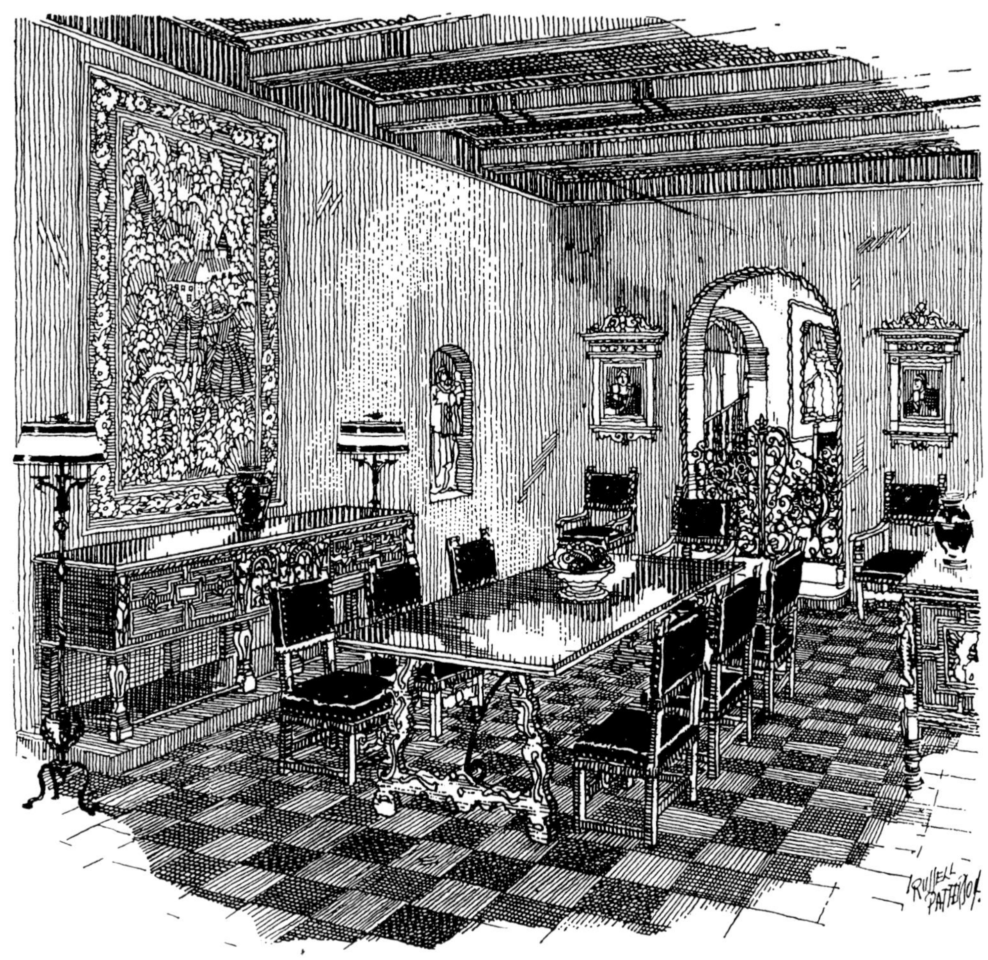

The first ten years of Patterson's career were spent on interiors for large department store ads and catalogs.

a luxury magazine co-edited by Lepape and Lucien Vogel and universally recognized as the standard bearer for the new trend in art and fashion.

La Gazette du Bon Ton had the highest aspirations, as proclaimed in the promotional first issue:

> *This revue will also be a work of art. Everything about it will please the eye: its format, characters, texts, illustrations, and the couturier's models will not be simple reproductions, but genuine portraits of dresses painted and drawn by the finest artists of the day.*

Lepape and Vogel recruited other like-minded Young Turks, brash artists, who for the most part had recently studied together at the Ecole des Beaux-Arts in Paris, but whose work was hardly academic or traditional. Among the notables were Charles Martin (perhaps the most Patterson-like), Georges Barbier, Eduardo Benito, Pierre Brausad, Umberto Brunelleschi, and Andre Marty. They incorporated many diverse and exciting elements including Japanese woodblock prints, decadent Orientalism, and African tribal masks, all of which can be felt in the extravagant costumes of Leon Bakst for the *Ballets Russes*.

Through an elaborate printing process called *porchoir*, the fashion illustration contained in the magazine was marked by incredibly delicate watercolor and an essential abstraction of the figure into elegant, elongated, narrow, vertical columns of color and line, with no modeling within the figure. The faces were exaggerated stretched ellipses on long necks, and the features—inscrutable eyes and crescent lips—a repetition of smaller ovals.

Although it's hard to say how much Patterson's art changed after Paris (almost none of his early work has survived), it's relatively easy to speculate as to the impact it had on him. American illustrators who matured during the first two decades of the 20th century, particularly pen-and-ink artists, were heavily influenced on one side by the idealized, romantic, and realistic styles of Pyle, Gibson, Flagg, Joseph Clement Coll, Franklin Booth, and Edwin Austin Abbey, and on the other side, by the unapproachable Art Nouveau virtuosity of Winsor McCay and his *Little Nemo in Slumberland* and the more modern brilliance of George McManus and his *Bringing Up Father*. After a short stint in the City of Light, Patterson came back with the revolutionary idea that there could be another way—it didn't have to be painting with a pen.

As it turned out, Patterson wasn't the only American artist so affected. For example, one of his oldest rivals, Ralph Barton, came back from his sojourn in pre-war Paris far less tight and representational than when he left. The French style could also be found in the work of theater designers such as Florenz Ziegfeld's Joseph

Urban and Erté, the *Vogue* illustrators Helen Dryden, René Bouché, and Carl Ericcson (Eric), and in the work of movie and Broadway poster illustrators Allan Cordell "Hap" Hadley, William Galbraith Crawford, and Marcel Vertès.

Patterson never directly cited the French influence, but the sole example of his writing from the period eloquently portrays him in the thrall of art and in the thick of Modernism:

> *The Morris Rosenwalds [according to Eliza, head of Sears and Roebuck] supported a young artist Harry Lachman [a former student of Howard Pyle] who had been living in France for many years. He was very kind and introduced me to many of his artist friends. One of his pals was a skinny little man with thick glasses and he had a skinnier, domineering wife—Mr. and Mrs. Pierre Bonnard. When Lachman went back to the states for his yearly three months exhibit, he let me use his studio apartment. When he returned, he invited me to his place in Petite Andle, a small town on the Seine, two hours out of Paris. I rented a room at the Hotel de Normandie for the summer. The Bonnards visited Lachman often and through them, I met other artists who had homes there—Warshaski, Paul Signac, Gilbert White, and the Pissarro sons who were married and lived in their father's old farmhouse. Claude Monet lived an hour's drive down the road. We went to visit him now and then...I painted and they all helped me.*

Another revealing example of early Art Deco Patterson, a snapshot of the artist when he returned from France, are the 20 lessons from his self-titled art instruction course, "The Last Word in Humorous Illustration," which he created and distributed circa 1922-1925.

Again, Patterson's brother Tom figures prominently. As Patterson started to gain new work featuring his sexy flapper, his brother noticed style sheets around the studio that Patterson had created to insure that he turned out consistent work. His brother quickly realized that budding artists would find these useful, and with a standing offer from *College Humor* publisher Bill Ziff to trade advertising space for drawings, a school was launched. It became such a success that Patterson couldn't keep up with his students and administrative costs (the mailing costs alone were eating him alive). He eventually sold the school to the Chicago-based Meyer Both company, "the largest art and advertising service in America," which continued it for several years under Patterson's name.

The course consisted of 20 lessons, with 15-inch-tall single sheets sent to students one lesson at a time:

1. Outline Construction of the Female Figure
2. Construction of the Female Head
3. Advanced Construction of the Female Figure—construction of hands and feet
4. Drapery of the Female Figure
5. Construction of Male Figure
6. Drawing of Children
7. Animal Draftsmanship
8. Adaptation of Female Figure to humorous and comic illustration requirements
9. Adaptation of Male Figure
10. Simple Perspective
11. Study of details
12. Simple method of attaining action
13. Types of Lettering used with humorous illustration. Means of carrying out a comic strip.
14. Composition
15. Group Drawings
16. Technique Development
17. Simple methods of carrying out pen and ink and pen drawings
18. Different pen and ink treatments of the same subject
19. The construction of the complete drawings
20. General Review and Examination

The booklet Meyer Both sent upon request to prospective cartoonists gave the course outline and noted how successful, young and handsome Patterson was and how this style was fresh and state of the art. It also claimed there was big money to be had for just a few hours of work, and that the routine company of beautiful, half-draped figure models was an occupational hazard.

Unfortunately, Patterson's text explaining his lessons has been lost. There may have been very little text anyway. Later, when Patterson talked about his art or illustrated a brief lesson, as he did in Gene Byrne's *Complete Guide to Drawing, Painting, Illustrating and Cartooning* (1946), he allowed the pictures to teach the lesson and told artists asking for his advice to start by observing live models, elongate the figure to 8 1/2 or 9 heads tall as the drawing developed, look for a "line of balance" to keep figures simple and easy to read, and compose with blacks shapes forming strong lines of action. (This black spotting was Patterson's own unique departure from the French style, and for that matter, every other cartoonist.)

Patterson was proud of the course and recounted a comment made by Walt Disney when the two bumped into each other one evening: "Patterson, you bastard, you got me into all this," meaning that Disney had been a Last Word student. The timing of the comment, however, is slightly off, 1924 to 1934 or so, which would be too late for Disney himself to be at a drawing board. Perhaps Disney was referring to using the course to strengthen the drawing skills of his animators, particularly its emphasis on drawing from life, an emphasis Disney was very well known for having

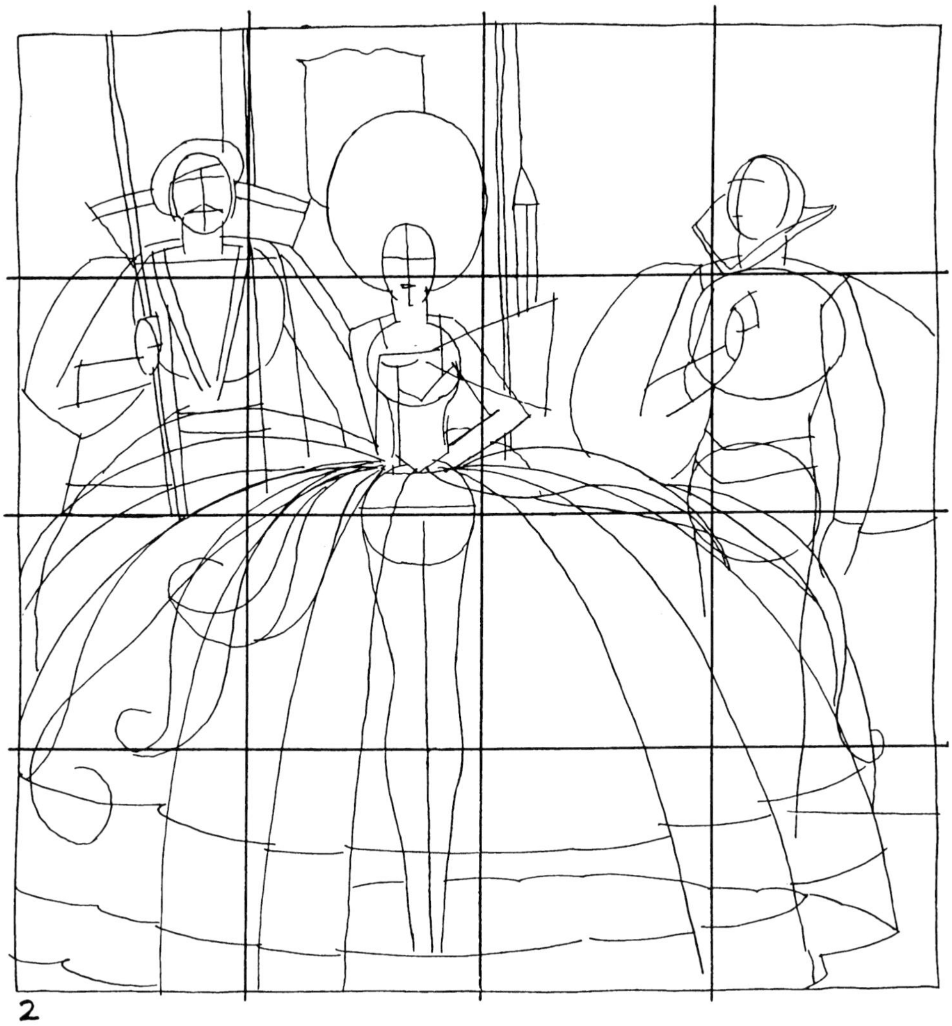

1

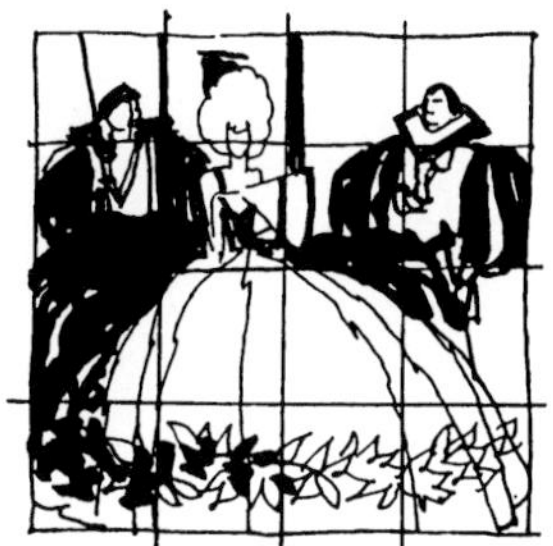

A

B

C

D

2

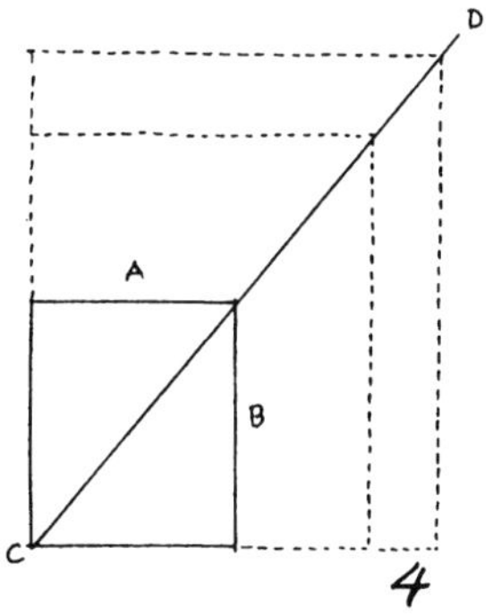

4

LESSON 18

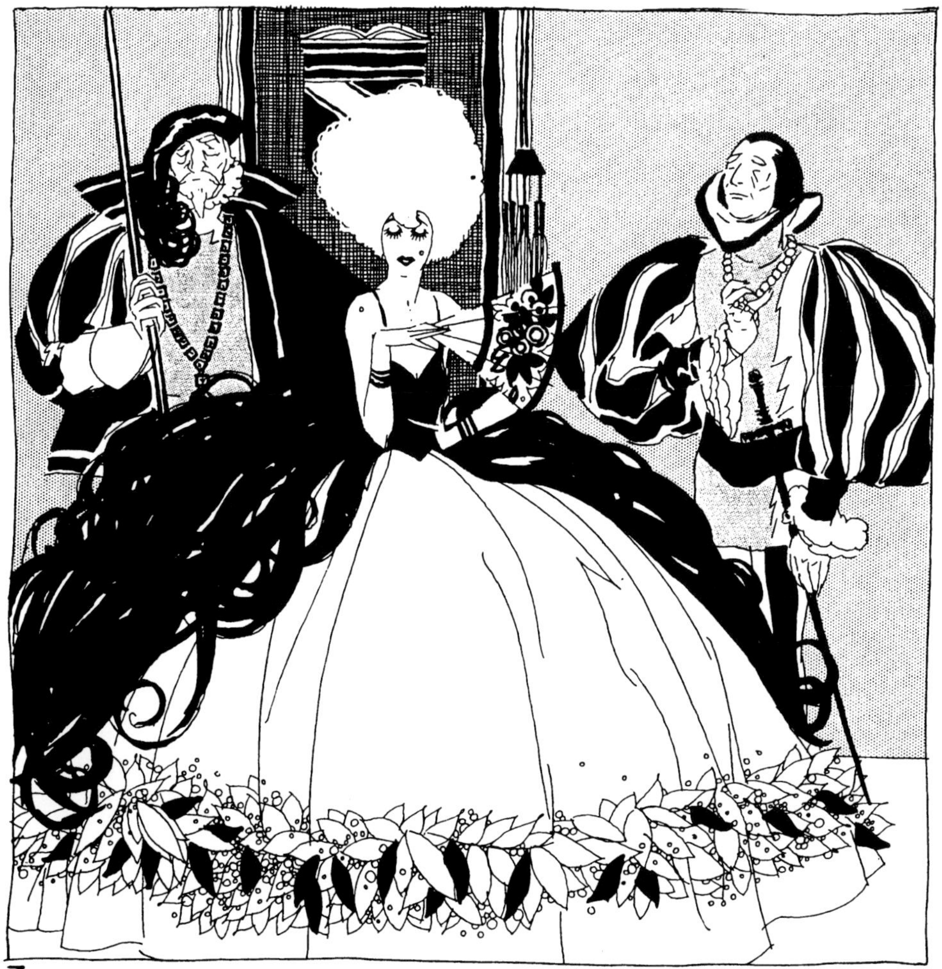

3

Page from Patterson's correspondence art course from the mid 20s, The Last Word in Humorous Illustration, stressed striking composition.

COPYRIGHTED 1926

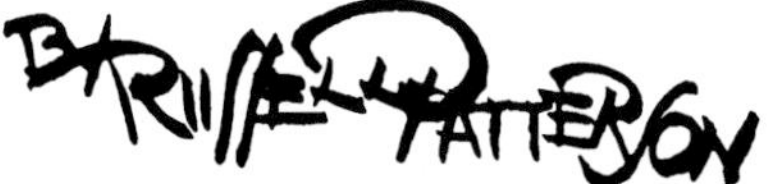

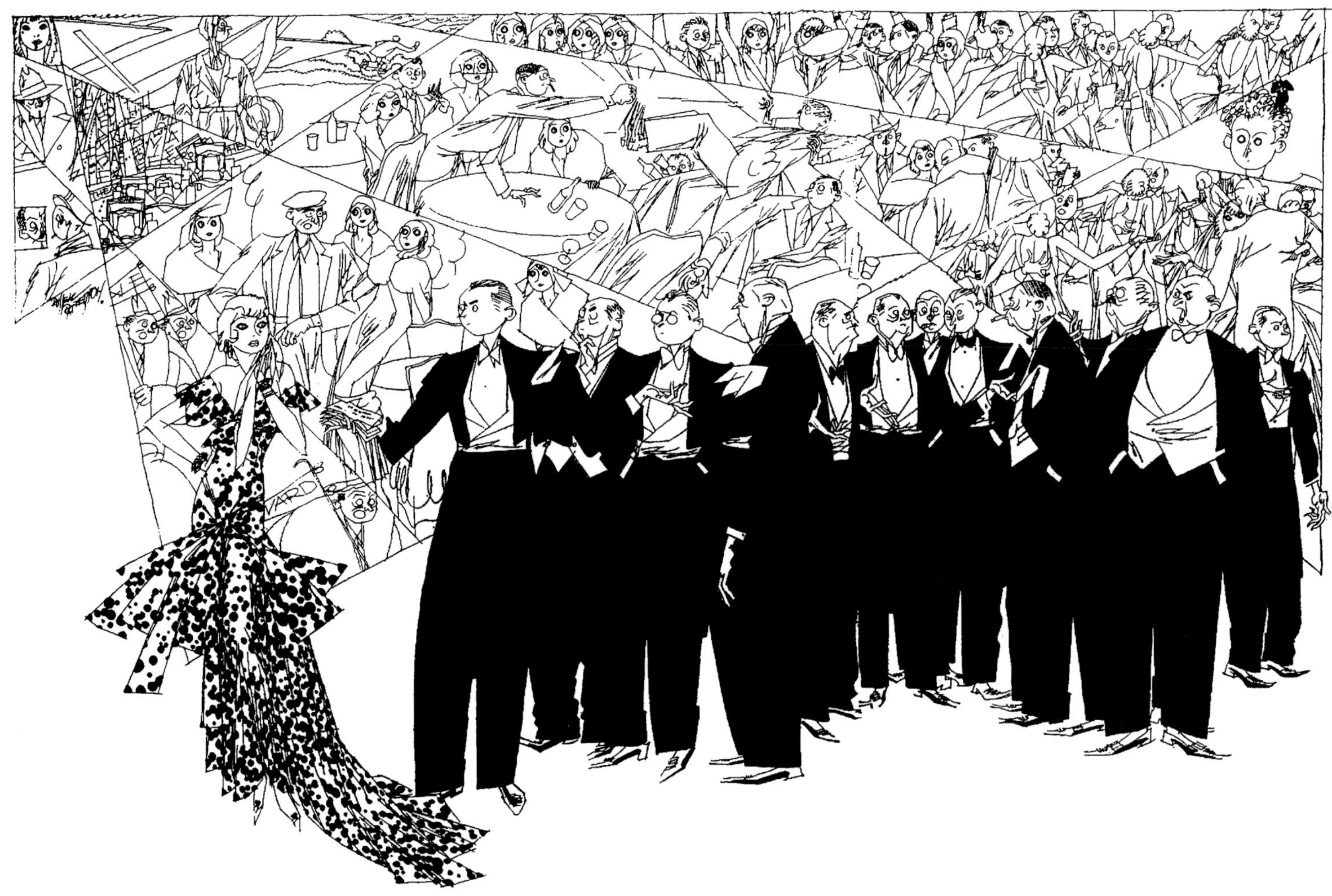

and would eventually become Chouinard Art School instructor Don Graham's rigorous training program for new studio hires in 1932. Or maybe Disney was referring to the impact Patterson's work had on him and the rest of the growing animation industry at the time.

Whatever the case, there was no doubt that by 1926 Patterson was a force to be reckoned with, and he soon supplanted John Held, Ralph Barton, and Miguel Covarrubias as the most popular cartoonist appearing in major magazines. Or, as the late Al Hirschfeld noted when asked to explain why Held disappeared so suddenly as the decade drew to a close, "Short skirts went out, long skirts came in. John couldn't draw long skirts so Russell Patterson took his work away from him."

WE'LL HAVE MANHATTAN

The great big city's a wondrous toy
Just made for a girl and boy.
We'll turn Manhattan
Into an isle of joy.
—Richard Rodgers and Lorenz Hart,
"Manhattan," 1925

The verses in this volume show only one side of Manhattan—the light, sophisticated, supposedly smart and somewhat—I hope—amusing facets that flash and glitter as you casually turn the gem of the town around in your fingers.
—Wilfred J. Funk
Manhattans Bronxes and Queens
Illustrated by Russell Patterson, 1931

In a survey of the lost era of entertainment called *Nightclub Nights*, Susan Waggoner blames the onset of prohibition, January 16, 1920, for the frantic, heedless rush to experience life that was the Roaring '20s. She noted that the prospect of no alcohol sales prompted mock wakes and solemn rituals throughout the country. "To accommodate the disaster of going dry, club owners and managers came up with a series of dodges and diversions." The end result, as Waggoner writes, "was a circus of distraction so booming and spectacular it almost seemed to have been invented by design."

No other visual artist caught the circus of distraction as effectively and affectionately—as full of electric energy and life as the period itself—as Russell Patterson. F. Scott Fitzgerald ultimately saw emptiness and false values in the era, "the foul dust" that floated in the wake of Gatsby's dreams and saw his own youthful participation as a long soul-killing hangover, and Held, who retreated to an immense Long Island estate in 1919, said he "was only commenting on what I saw going on around me" and "...I made so many drawings that I grew to loathe the little characters...."

Long skirts or not, there was no such hangover or loathing in Patterson's spot, story, ad, and cover illustrations that appeared in *Life, College Humor, Judge* or *Ballyhoo* between 1925 and 1933. So rather than Fitzgerald or Held, the two most celebrated chroniclers of the era, a closer parallel to Patterson can be found in the Great American Songbook of the leading musical theater composers Irving Berlin, the Gershwins, Cole Porter or Rodgers and Hart. It was the era of "Putting on the Ritz," "I'll Build a Stairway to Paradise," "Manhattan," and "Let's Misbehave."

The music of the time had the same sort of *joie de vivre* Patterson brought to his work—bright and witty surfaces, the optimism tinged by flattened notes of loss and memory, the joy and pain of being young and alive in an exciting city, easily falling in and out of love, even as the Depression began to cast a dark pall on the country. Like Cole Porter, who has been compared to Patterson because of their shared Midwestern background, cosmopolitan manners and university training, and the witty, sexy, sly style both displayed throughout their careers, Patterson reveled in what made city life so fascinating: kohl-eyed chorus girls, off stage resting, and watching the show from the wings while the leads belted out solos; doormen standing erect with lobby cards announcing the midnight show; Greek columns and vaulted ceilings; sleek open roadsters; excited, buzzing opening-night crowds; modern art sculpture; streamlined furniture and curved staircases; prizefights; crowded steamship staterooms; orchestra pits; a line of bathers at the seashore; sidewalk tables and small intimate bistros; and young coquettes changing into evening wear after a full day of shopping.

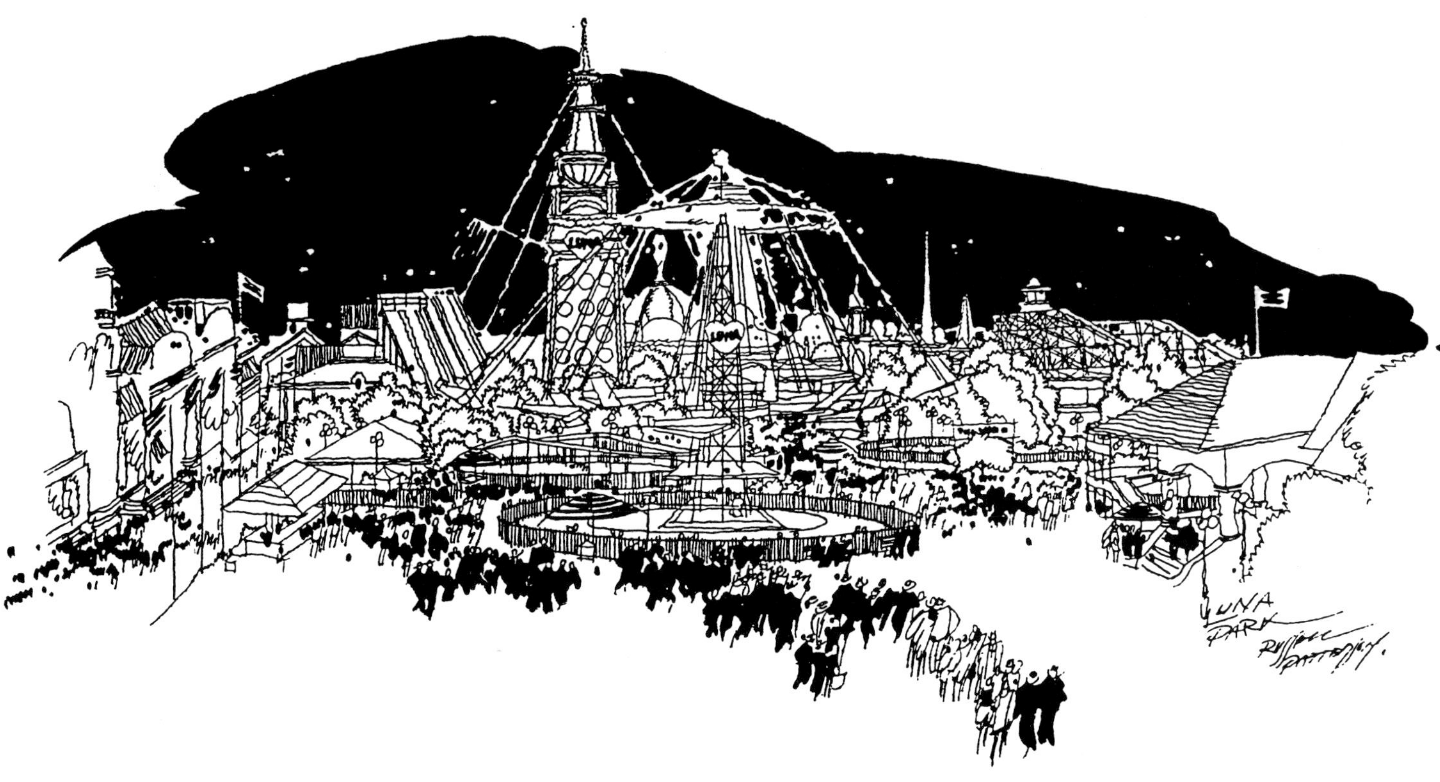

Patterson was not afraid of portraying multitudes and deftly gave the impression of a moving, living throng—the cheering crowds at the bike races, the horse track, or an almost eerie impression of glittering lights, rides, and booths of an airy Luna Park at night.

Patterson's black-and-white work doesn't mock its participants, but demonstrates a genuine love for the crazy, impulsive, vain, attractive, maddening, amusing people who lived in the city. Patterson was a social animal and insatiable people watcher, a sympathetic portrayer of his times. Even his caricatures of such easy targets as Mayor Jimmy Walker, Texas Guinan, Helen Kane, Alexander Wolcott, and Jack Dempsey were always done with good will, never viciously.

Patterson's second wife Ruth mentioned how even when he was close to 50 years old, after a full day and evening of being out in the city, Patterson would retreat to his studio and sketch out ideas and scenes he had savored that day.

He was so much a part of the parade, a part of the circus. Patterson illustrated monthly columns for Hearst's *Cosmopolitan* and Charles Dana Gibson's old *Life* magazine for authors like O.O. McIntyre and Walter Winchell with the banners "New York Life," "That's Life!," "What College Did to Me," and "Broadway Novelettes." He even penned a *Life* column himself, "For Men Only," showing just how engaged he was in the New York City lifestyle and how closely he observed the whirlwind around him.

His columns followed a regular pattern: first, a lighthearted apology to his editor for submitting his column late, a review of the latest men's fashions he hoped to acquire ("if I can make enough drawings"),

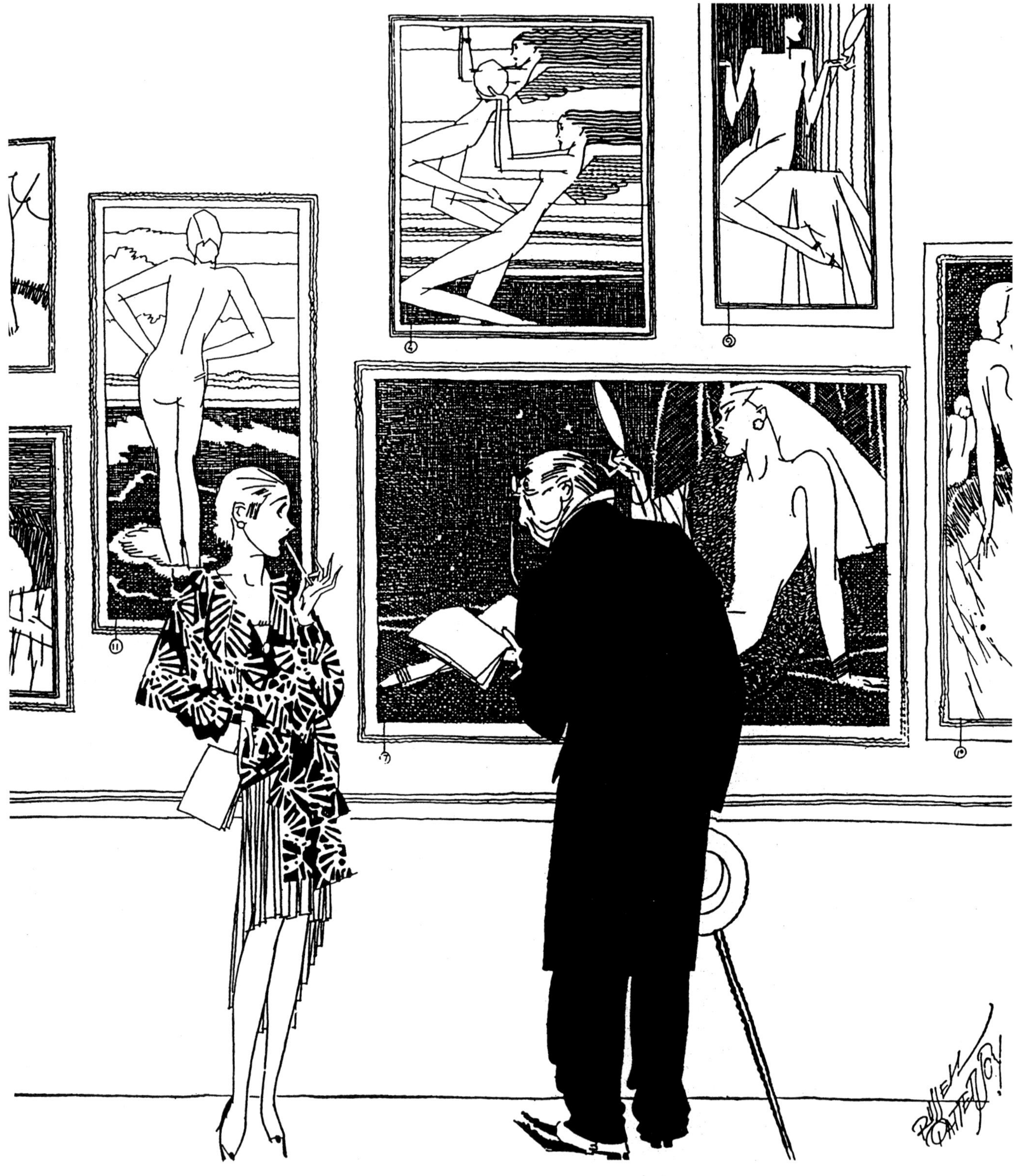

May I show you anything, Sir?

then plugs for his latest ventures, usually a theatrical production or an appearance at a beauty contest as a judge. He made sure to mention all his illustration buddies, too.

In one column from 1932, after a walk through one of his favorite stores' latest shipments, Patterson drops in a few paragraphs about designing Corey Ford and Russell Crouse's Broadway play *Hold Your Horses*, confesses his admiration for the performers and others involved in the show, and admits "It is swell to know all of these different people, see them work, design for them, and watch a tremendous undertaking like a revue develop."

Patterson also spent some time defending his profession (and friend Rube Goldberg) against fine art and illustration snobs who claimed cartooning "drags art into the mud" but which he felt was every bit as accomplished since a good cartoonist knows "the human side of life and [has] imagination." He mentioned rival cartoonist and pal Gladys Parker, who, tired of unacknowledged swipes of her strip *Flapper Fanny*, was opening her own dressmaking business. He announced a new drawing talent, who would collaborate with Patterson on a theater curtain containing 150 caricatures of celebrities they both know, including Walker, Dempsey, Gene Tunney, Joe Connolly, J. J. Shubert, Arthur William Brown, Earl Carroll, Peter Arno, Herbert Ross, and Heywood Broun. He also writes that he bumped into illustrators John La Gatta, McClelland Barclay, and Tony Sarg at a beauty contest, then briefly opines why the best models come from the South—Texas, Alabama, and Georgia.

Patterson ends his column with suggestions for those visiting New York, but it seems more like the program of his busy, creative life:

> When in New York, if the theater interests you, try to see *Take a Chance*, *Goodbye Again*, *Twentieth Century*, and *Strike Me Pink*; have dinner at *The Tavern*, *Sardi's*, *La Rue* or Tony Sarg's *Bohemia*; dance at the *Biltmore*, the *St. Regis*, the *St. Moritz*, the *Carlton*, *Place Pigalle*, or the *Ha-Ha*. Drink, by all means, at the *Surf Club*, *Leon and Eddie's*, *Moriarity's*, *The Stork Club*, *Tony's*, *Barney's*, *Louis and Armand's*, *The Press Club*, *Merry-Go-Round*, *Jack and Charlie's*, *Frank and Jack's*, or *Gus's*. And after that, *Rueben's* or *Dave's Blue Room*....
>
> And so to bed—where I am going now.

When looking at the illustrations from this period, one is struck by their cohesive black spotting, primarily on male characters. Patterson's ability to mix air and dark was admired and unmatched by those in the industry. The solid black of male clothing was contrasted by the more fanciful women's dresses and swimsuits, which were often textured with intricate geometric patterns and given a slight twist to the torso.

Patterson once wrote that he first conceived of an illustration as an arrangement of blacks, which were then tied together with thin, active, light lines. His figures, especially females, were open and suggestive, merely a contour, anchored in place by the blacks and precise architectural rendering.

He was equally accomplished at color. On covers, he simplified the elements in a picture, with just one or two figures with a single central female. The penciled under-drawing remained visible, which gave the picture character, while the delicacy of the watercolor wash and his lightness of touch bestowed grace and beauty. Patterson typically showed his girl in profile, always emphasizing her long legs. He was especially adept at legs, and his trademark idealized elongated figures showed his Patterson girls' legs to their best advantage, complemented by dark hose, tops of stockings and punctuated by two incredibly small, pointed, and turned-in feet simply and quickly executed.

ALWAYS TRUE TO YOU IN MY FASHION

> *Russell Patterson has an inventive mind that goes on and on...For years he suffered at the sight of twisted seams in silk stockings and finally invented a garter that keeps them on a straight path. He's invented many other things but his big ambition is to architect an entire city. He is a dandy in every sense of the word and likes publicity and red heads with green eyes. He seldom wears a hat and never worries about money. The worst thing I know about him is that he likes to judge beauty contests.*
>
> —Henry Birchman
> *Faces and Facts: By and About 26 Contemporary Artists, 1937*

Today, it's commonplace for designers and celebrities to branch out to different areas, lending their names to ventures far removed from the field where they initially gained prominence. Russell Patterson was a brand name before such things existed, arguably the most versatile graphic artist of his generation. His name was attached to a wide variety of projects once his magazine illustration period tapered off around 1933.

He joined a men's social group called The Dutch Treat Club and became part of its annual production. The Club, established around the turn of the century, included by 1930 virtually every celebrated editor, publisher, writer, and illustrator living in New York City, from the famous Algonquin Round Table and the

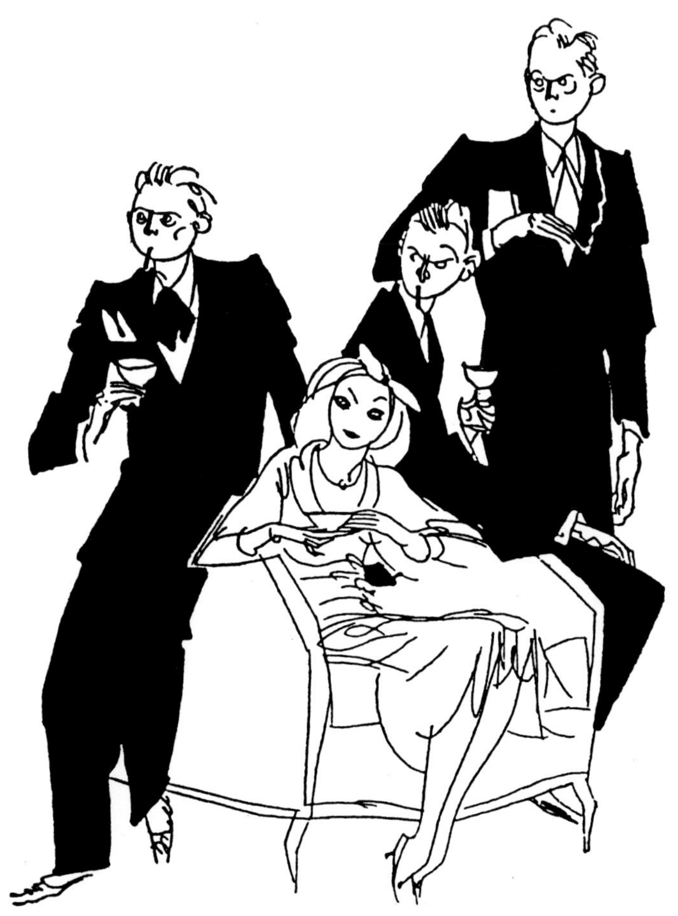

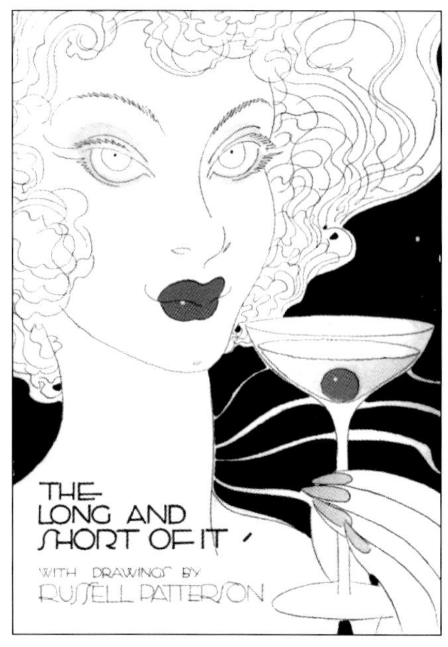

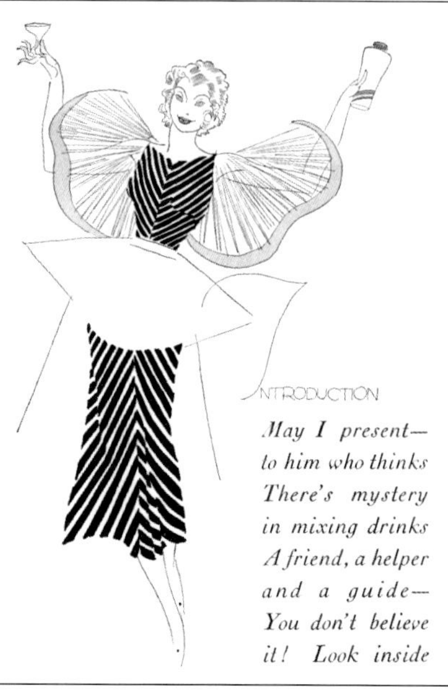

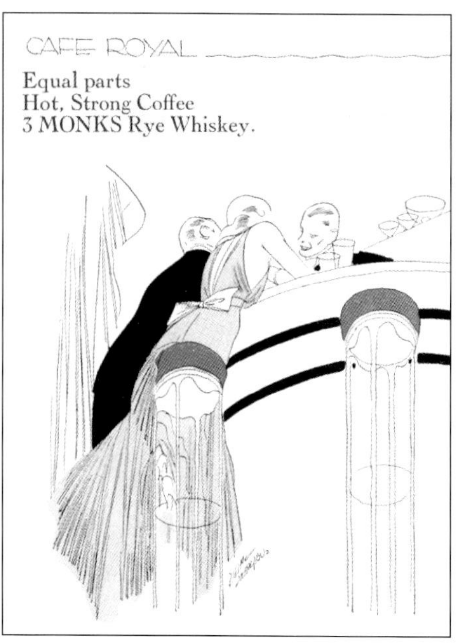

likes of Robert Sherwood and George S. Kaufman, to Jazz Age authors Ring Lardner and Marc Connelly, sportswriter Grantland Rice, publishers Richard Simon, William Morrow and Alfred Knopf, and CBS radio head William S. Paley.

Not only did he design for the shows, he also contributed cartoons and spot illustrations for the *Dutch Treat Annuals*, a sort of high-class men's periodical before such a thing existed on the newsstands. Each annual report to the members had program bills for the shows and credits of the sketches and songs, parodies of "state of the club," speeches from the President and other elected committee officials and columns about issues of the day, verse by member Ogden Nash, addresses and phone numbers, and illustrations by club members, usually sensual nudes or cartoons (often in color) by the likes of Dean Cornwell, Loren Stout, Rea Irvin, John La Gatta, John Sheridan, Flagg, W.T. Benda, Albert Dorne, Bradshaw Crandell, and Jefferson Machamer. Patterson's girls, probably the most frank and sensual he ever produced and most akin to his French beginnings, were often the longest feature, the piquant, charming decoration that pulled the intimate privately printed book together.

These annuals foreshadowed Patterson's work in various bartender guides. As early as 1931, his Girl and his designs decorated book pages devoted to cocktails and cordials and nightclub menus. Patterson produced this type of work regularly for 20 years, with Ted Saucier's *Bottom's Up* (1951) the closest to the Dutch Treat *Annuals* (since it included illustrations by Dutch Treat alumni Flagg, Brown, Dorne, Bundy, and La Gatta). Years before the artist Leroy Neiman would decorate *Playboy* magazine's joke page with his diminutive Femlin, Patterson had a drink-sized Patterson Girl slumped in a champagne glass and cavorting across the page in similar petite Femlin fashion.

Patterson also contributed to Broadway and off-Broadway productions. Beginning in 1927, he started to design costumes and sets for the Society of Illustrators "Artists and Models" revues. Originally recruited by Arthur William Brown, his first effort was a combination of Held, Machamer, and Patterson marshalling their forces.

The early '30s were a busy time for Patterson, as he had a hand in such shows as Oscar Hammerstein's *The Gang's All Here* (1931), the aforementioned *Hold*

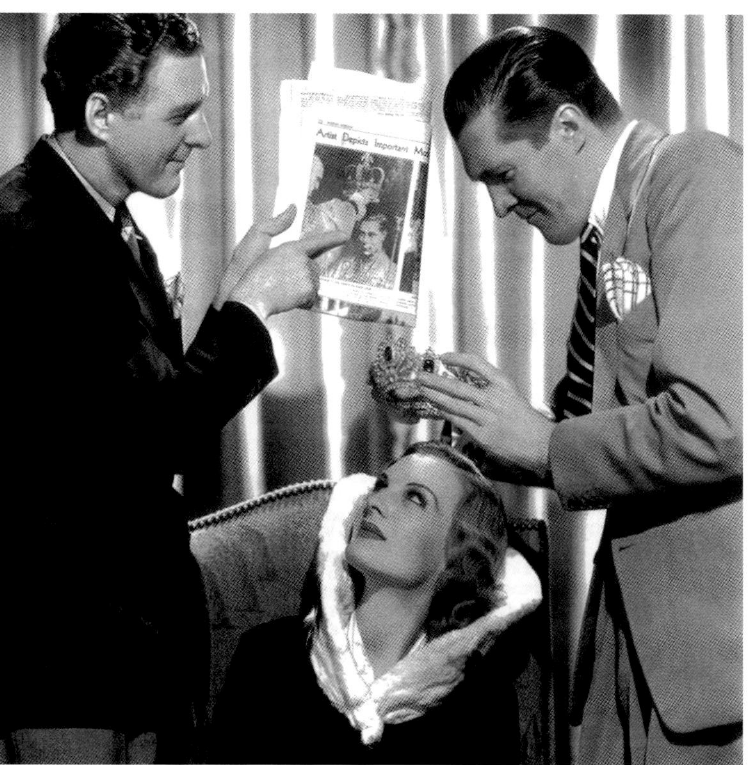

Top: Patterson's illustrations for sexy bar and drink guides throughout the '30s and '40s set the standard for masculine entertainment well before the Rat Pack and *Playboy* magazine.

Above: Patterson with *Artists and Models* co-star and *New Yorker* cartoonist Peter Arno.

Opposite: Set design for the 1933 film *Stand Up and Cheer*.

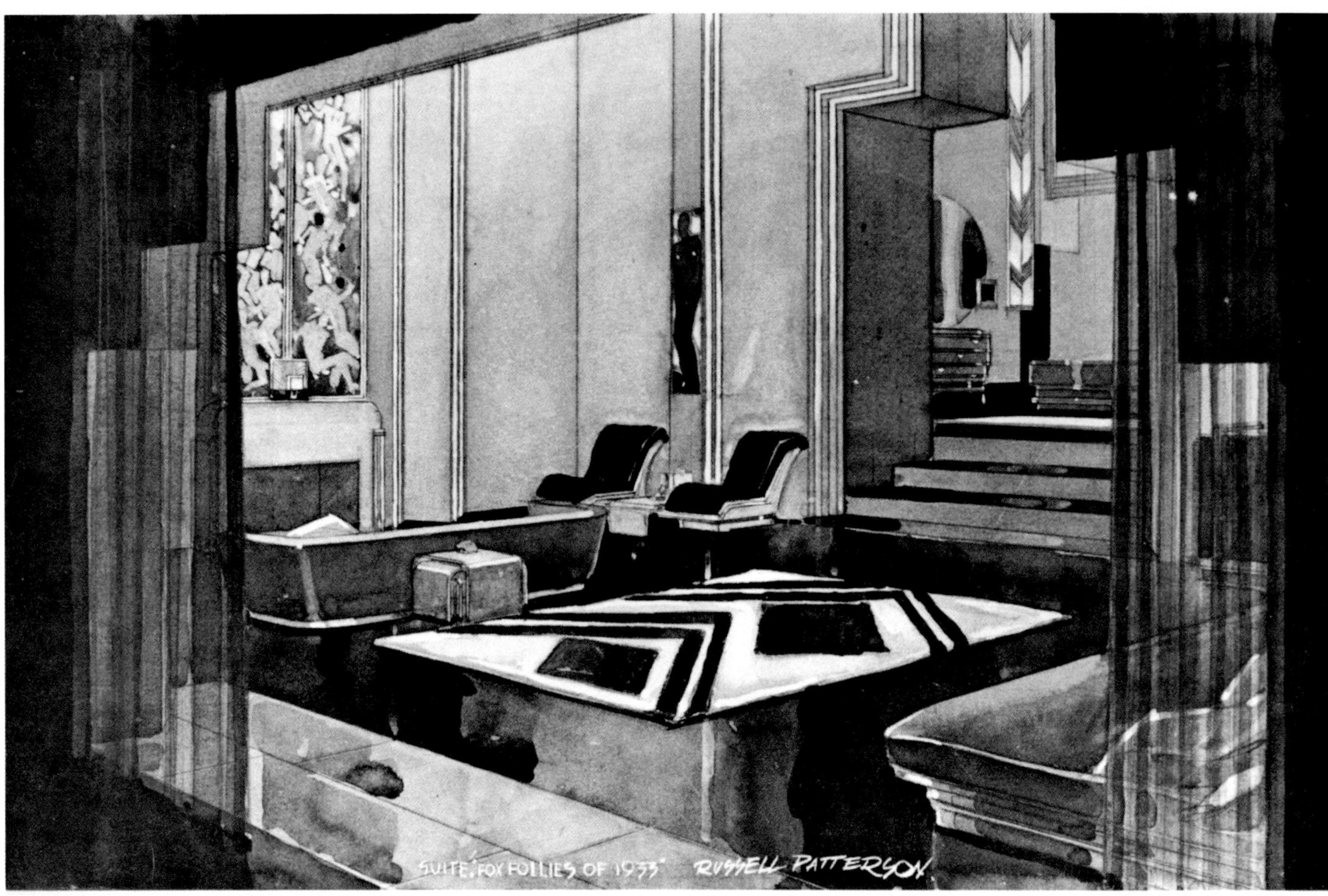

Your Horses (1933), and finally, *Ballyhoo of 1932*, a production remembered not only as a showcase for the Patterson Girl and the magazine, but also for the first appearance of Bob Hope in a lead role.

Nineteen thirty-three through 1934 found Patterson in Hollywood, mainly working at Fox and Paramount and later at Columbia and RKO from 1937 to 1938. According to Stephen Rebello in his book about the golden age of movie posters, *Reel Art*, Patterson was all over the lots working in the set, costume or promotion departments for *Stand Up and Cheer* (1934), *Babes in Toyland* (1934), *The Gay Divorcee* (1934), *Bottom's Up* (1935), *True Confession* (1937), *Artists and Models* (1937), and *Bluebeard's Eighth Wife*, *The Big Broadcast*, *College Swing*, *Tropic Holiday*, *Give Me A Sailor* (all 1938) and *St. Louis Blues* (1939). Rebello notes Patterson's work in Hollywood, perhaps the most elaborately rendered and colored of his entire career, contained "witty design, dense, mirthful detail, and ubiquitous, minx-like glamour pusses."

The '30s were busy and unsettled. Like many actors, writers, artists, and songwriters, Patterson shuttled between coasts until the end of the decade, with the West offering steady movie assignments and the East representing more personal, fresher, but often lower-paying work. He learned, as most did, to live with the tradeoff. Along with Flagg and Crandell, Patterson was one of the nationally known cover illustrators whose Columbia movie posters were reworked by anonymous staff artists (Hirschfeld called them "ear, eye, and nose" specialists) employed by nervous studios to guarantee a near photographic likeness of the stars One account has Patterson returning to New York City in the mid '30s, determined to "cut expenses to the bone," renting a studio apartment and devoting himself only to his growing list of personal projects.

His second extended stay in Hollywood was prompted by the opportunity to combine studio work with his latest personal creation, marionettes. In the mid-'30s, Patterson designed and produced "Patterson Personettes," an ambitious puppet show conceived as a full-blown Busby Berkeley musical. Following its debut in East Coast nightclubs and casinos, Paramount featured the Personettes performing "Mister Esquire" in its 1937 Jack Benny vehicle directed by Raoul Walsh, *Artist and Models*, based on the shows of the same name by the Society of Illustrators. Patterson also kept busy by designing the annual Christmas windows for Macy's and other department stores (he tried to get Held a similar job but Held refused, and turned instead to writing novels), and judging beauty contests (Patterson judged every Miss America contest from 1927 to 1945). It was also in 1937 that he met musical composer Ruth Cleary, who was hired to accompany his Personettes on stage. They married a year later, and in 1939, his second daughter, Russelle, was born.

According to Stephen Becker in his 1959 book *Comic Art in America*, Patterson had one indispensable

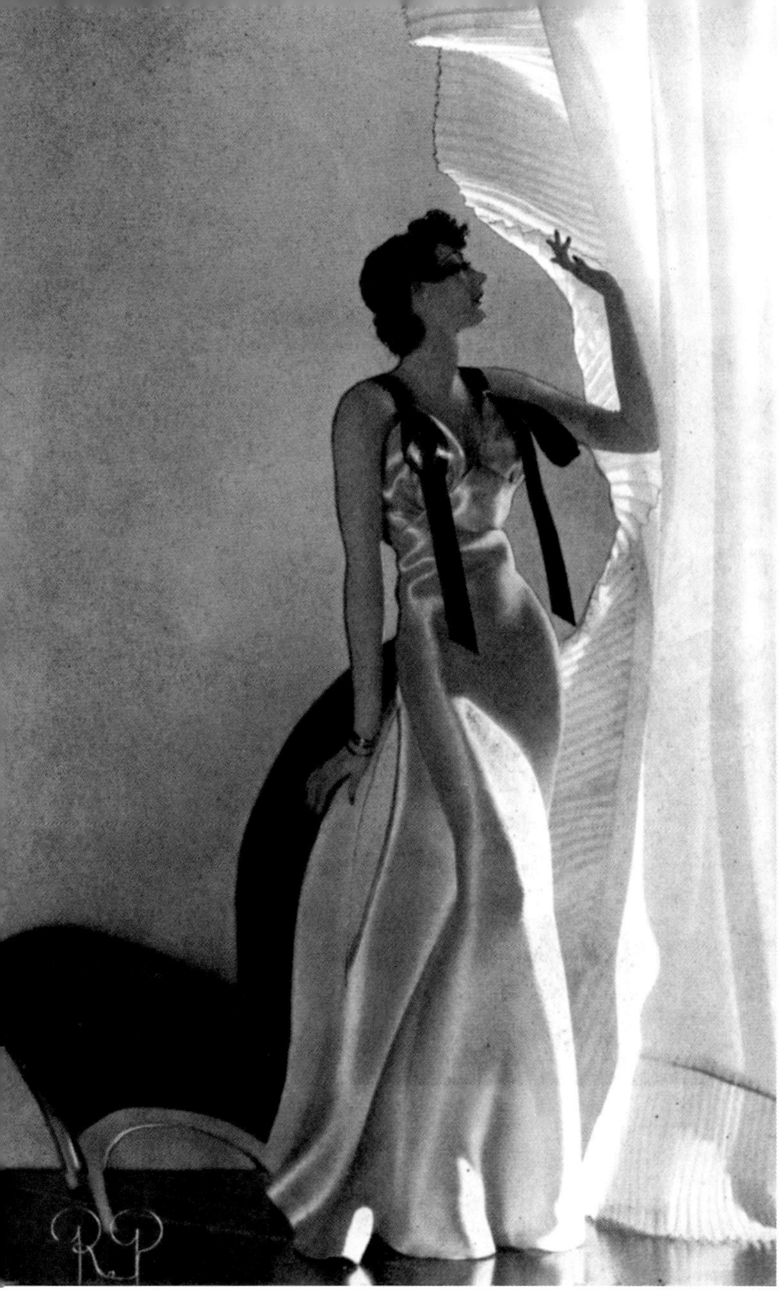

quality for real creativity: "No one knows what he will come up with next." In the 1930s and 1940s, he developed a 3-D process for ads appearing in *American Weekly* (which had a Personette wearing Patterson clothes in a Patterson-designed set with Patterson artwork on the walls) and designed Fall coats for men and women using maquettes to model his designs. His Christmas window arrangements such as *The Wedding of the Wooden Soldier and the Painted Doll* inspired seasonal children's books based on his display. He collaborated with his wife and a writer on another display-based book about the adventures of a young Mexican boy, *Rolito* (1941), which included a Decca recording of simple songs designed to instruct children about Mexico's culture and language. Patterson also designed hotel lobbies, supper clubs, bars, restaurants, and the interiors for 15 Western Pacific club cars and five off-Broadway theaters. As if that weren't enough, he also appeared in ads for whiskey and pens, designed swimsuits, and operated a dress-pattern company for teen fashions called "Pattikins."

Another idea that intrigued him was a social group exclusively for cartoonists. Patterson said his first goal when he came to New York was to meet all his illustration role models. For the rest of his life, he was proud of the fact that his heroes, men like Gibson and Harrison Fisher, were likewise seeking him out. He often told the story of getting into a shouting and shoving match at a Society of Illustrator's *Artist and Models* rehearsal with a fiery James Montgomery Flagg and ending the dispute by announcing that the proud older man was about to exchange blows with "your biggest fan."

During the war years, the Theatre Wing organized Camp shows—a USO affair with the illustrators as performers. The group consisted of artists like Ernie Bushmiller (*Nancy*), Otto Soglow (*The Little King*), Milton Caniff (*Terry and Pirates*), Bob Dunn (*They'll Do it Every Time)*, and Russell and Ruth Patterson. Rube Goldberg (his unique *Crazy Inventions* was appearing then in Hearst newspapers) served as emcee. At one of their stops, Patterson convinced Goldberg that a small group composed entirely of their NYC circle of friends/cartoonists would be a perfect unit. Goldberg finally relented and the small group that later expanded into the National Cartoonists Society was born. Patterson served as the NCS President from 1952 to 1953.

Then, of course, there was his career as a cartoonist and comic-strip artist. At the same time his illustrations were appearing in *Collier's, Liberty, Photoplay, Women's Home Companion,* and *Redbook*, Patterson was also writing and drawing serialized strips for Hearst's Sunday supplement, *The American Home Journal*. Among the titles were "Cookie"(1928), "Runaway Ruth" (1929), "Whoa, Nellie" (1930), "Almost a Bride" (1932), and "Get-Your-Man Gloria" (1932), all featuring the romantic misadventures of a girl from the chorus line, a genre first popularized in 1925 by Anita Loos' *Gentlemen Prefer Blondes*.

By the end of the 1930s, Patterson would switch from chorus girls, transatlantic voyages, and incognito millionaires to the home front. Patterson's latest incarnation of his Girl, the irresistible and irrepressible (and surprisingly clumsy) Flossy Frills, did her wacky bit for the escalating war effort as a cover feature for *American Weekly*. Patterson produced three 12-week Flossy Frills series: the first began in 1939 and was written by Carolyn Wells, followed in 1941 by "New Adventures of Flossy Frills" and then the 1942 "Flossy Frills Helps Out," now penned by Perry Shaw.

When the series finally ended in 1943, Patterson illustrated a *Weekly* cover feature called "Hits to Be," the songs purportedly chosen by famous entertainers like Vaughn Monroe and Tommy Dorsey, which was followed in 1945 by the King Features strip "Pin Up Girls."

Patterson's last girl strip was *Mamie*, which ran from 1951 to 1955. *Mamie* was a Sunday only glamour-girl strip that told simple, dumb-blonde gags and included girl-friendly features like paper dolls. His last comics work was the series *Over Sexteen*, an uneven collection of adult humor that presented crude

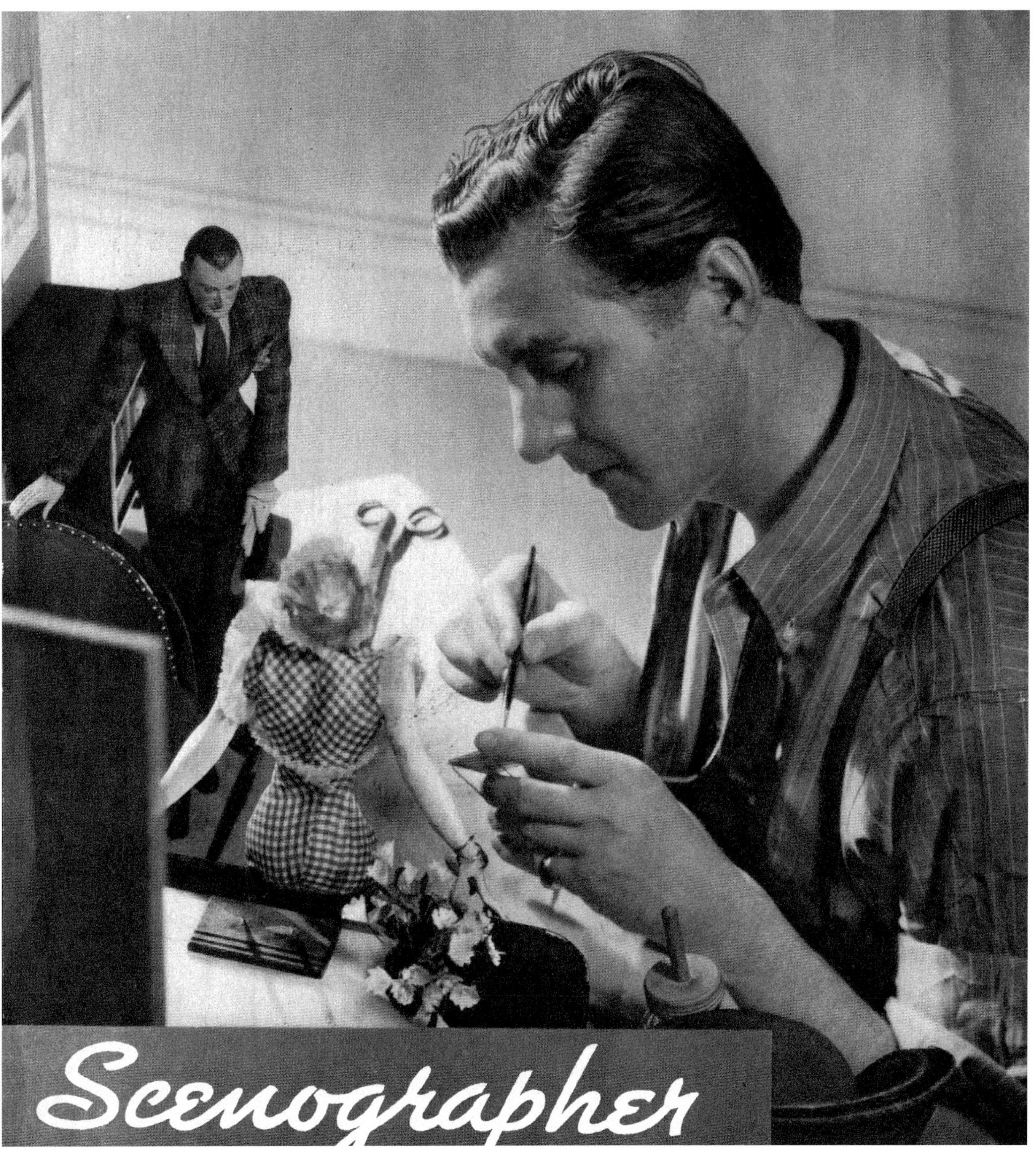

verse and corny jokes alongside cartoons, many in color. Patterson illustrated two volumes, one in 1958 and the second in 1960. It's somewhat sad to see this final phase, marked by an over-the-top exaggeration the Patterson Girl had never previously succumbed to, a strident approach popularized by the post-World War II bombshell era.

Looking at his career in its entirety, Patterson was far more a leader than a follower. Among his most obvious disciples was Elmer (E.) Simms Campbell, who became a girlie cartoonist on Patterson's advice, "you can always sell a pretty girl," and who was cheap enough to be hired by the start-up magazine *Esquire* as well as another fledging upstart, *Playboy*. There also was Don Flowers, who freely admitted his debt to Patterson. There were many others, like Chicago pals Floyd Davis and John Streibel (*Dixie Dugan*), Russell Keaton (*Flying Jenny*), and humor magazine illustrators Gilbert Bundy and John Holmgren. In fact, it can be said with confidence that Patterson's trademark girl touched virtually every girlie comic artist working between 1930 and 1960.

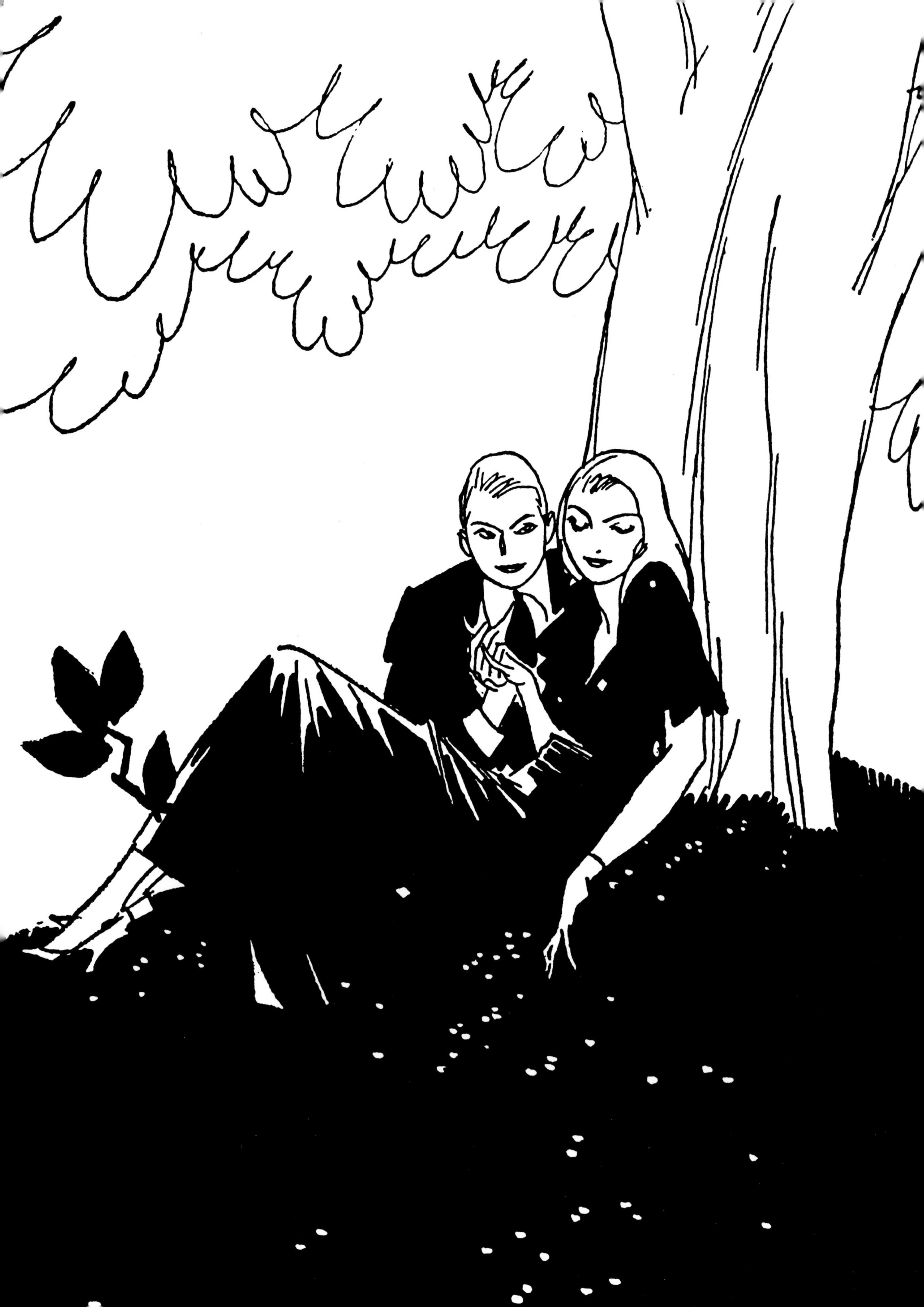

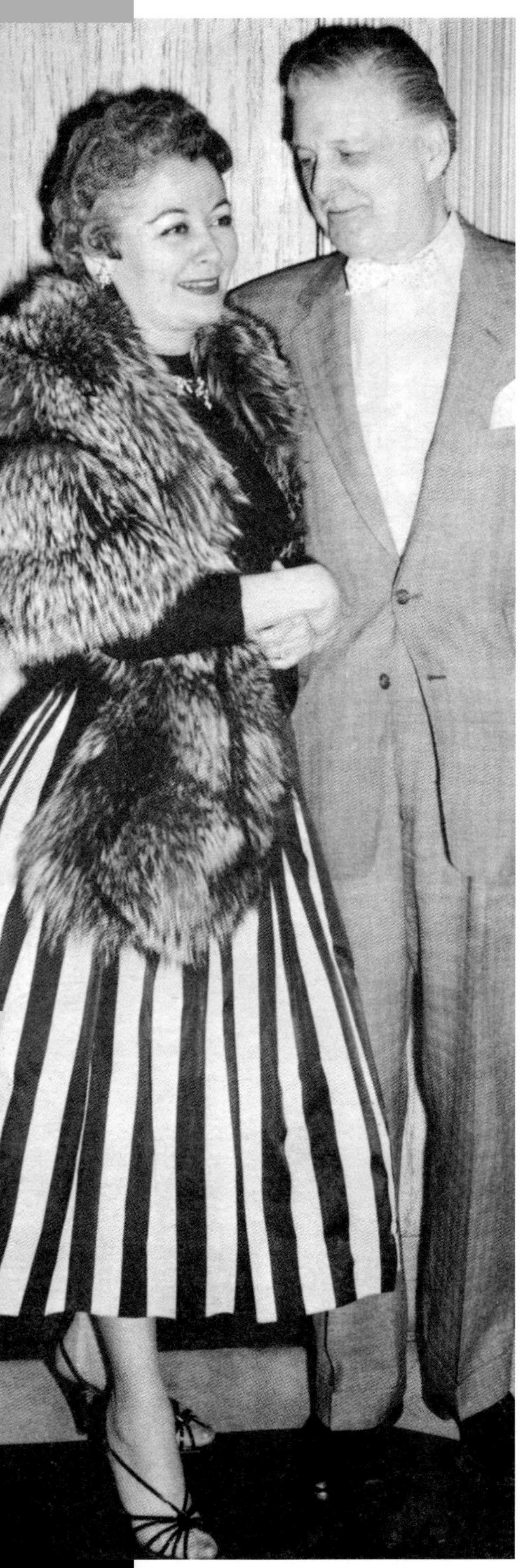

Patterson and his second wife, Ruth Cleary Patterson. By the time this photograph was published, Patterson had ceased drawing.

In a tribute he wrote after Patterson's passing, Milton Caniff said it was Patterson, not Held or F. Scott Fitzgerald, who best defined the strut and fret of American life between the two World Wars, concluding: "He had the flair. He had the touch."

SO WHAT?!

Patterson worked and worked and worked until he physically couldn't.

Unfortunately, the perfect sense of timing that served Patterson so well throughout his career eluded him at the end. In the early 1960s he developed arthritis in both hands and as a result needed a specially constructed glove to help him hold a brush. He stopped working altogether in 1966, and until his death 11 years later, was unable to add to his amazingly varied body of work.

Unable to draw, he channeled his energy toward mentoring younger artists. He was on the faculty of National Institute of Art and Design with director Frank Reilly, and wrote short pieces about his life and times for the National Cartoonists Society. While he changed minor details in each retelling, Patterson never tired of telling his story. He saw his life as blessed, rich in friends and incident, yet recognized that you shouldn't dig too far. At the close of his self-lettered biographical caption for the 1965 NCS annual that recapped some of his career highlights, he was unable to sign his entry with his familiar dashing chop, so he challenged his fellow members with the breezy "*So What?!*"

Effervescent. Smart. Sexy. Fun. Tasteful. Something like a wicked lyric with a heartbreaking melody by Cole Porter or Rodgers and Hart.

That was the top. That was Russell Patterson.

THE ART OF

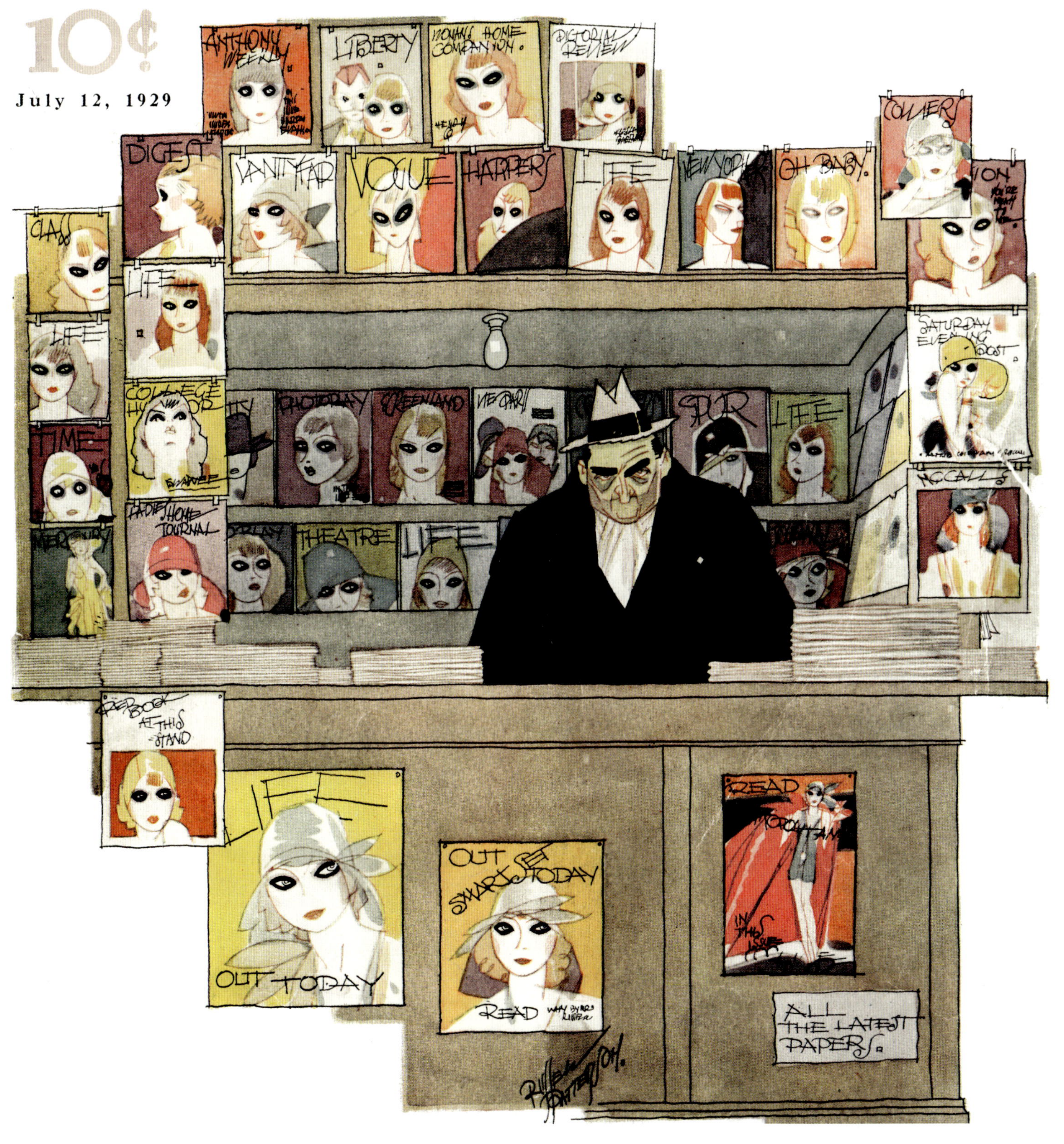

RUSSELL PATTERSON

Life

August 30, 1929

10¢

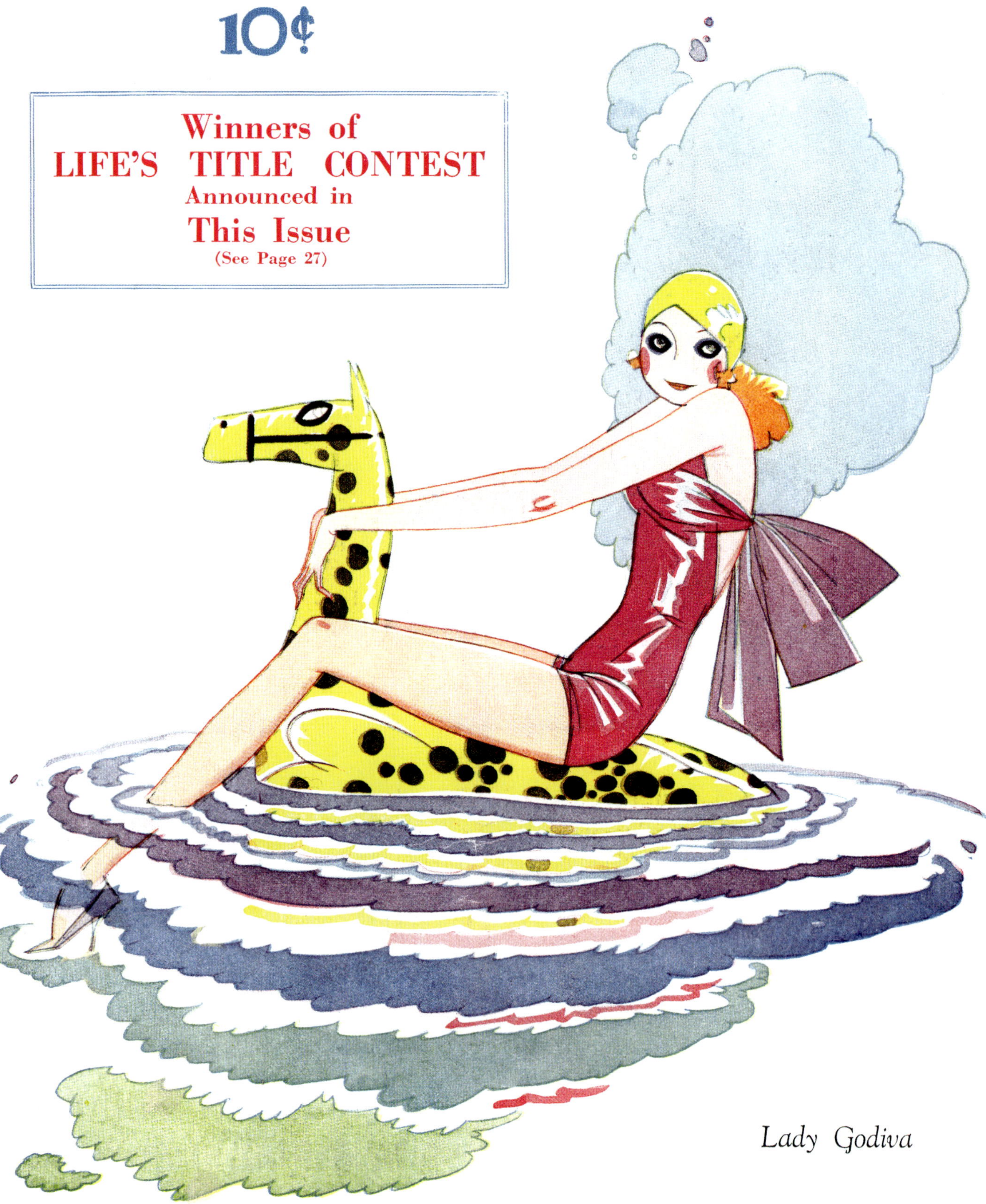

Winners of
LIFE'S TITLE CONTEST
Announced in
This Issue
(See Page 27)

Lady Godiva

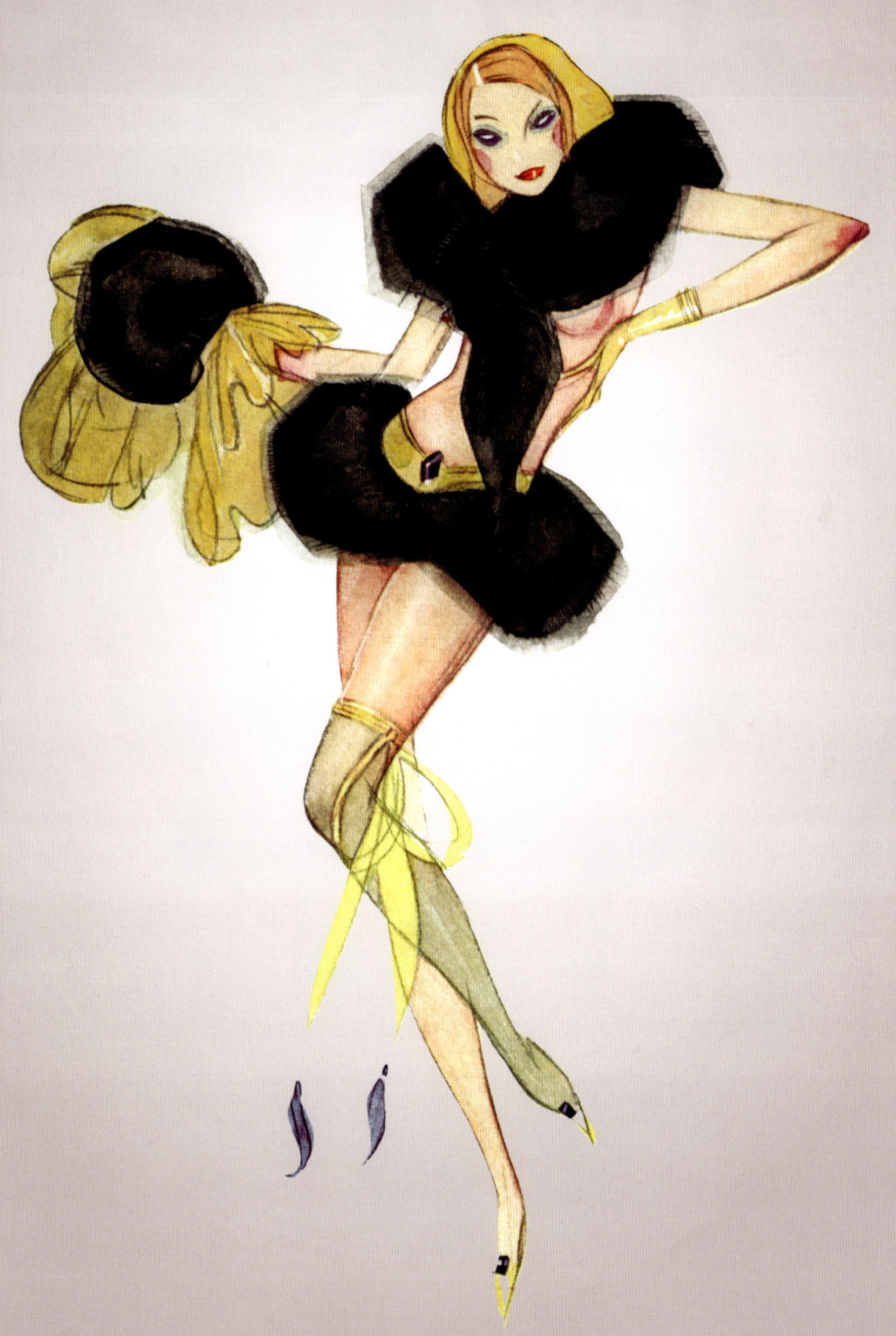

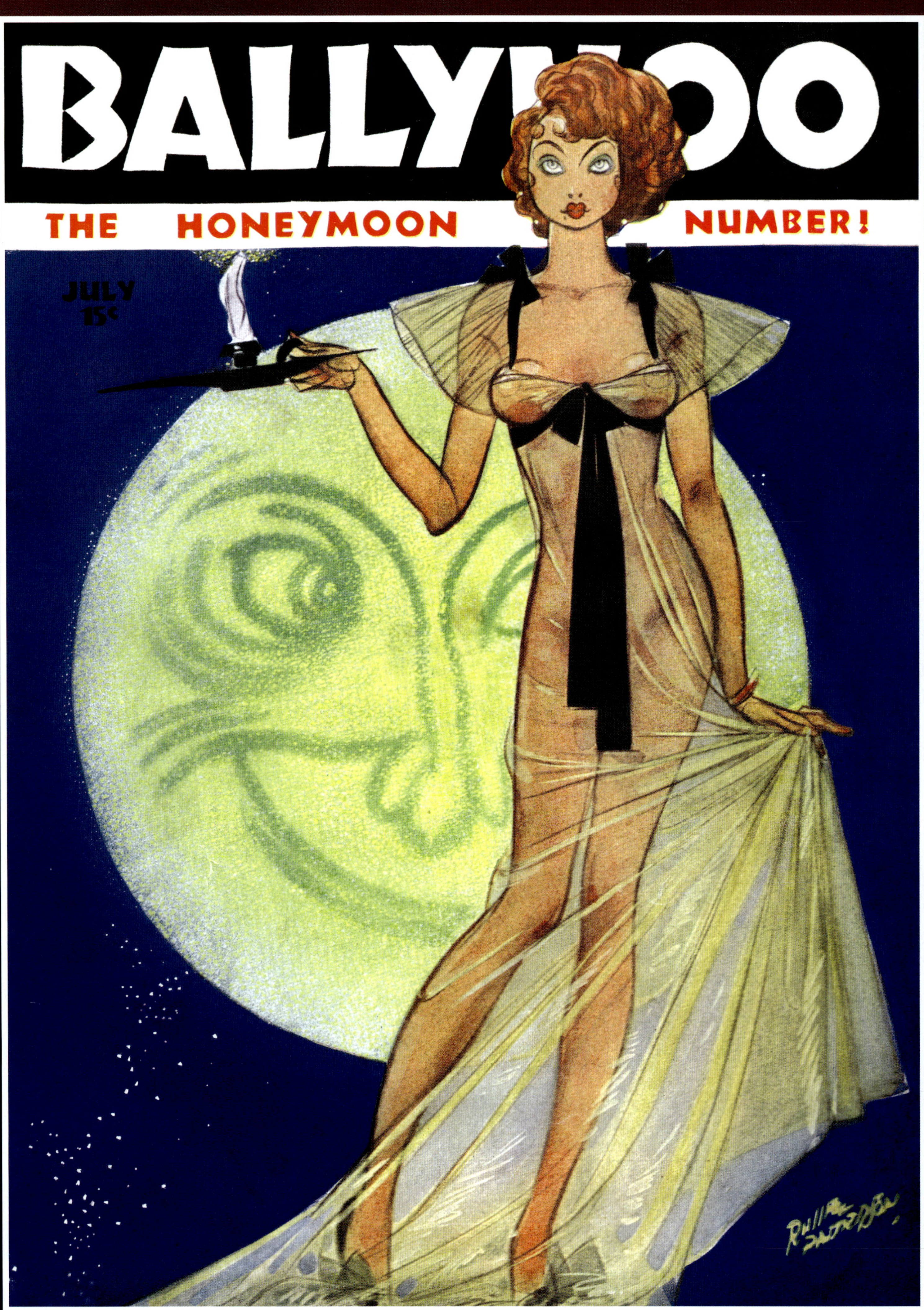
BALLYHOO
THE HONEYMOON NUMBER!
JULY
15¢

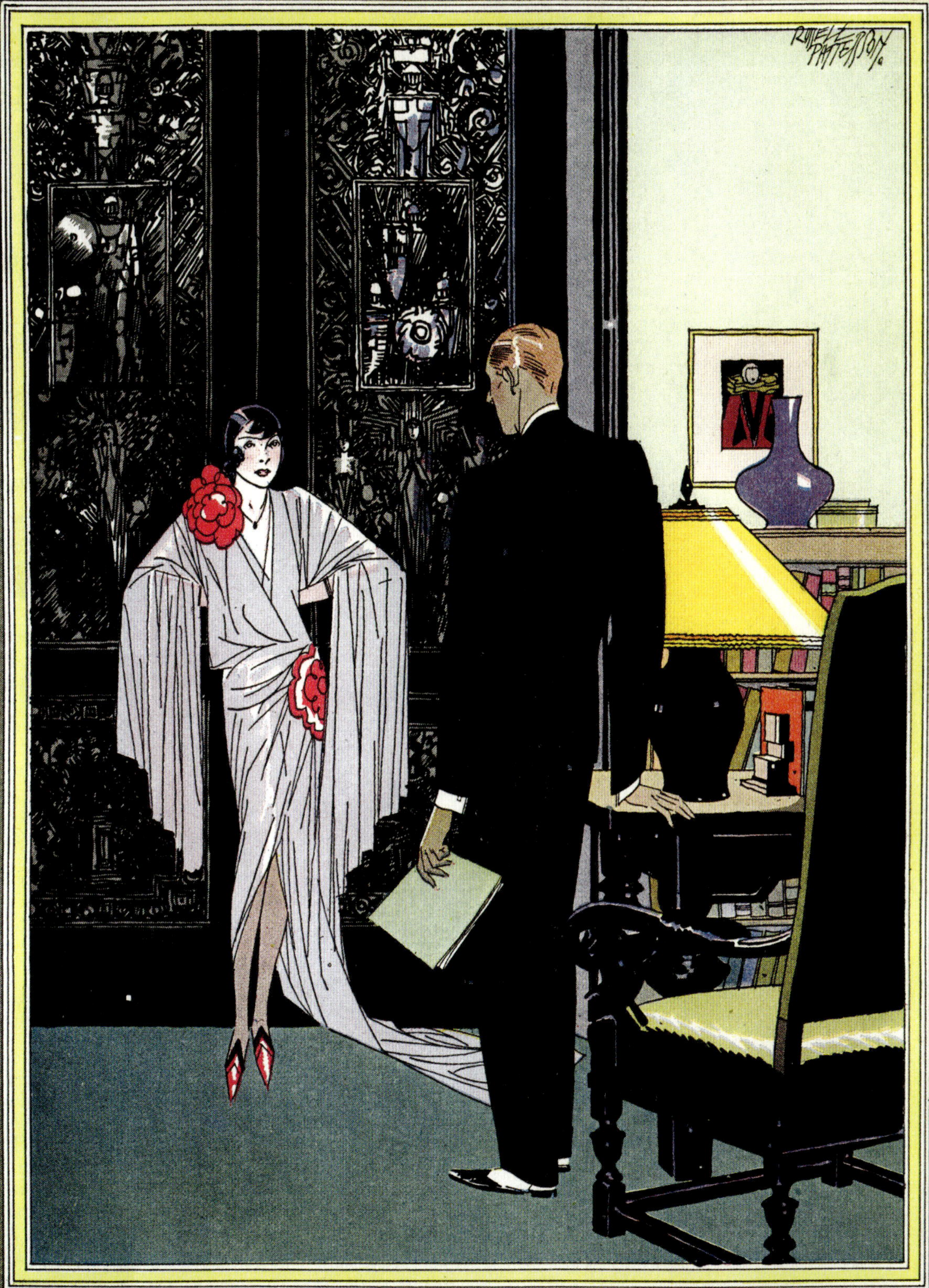
RUSSELL PATTERSON

BALLYHOO

DECEMBER

15 CENTS

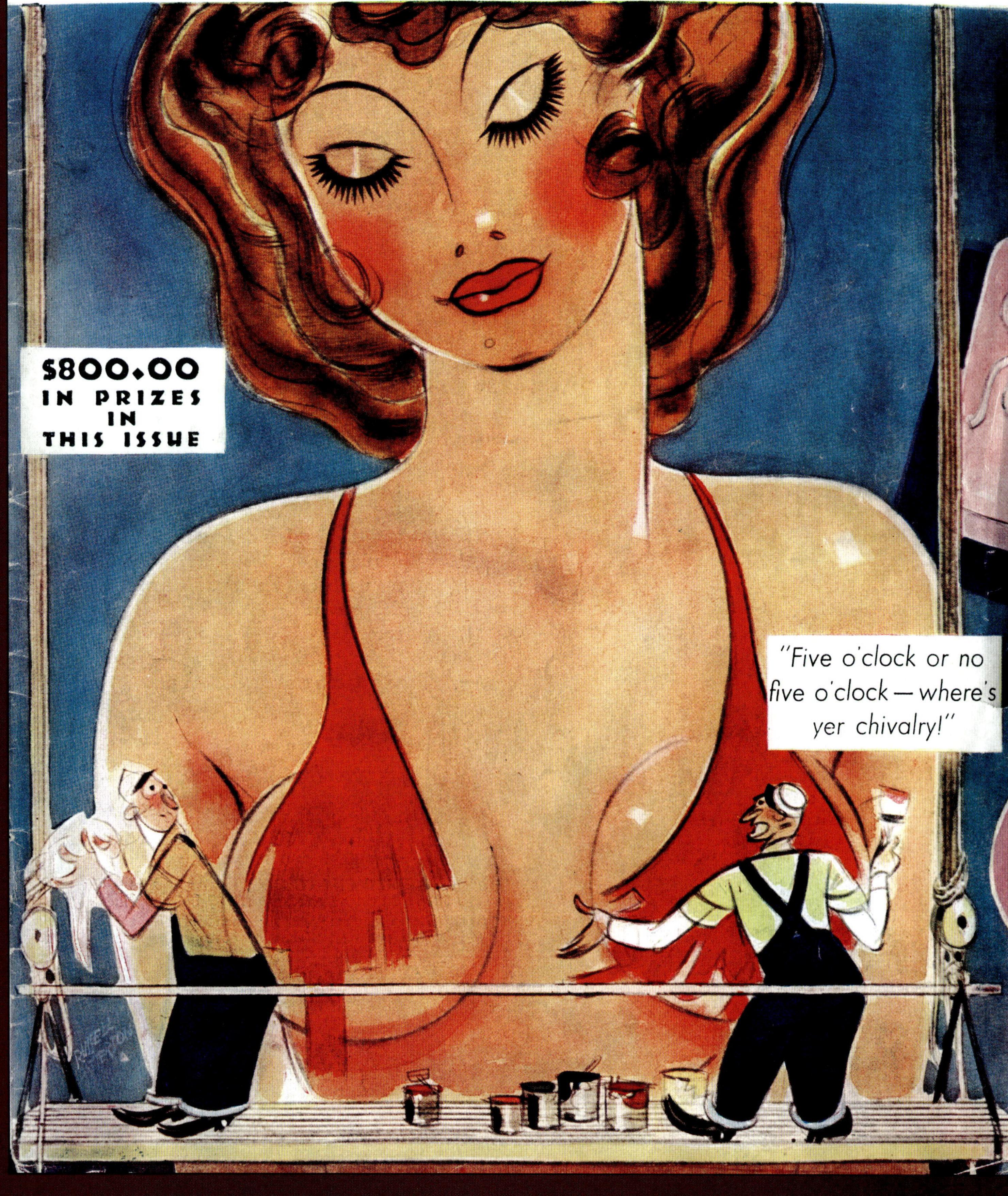

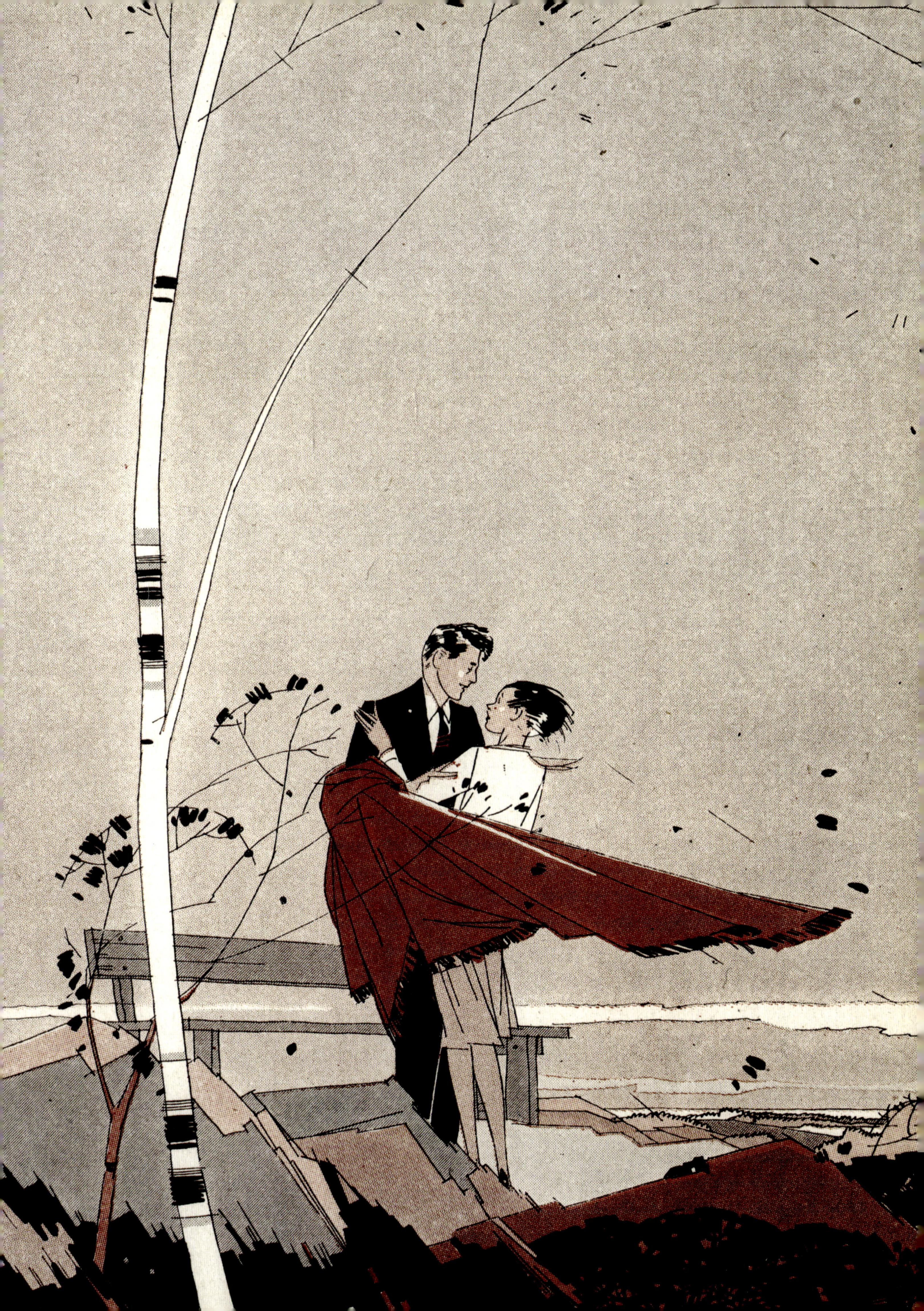

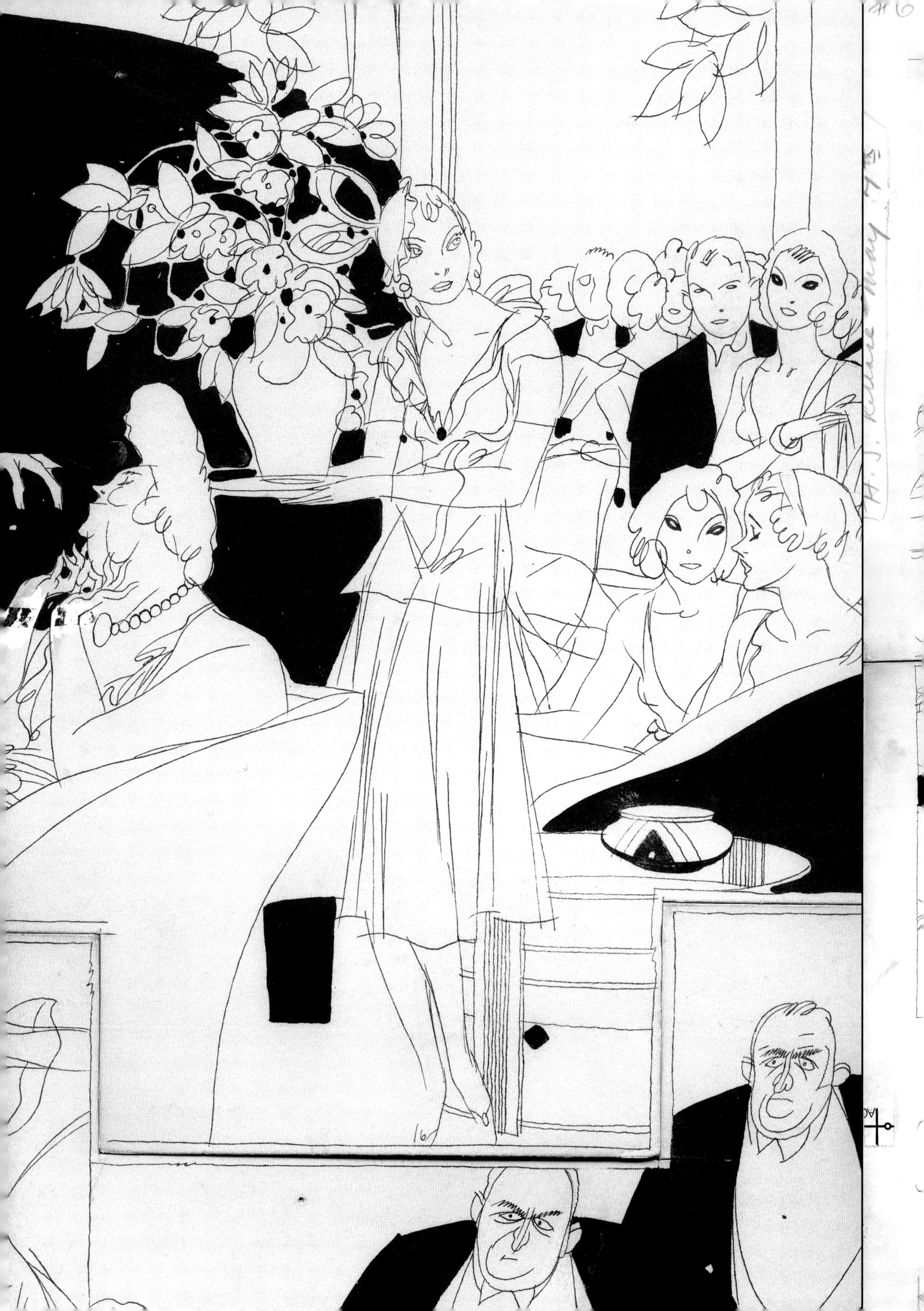

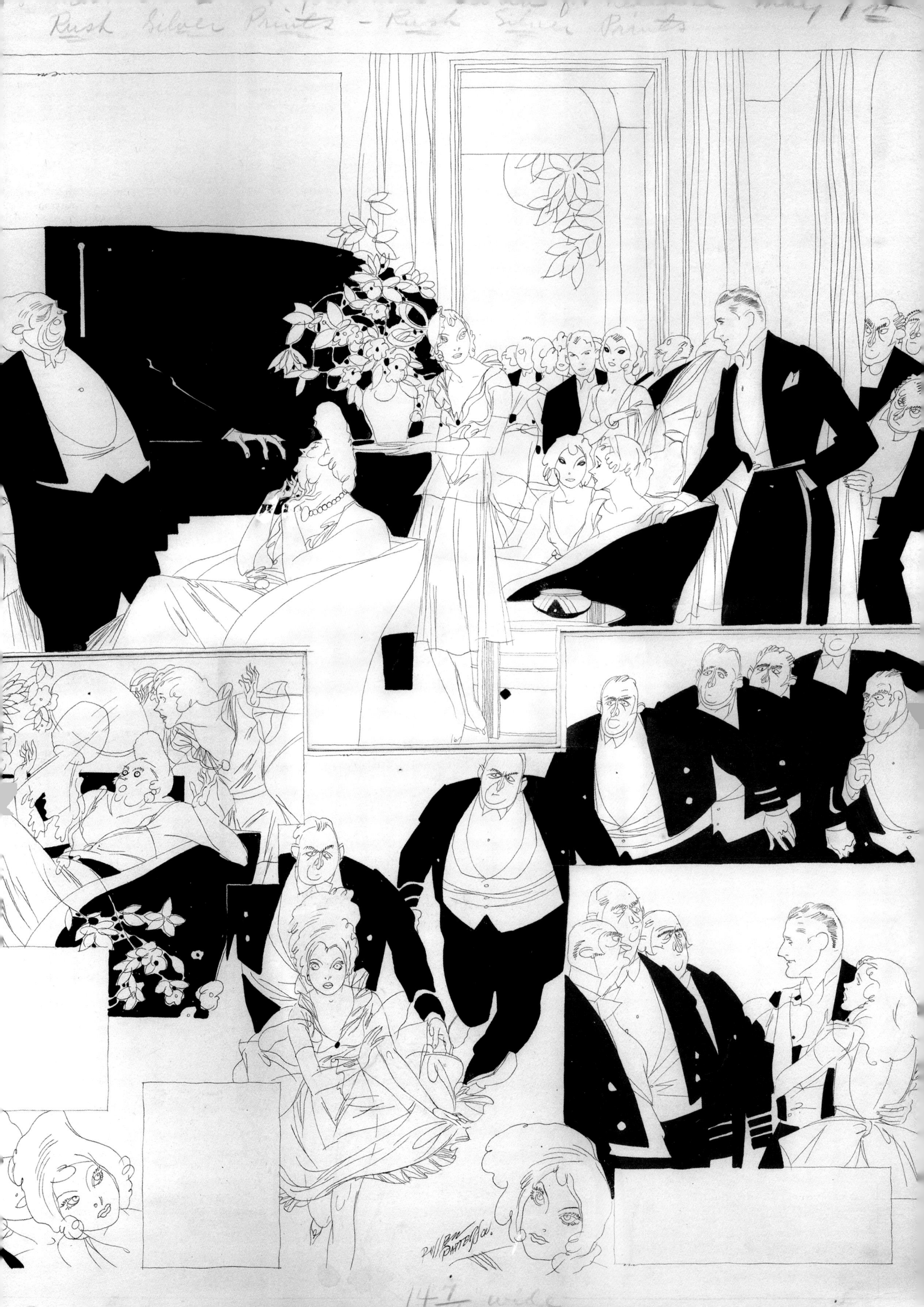
Rush Silver Prints - Rush Silver Prints

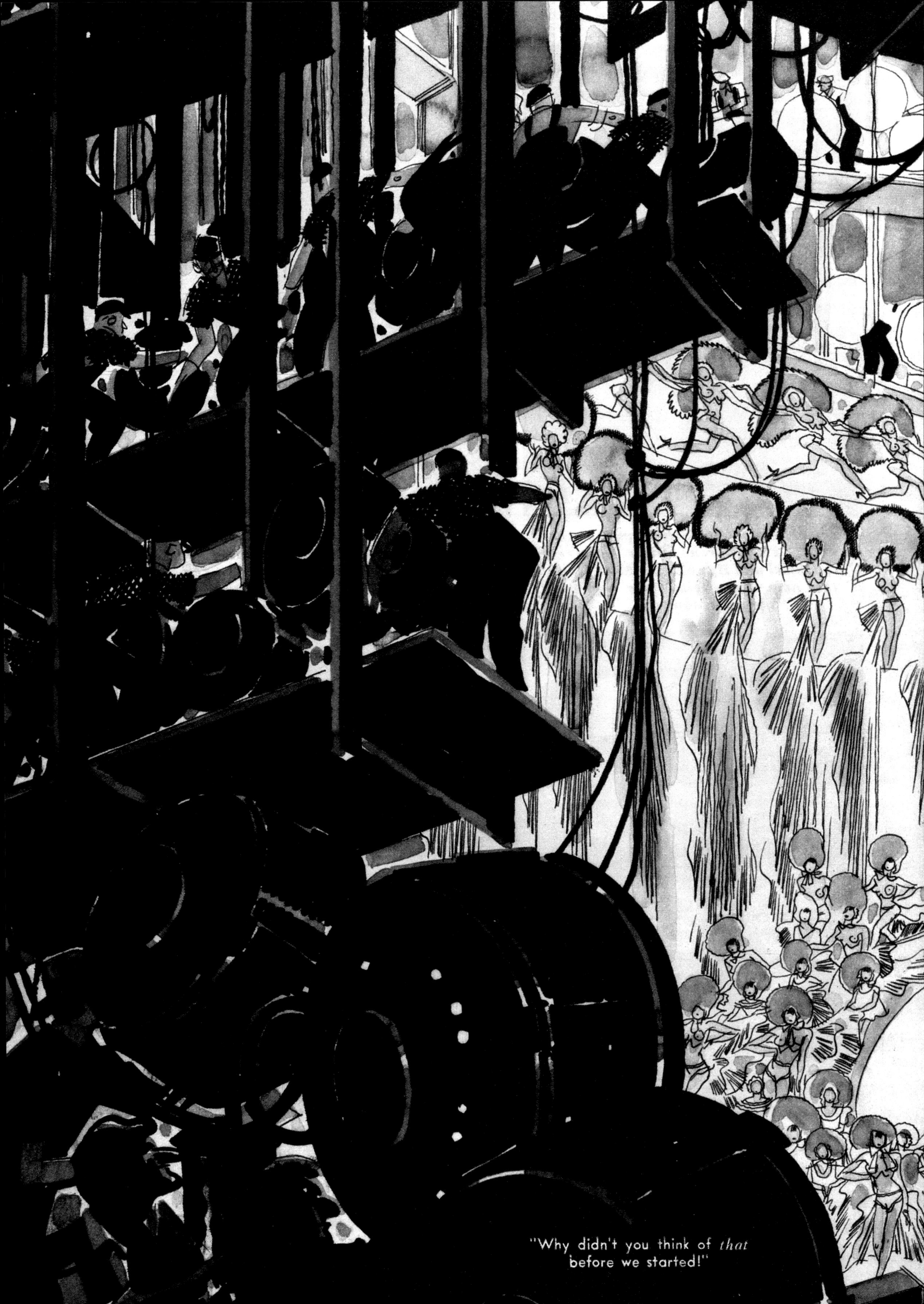

"Why didn't you think of *that* before we started!"

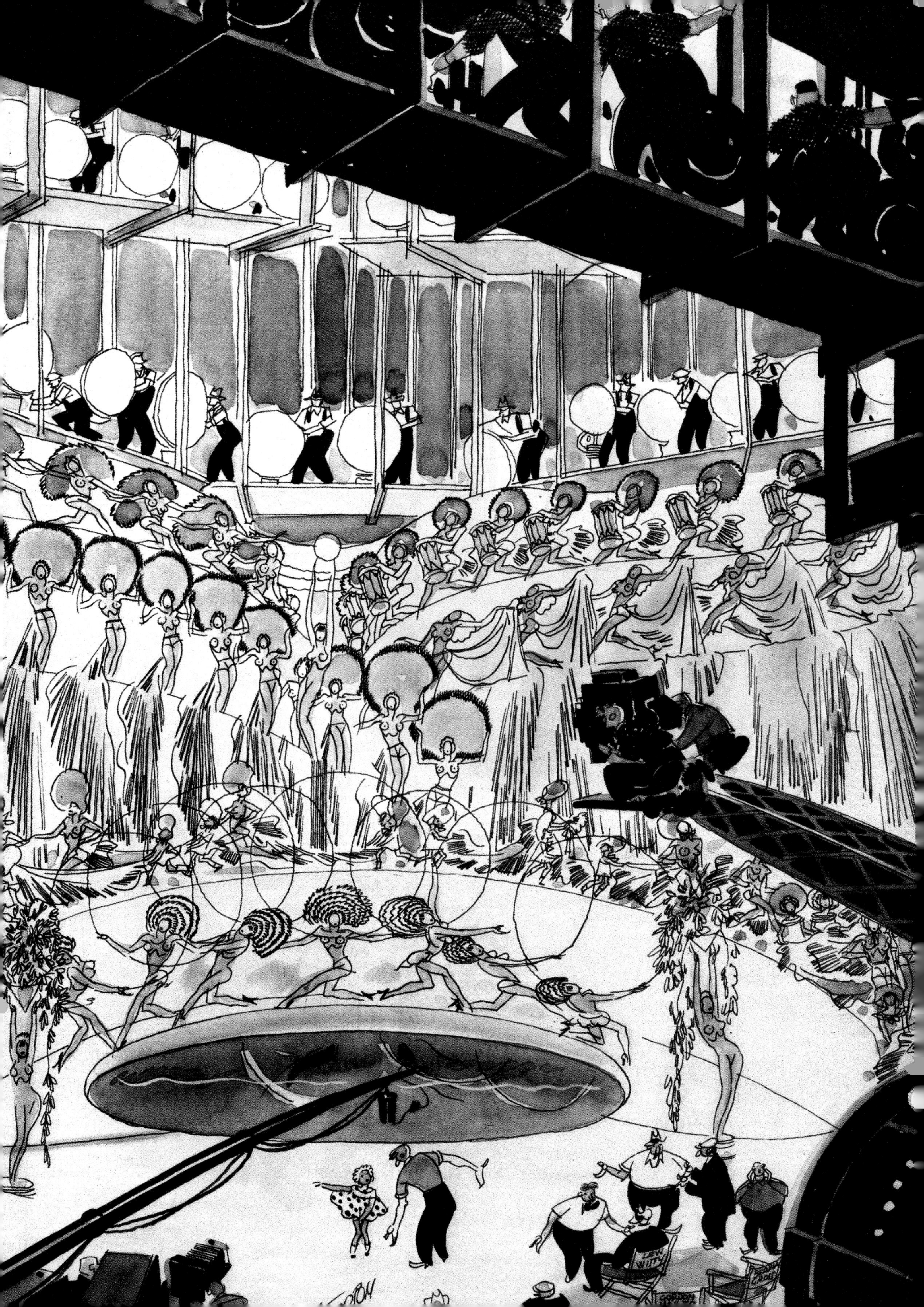
LEW WITTY
GORDON

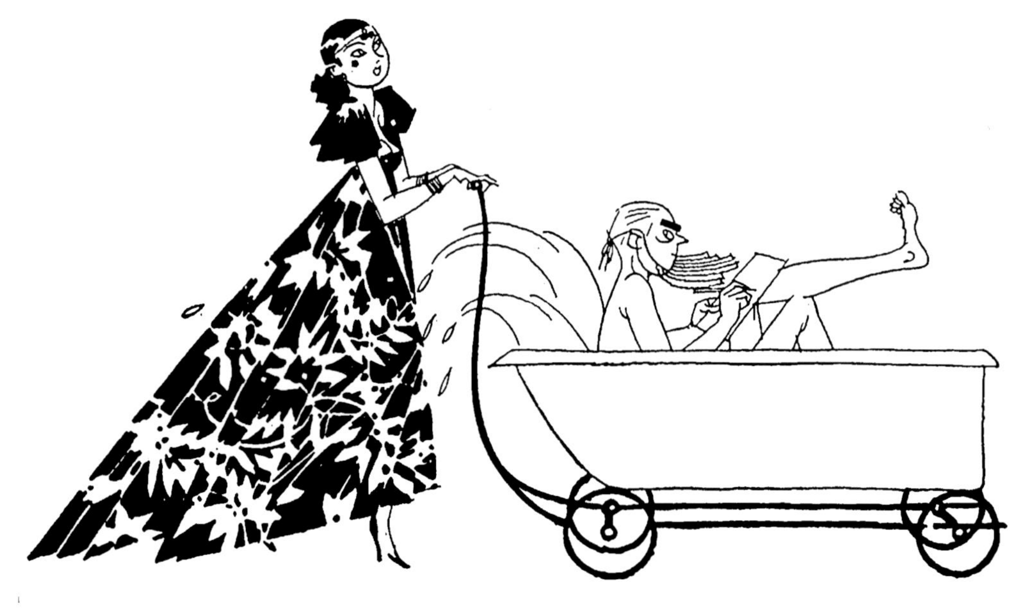

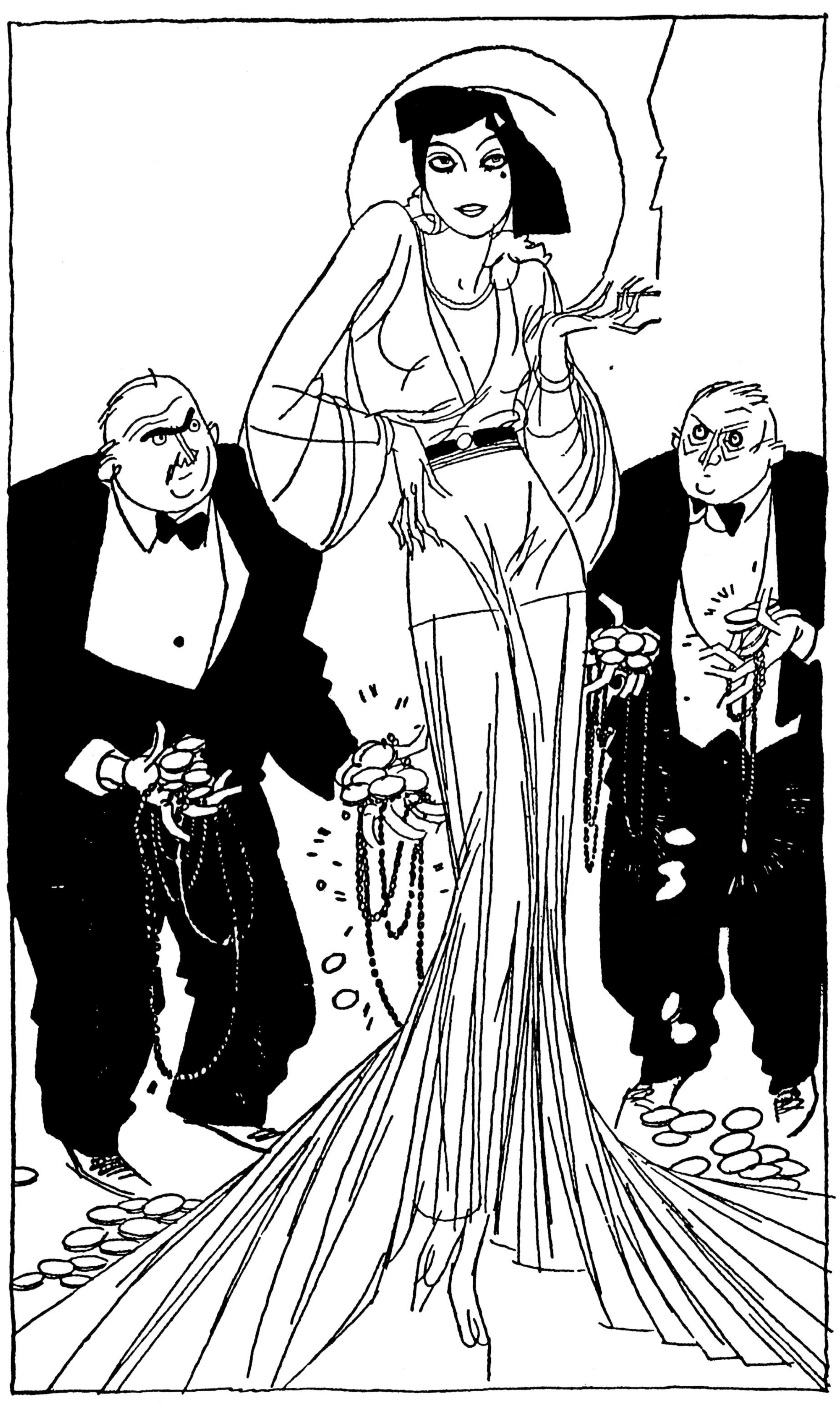

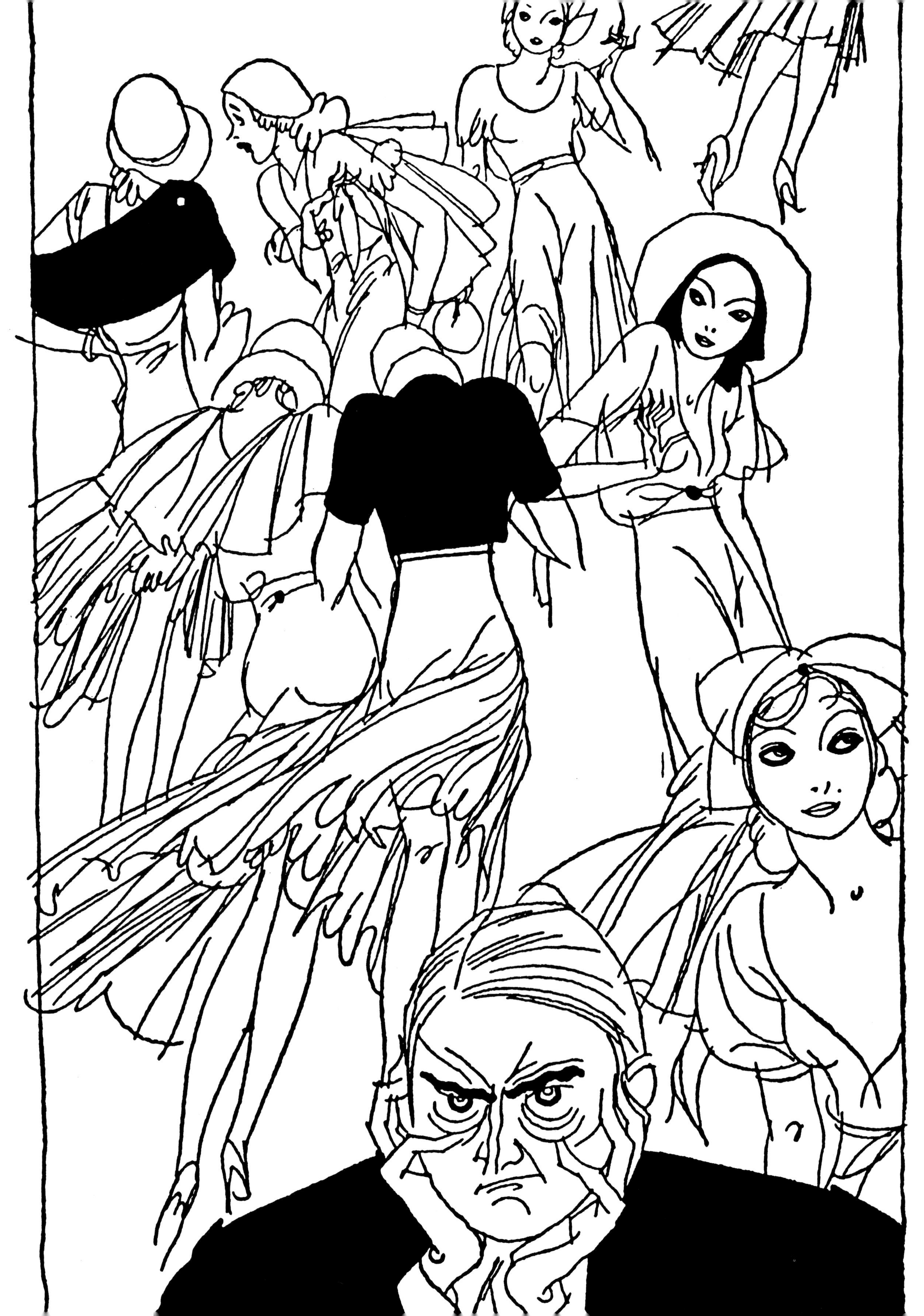

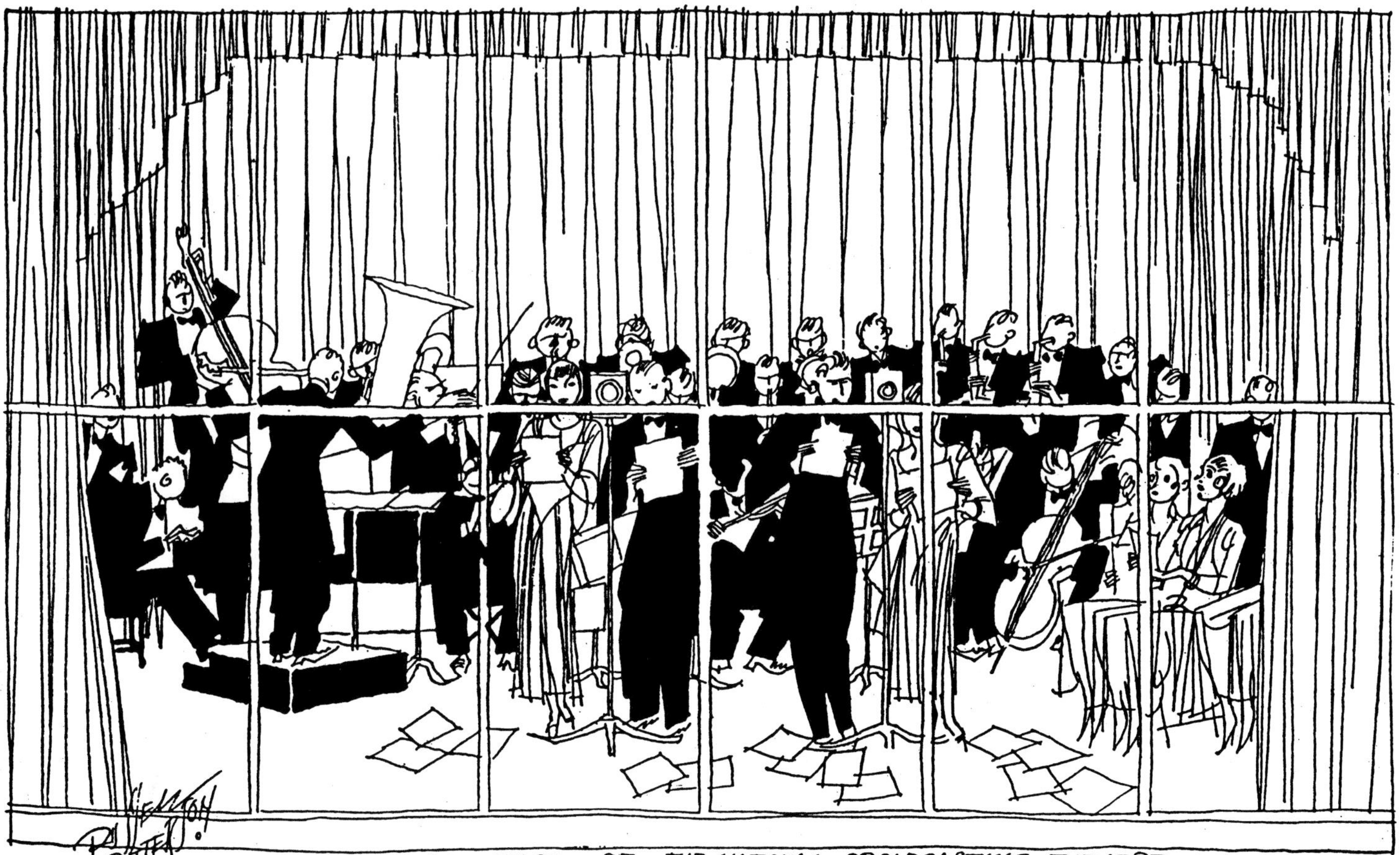

THE GLASS ENCLOSED STAGE OF THE NATIONAL BROADCASTING THEATRE ON THE ROOF OF THE AMSTERDAM.

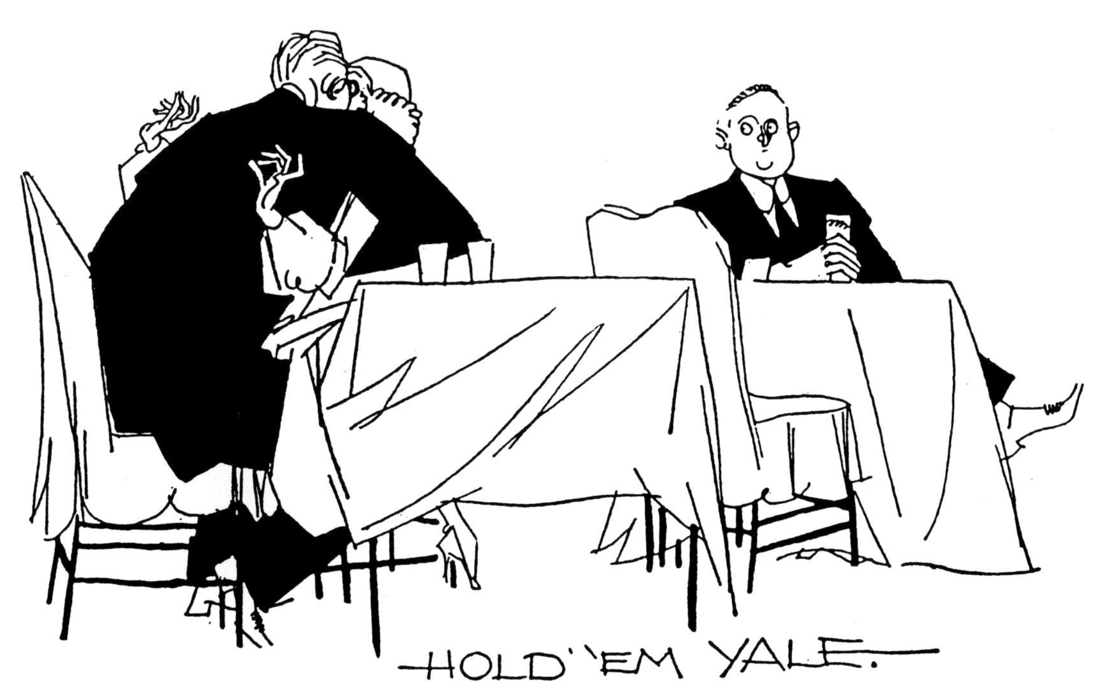

HOLD 'EM YALE.

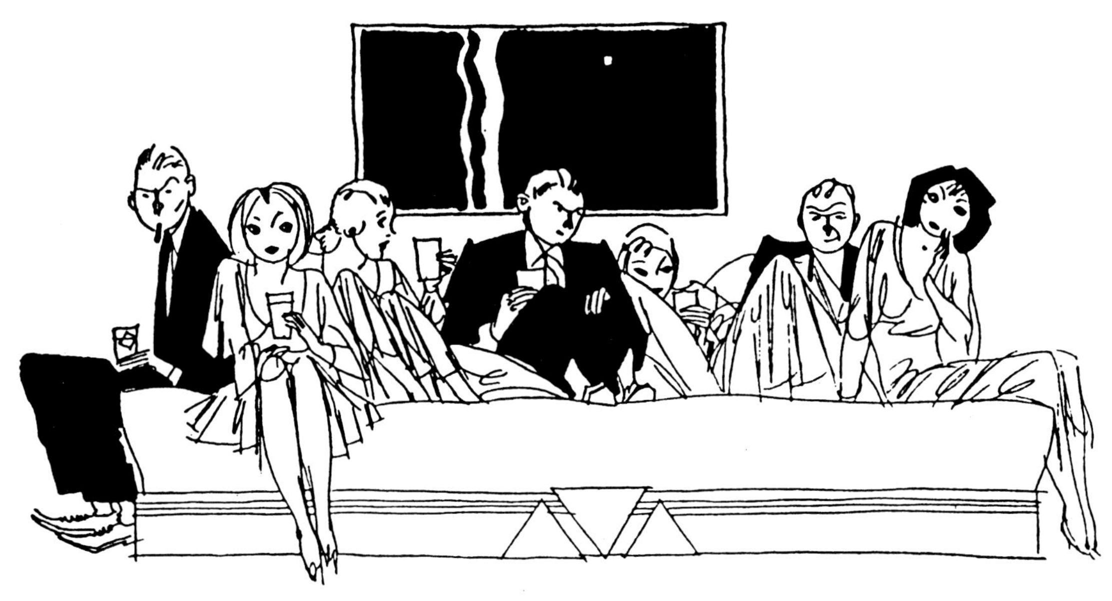

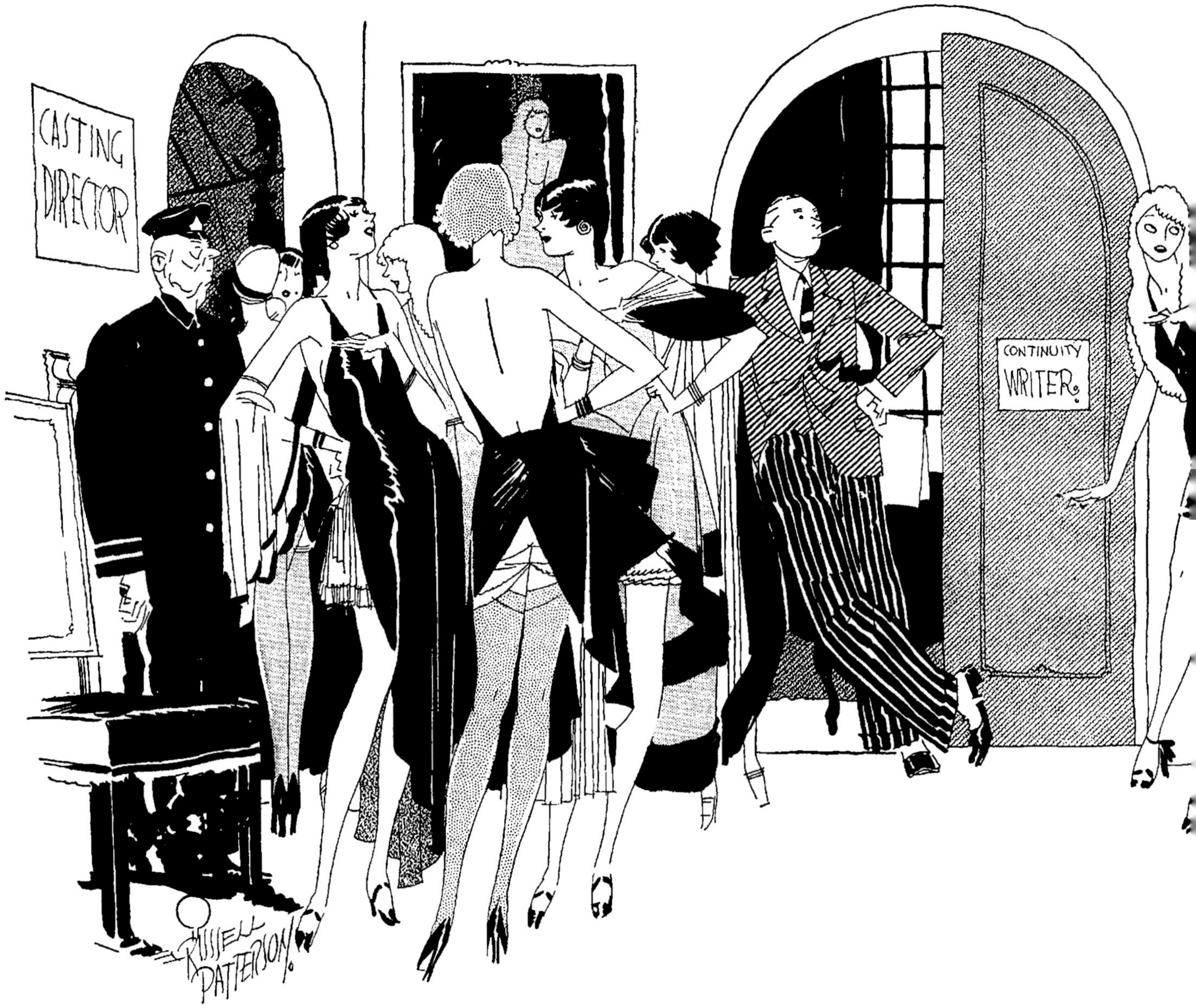

CASTING
DIRECTOR
CONTINUITY
WRITER
RUSSELL PATTERSON

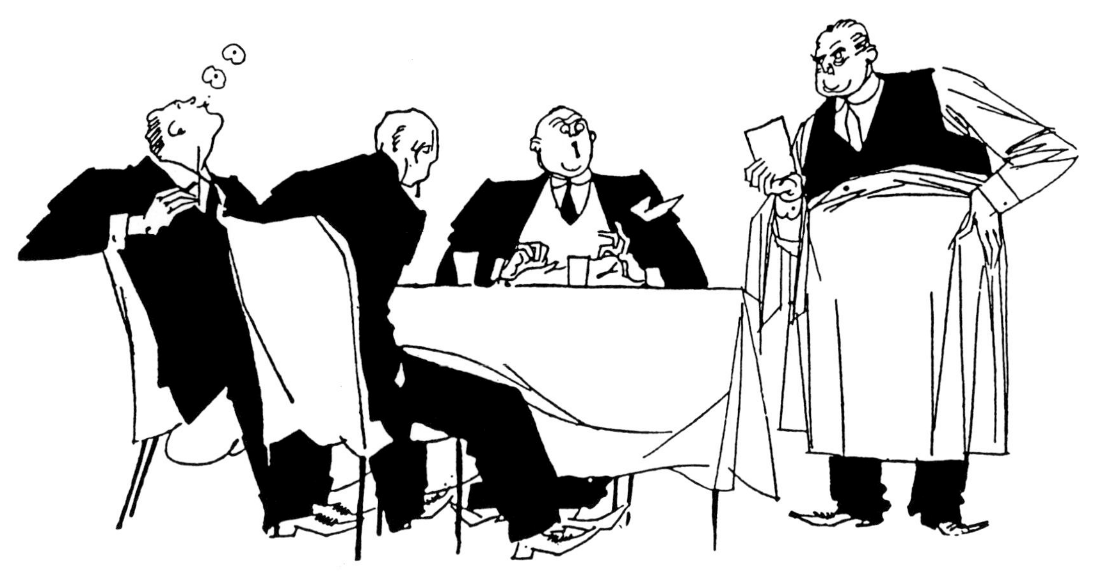

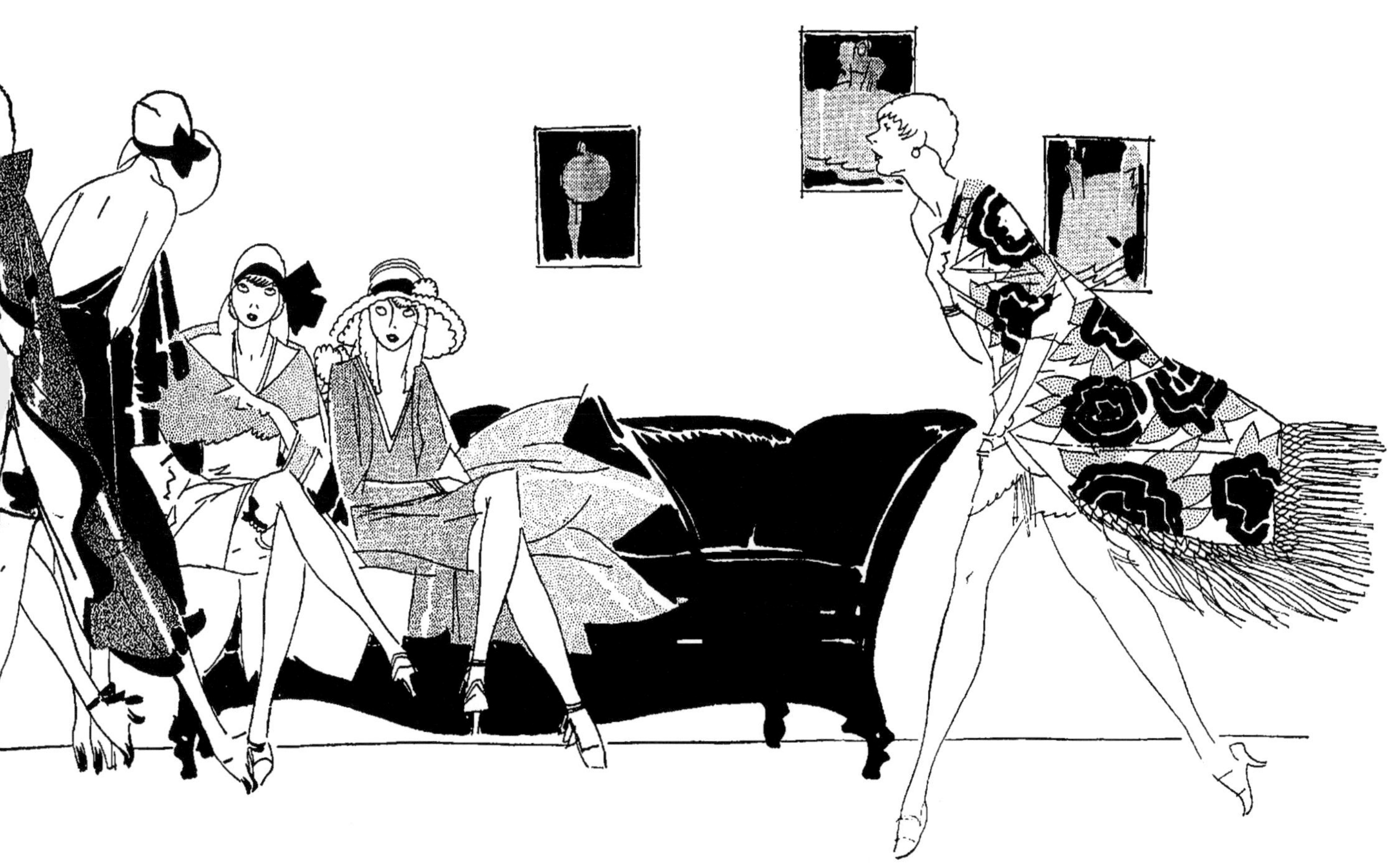

Here is a continuity writer in the act of concentrating. Observe the keen, active mind at work, ingeniously creating big scenes for his boss. No, dear readers, he isn't giving a thought to the cuties

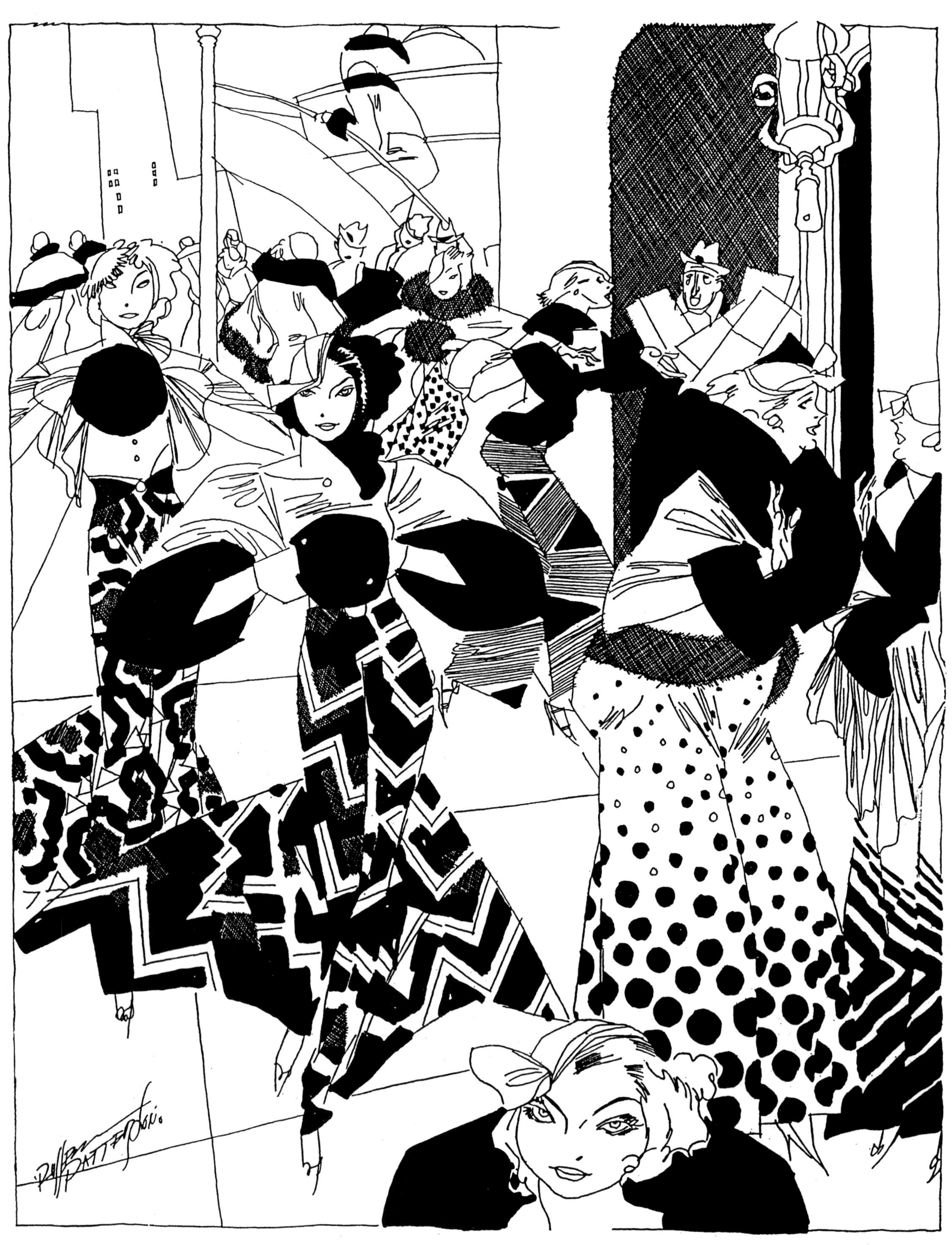

Why not brighten up the holiday season with beach pajamas?

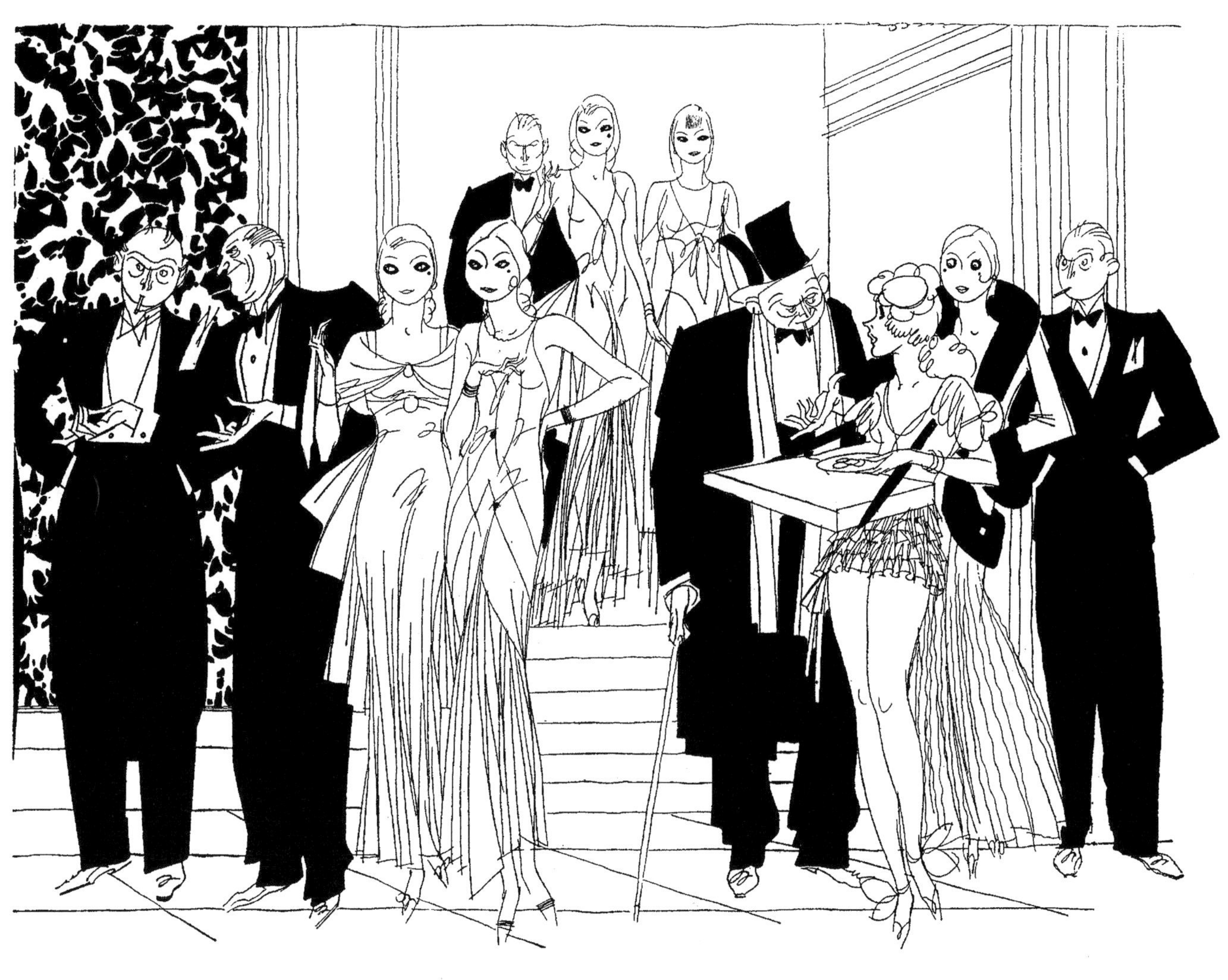

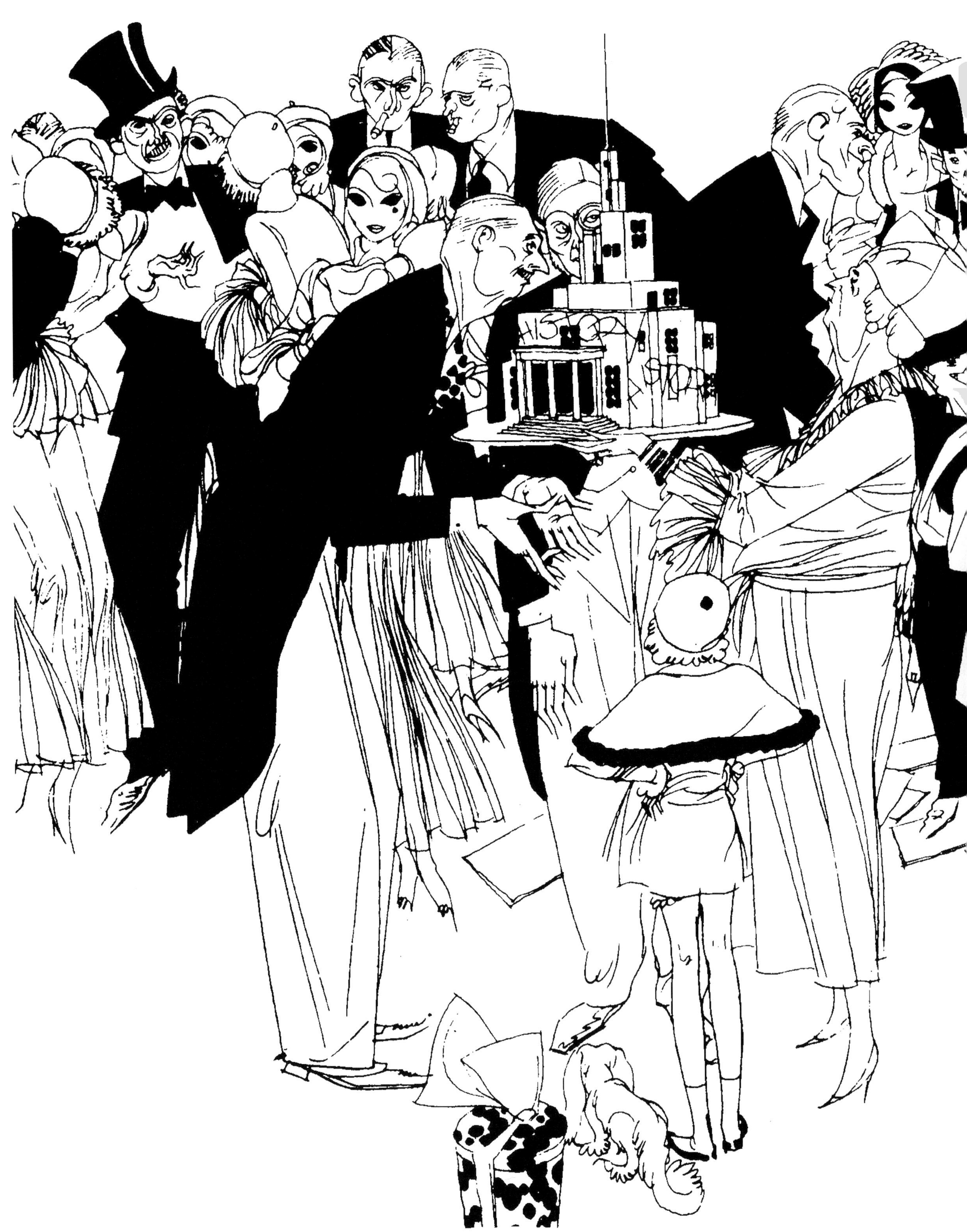

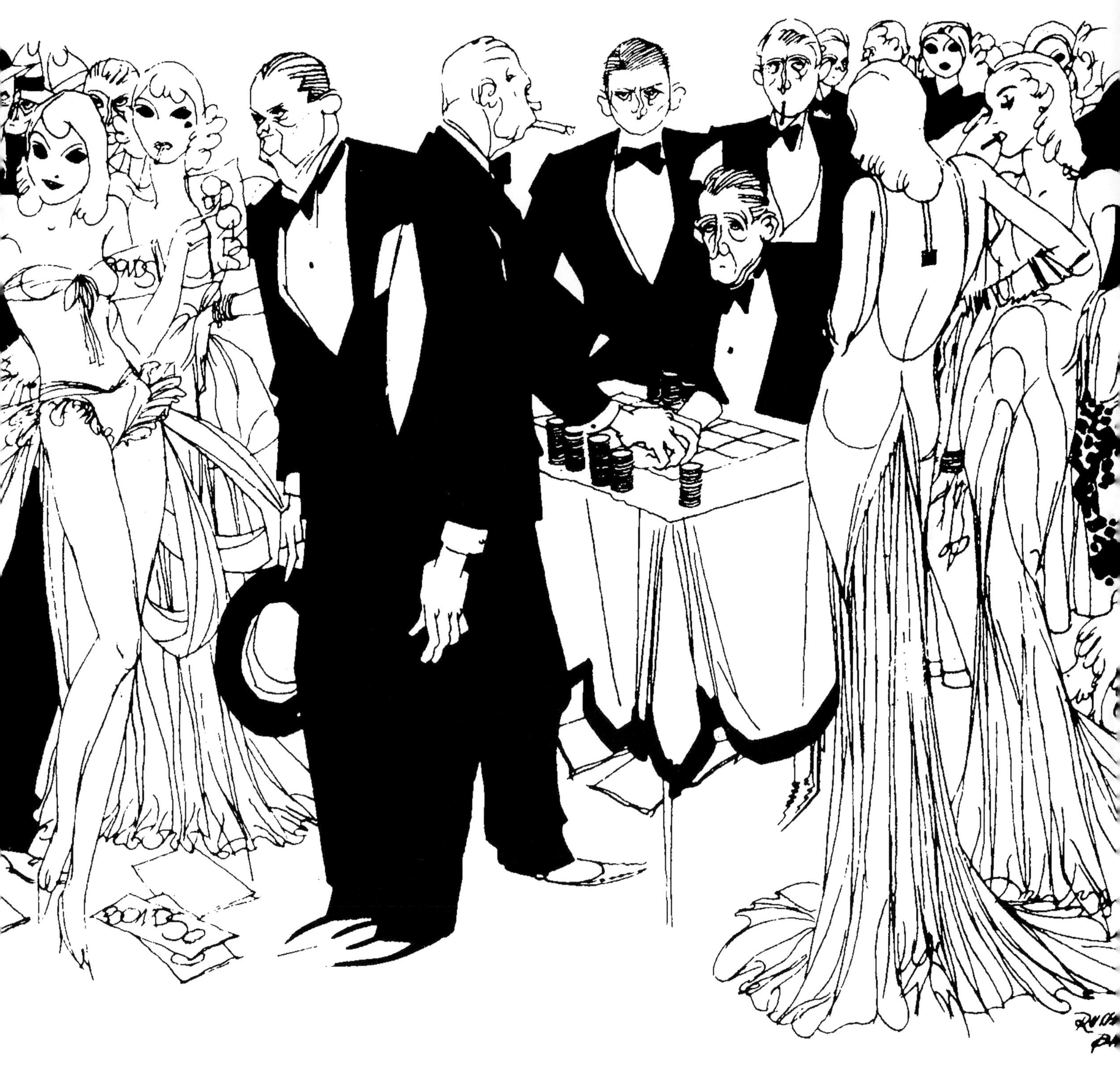
BONDS

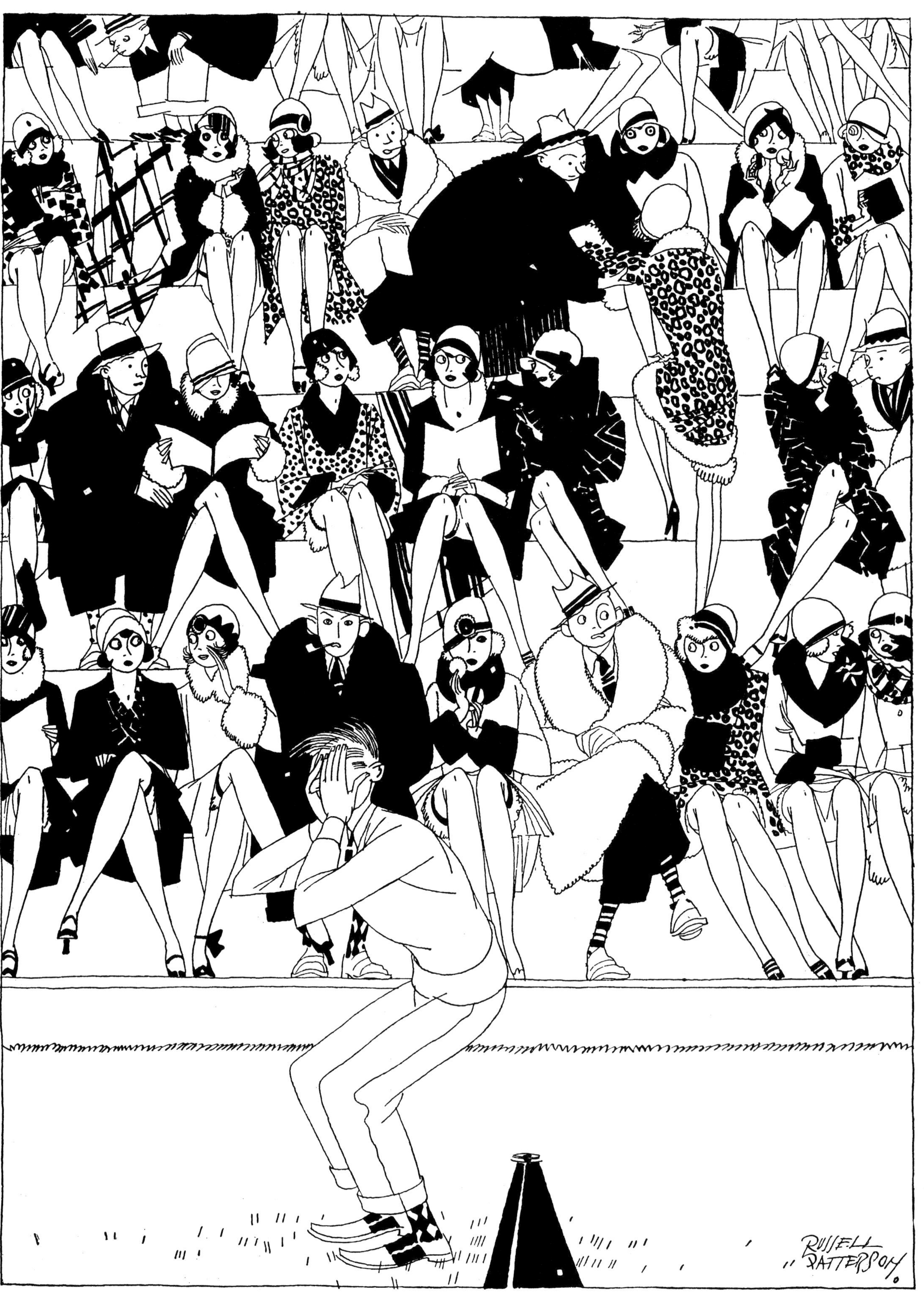
RUSSELL
PATTERSON

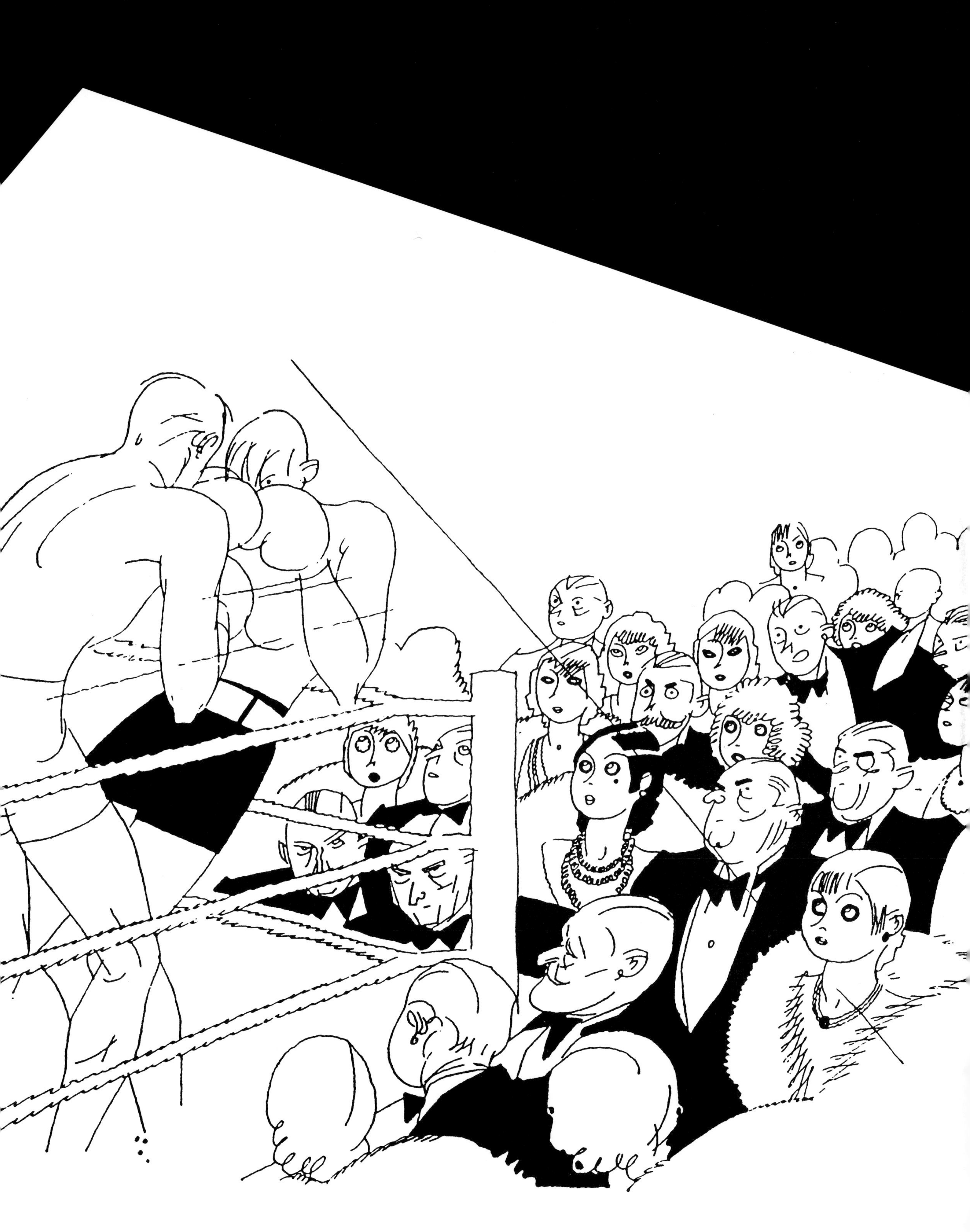

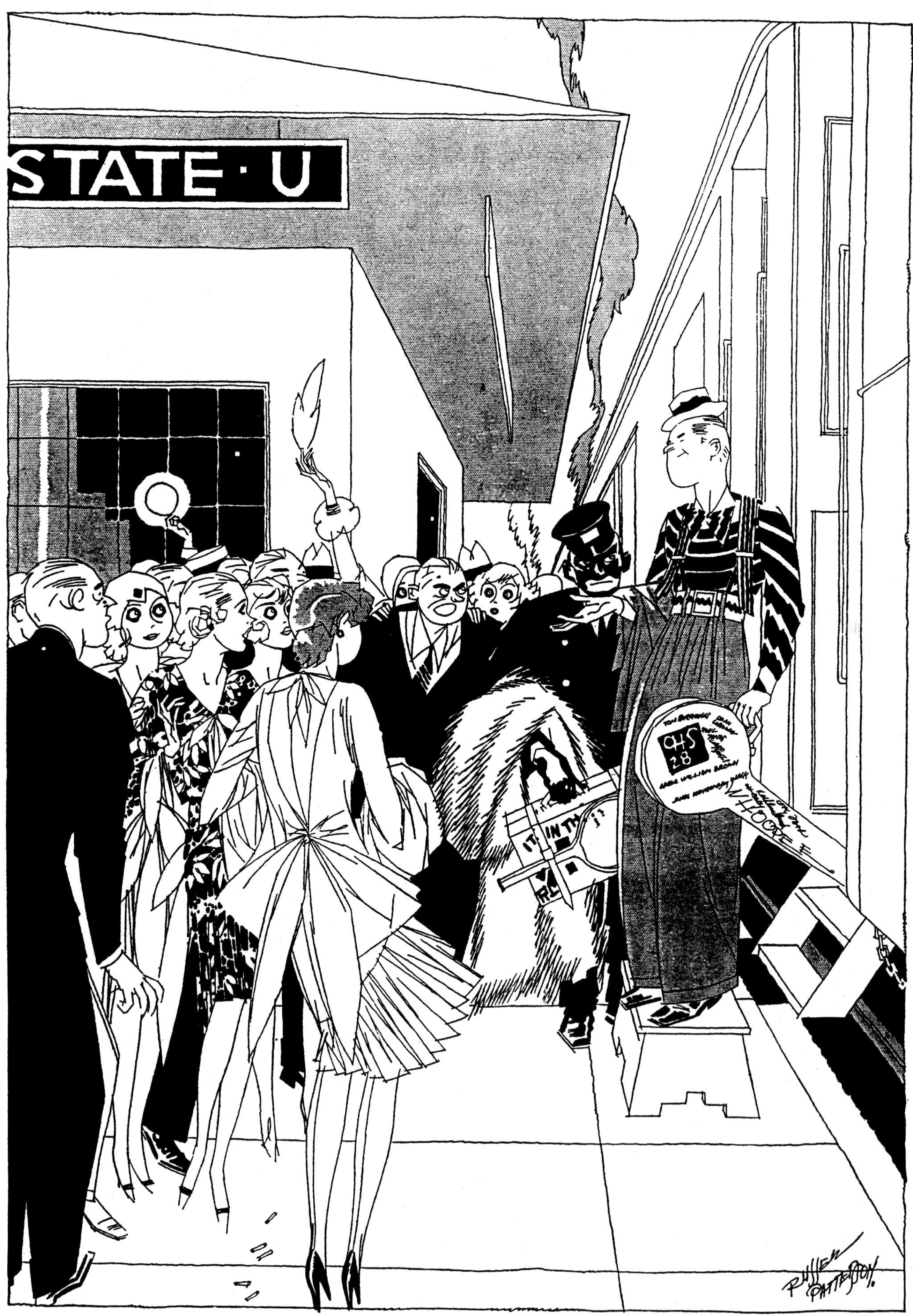

The High School Graduate Makes Good

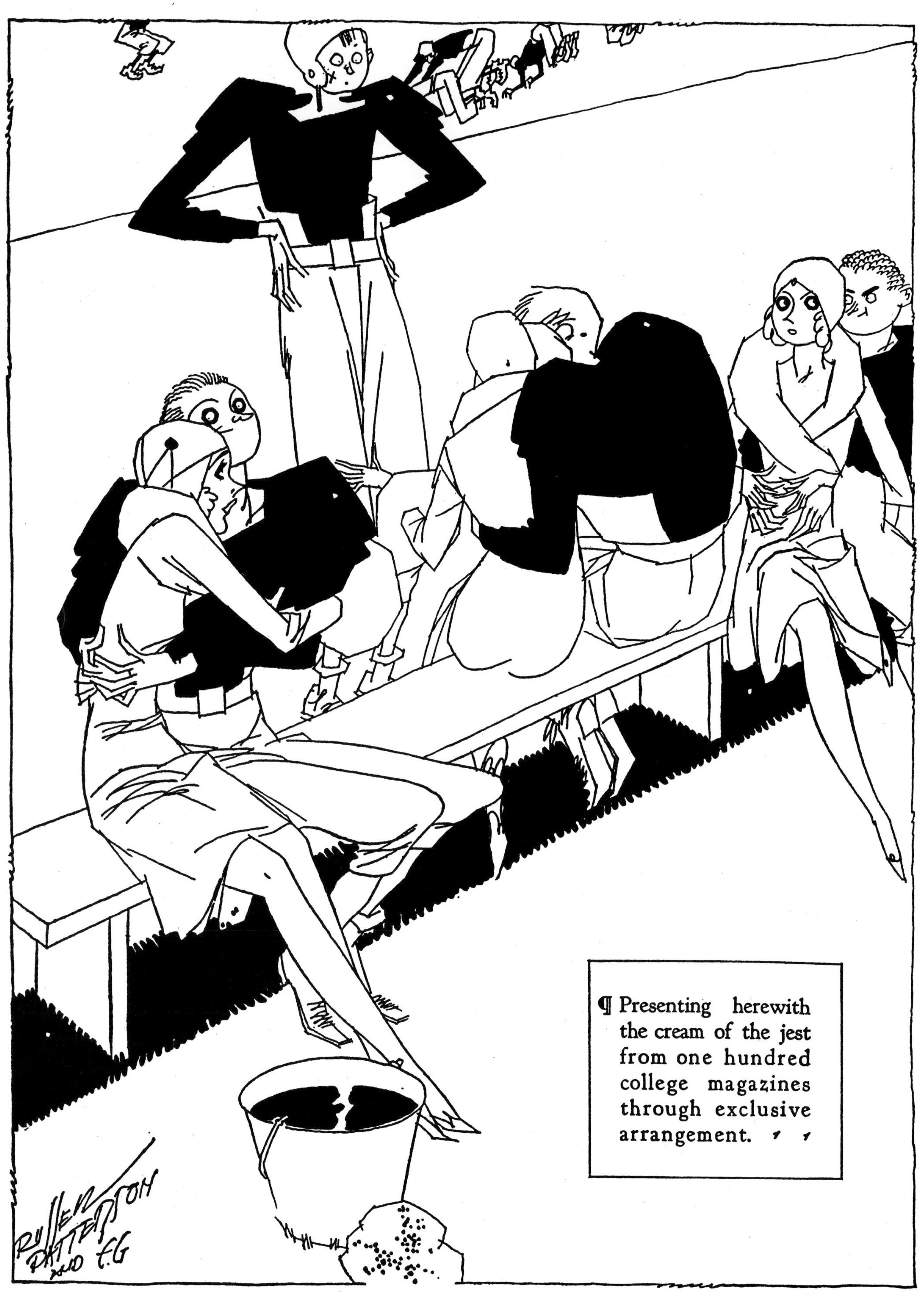

Warming Up the Substitutes

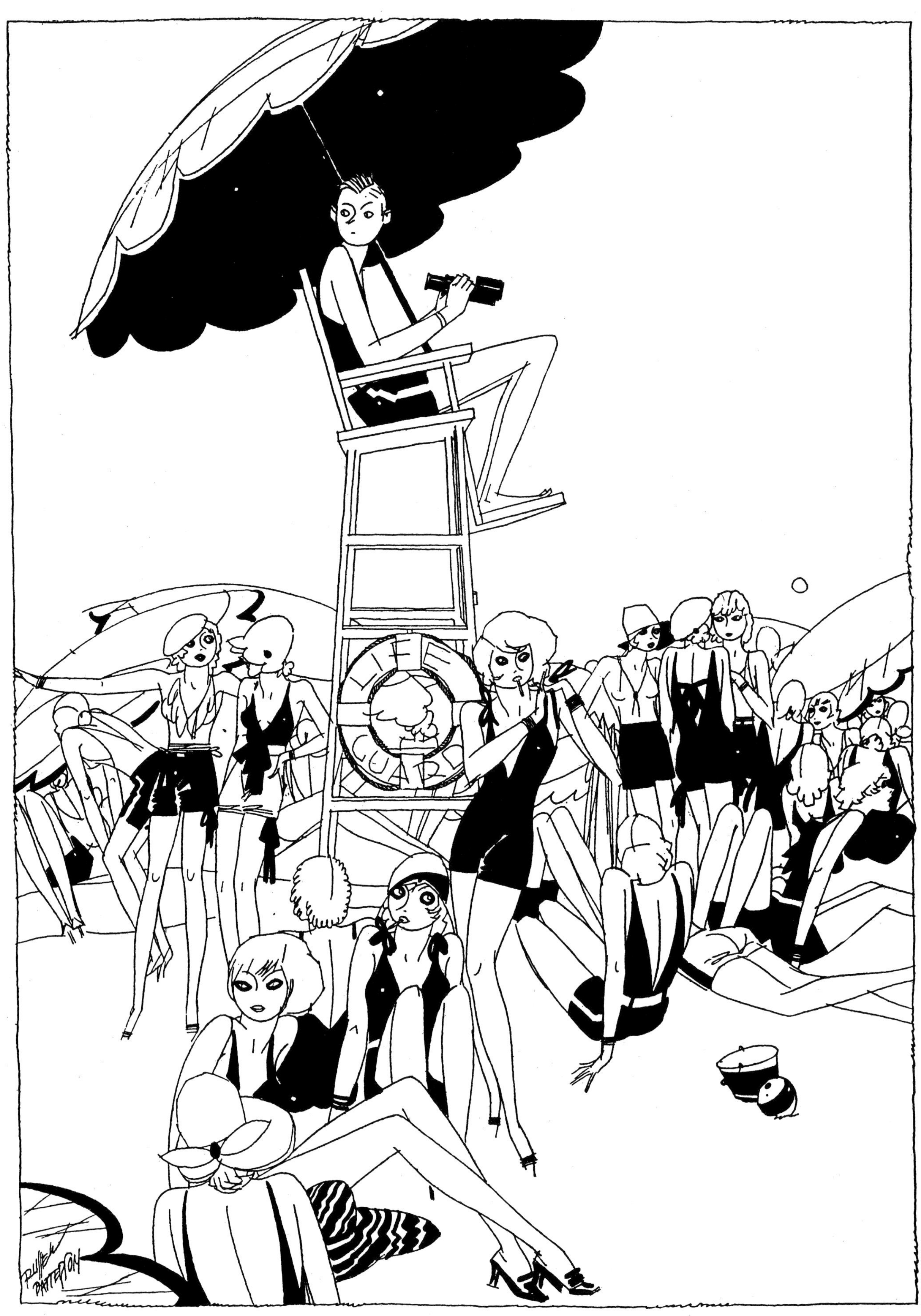

The Poor College Boy Who Had *to* Work During His Summer Vacation

JUST BETWEEN US GIRLS

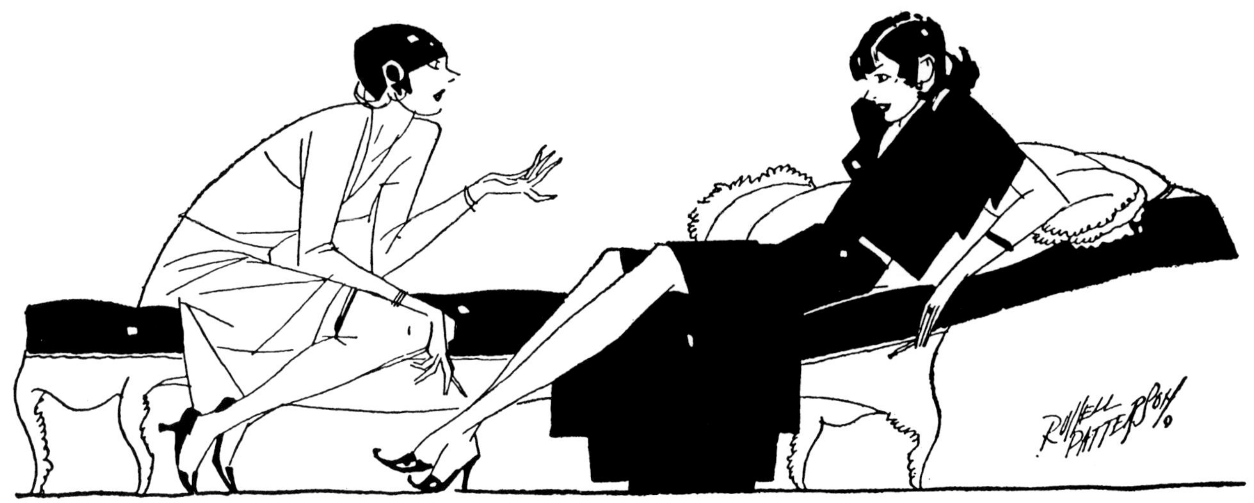

JUST BETWEEN US GIRLS

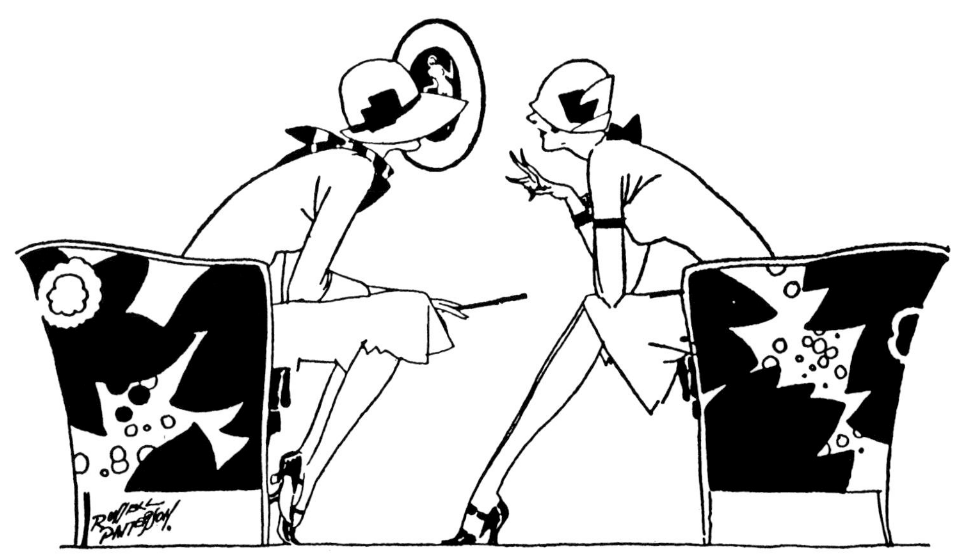

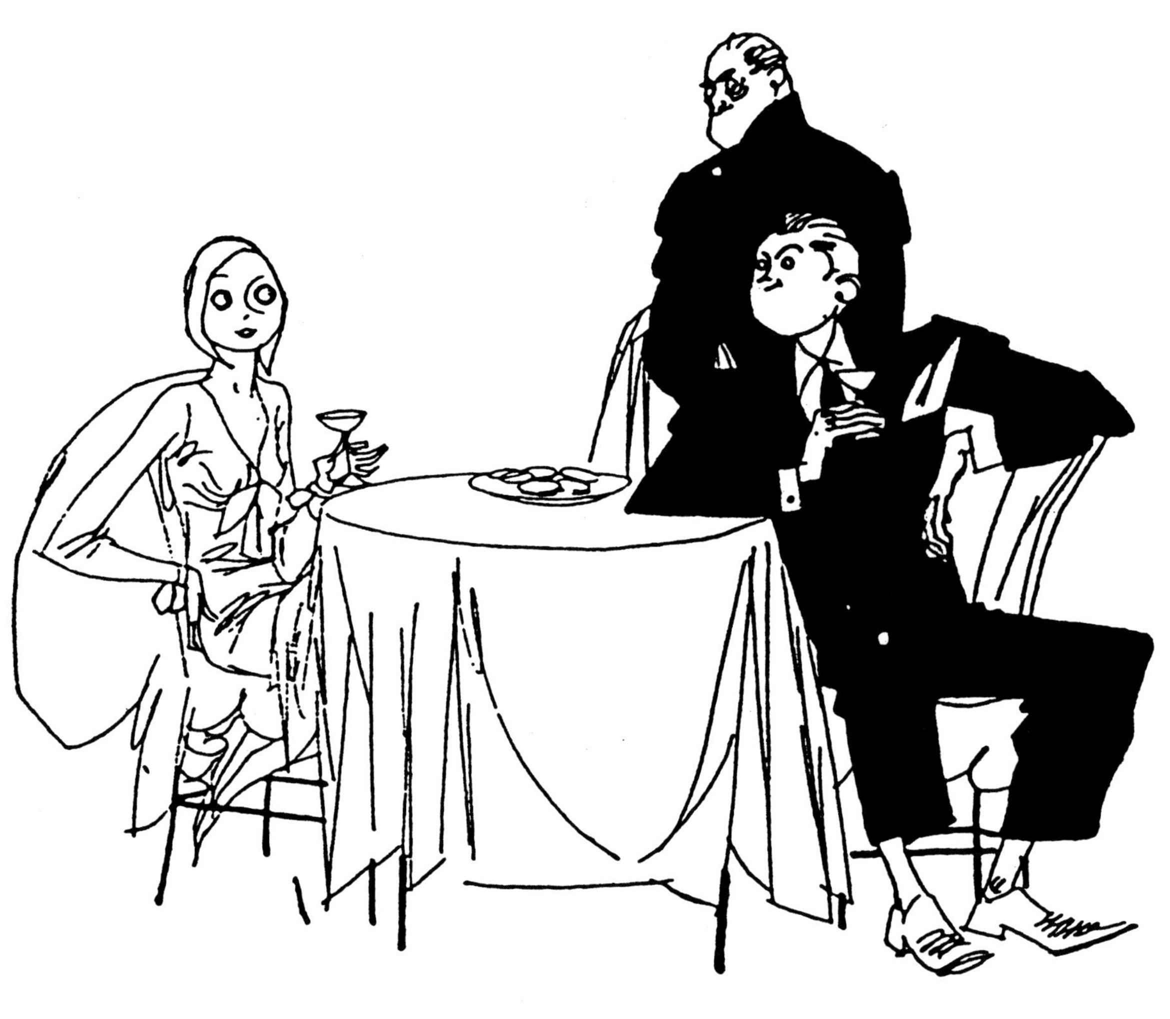

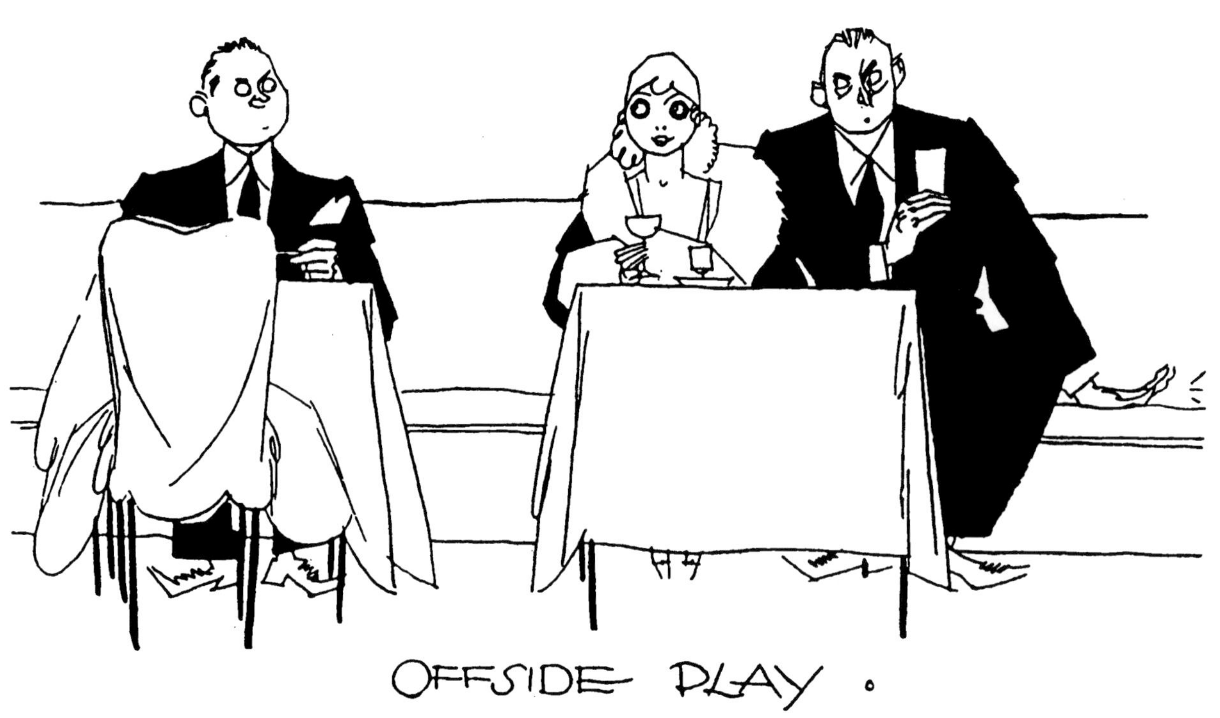

OFFSIDE PLAY.

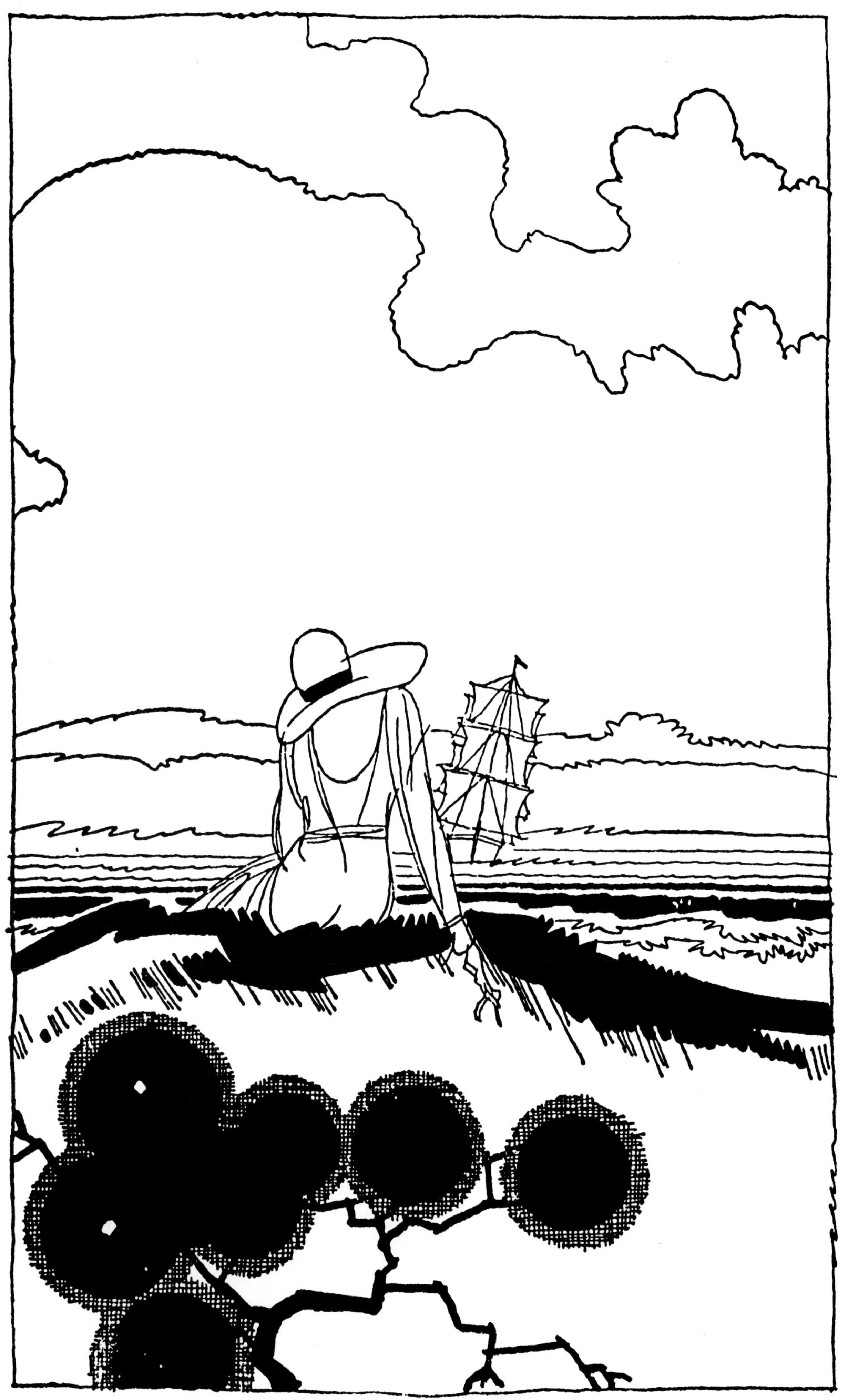

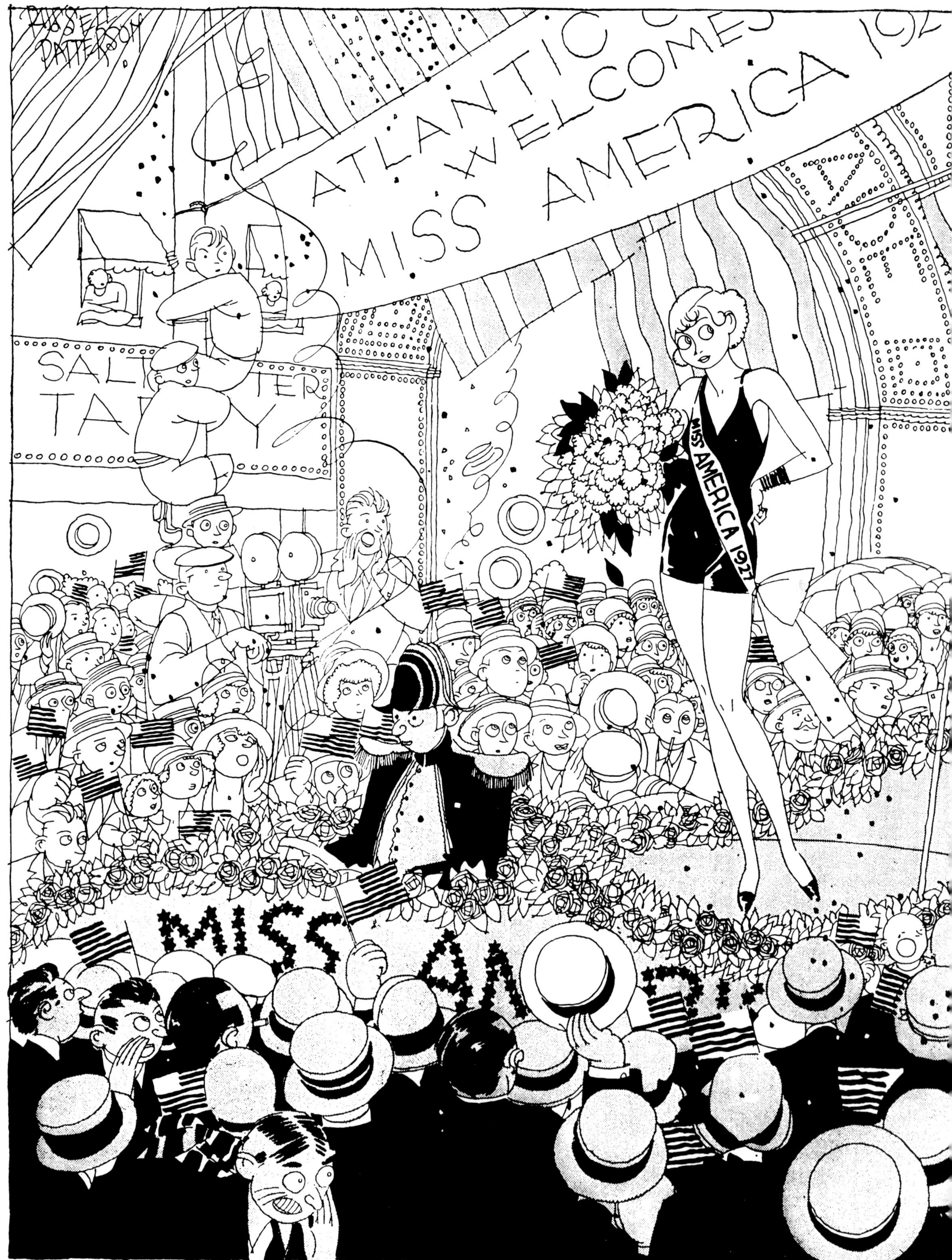
RUSSELL PATTERSON
ATLANTIC
WELCOMES
MISS AMERICA 192
SALT
MISS AMERICA 1927
MISS AM

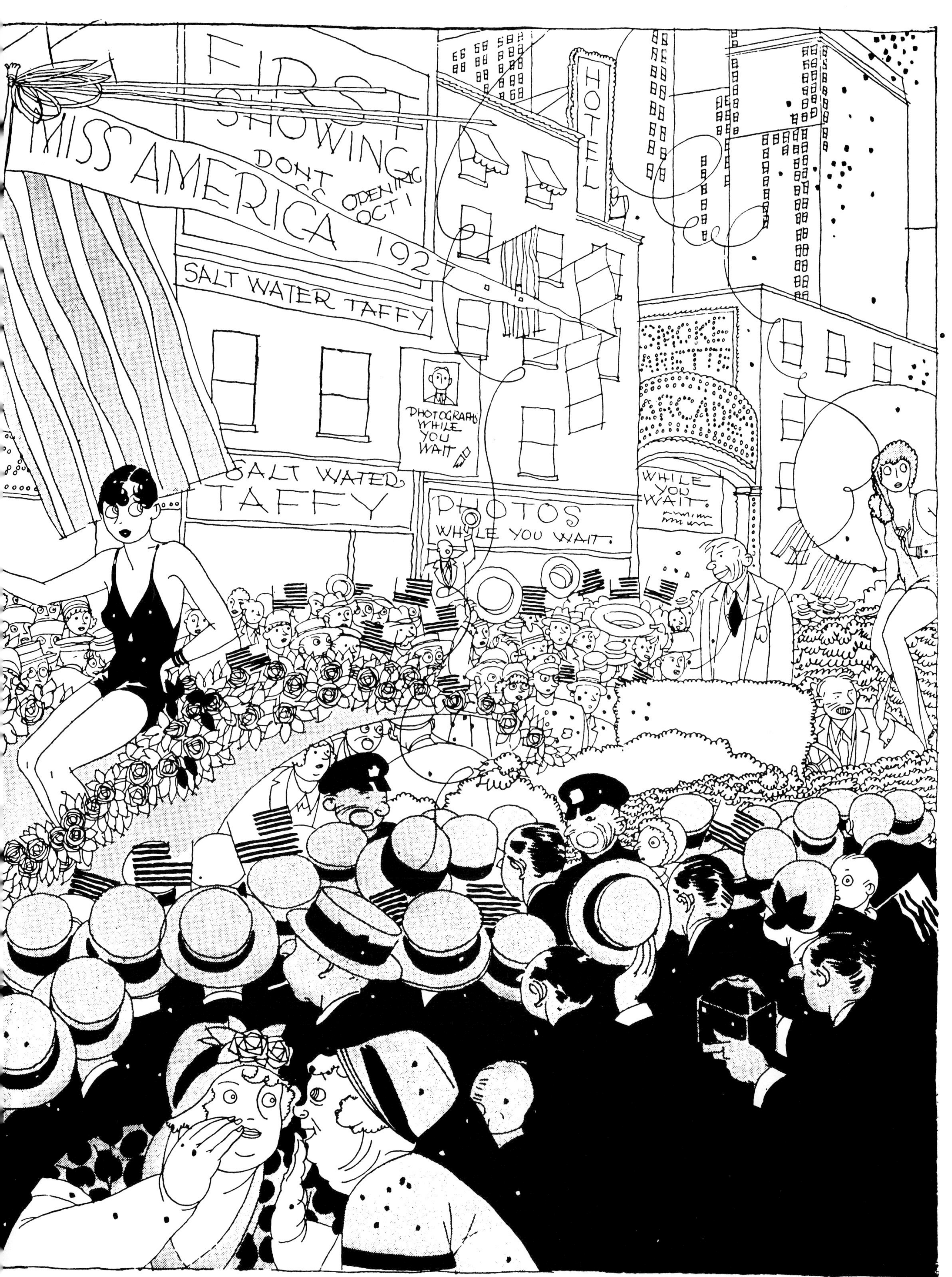

"Look, Emma! They call *that* beauty!"

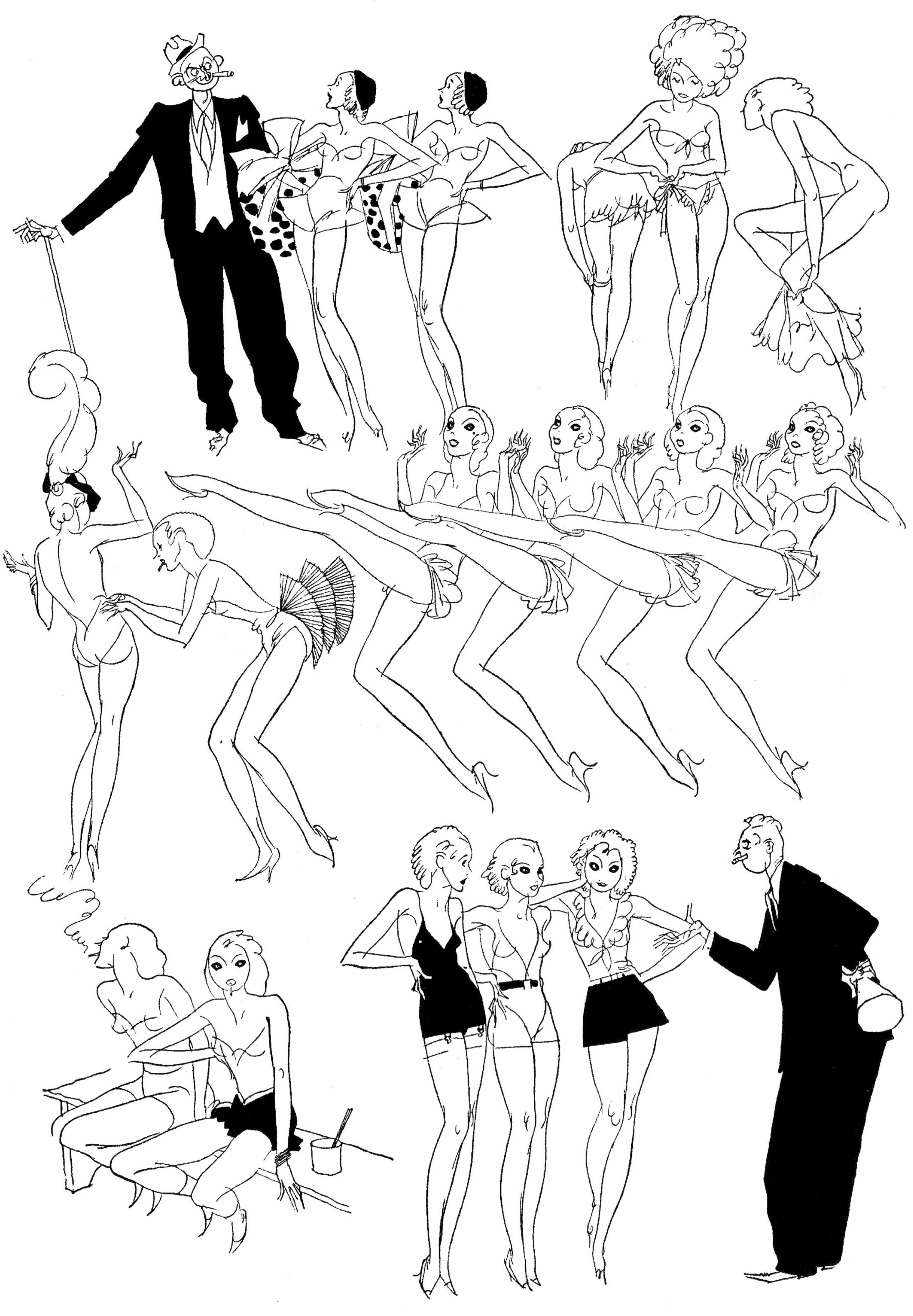

The Nudities of 1931

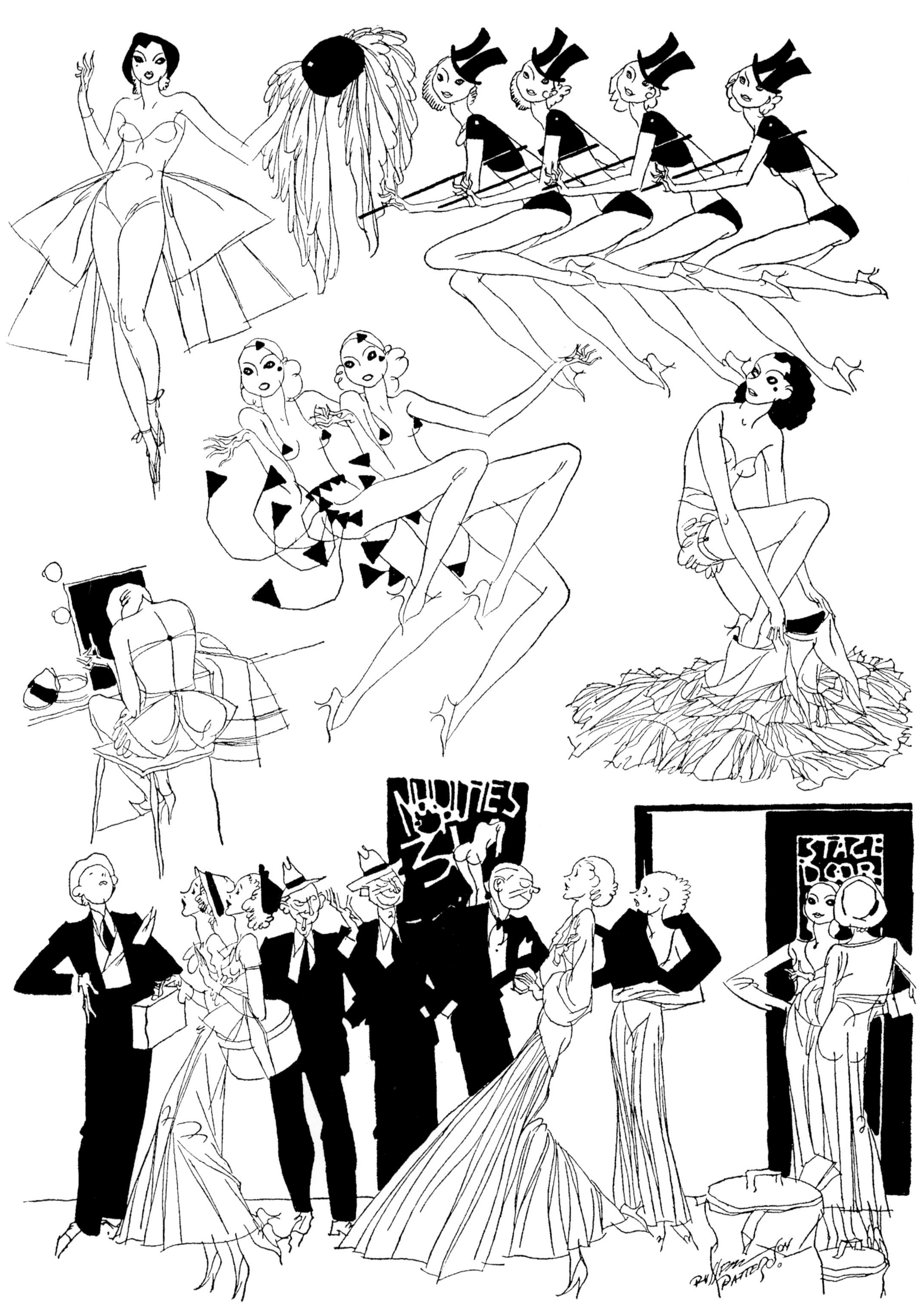

New York Life

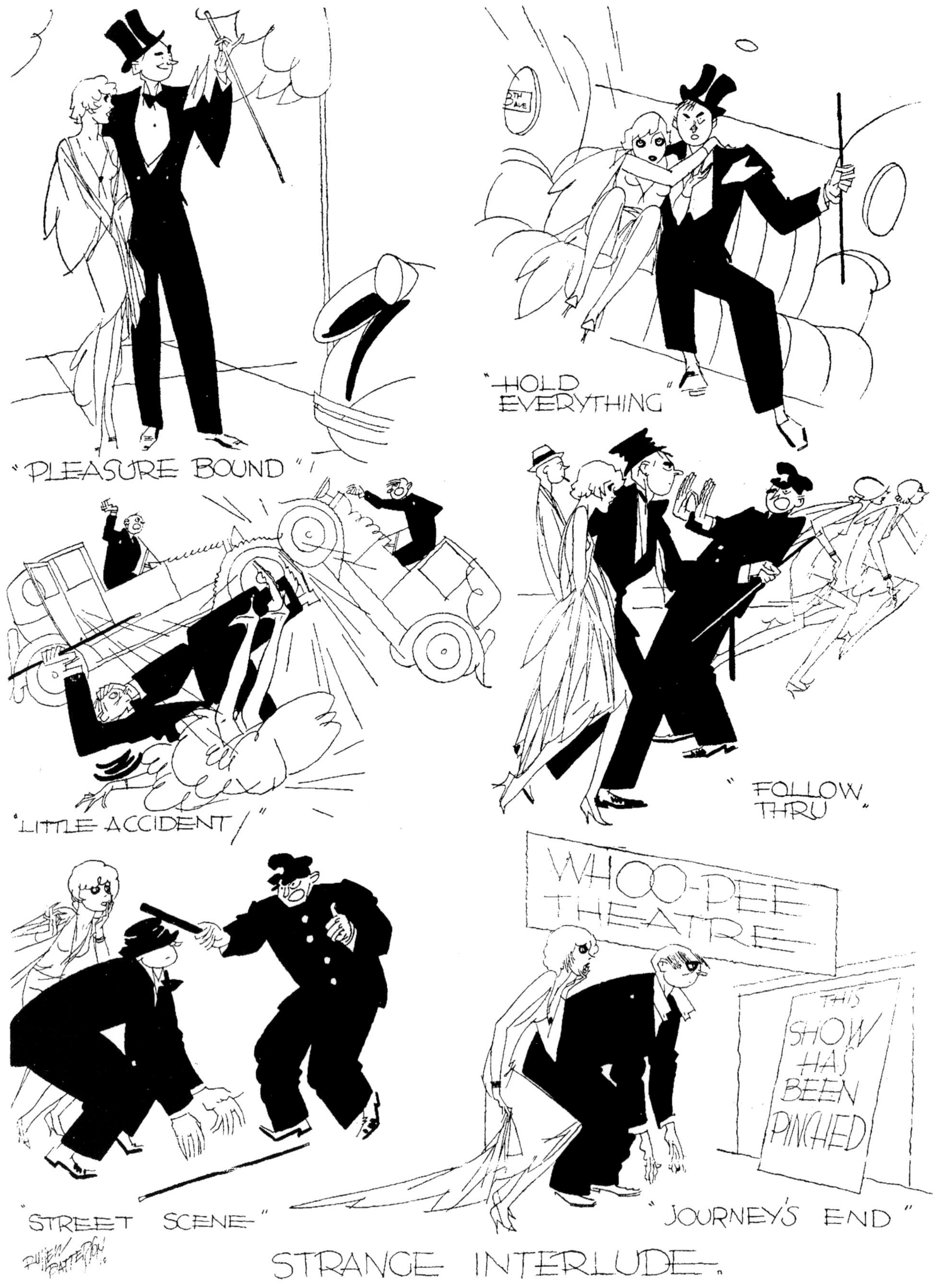

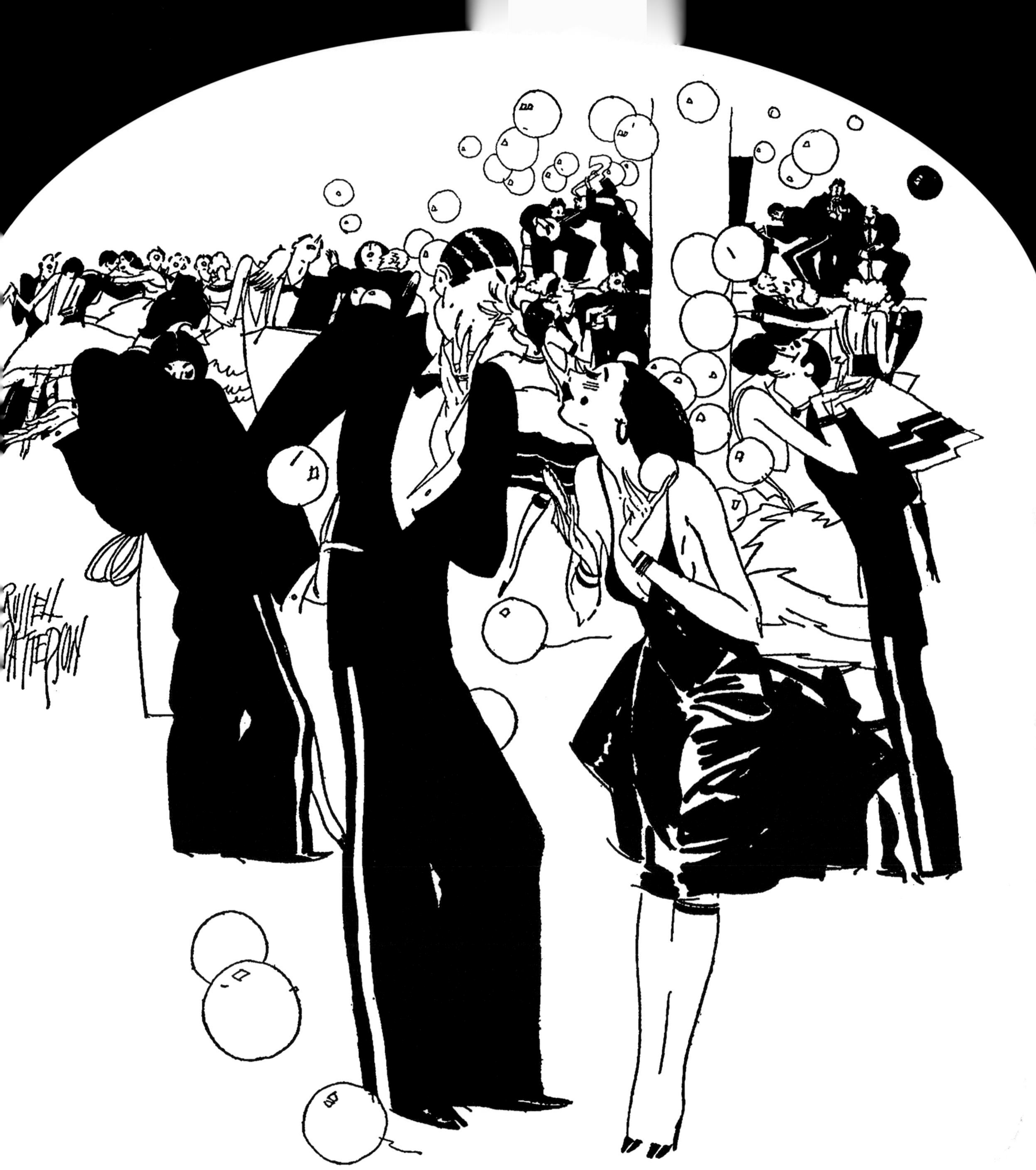

¶ "Kid," said Zora Fipps, as she paused after the tenth fox-trot to powder her nose or, as some would say, proboscis, "I don't know who you are but you are sure a nifty dancer."

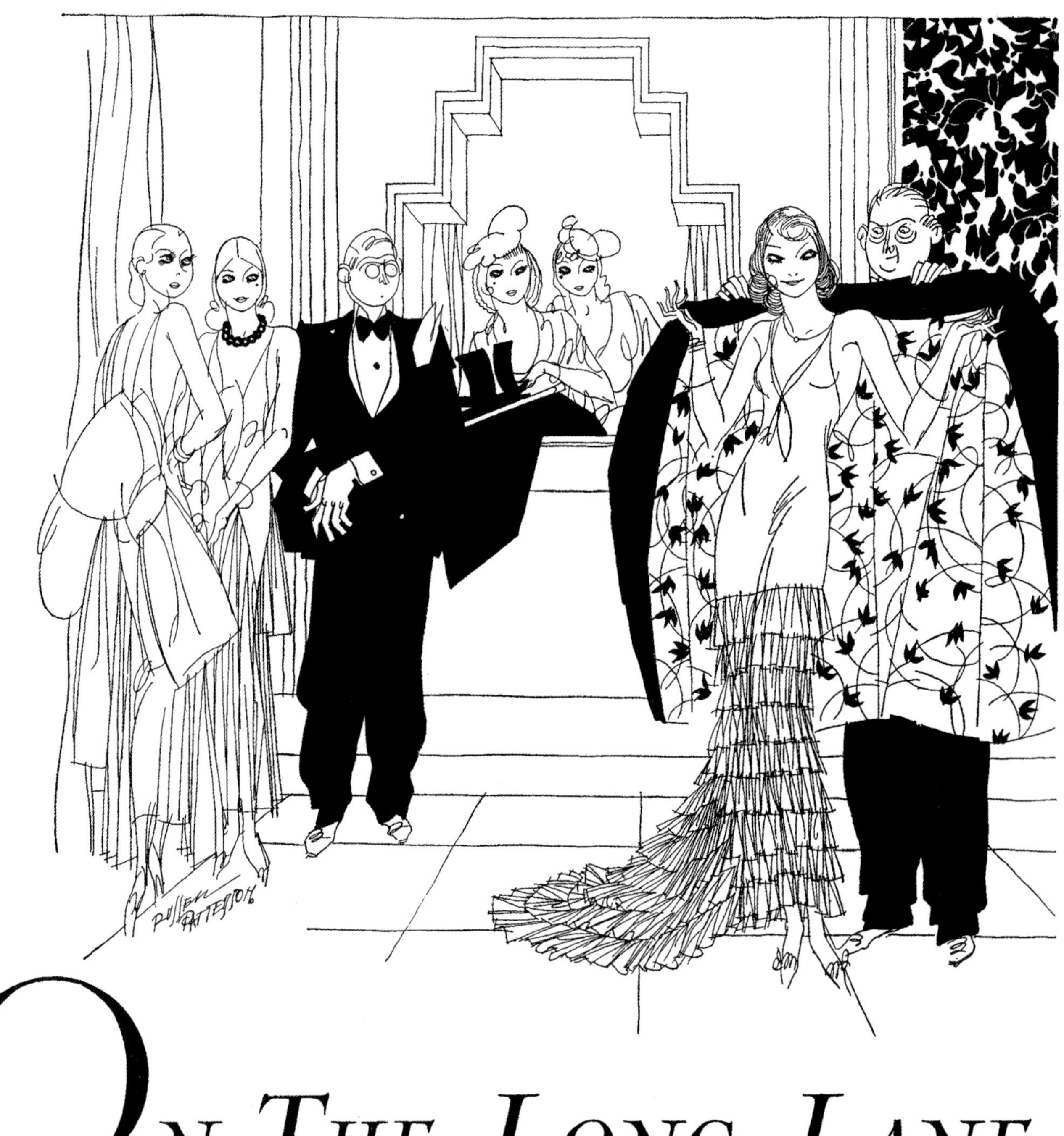

ON THE LONG LANE

THE scene was on the pavement in front of Mr. Ziegfeld's handsome playhouse on Sixth Avenue. The event was the première of Ziegfeld's new Ed Wynn show, *Simple Simon,* and the news photographers were bunched near the foyer to snap-shoot the town's élite and worthwhiles.

The hocus-focus lads, however, passed up such well knowns as Ring Lardner, Anita Loos, Lillian Gish *et al* to take pictures of anything in a tall hat or ermine wrap.

A pair in evening clothes hopped out of a cab and appeared to be Big-Shotty.

Boom! boom! boom! went the flashlight explosions.

When the pictures had been snapped, a photographer cornered the man and asked for his name. "And," whispered the lens toter, "who's the woman?"

"I don't know," replied the fellow. "I just picked her up in my hotel lobby."

Illustration by

Russell Patterson

SPEAKING of Mr. Ziegfeld's premières, which are always the smartest, unless you pause to salute those who collect for the premières sponsored by Charles Dillingham, at the *Simple Simon* opening almost every spectator was attired in dress clothes. The swankiest of audiences attended and you went deaf from the crunching of starched shirts.

The only man in the gathering who Acted His Age and wore his baggy pants and blue shirt and brown boots was Mr. Ziegfeld.

AMONG other gag wars now current is that between Phil Baker and Joe Frisco, two of the better wits. The feud this time is over a bit of repartee, which goes like this:

Frisco (or Baker) begins warbling lustily,

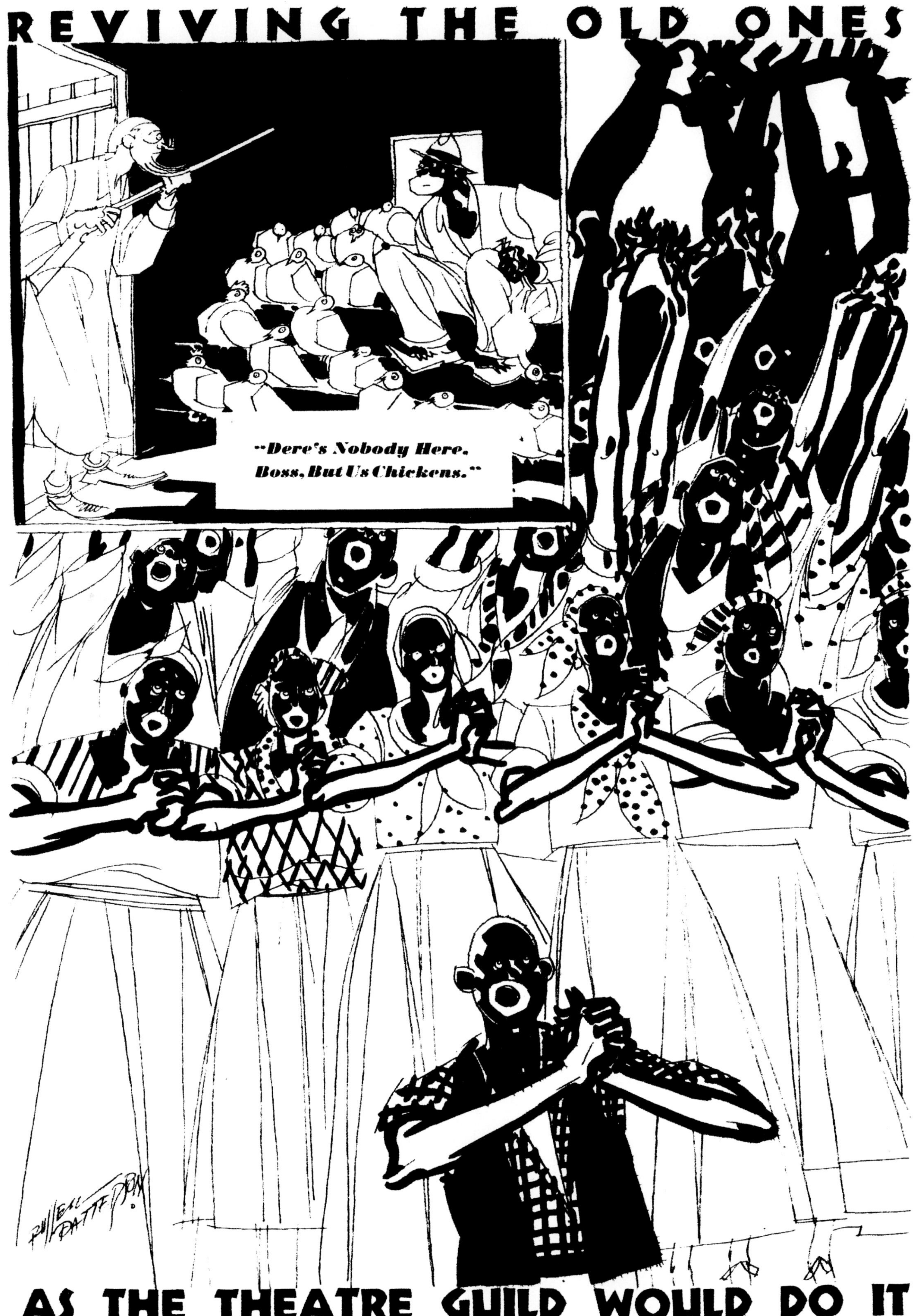
REVIVING THE OLD ONES
"Dere's Nobody Here, Boss, But Us Chickens."
AS THE THEATRE GUILD WOULD DO IT

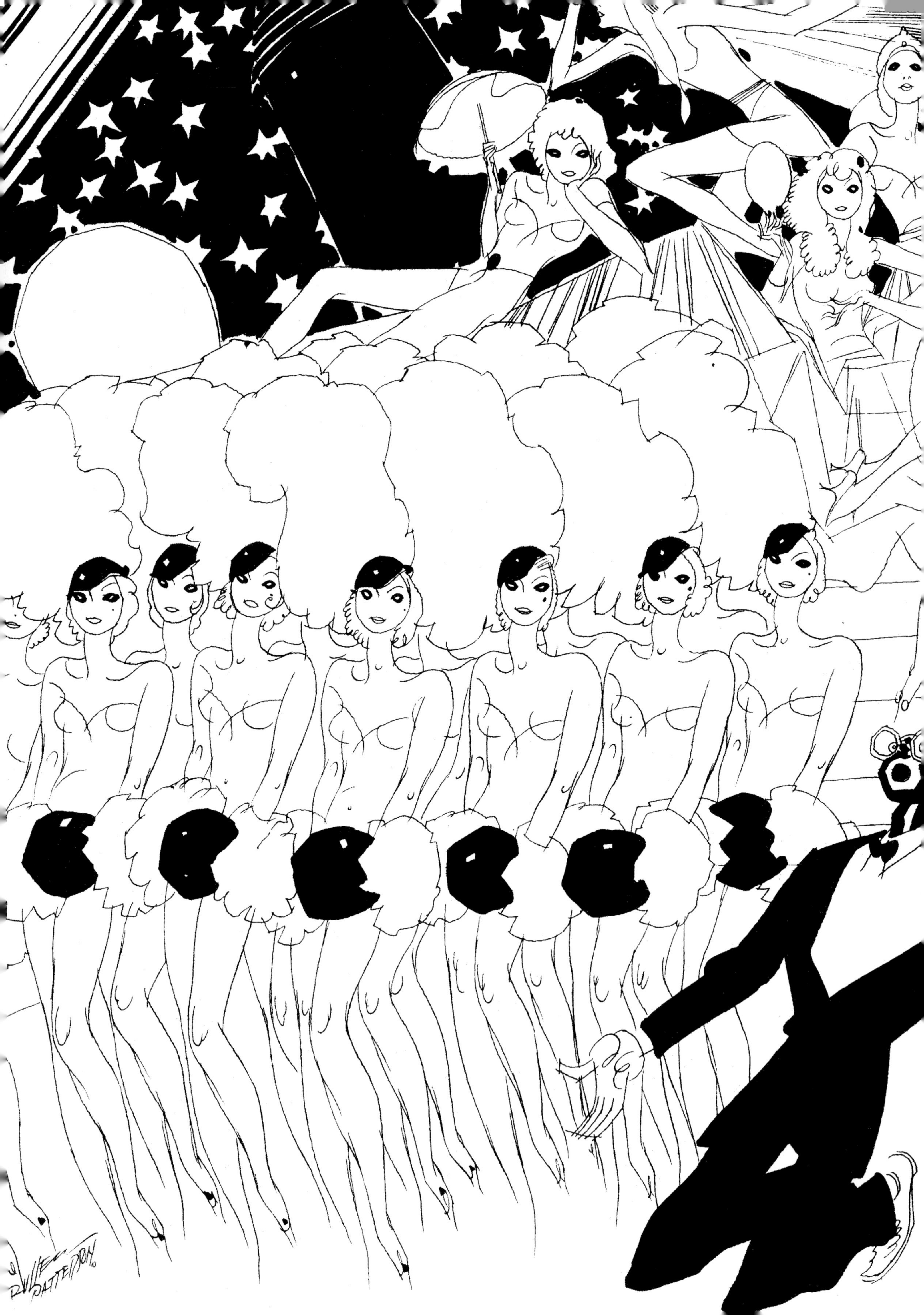

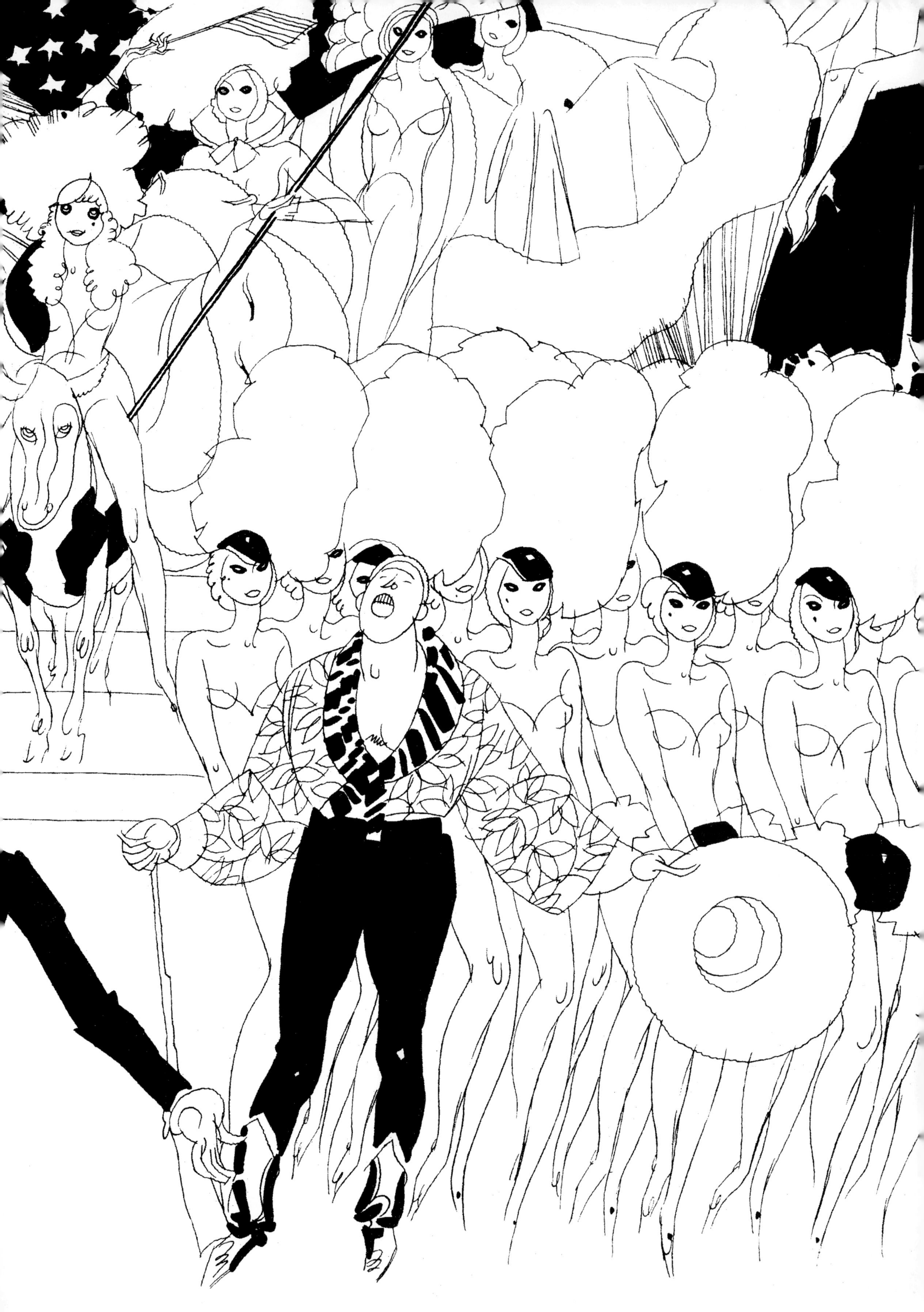

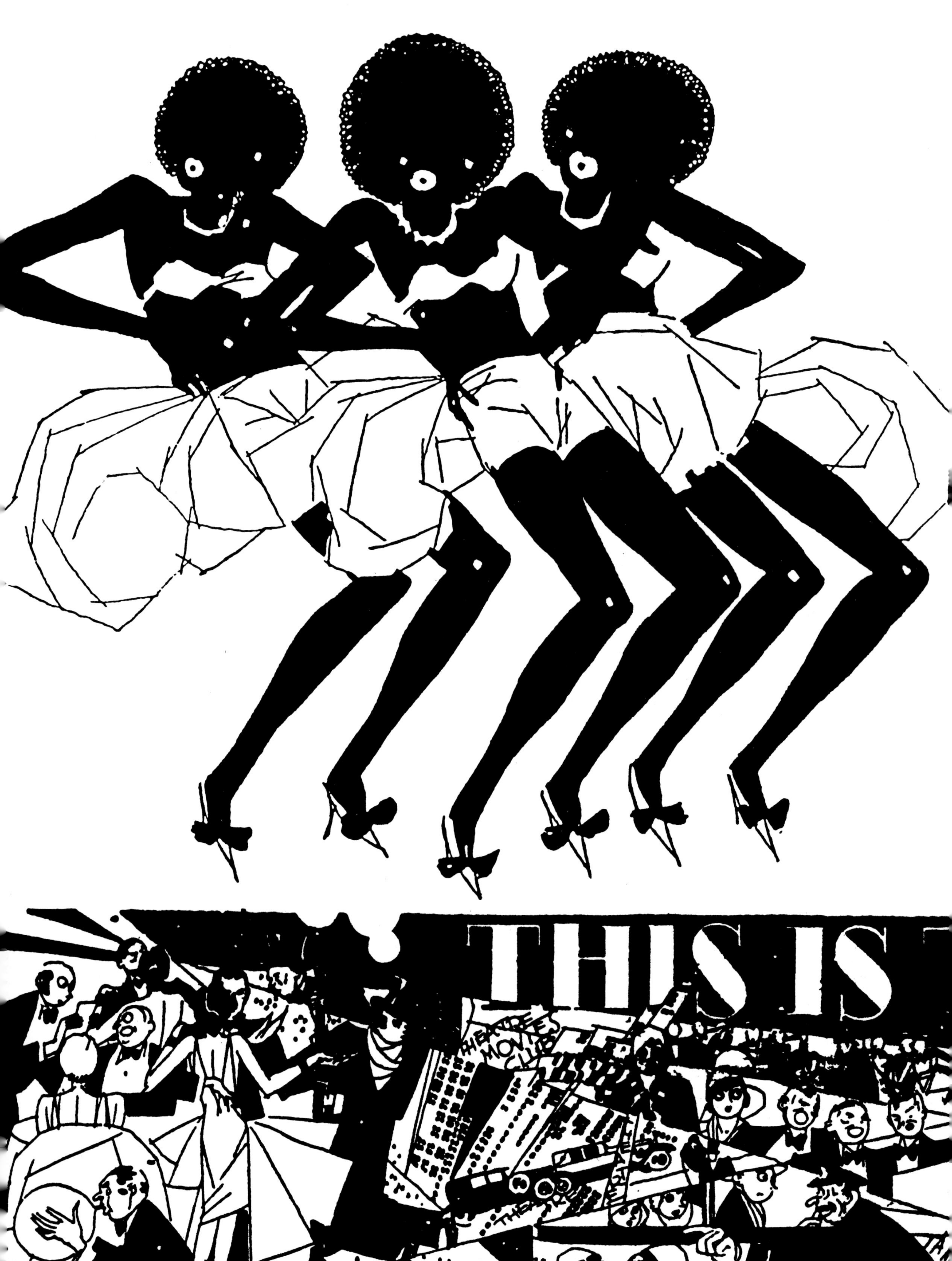
THIS IS

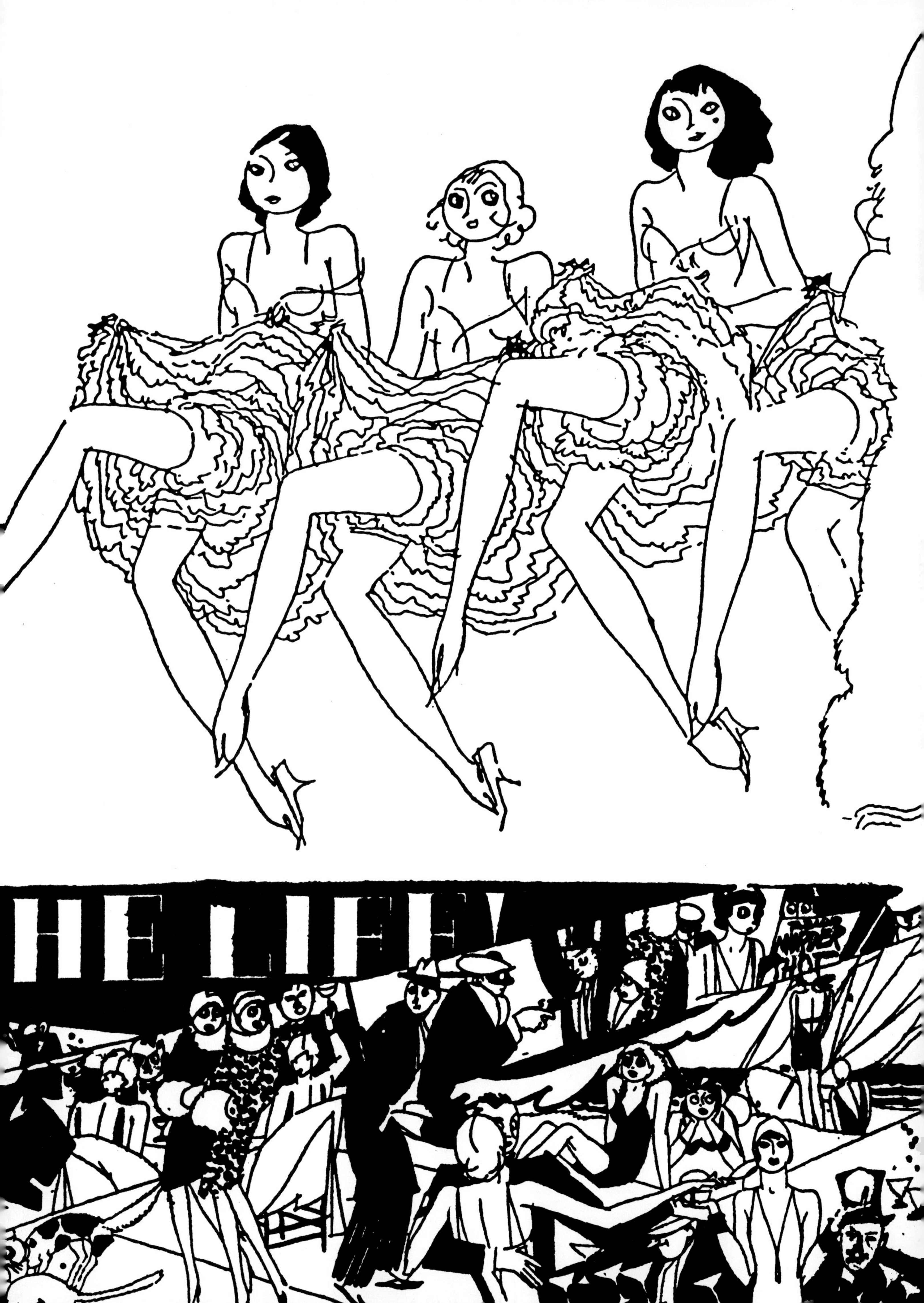
HE LIF

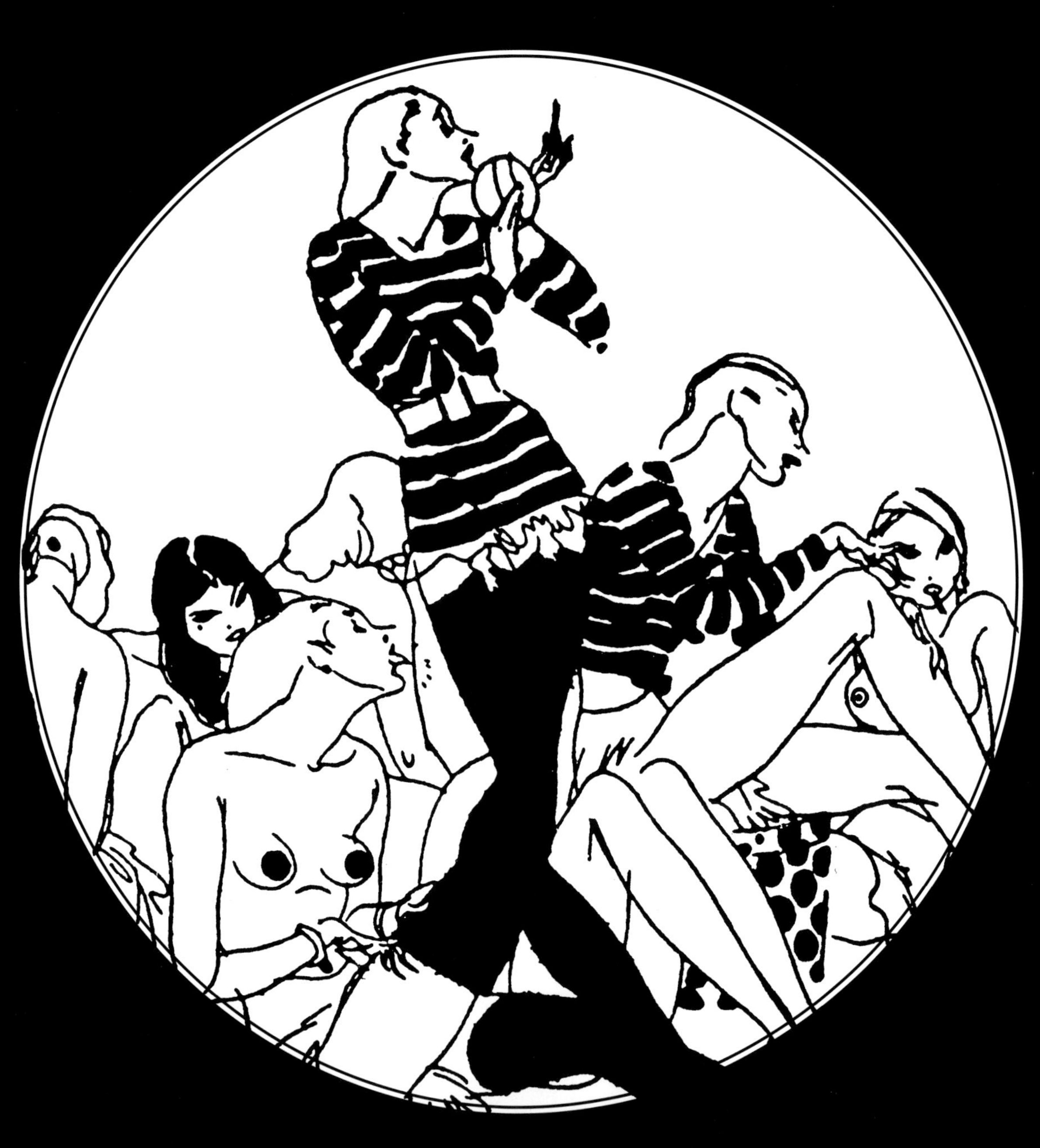

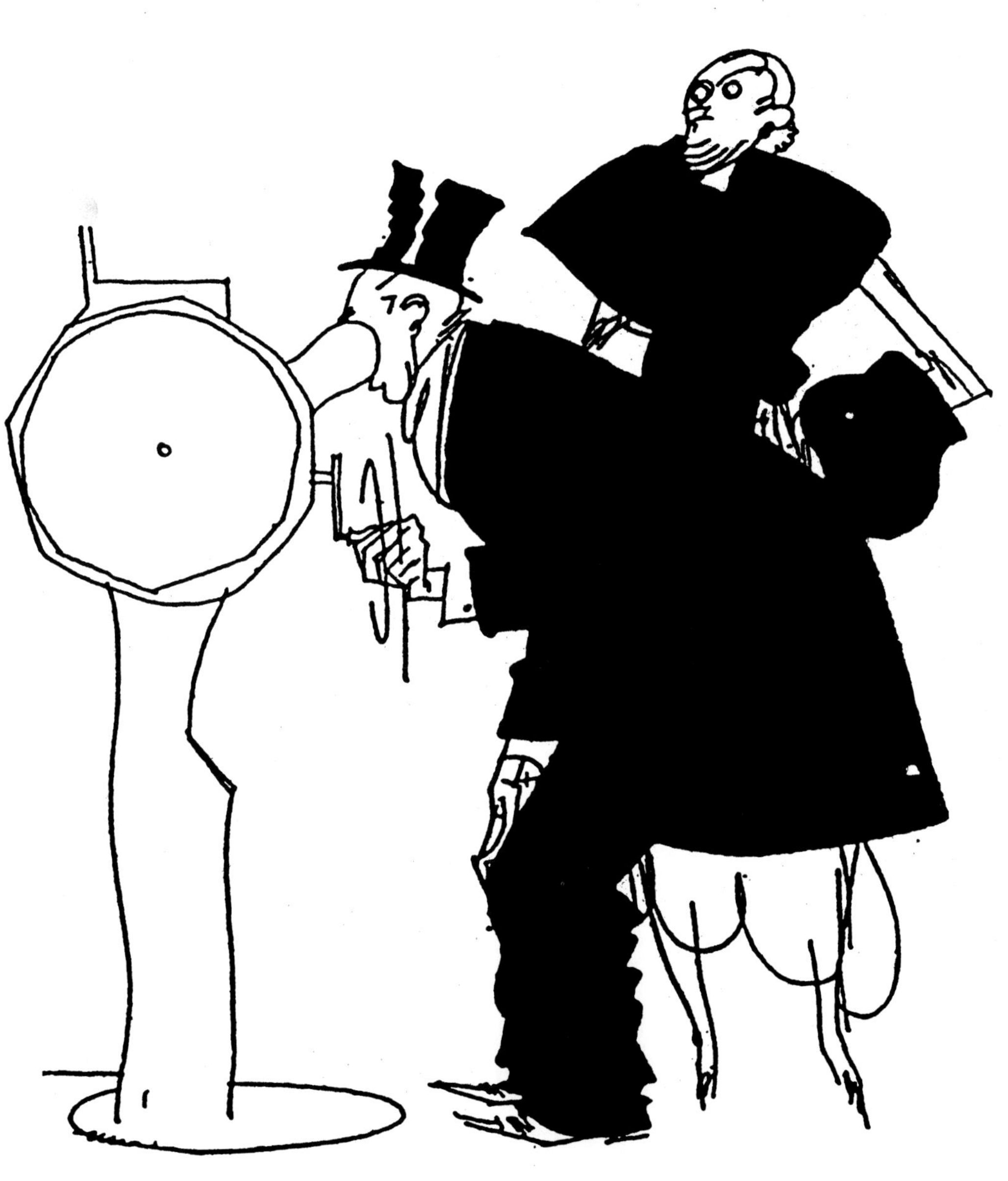

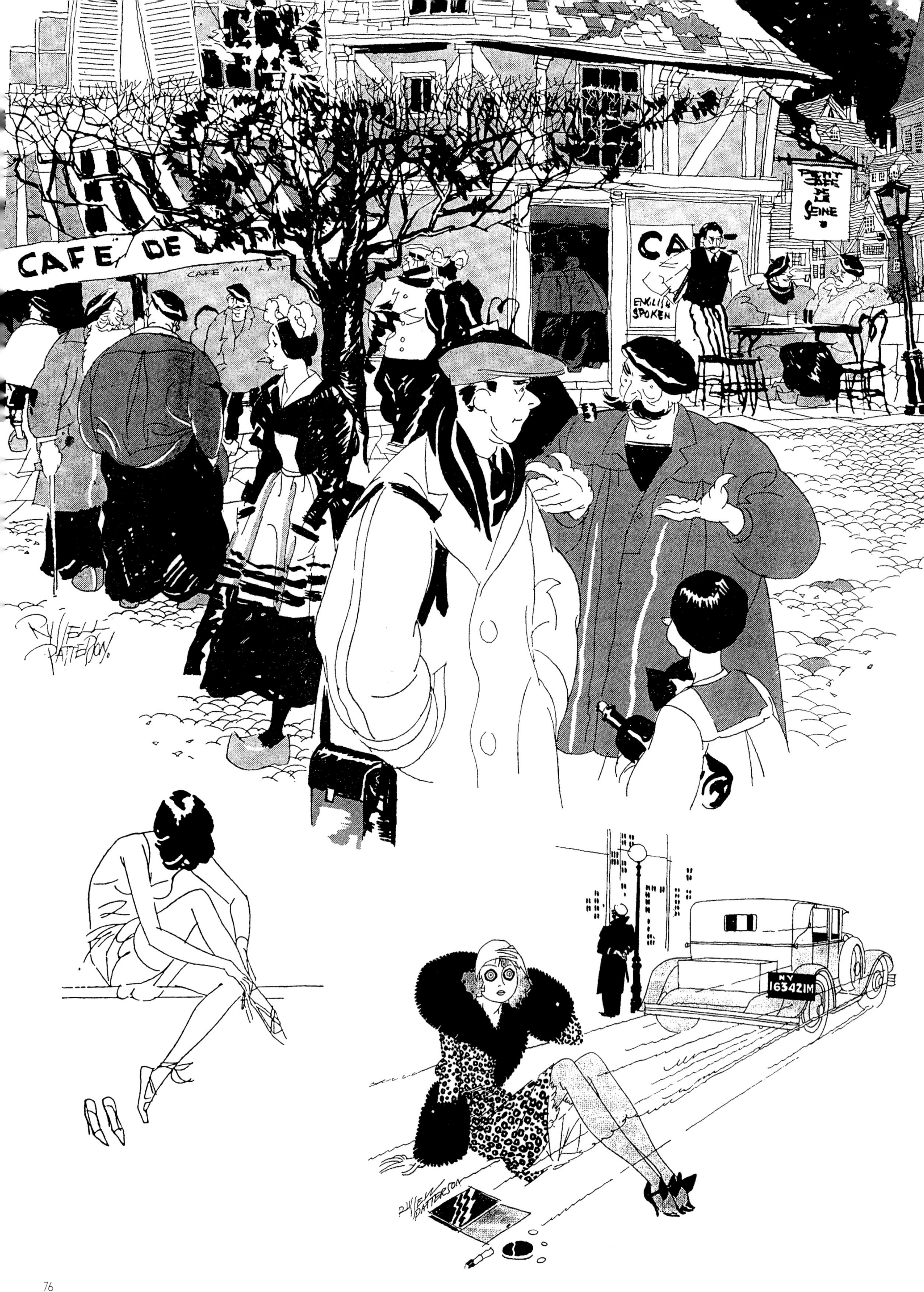
CAFE DE
PETIT CAFE DE LA SEINE
CA
ENGLISH SPOKEN
NY
16342IM

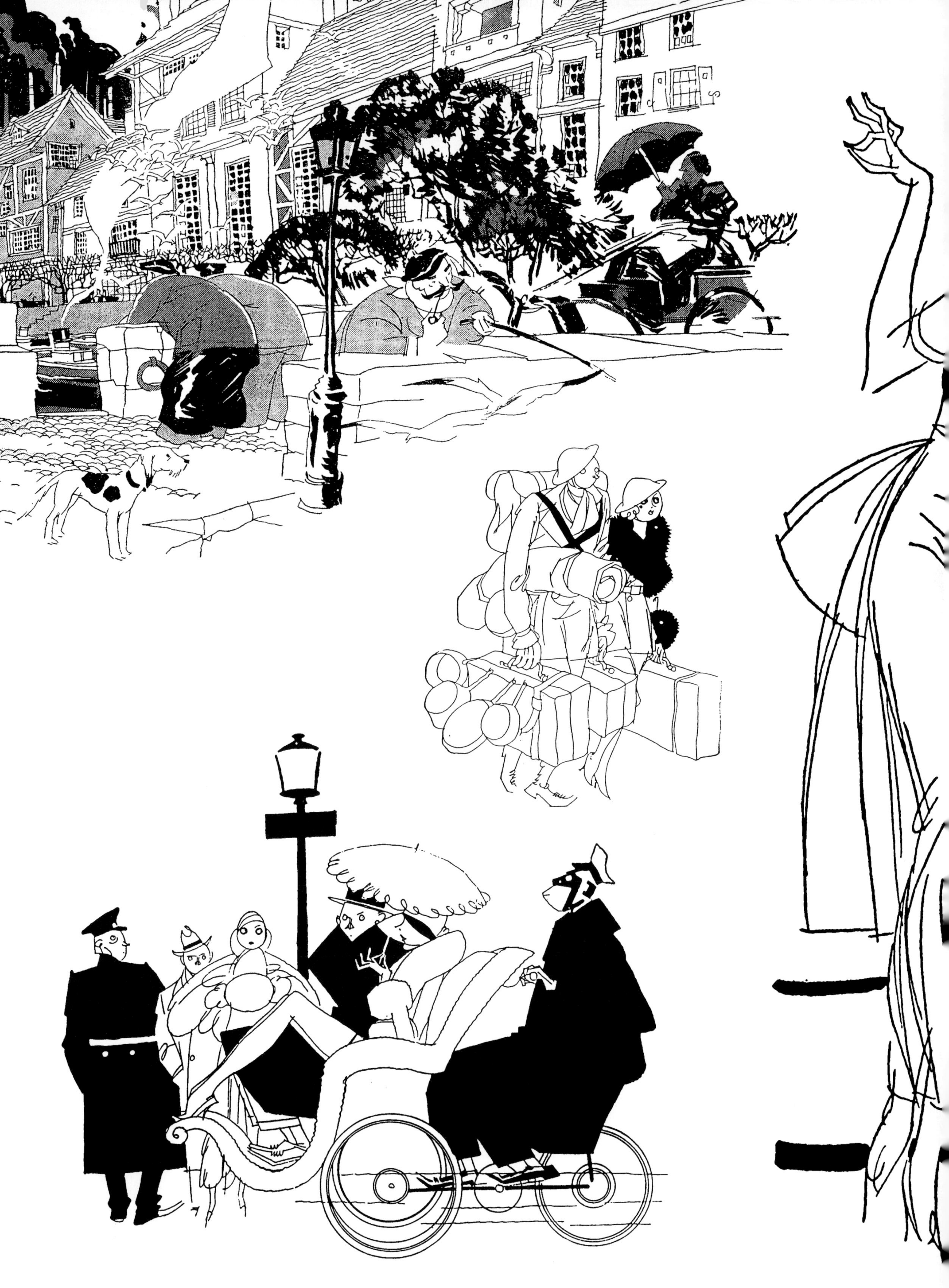

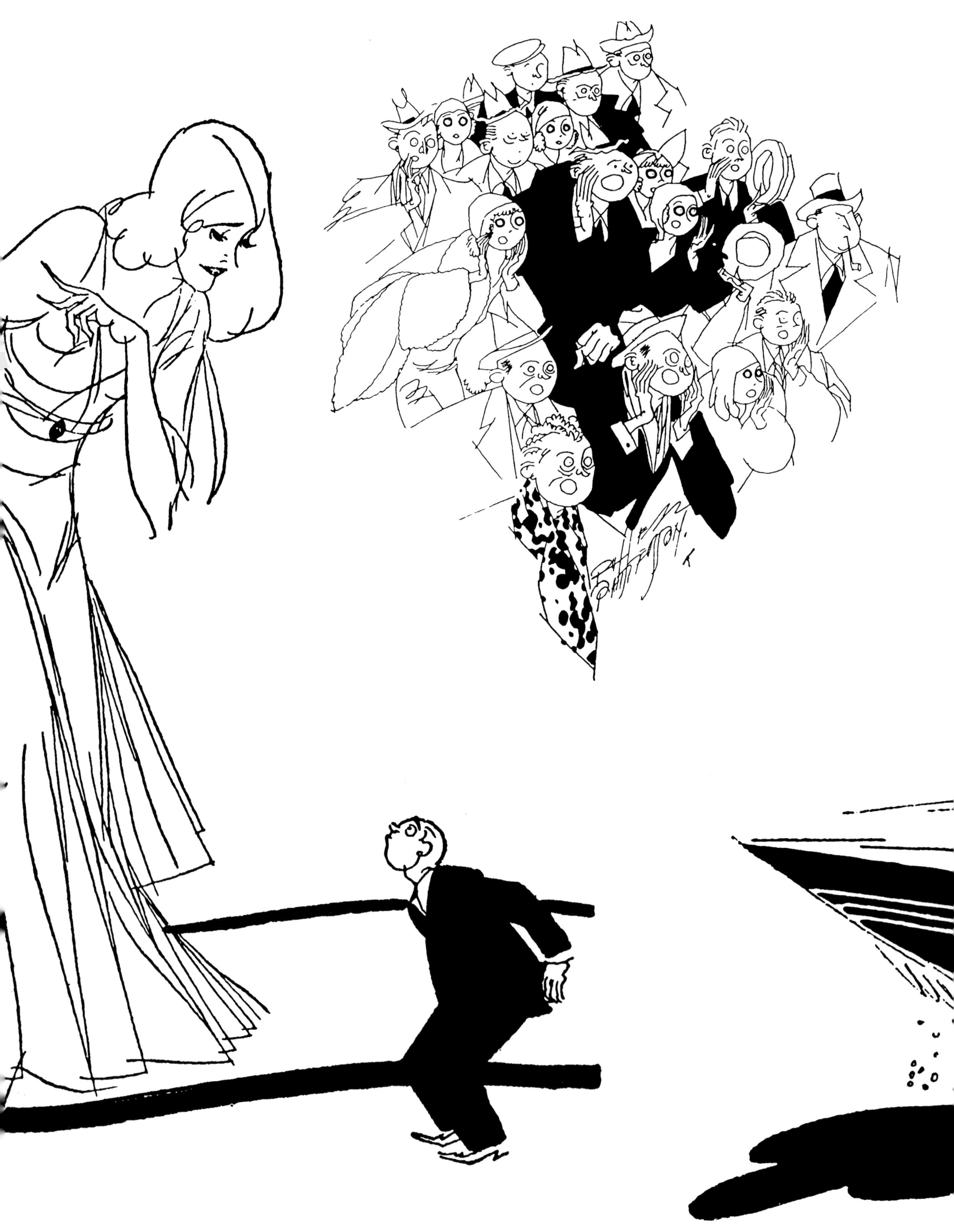

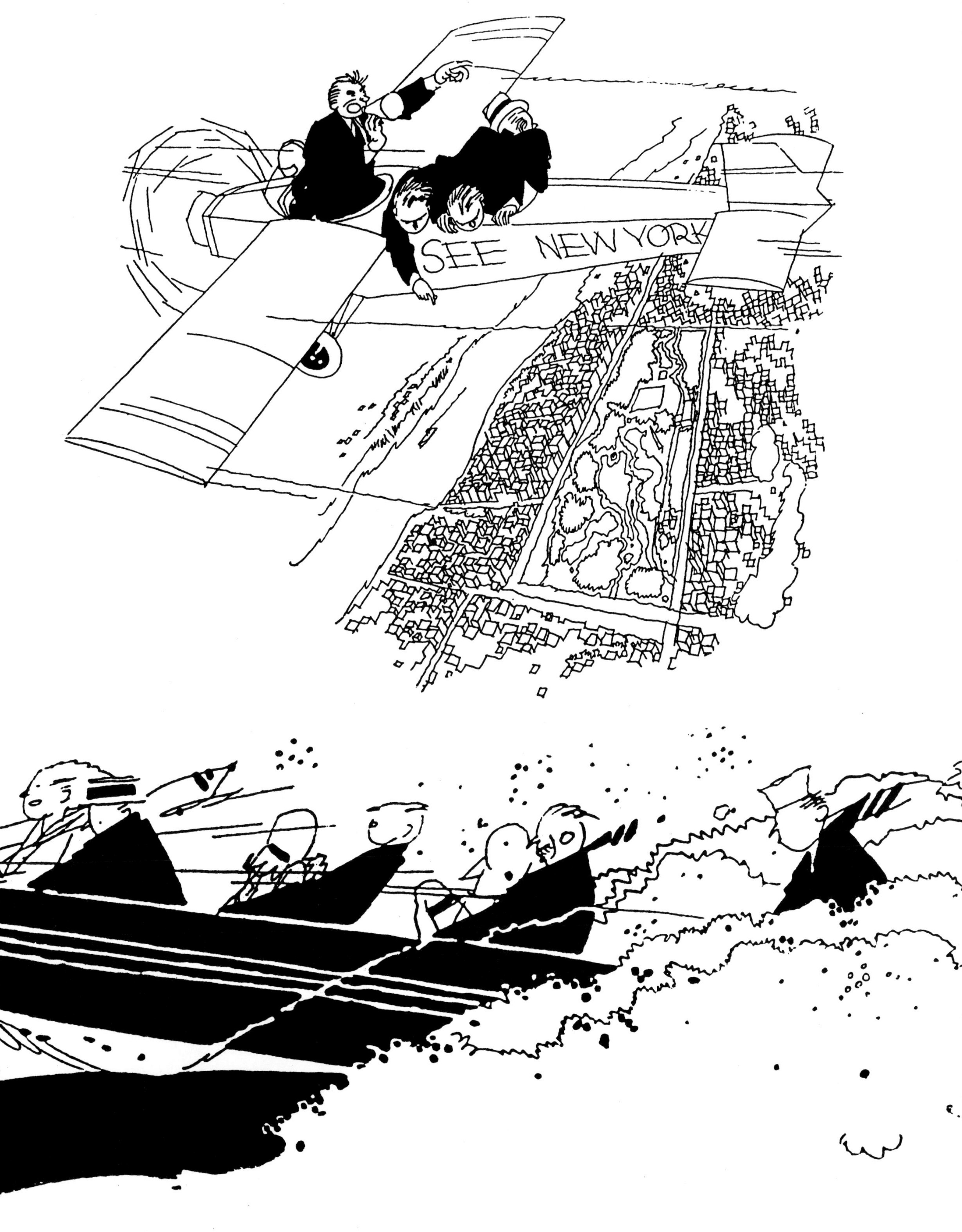
SEE NEW YORK

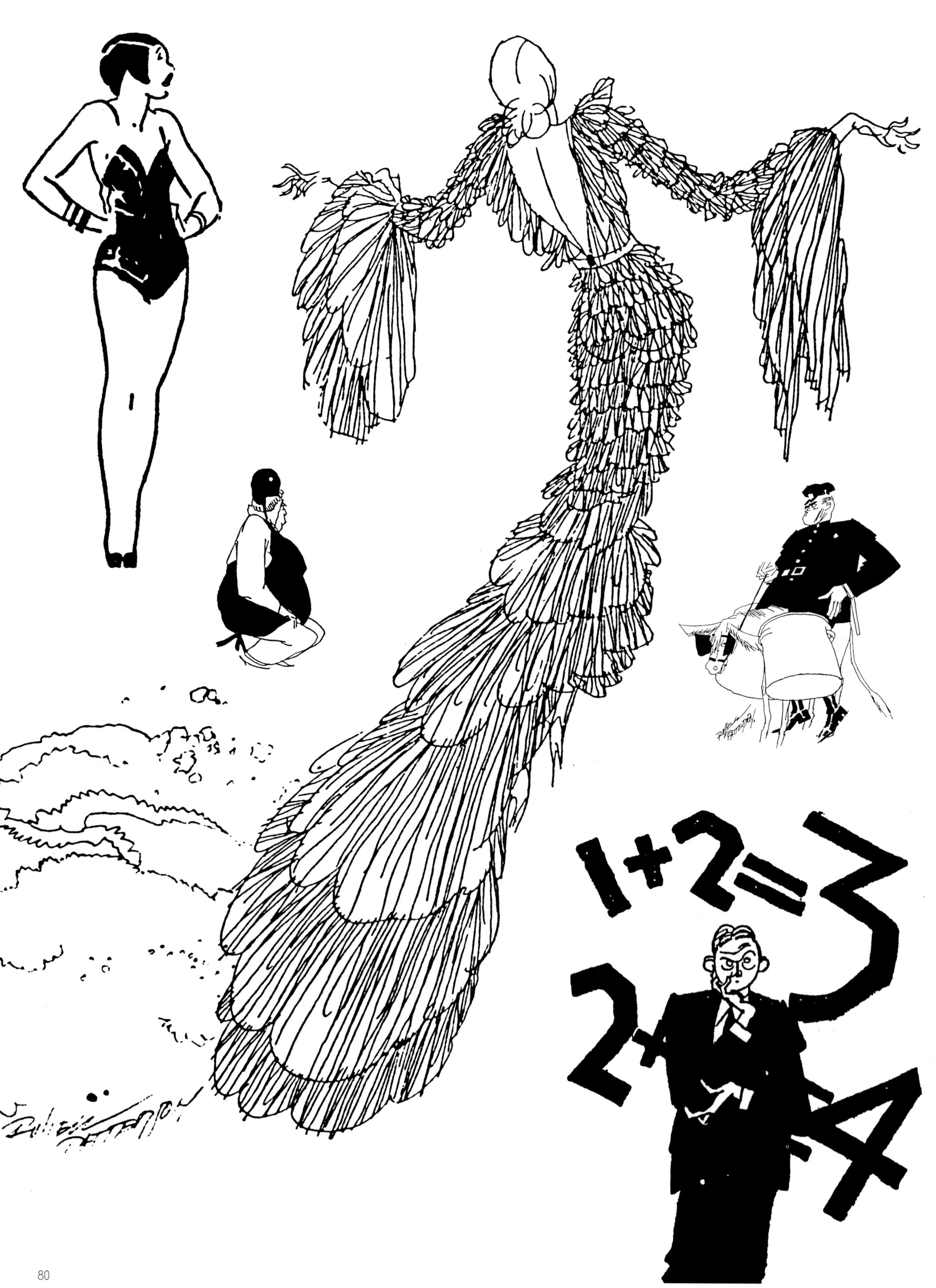
1+2=3
2+2=4

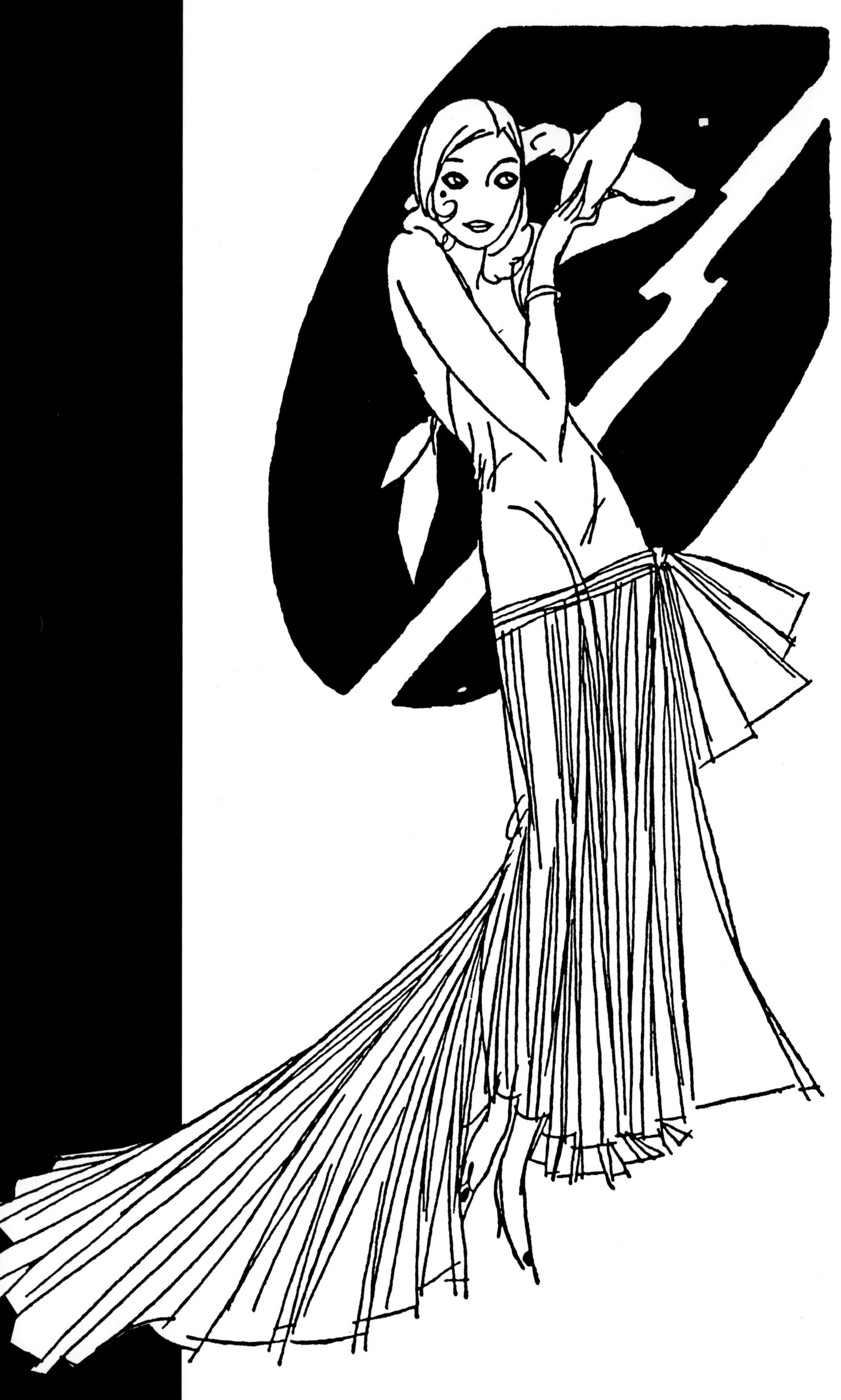

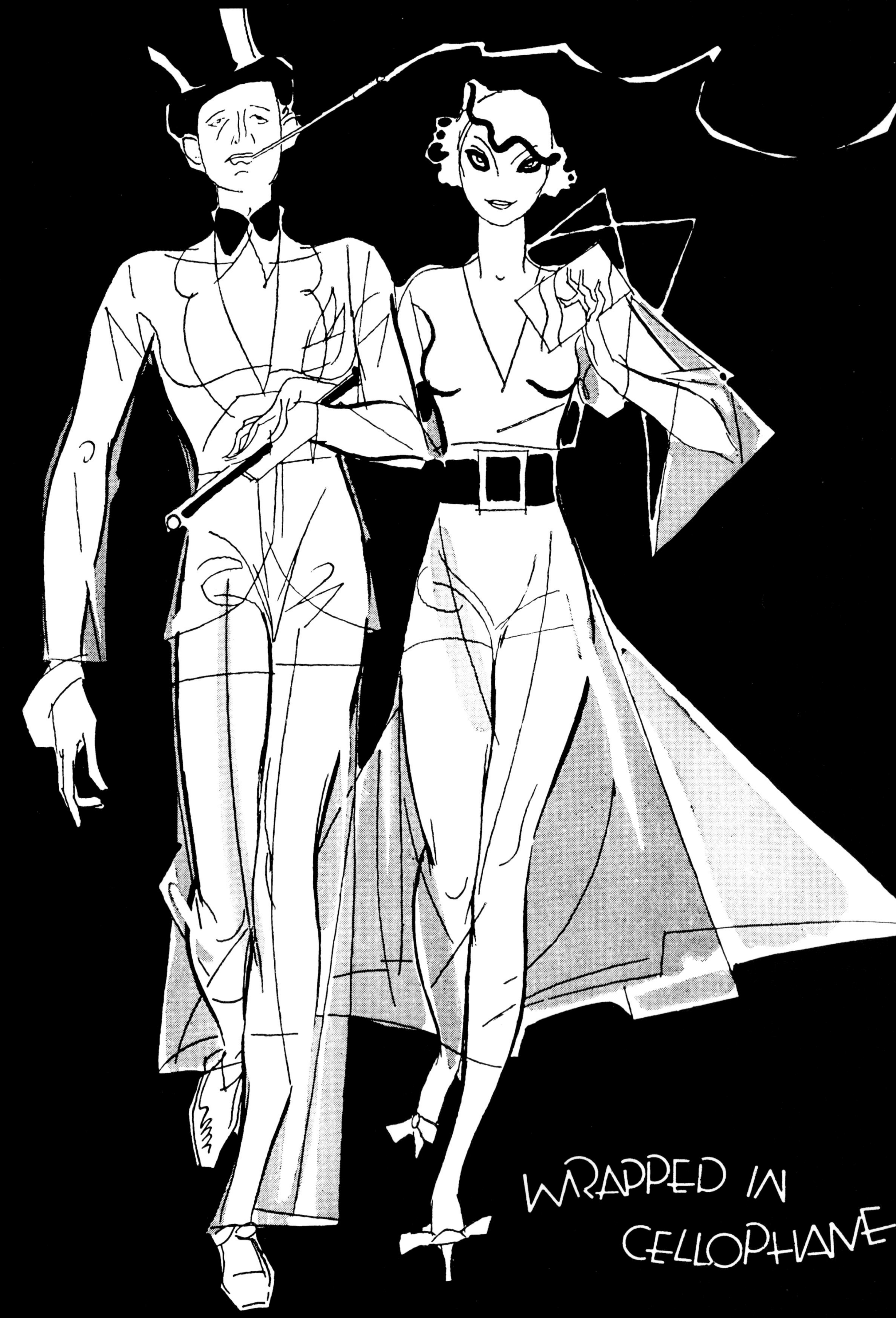
WRAPPED IN
CELLOPHANE

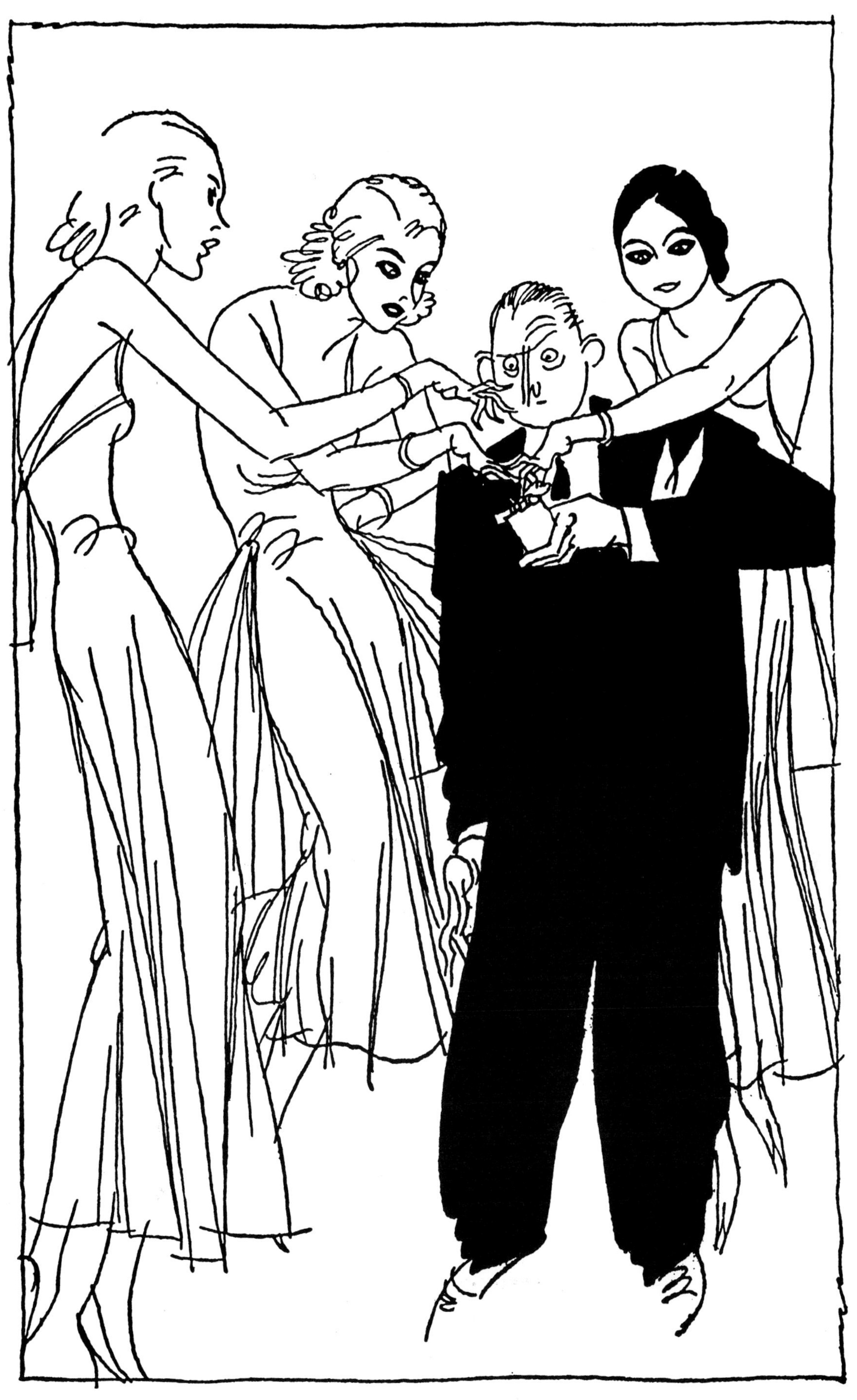

MODERNIZING THE OLD MASTERS

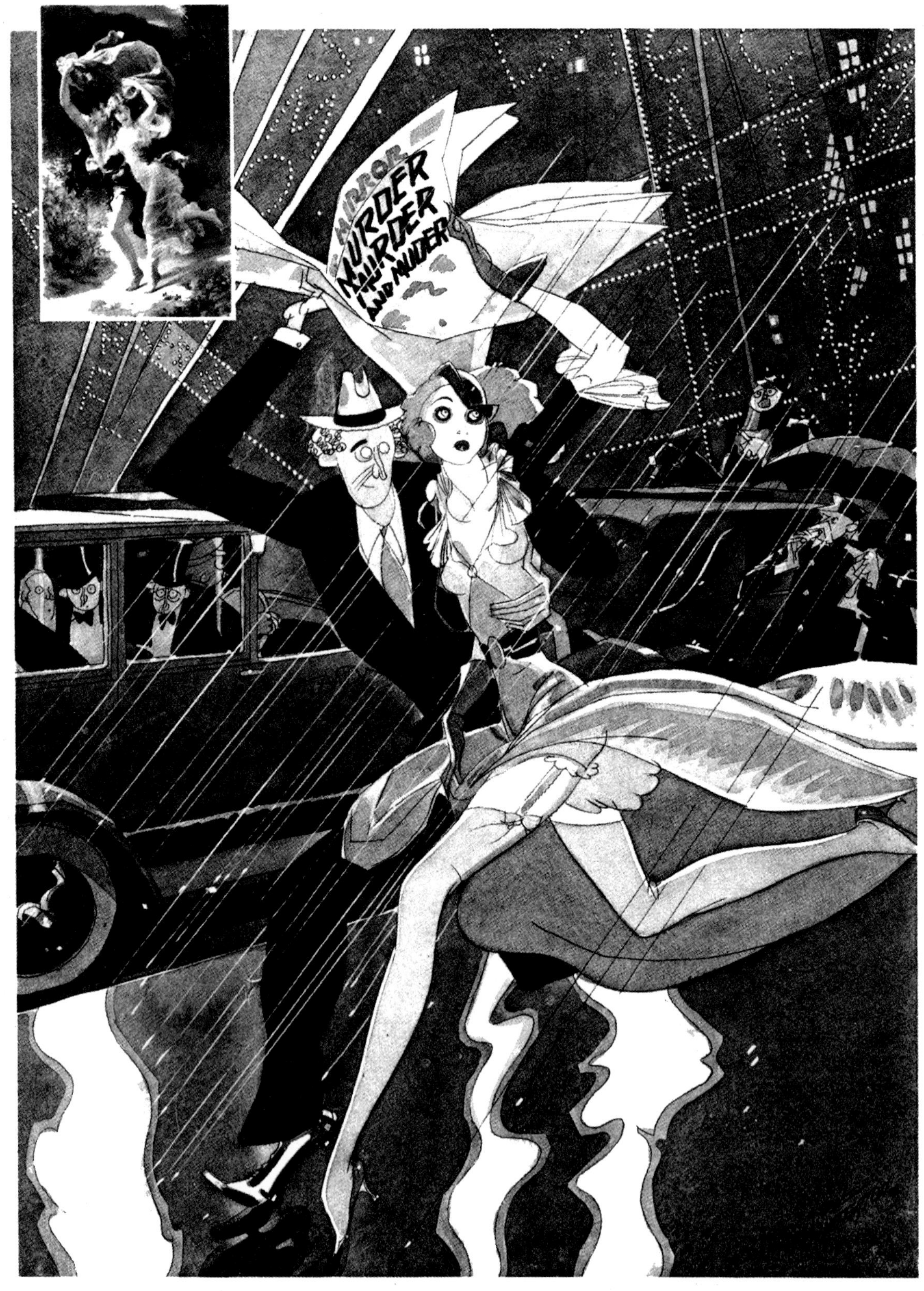

THE STORM

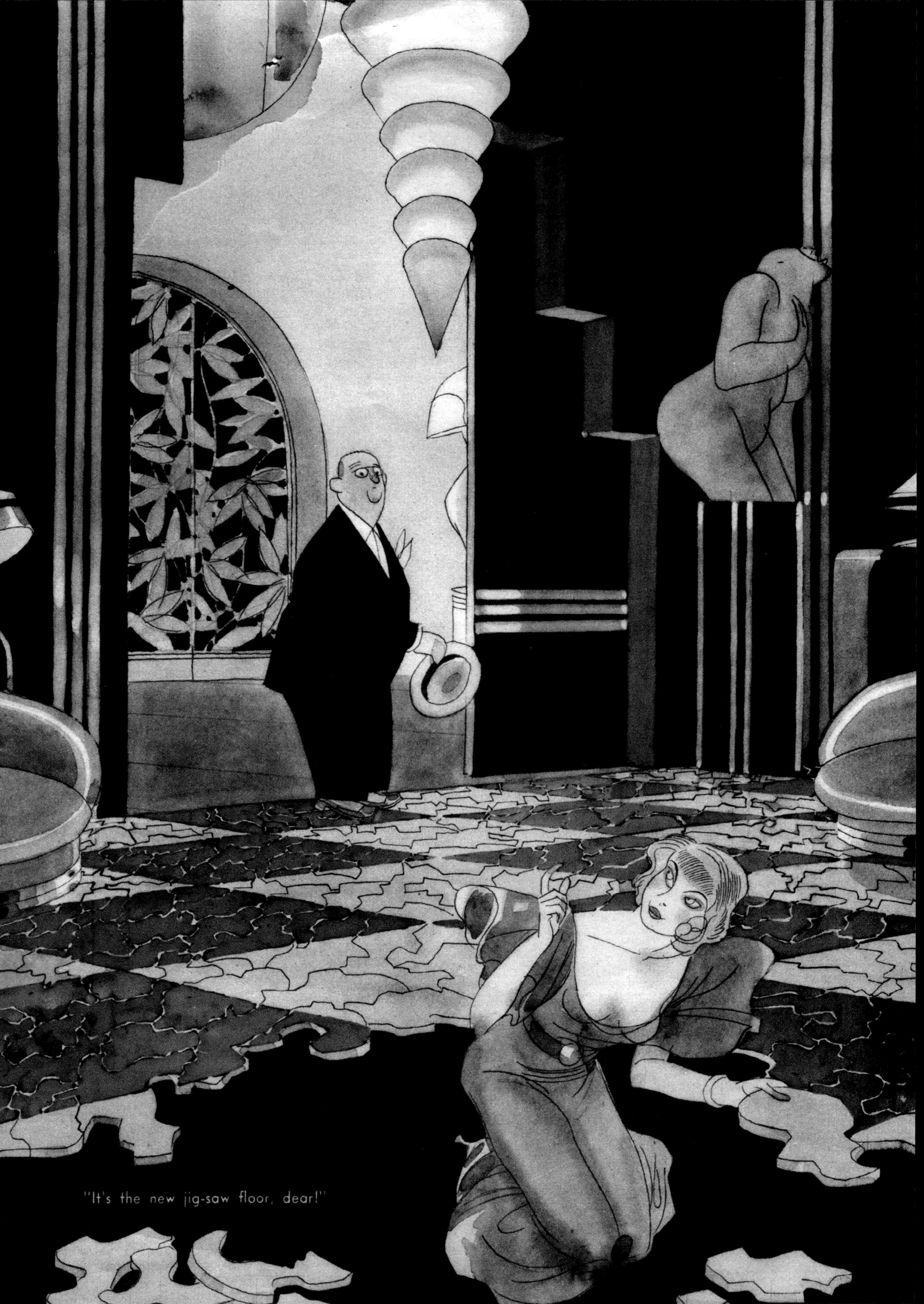

"It's the new jig-saw floor, dear!"

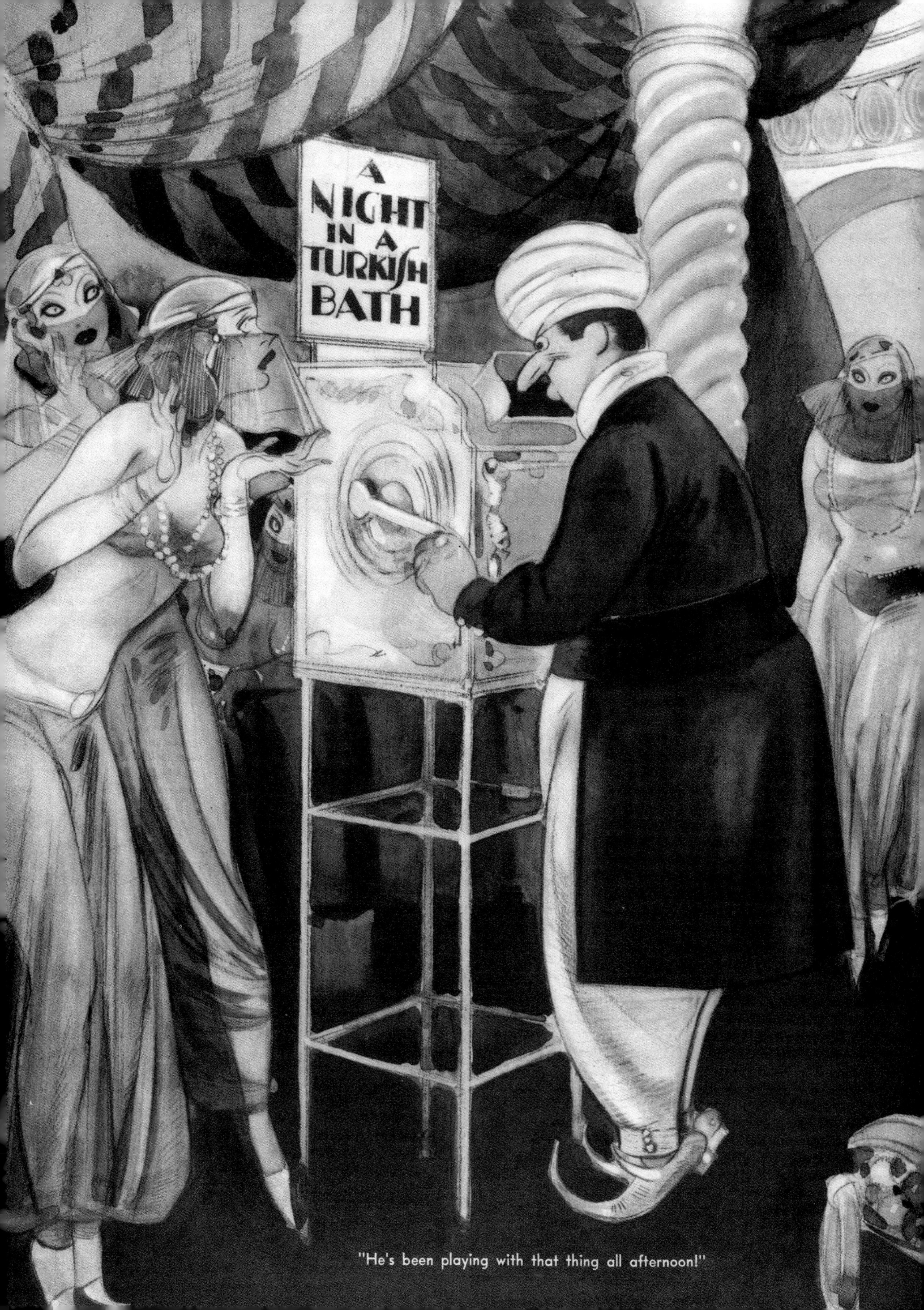

"He's been playing with that thing all afternoon!"

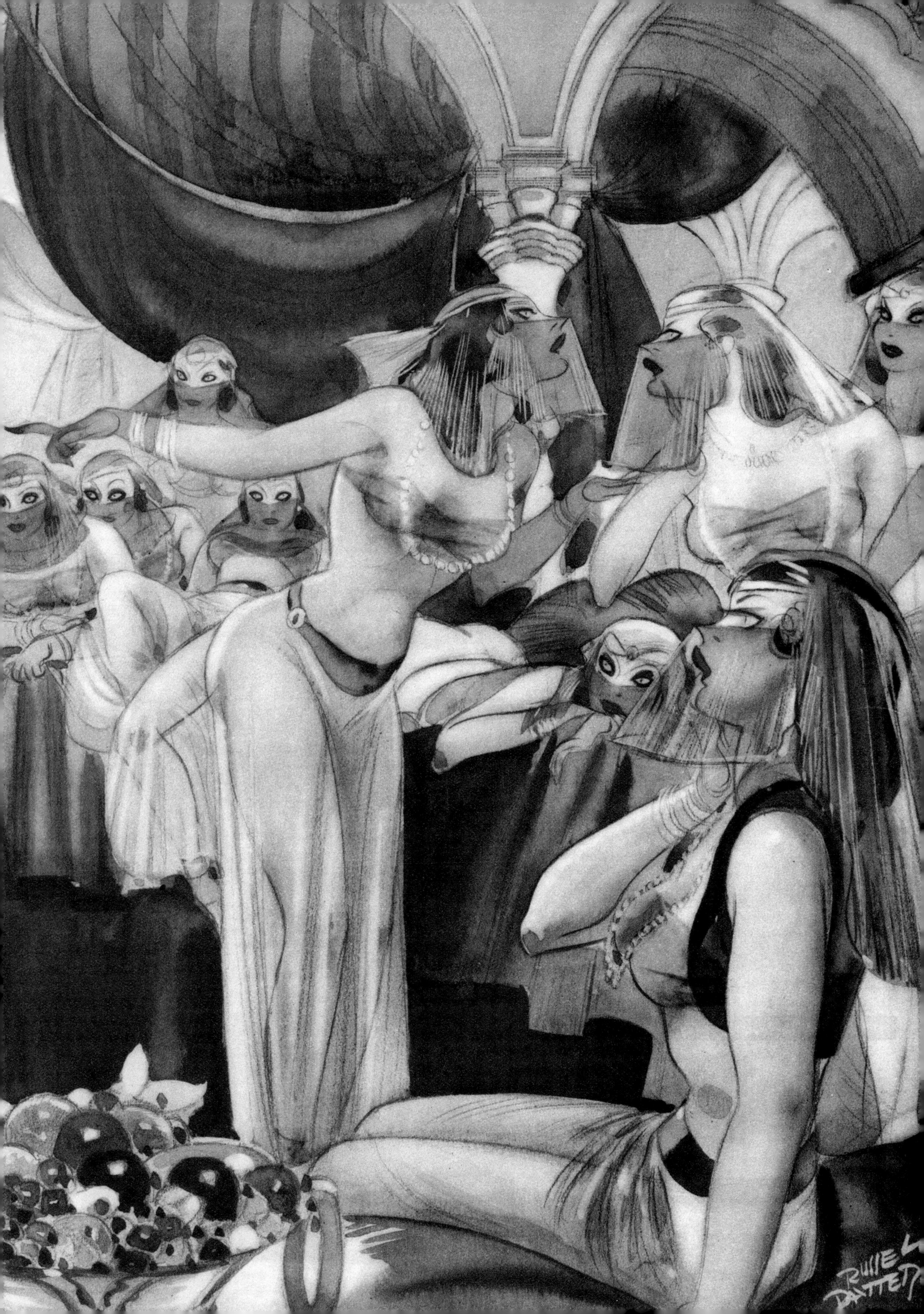

MODERNIZING T

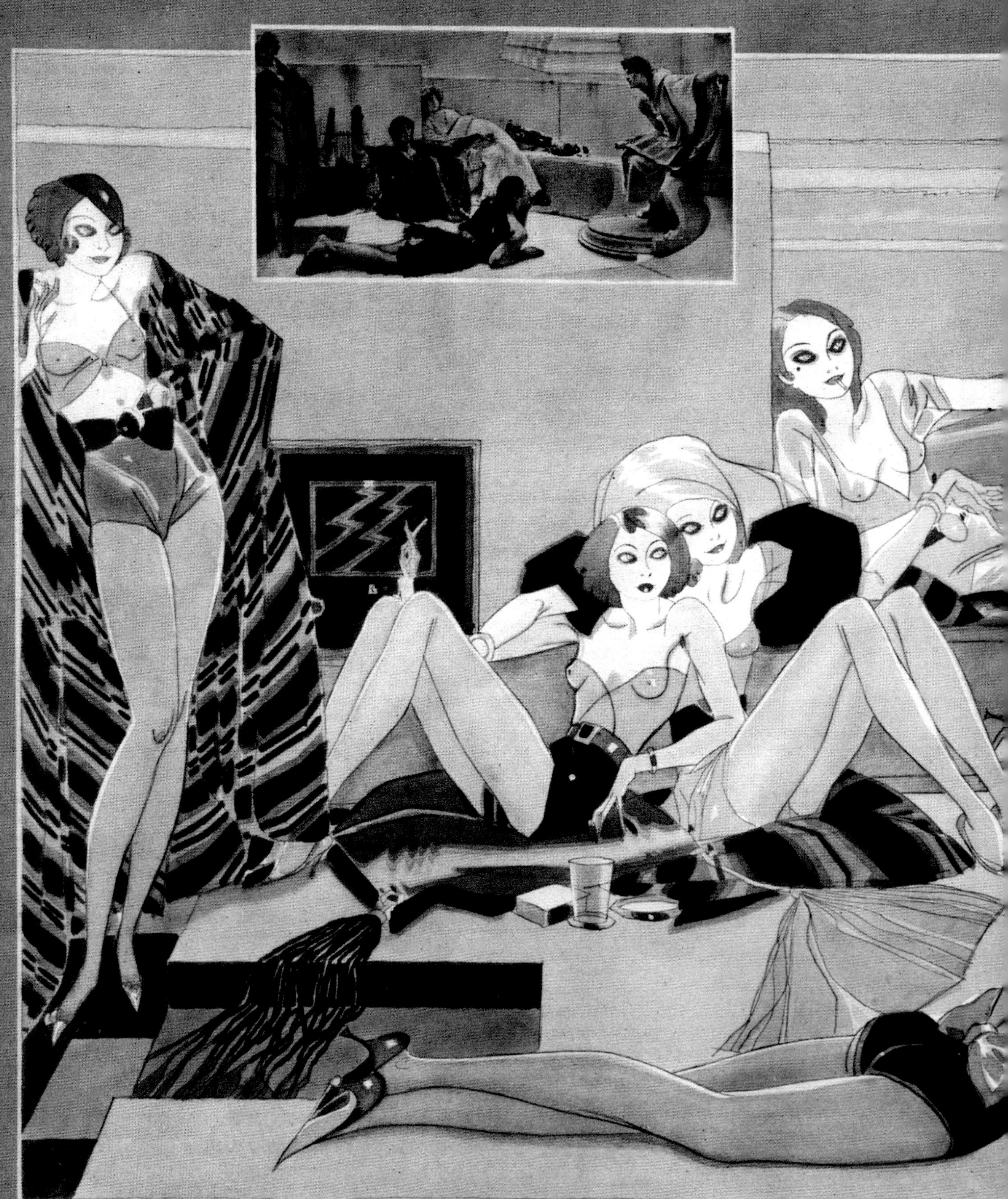

THE READIN

HE OLD MASTERS

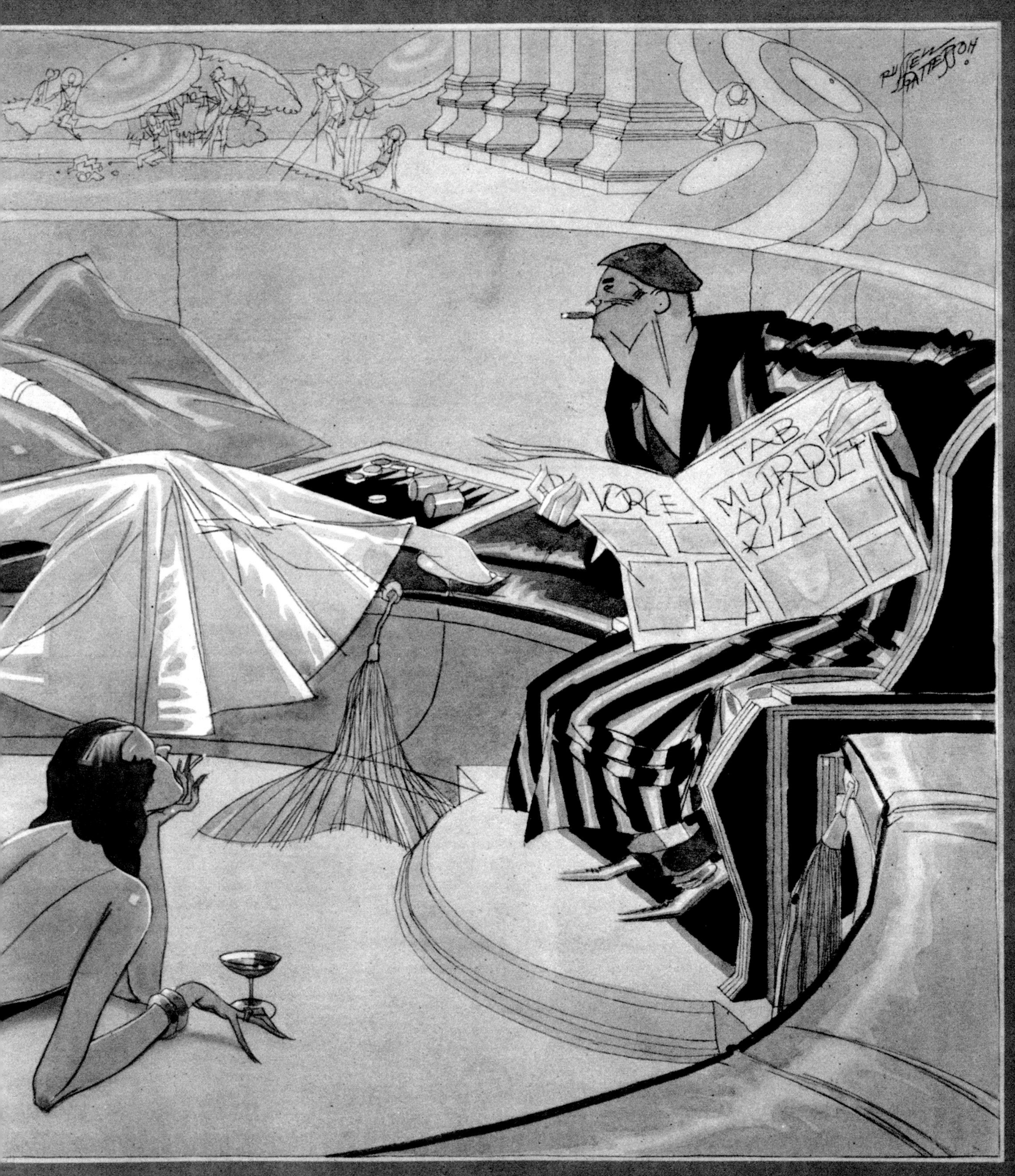

FROM HOMER

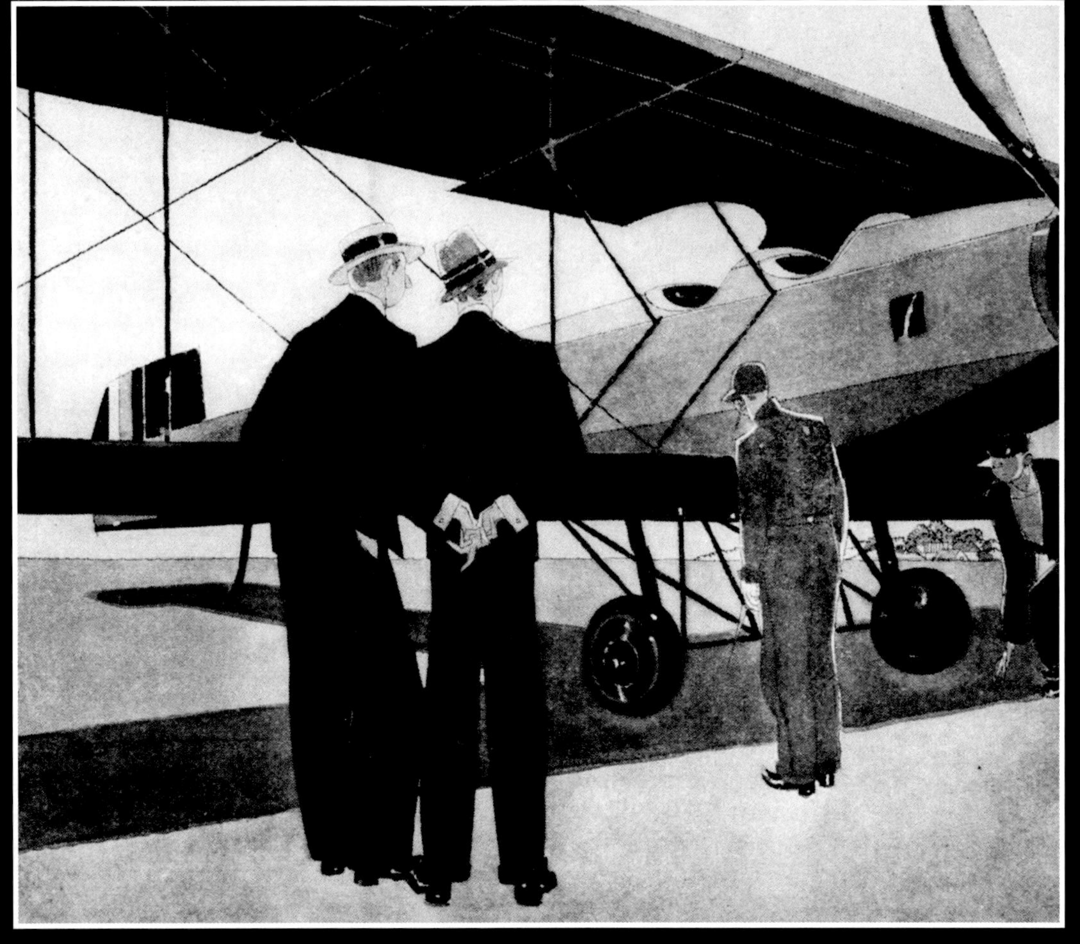

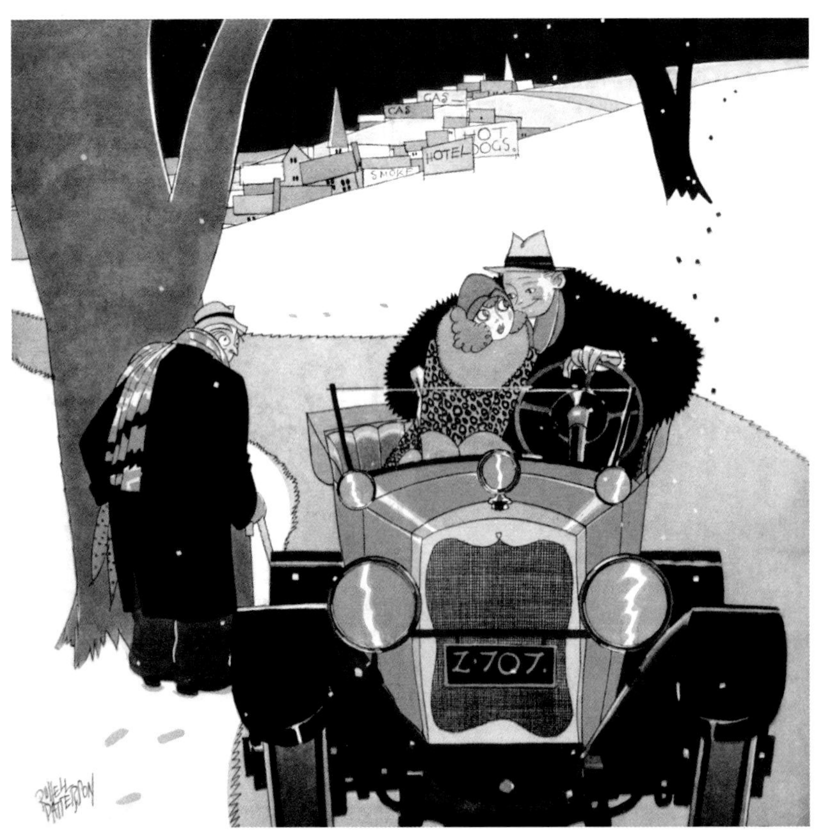
GAS
GAS
HOT DOGS
HOTEL
SMOKE
Z·707.
RUSSELL PATTERSON

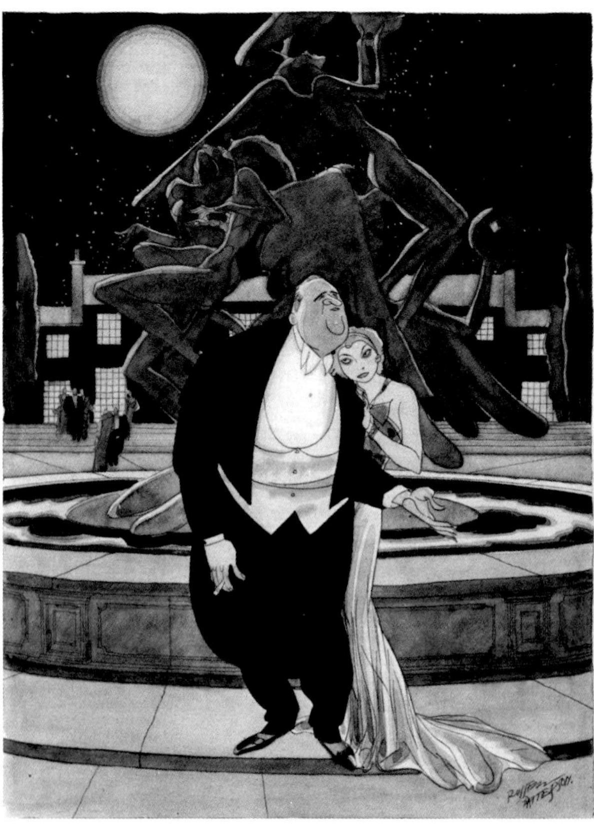
RUSSELL PATTERSON

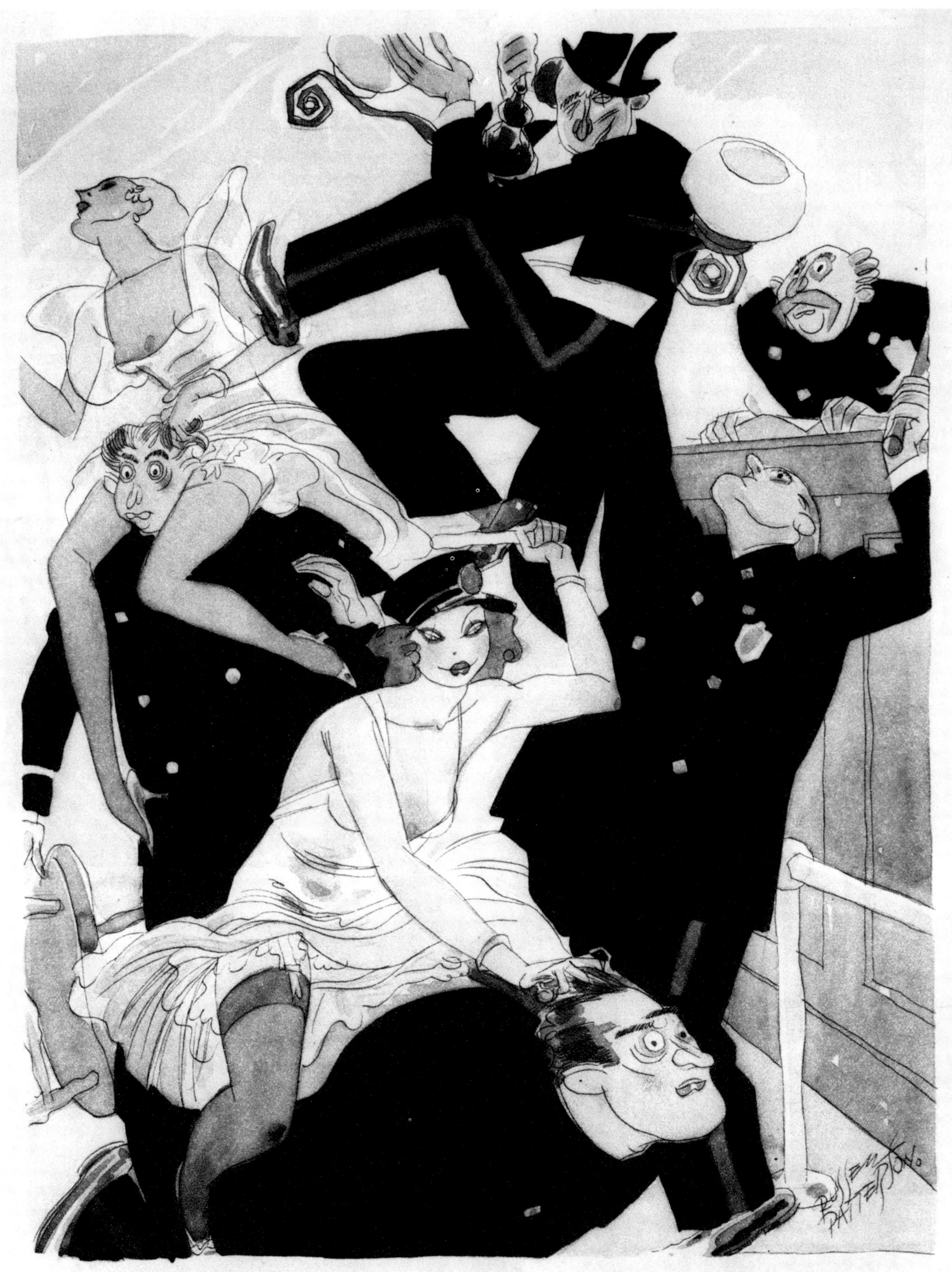

"We made a mistake pinchin' these birds, Sarge!"

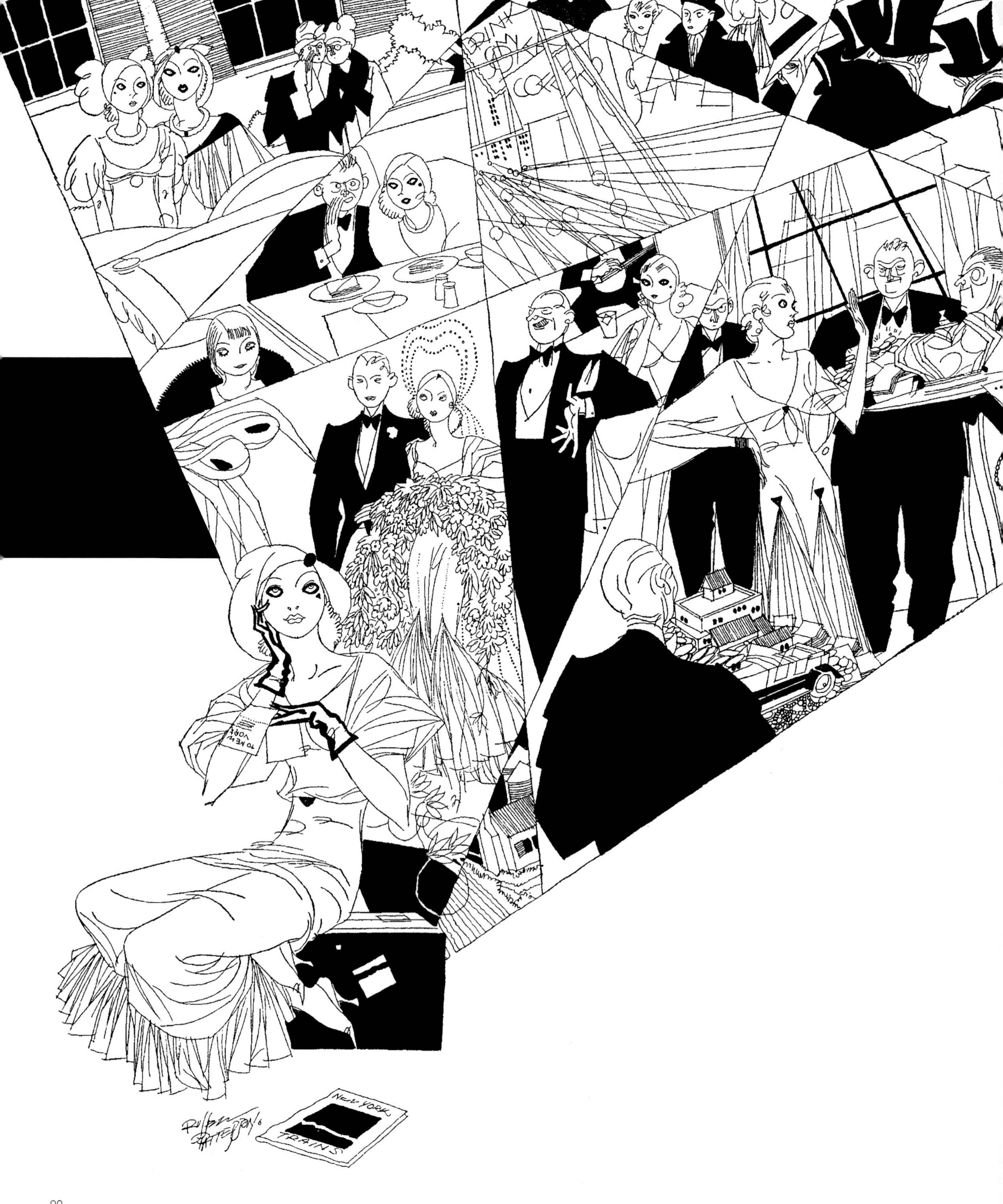
TO NEW YORK
NEW YORK
TRAINS

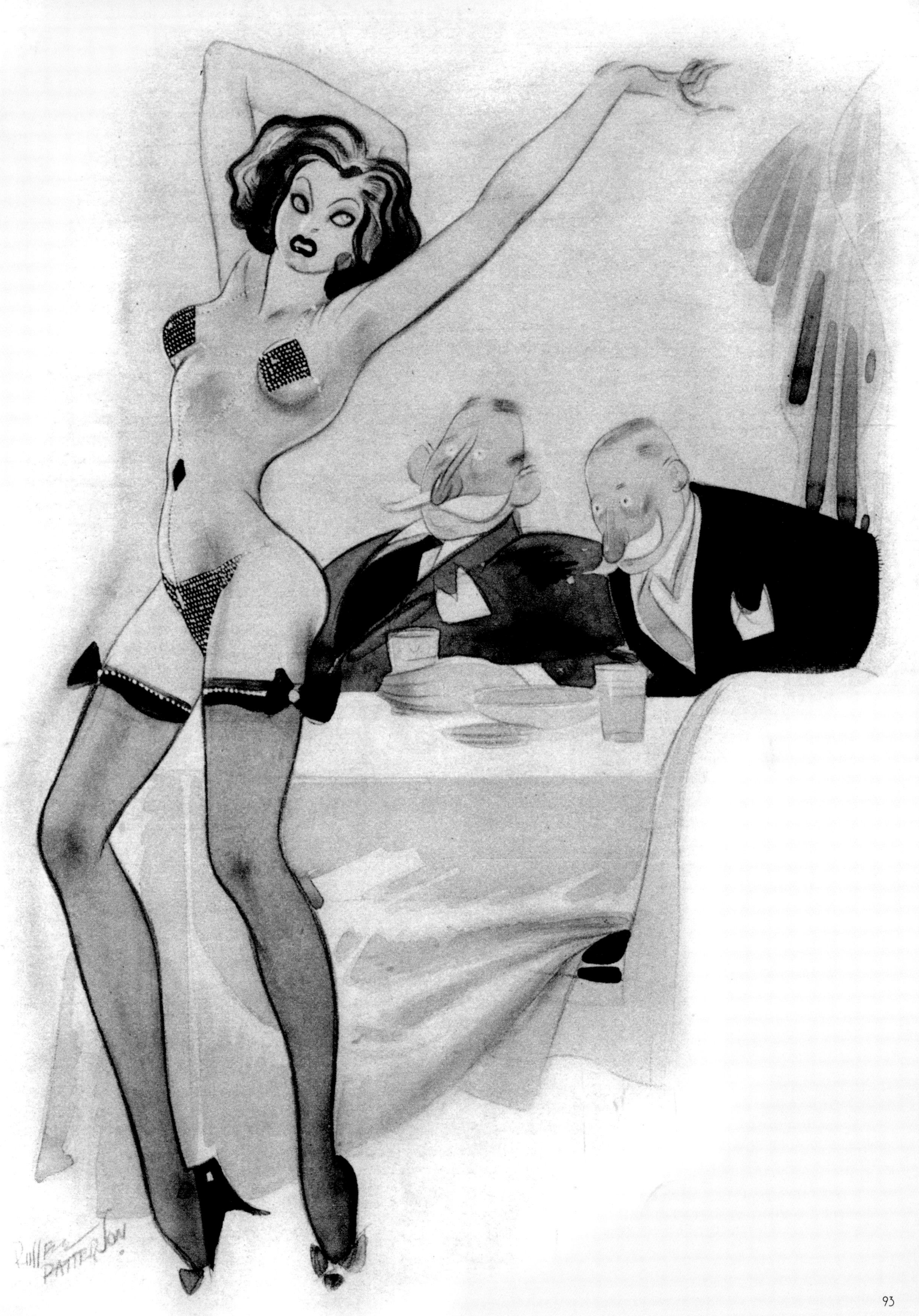
PATTERSON

Illustration by Russell Patterson

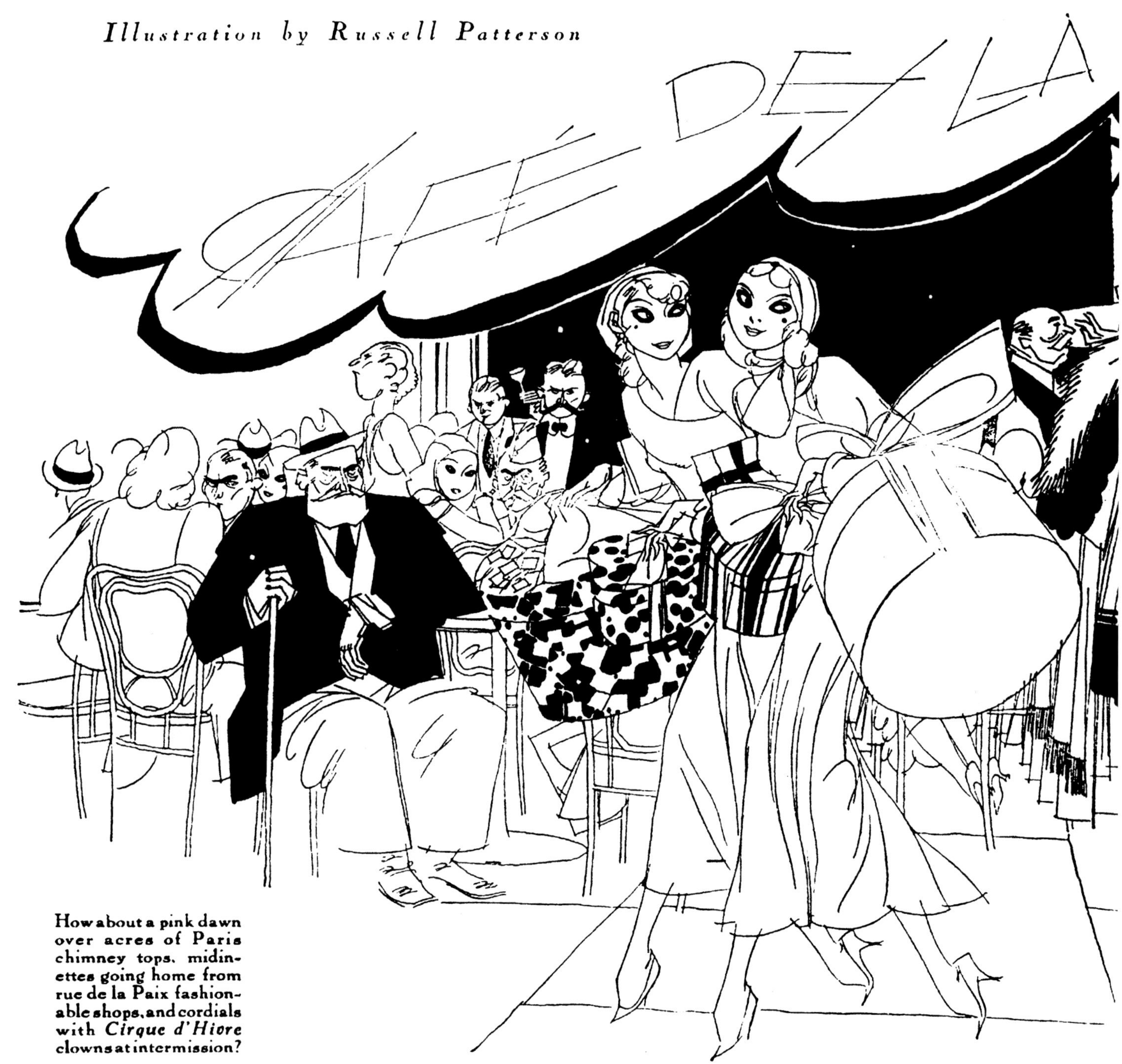

How about a pink dawn over acres of Paris chimney tops, midinettes going home from rue de la Paix fashionable shops, and cordials with *Cirque d'Hiore* clowns at intermission?

You Must SEE PARIS

THE older I grow—and what strides I make lately!—the more satisfied I am that Paris is only for Youth. In my early and late twenties Paris was the high spot of the universe, the top of the world.

It was Goethe who observed, "All of us must be drunk once; youth is drunkenness without wine." It seems to me before the age of thirty most of us could paraphrase that to read, "Paris is drunkenness without wine!"

I used to acquire a giddiness, without wine, from the moment I went down the gangplank at drizzling Havre or Cherbourg, and by the time I debouched at Gare St. Lazarre in Paris I was actually whooping and dancing in the streets. I even wanted to garland my hair. Whoops!

Everything was a thrill—the honking taxis; the narrow, cobbled, echoing streets; the madly pedaled bread tricycles; the caped and detached little *gendarmes;* the outside café tables dotted with blue seltzer bottles; the circular bars, the laughing-eyed midinettes; the cocottes flirting and looking back, the oppressive propriety of ancient streets, the gayety of the boulevards, the quick sad strokes of cathedral chimes—Paree! Paree!

But after thirty, Paris began to pall. How strangely "street carnival" and bourgeoise the city had become! Of

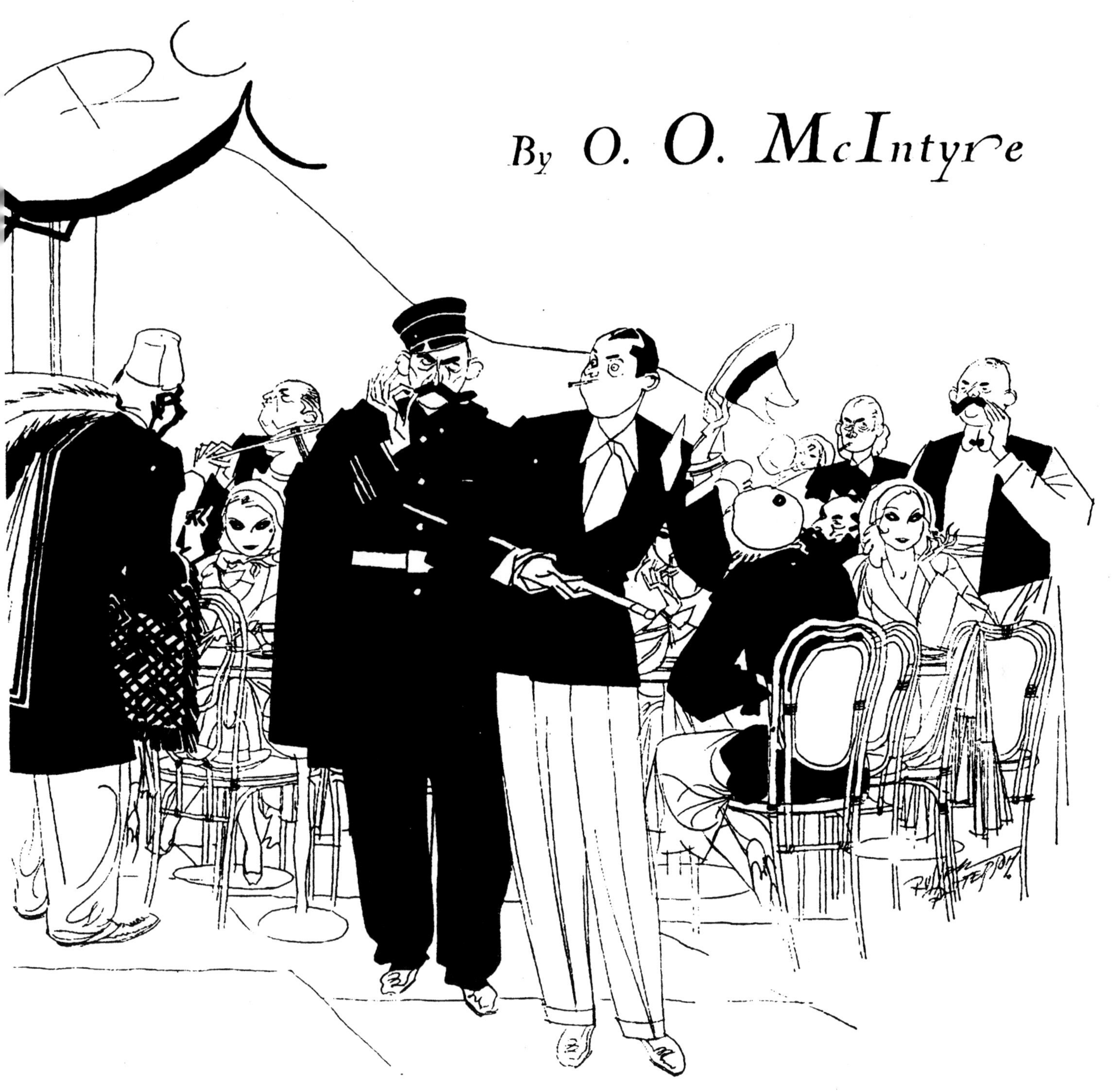

By O. O. McIntyre

BEFORE THIRTY!

course, the beautiful Tuileries with its caroling birds spiraling heavenward with glad cries, the treasures of the Louvre, the wooded loveliness of the Bois, the horticultural triumphs of the Luxembourg, the subdued dignity of the Bois de Bologne—all are there. But after a half dozen visits your excitement wanes.

And at forty Paris begins to be irritating—to make you terribly, terribly angry. You resent the gyppery of the *de luxe* hotels, the amiable insults of tradesmen with duality of prices aimed at Americans, the dirty post-card sellers under the ancient porticos of the rue de Rivoli, the snarling and thieving drivers of ramshackle mice-powered taxis, the mock condescension in the dressmaking *ateliers*, the *concierge* meanness and all the rest of the humbuggery that thrives in post war Paris.

You arrive in Paris at night and you want to be off in the morning for the cool, shrill air of St. Moritz, the languor of Florence or one of those frosted ginger-cake villages along the Rhine. That is, if you have passed the age of forty. And I have plenty.

And what wouldn't any of us antiquarians give to indulge a quick turn of the years back to the age of sixteen or even twenty-five to see modern Paris—the swiftly changing Paris of 1930—through the [*Continued on page 117*]

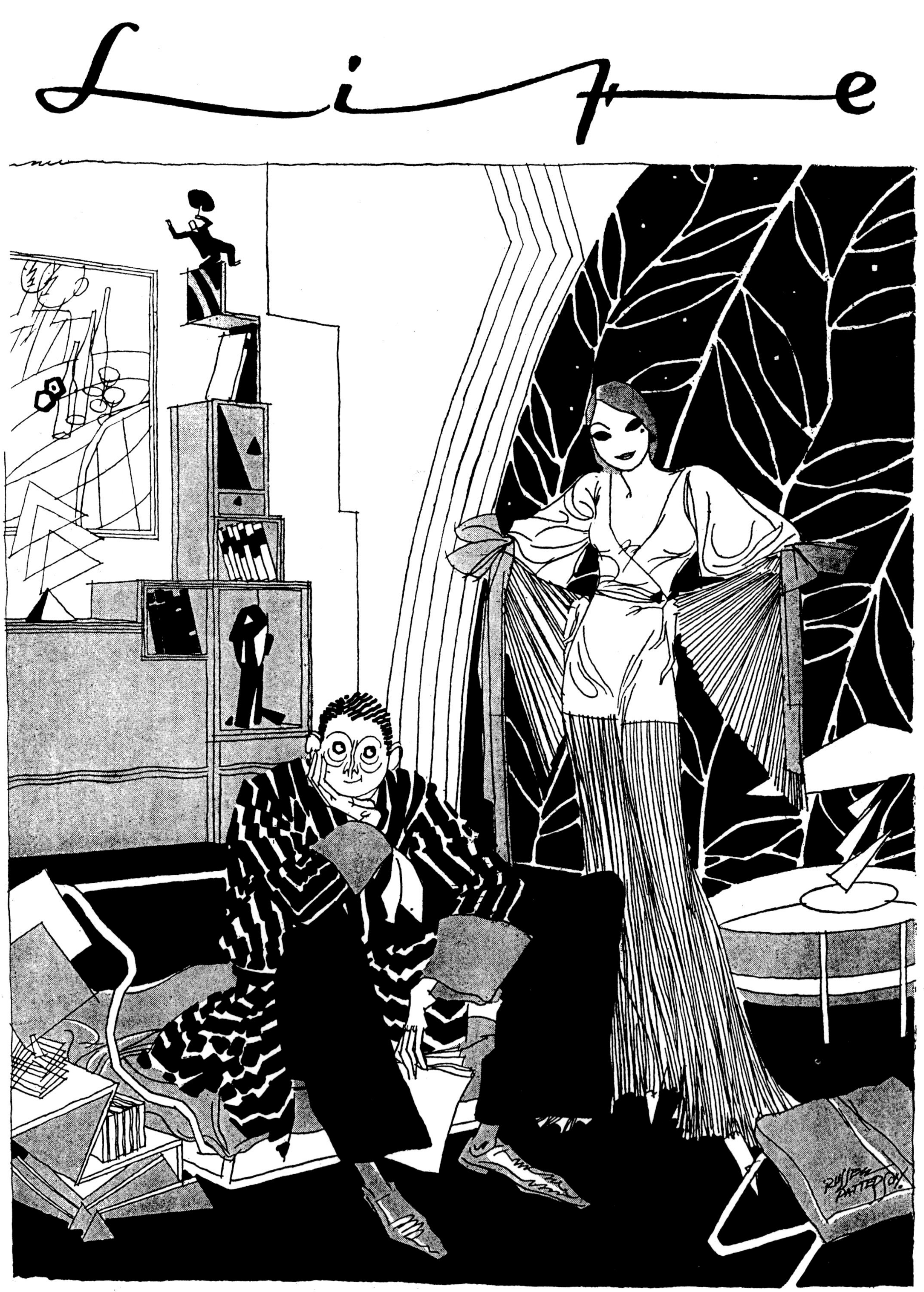

HUSBAND: *Thank Heaven! One more delinquent payment and this furniture is theirs!*

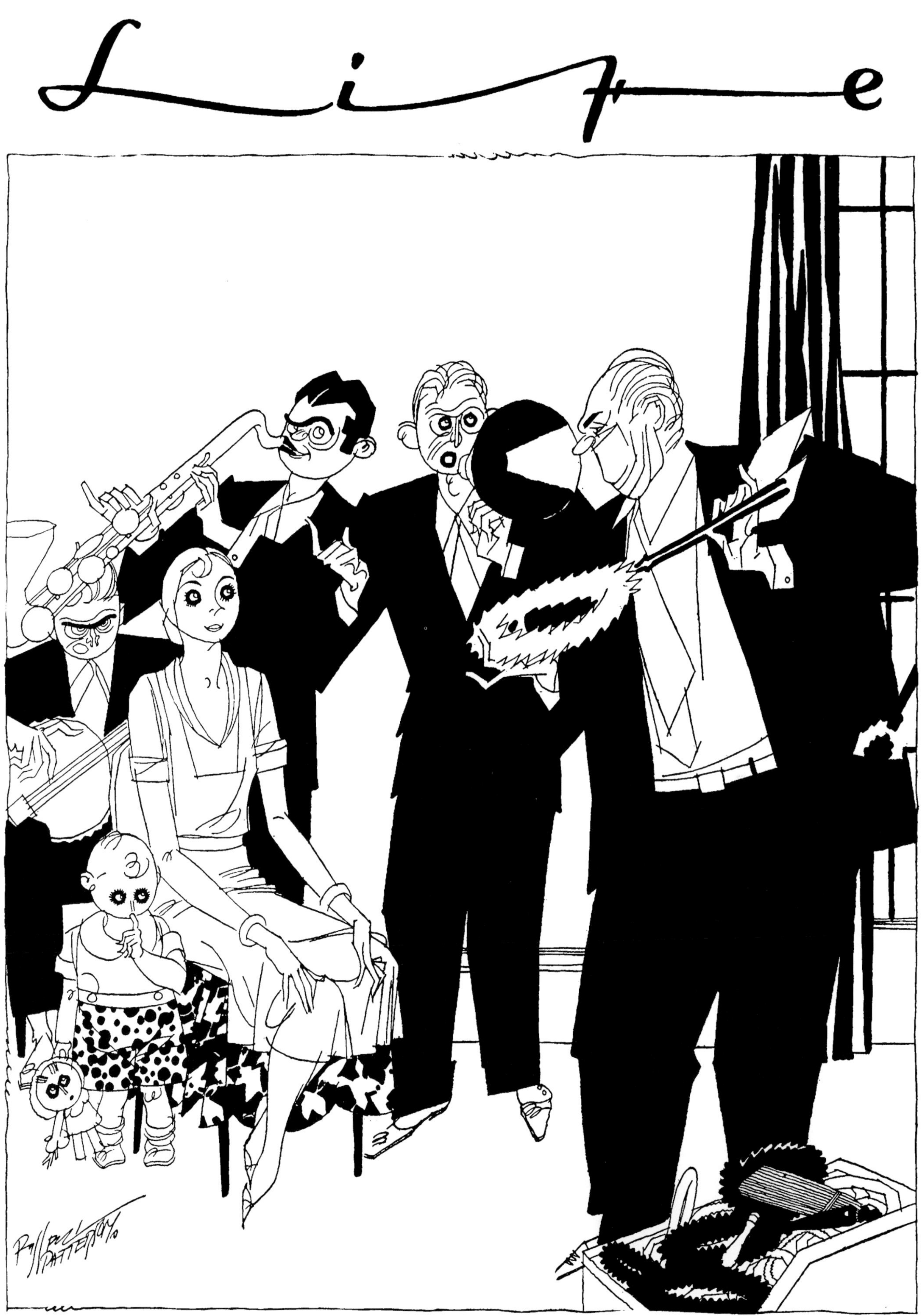

The Fuller Brush man meets radio competition.

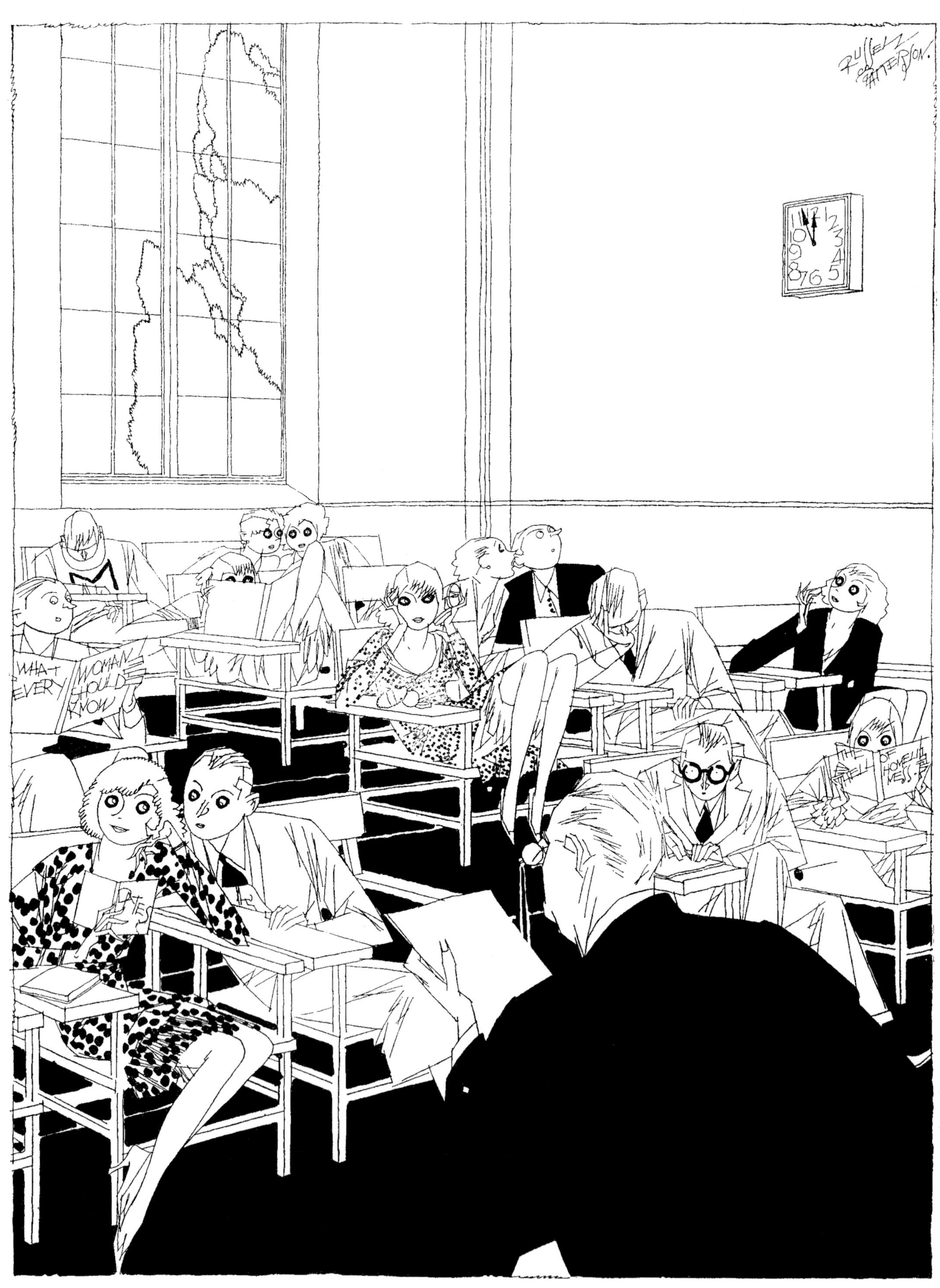

The Professor of Hygiene Delivers His Daring Annual Lecture on the Genesis of the Species

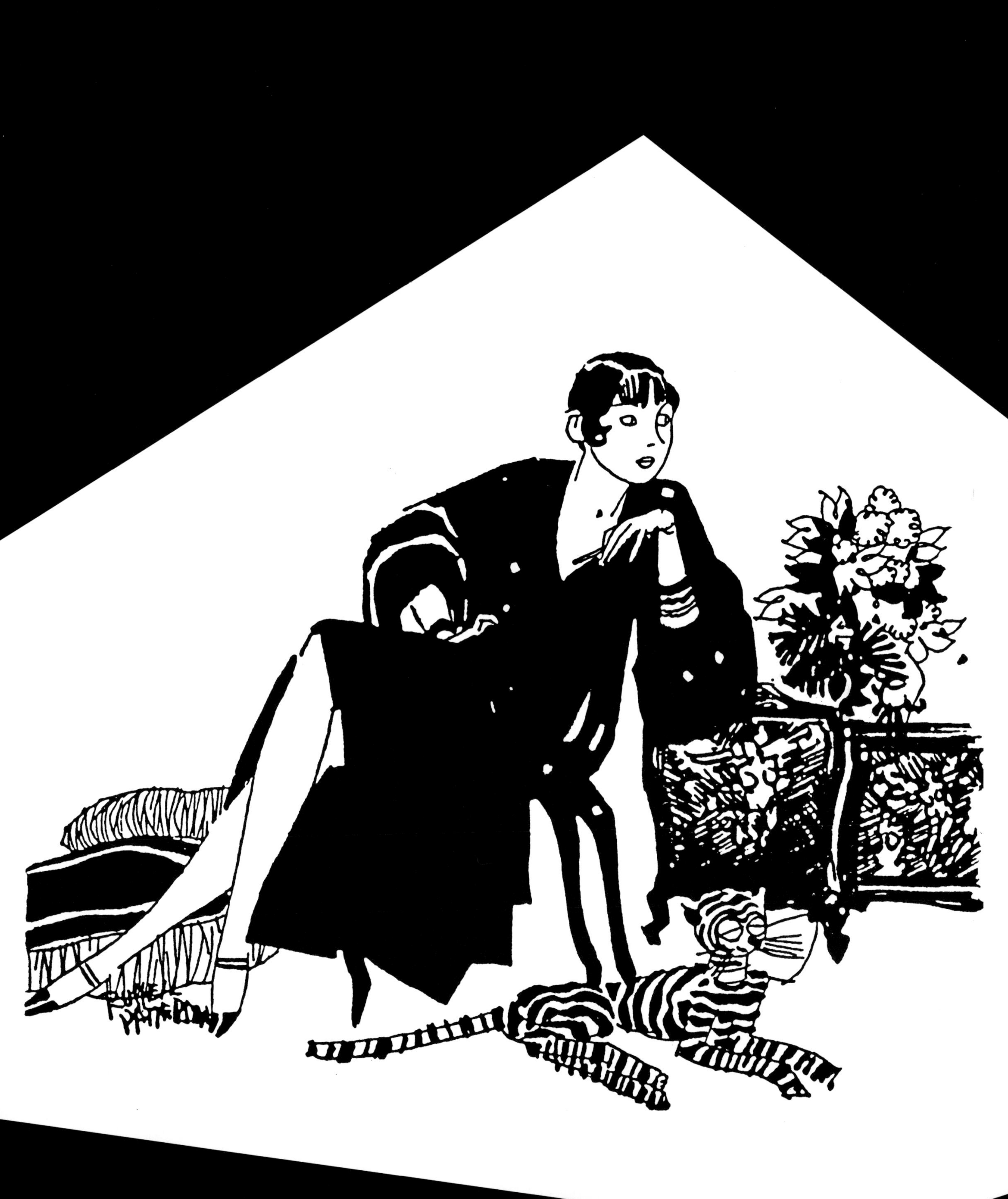

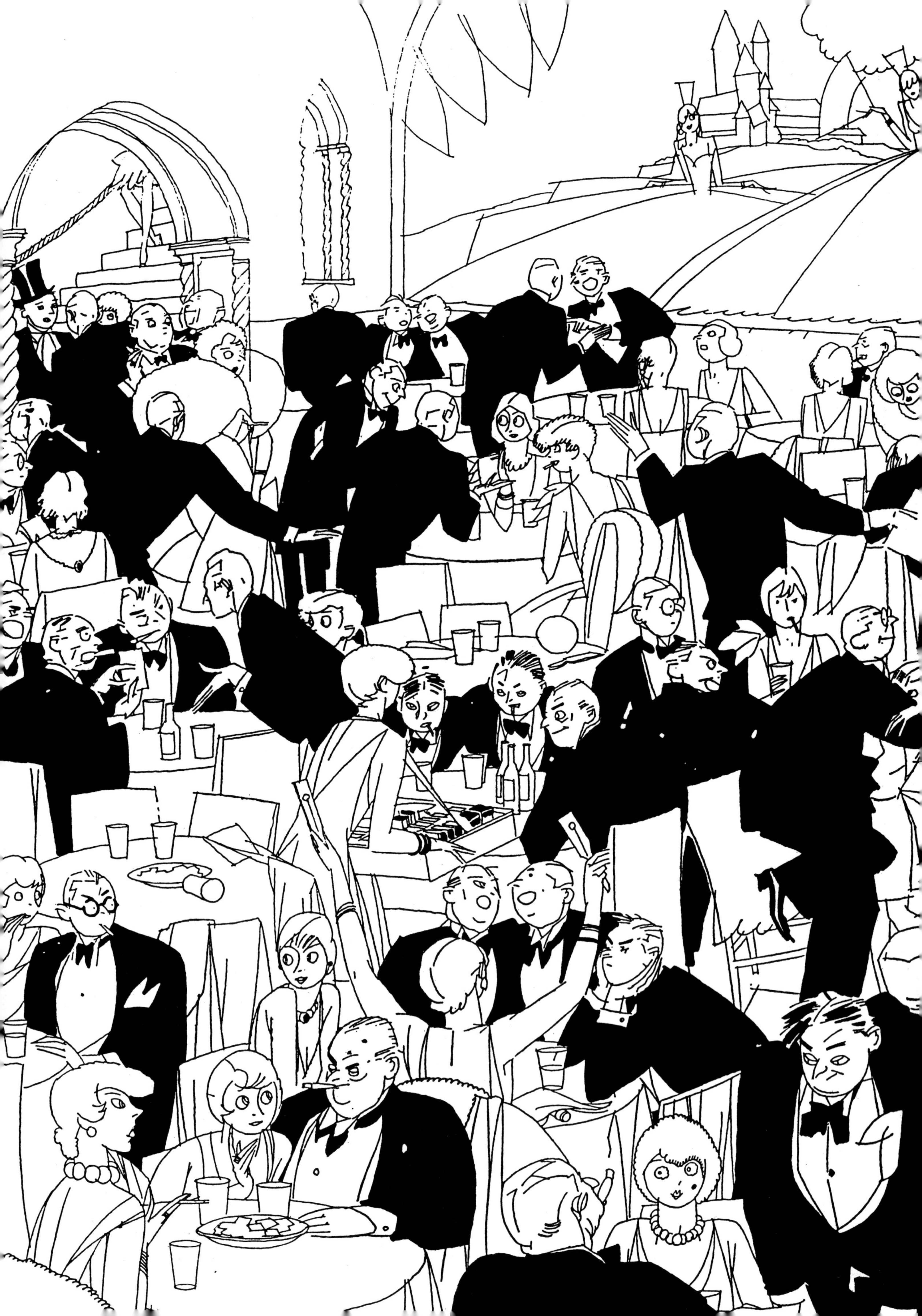

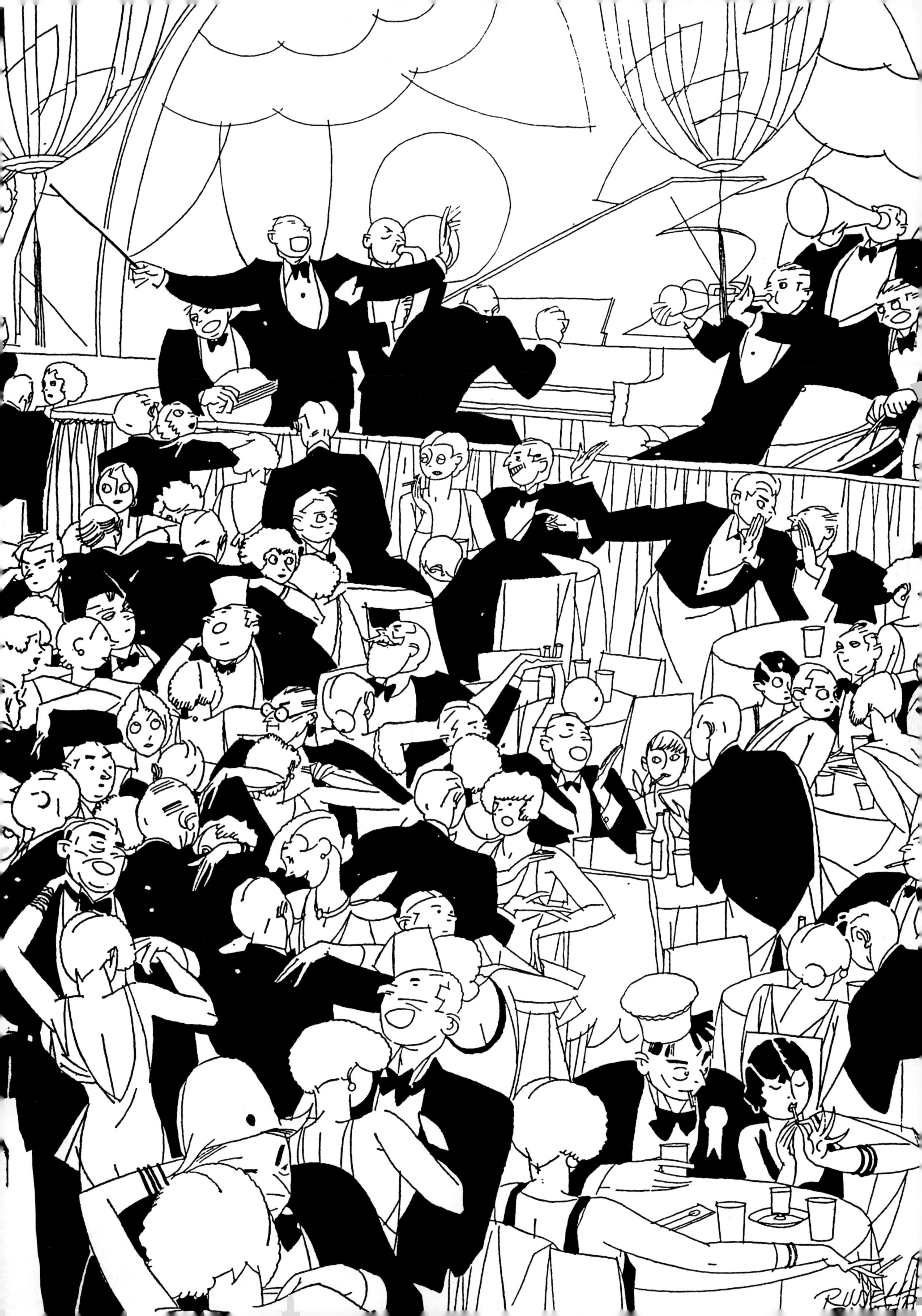

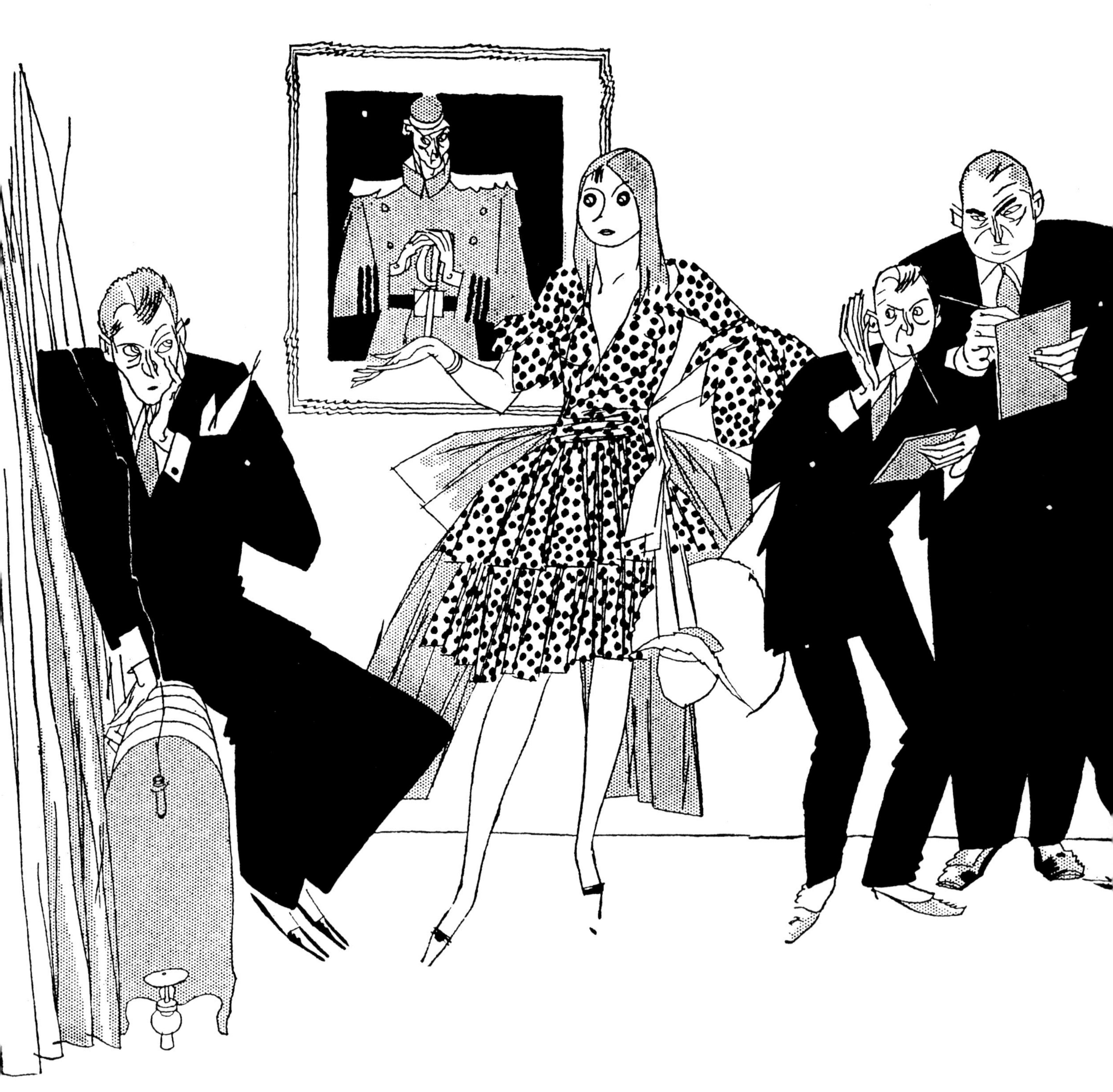

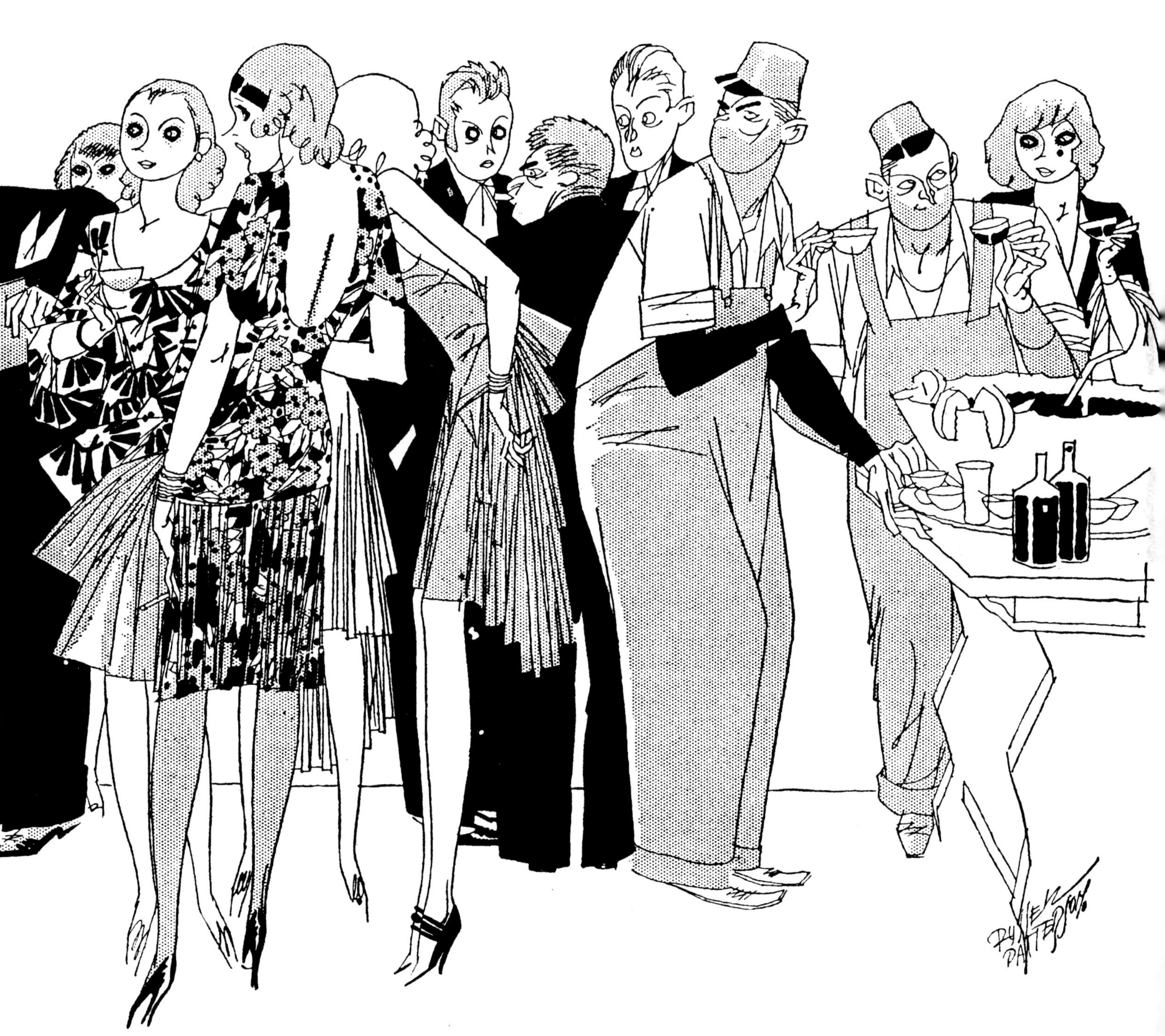

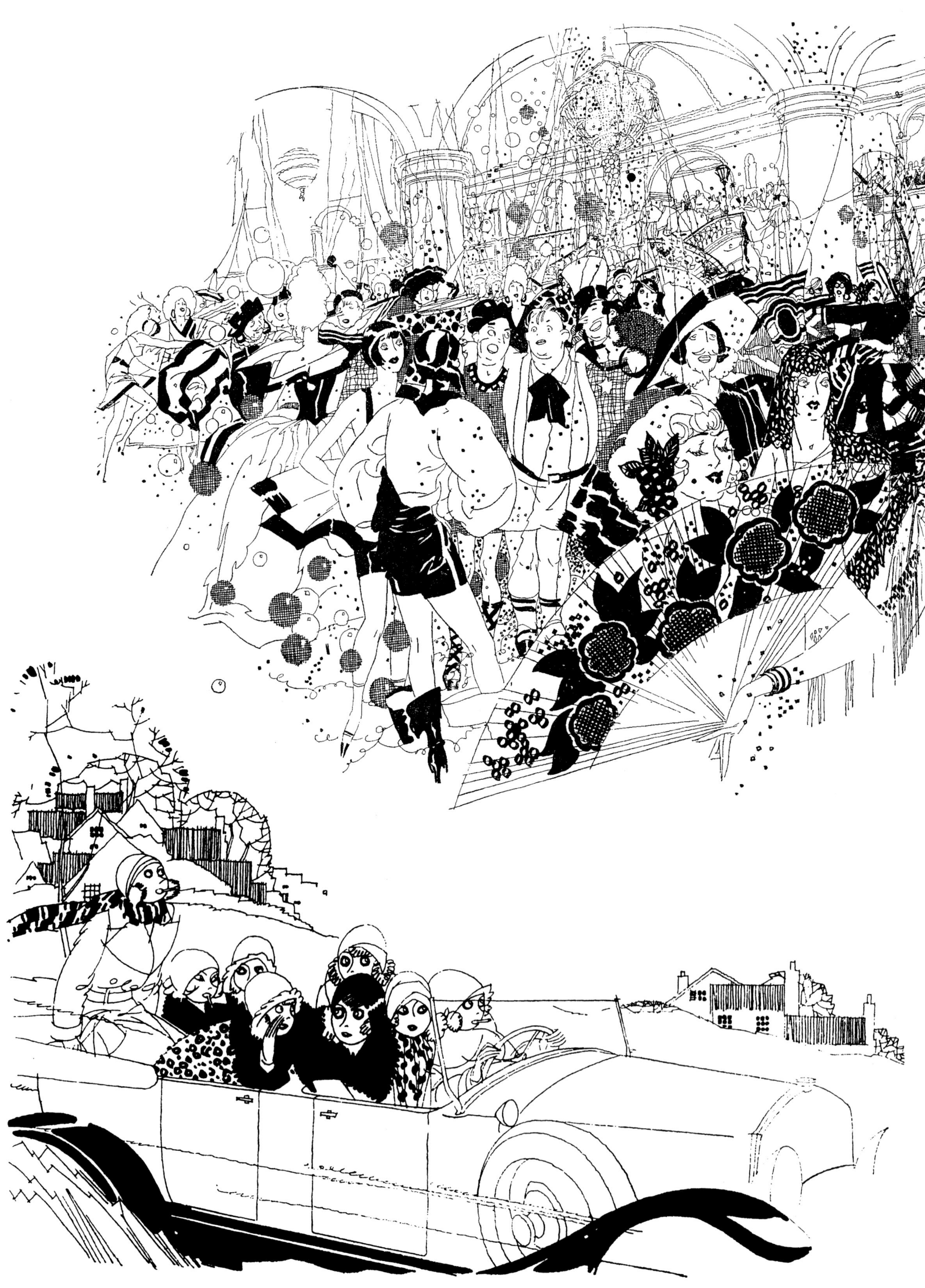

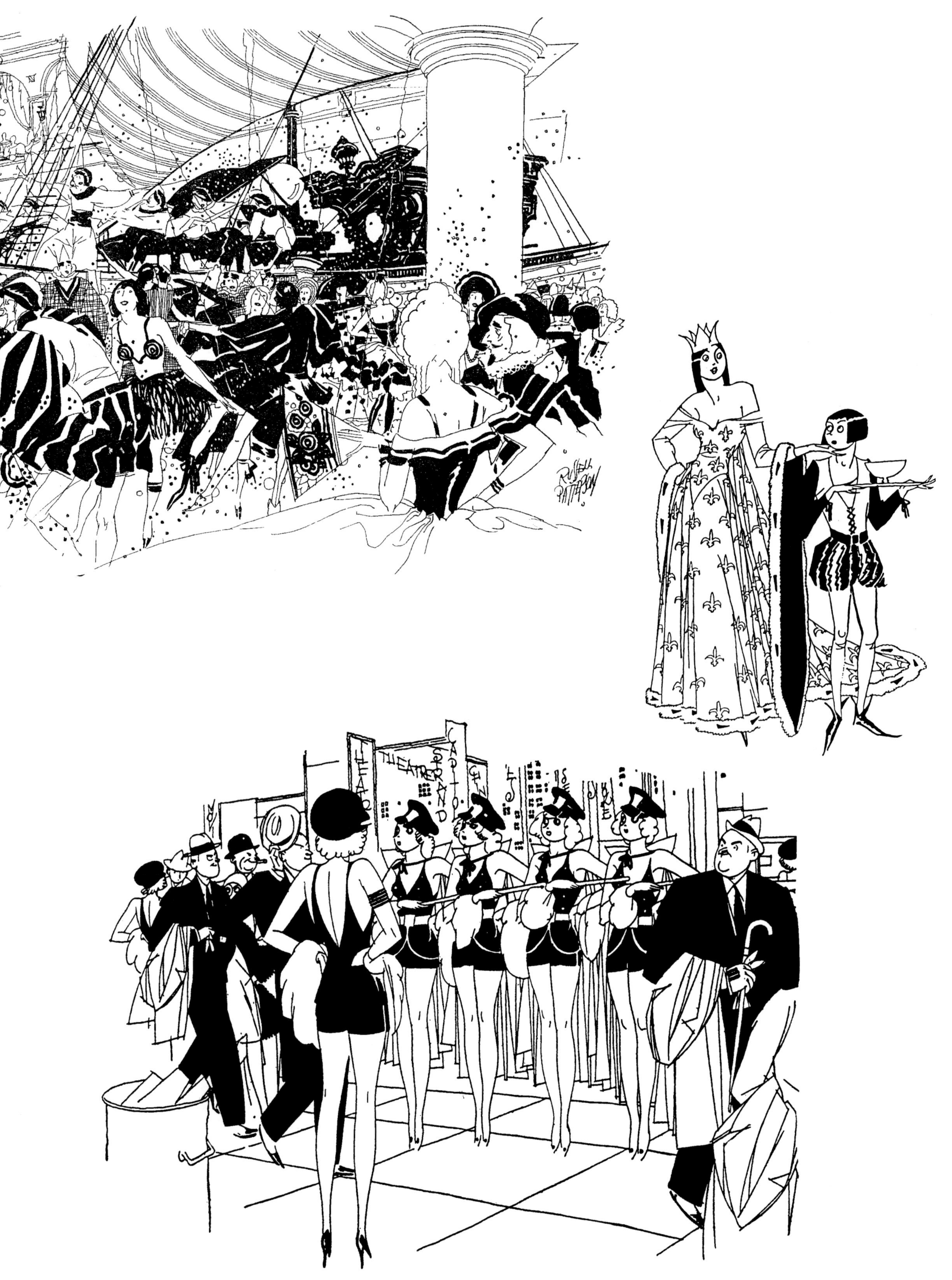
RUSSELL PATTERSON
THEATRE
STRAND
CAPITOL

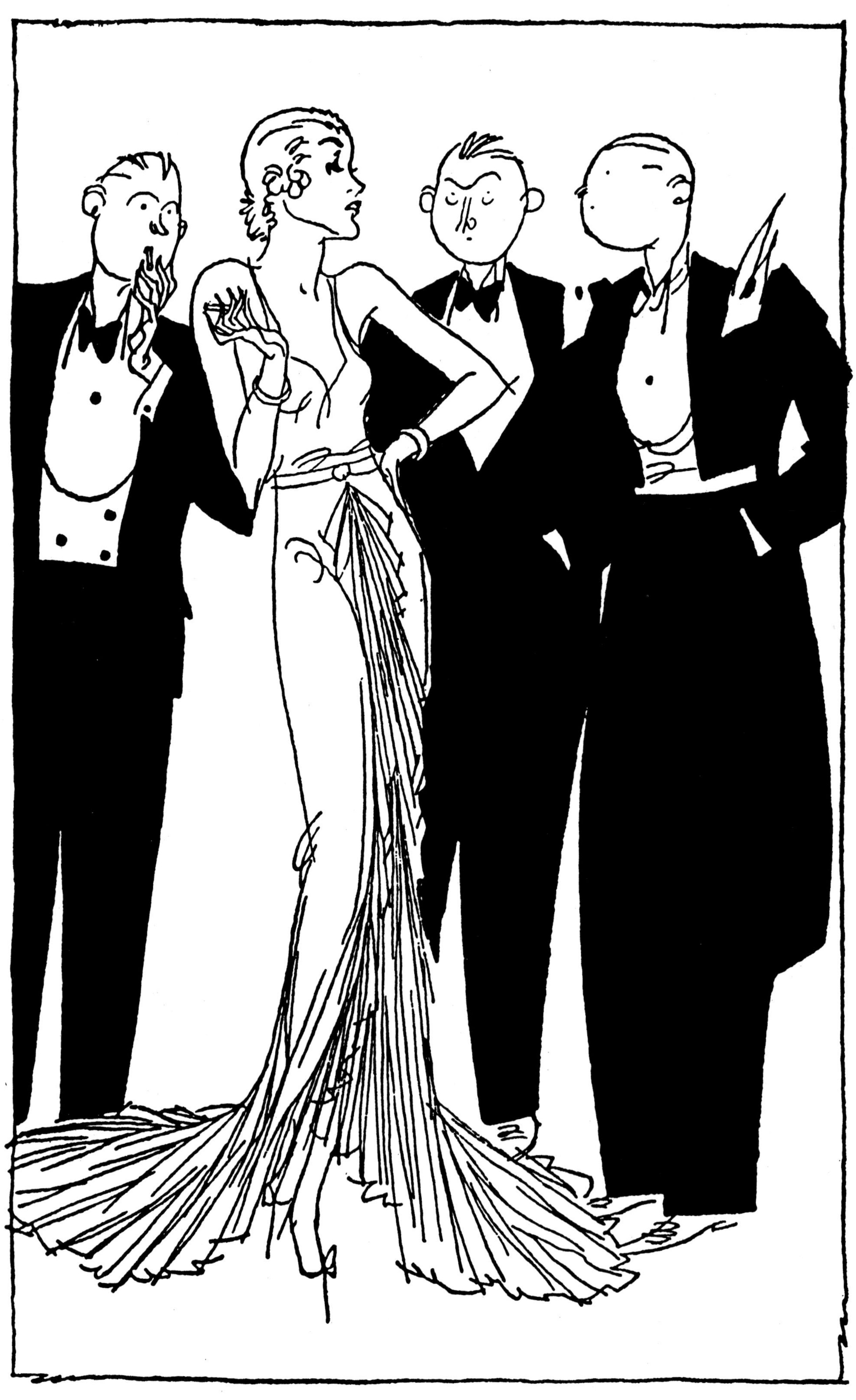

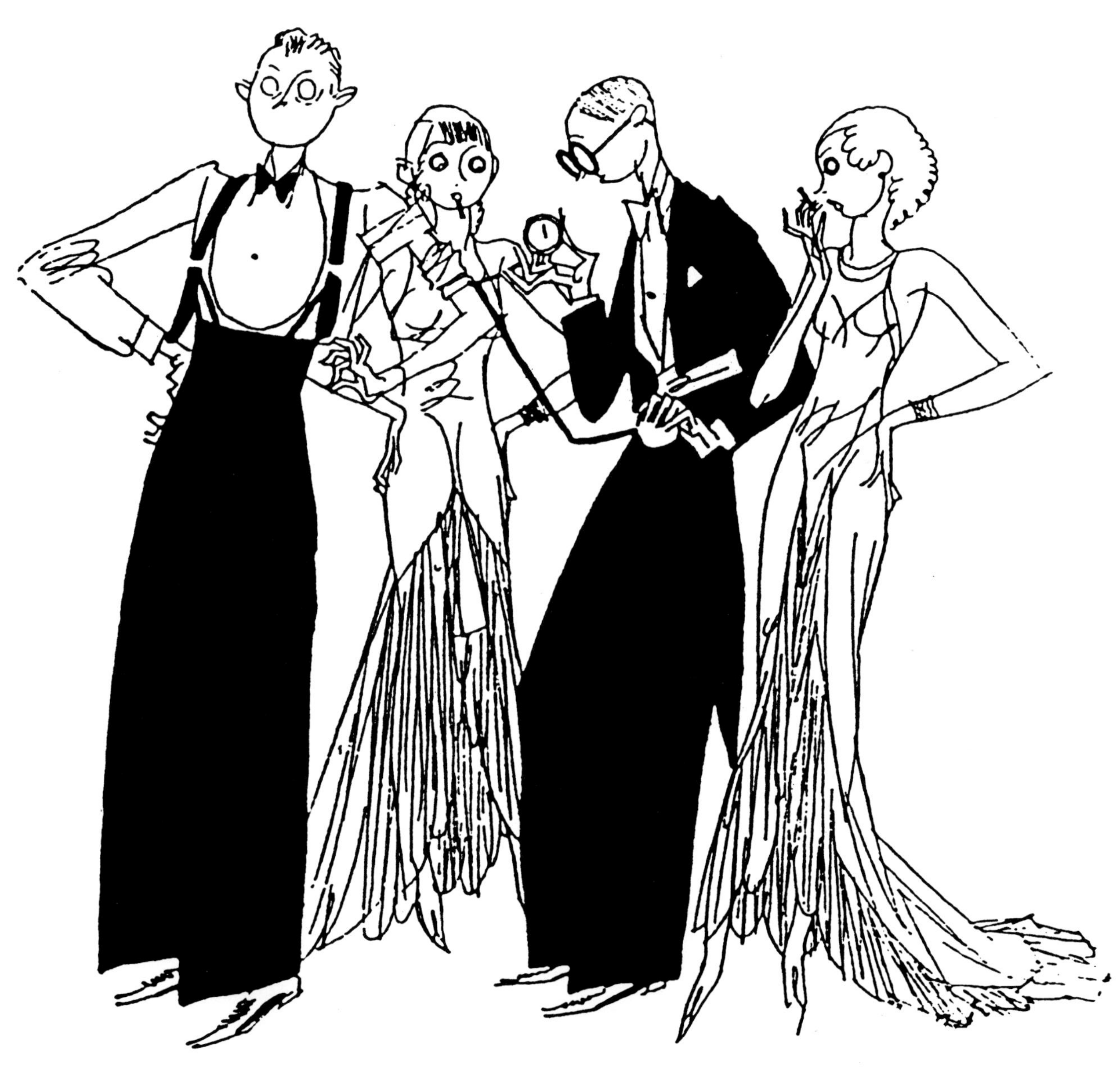

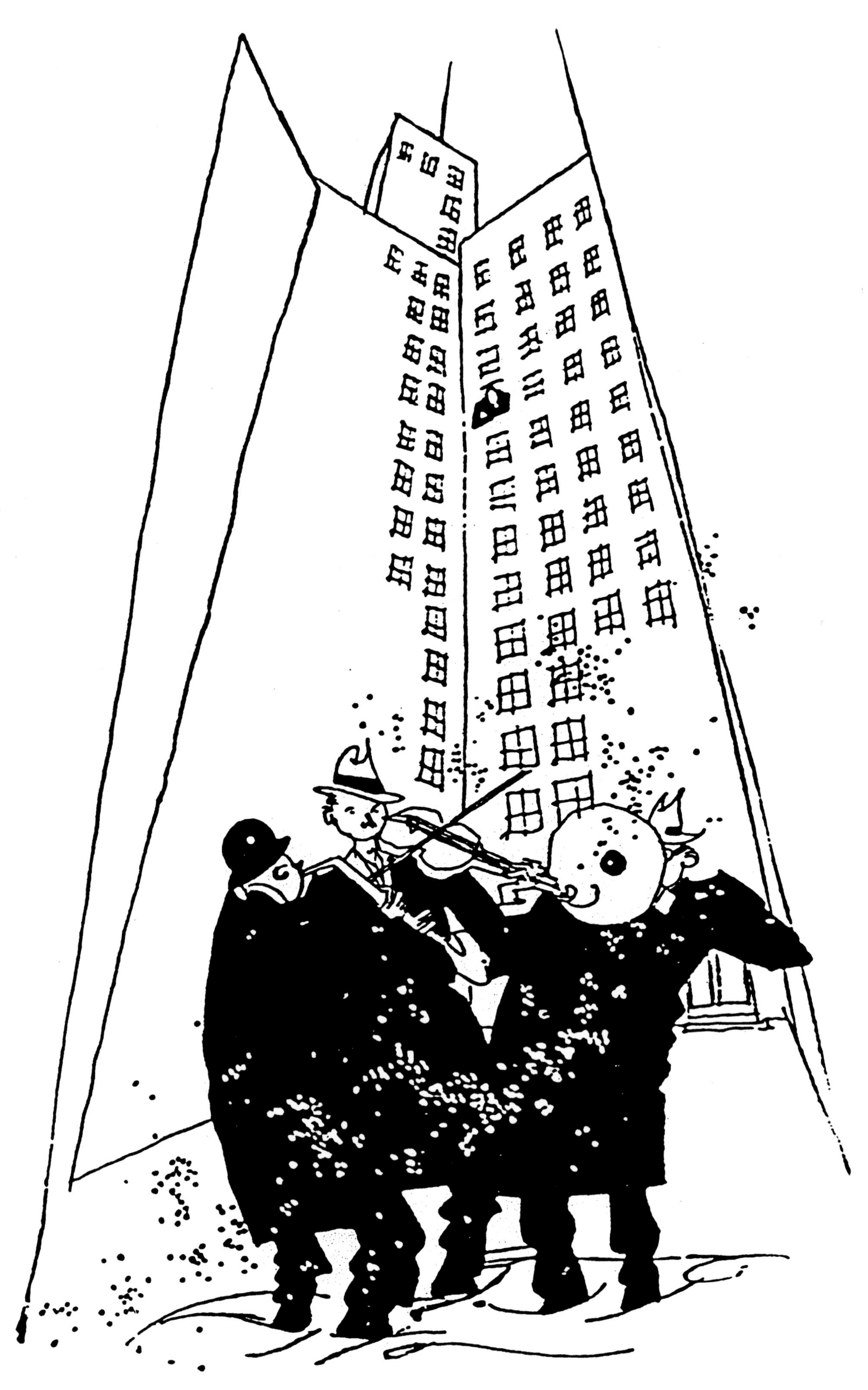

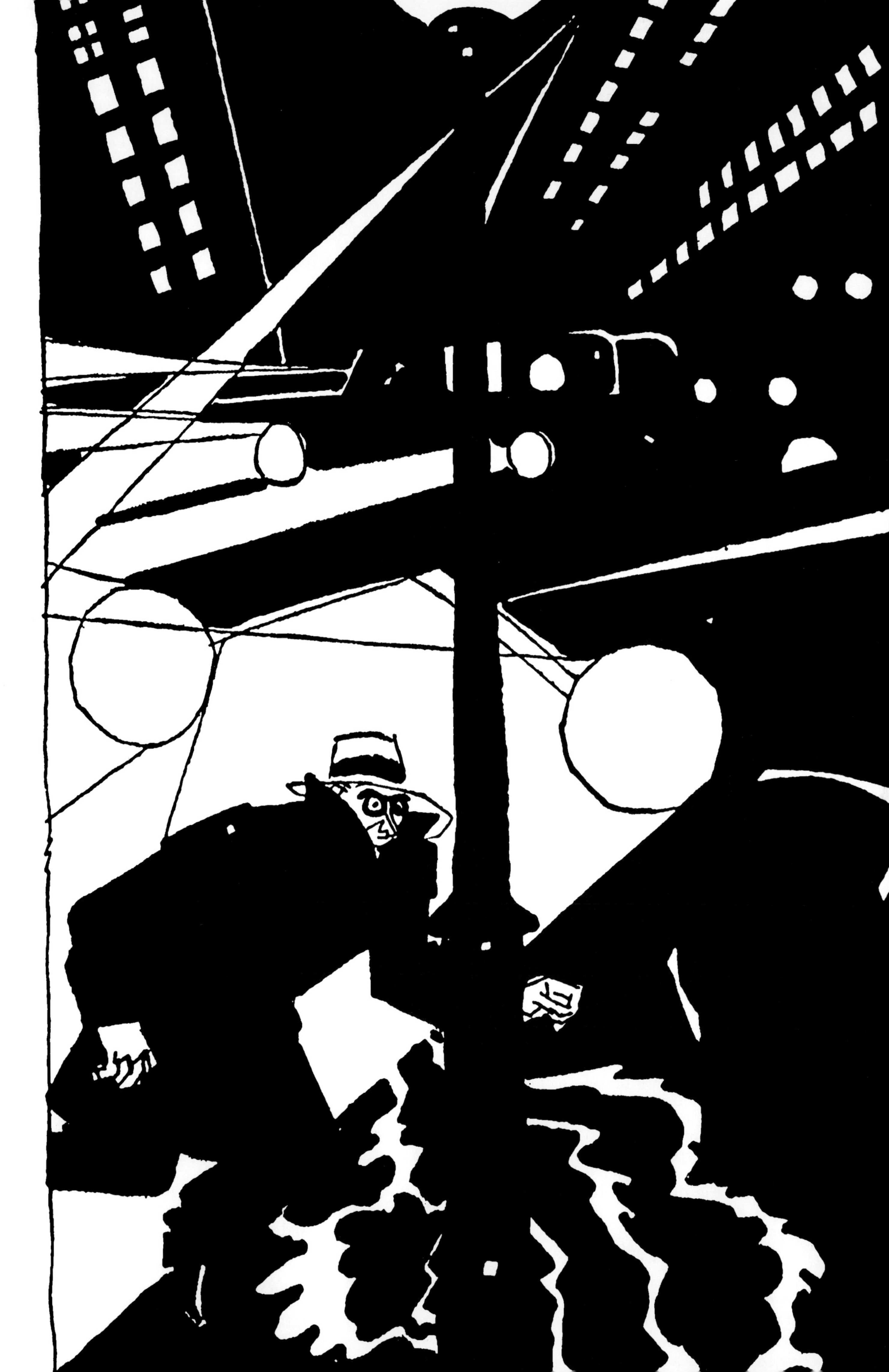

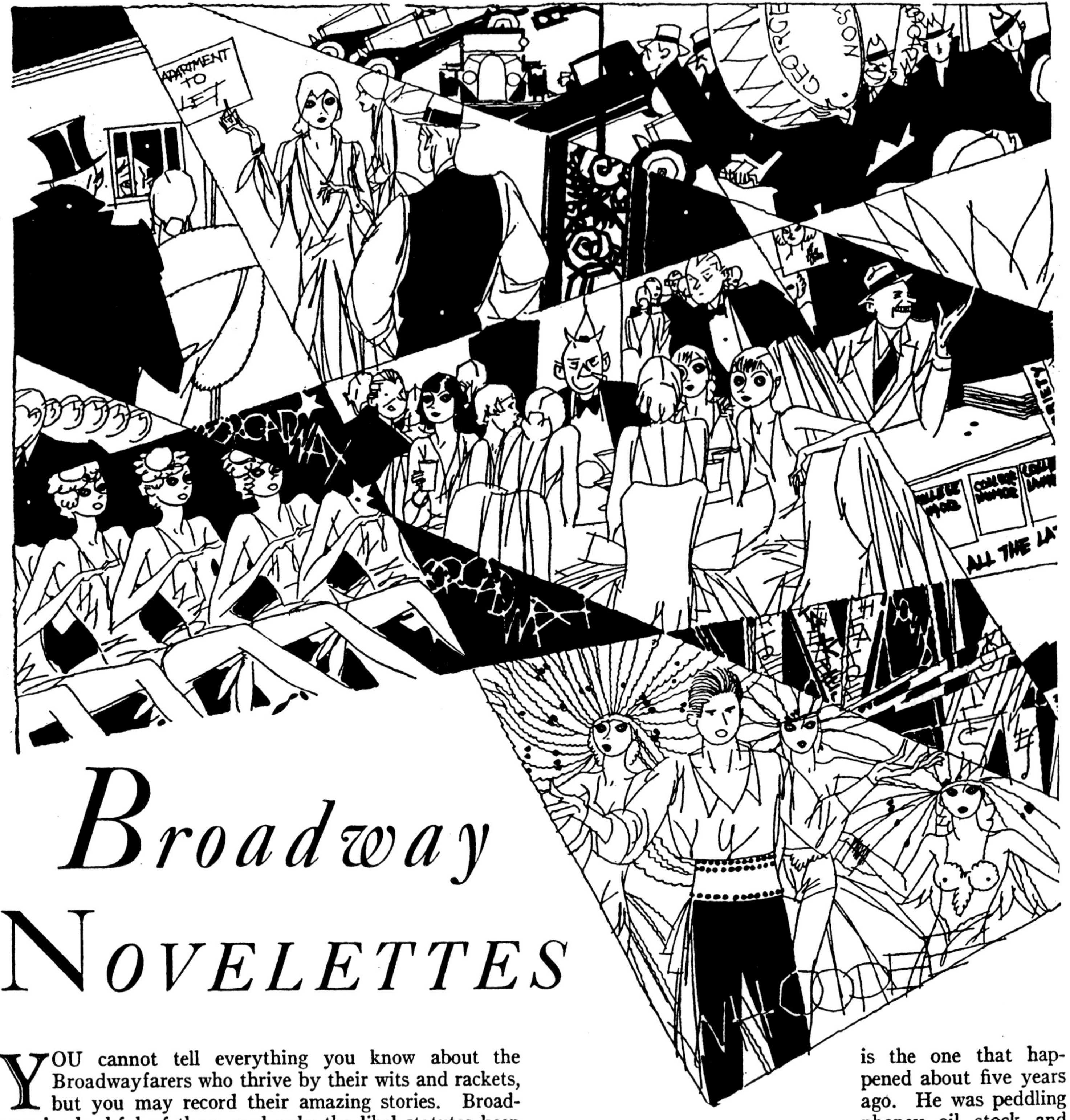

Broadway Novelettes

YOU cannot tell everything you know about the Broadwayfarers who thrive by their wits and rackets, but you may record their amazing stories. Broadway is chockful of them, and only the libel statutes keep the Main Stem historians from jotting down all the facts. In a recent number of this magazine, you probably recall, we chronicled the observation that the more interesting tales invariably concern the obscure natives of Giggle Water Gulch. The villain of the story to follow, however, is renowned along Broadway because of his gifts to gullible chorus girls and others, and most likely will become nationally famous when he is trapped by a mother who cannot be bought off.

He is the only "spender" left on Broadway. He thinks nothing of giving away one hundred dollar bills for tips to waiters, and his night club table is always crowded with pretty girl guests, recruited from here and there. Most of the gels are "young and high waisted," as they say when they refer to the beautiful but numb types. "Get 'em young!" he says. "They never know anything when they're young, and then they don't squawk!" You see, he knows his Broadway girls.

The most startling episode in his career, it seems to me, is the one that happened about five years ago. He was peddling phoney oil stock and got away with it until a little old lady from up New York State decided to complain.

It appears that he had gone to college with the man whom the government assigned to investigate the complaint. The investigator got in touch with the racketeer and said: "For God's sake, do something quick. I've learned that you didn't even try to discover oil on your Texas property. I can stall this case for a couple of years, but you must at least erect a derrick or so out there, so I can tell the people who are complaining that you are on the level and that you simply had bad luck. They are speculating with you after all and when you fail to click, they lose, too!"

He immediately arranged for diggers to dig his Texas sand lots, and settled back to await a dismissal of the little old lady's "beef."

Well, even Mr. Ripley is welcome to it for his book of *Believe It or Nots!* They cannot stop the oil gushers that have made him a millionaire over and over again! The boy will get along.

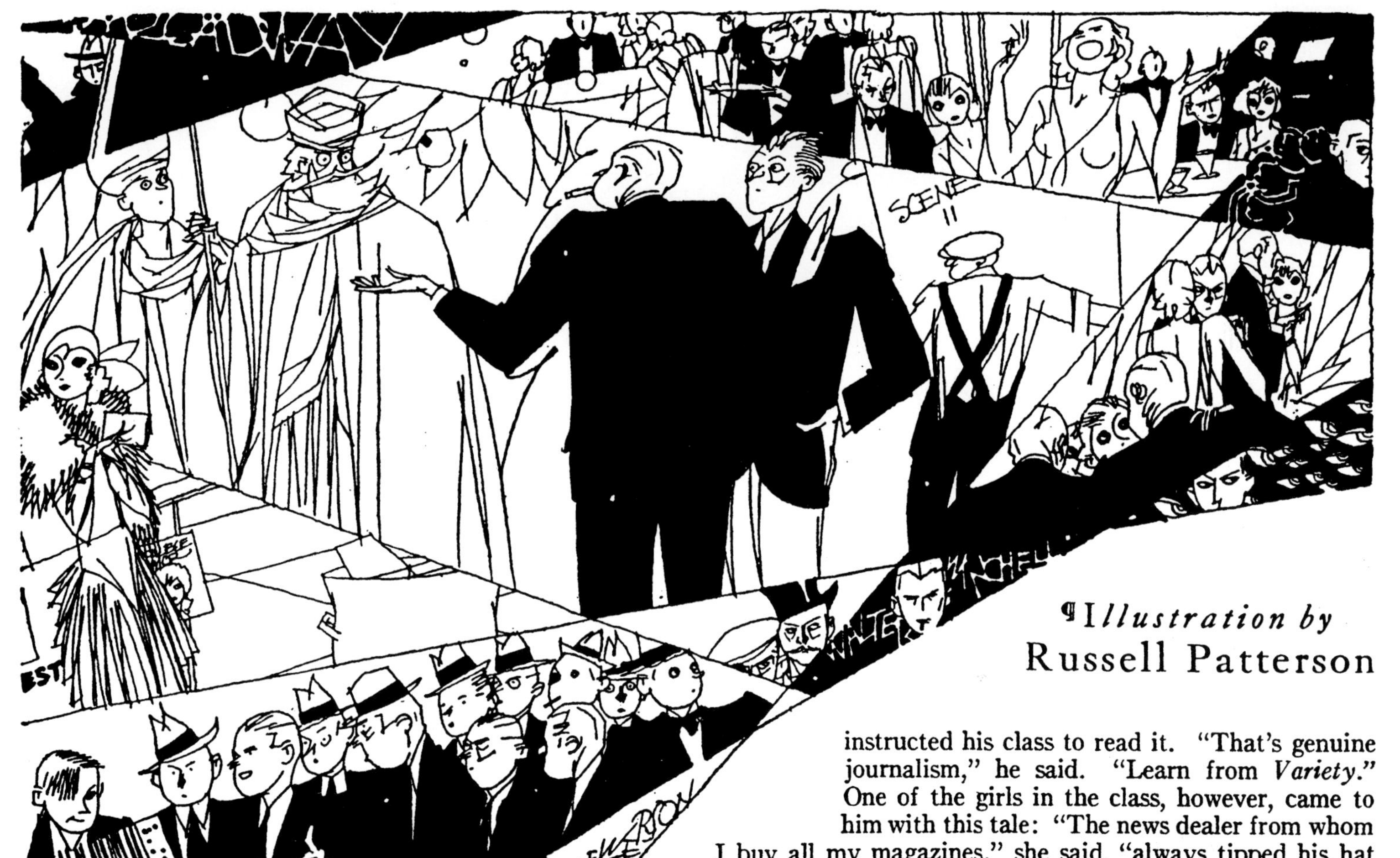

¶ *Illustration by*
Russell Patterson

THE collegiate and co-ed will appreciate learning that *Variety,* the theatrical weekly, has a staff consisting chiefly of college graduates, and not as the highbrows, who have only recently "discovered" *Variety,* would have you believe. The weekly, it appears, has caught the fancy of the literary scriveners, who adore the sheet's slang and "poor English." They have devoted several columns of praise to the paper and its staff, and assert that it packs the most fascinating vernacular ever jotted down on newsprint.

Well, the editor's son went to Manlius in New York State; Abel Green, the music critic, is an N. Y. U. man; Jack Pulaski, who covers the drama, is from Pennsylvania. The late Jack Conway, whose slang helped make *Variety* famous, was a Holy Cross grad, and most of the others went to American universities.

Sime, the editor, explains why his staff must write faulty English. "We cater strictly to hams and theater managers and acrobats, so we write their own language. If we started to get fancy, they wouldn't understand it and we'd lay an egg." That sums it up.

But the most amusing gag I ever heard about *Variety* is this one:

A professor at Columbia once told me that he was fascinated by *Variety* and instructed his class to read it. "That's genuine journalism," he said. "Learn from *Variety.*" One of the girls in the class, however, came to him with this tale: "The news dealer from whom I buy all my magazines," she said, "always tipped his hat to me and went out of his way to be polite because I bought *Harper's, The Atlantic Monthly, The American Mercury* and the *Review of Reviews.* But when I asked for *Variety,* he tried to make me!"

THEN there's the vastly amusing story about J. J. Shubert, the producer, who was once annoyed watching a Shakespearean revival because the famous bard "had lifted too much stuff!" Mr. Shubert decided to produce a piece written by an Eastern college man. At the second rehearsal when a player uttered, "I am Omar Khayyám!", Mr. Shubert jumped from his rear row orchestra chair and called out: "Just a minute. That should read 'I am Omar of Khayyám'."

"But," exclaimed the actor, the director and the rest of the company.

"Don't 'but' me," cried the producer. "Do as I say!"

And so the actor read it, "I am Omar of Khayyám!"

The next day the author sat with Shubert to see how the rehearsals were getting on. When he heard the revised line, he let out a roar. Then he told Shubert what he thought of a management that would permit such an error in a show. Shubert begged the playwright to soft pedal his remarks and say nothing to the cast. "I'll fix it," J. J. said, not a little embarrassed when he realized that it was not the name of a town, but a man's name.

When the player came to the line again, Shubert interrupted him. "Go back to the original way," he yelled. "Just say you are Omar Khayyám. Cut out the 'of'; the show is too long as it is!"

EDGAR ALLEN WOOLF, who writes sketches for Fannie Ward and other stars, started an argument recently which aroused the local dramatic critics. Mr. Woolf argued that too many of the New York journals hired critics who were not collitch trained. Then a sympathizer declared that Shaw and Mencken were [*Continued on page 121*]

By Walter Winchell

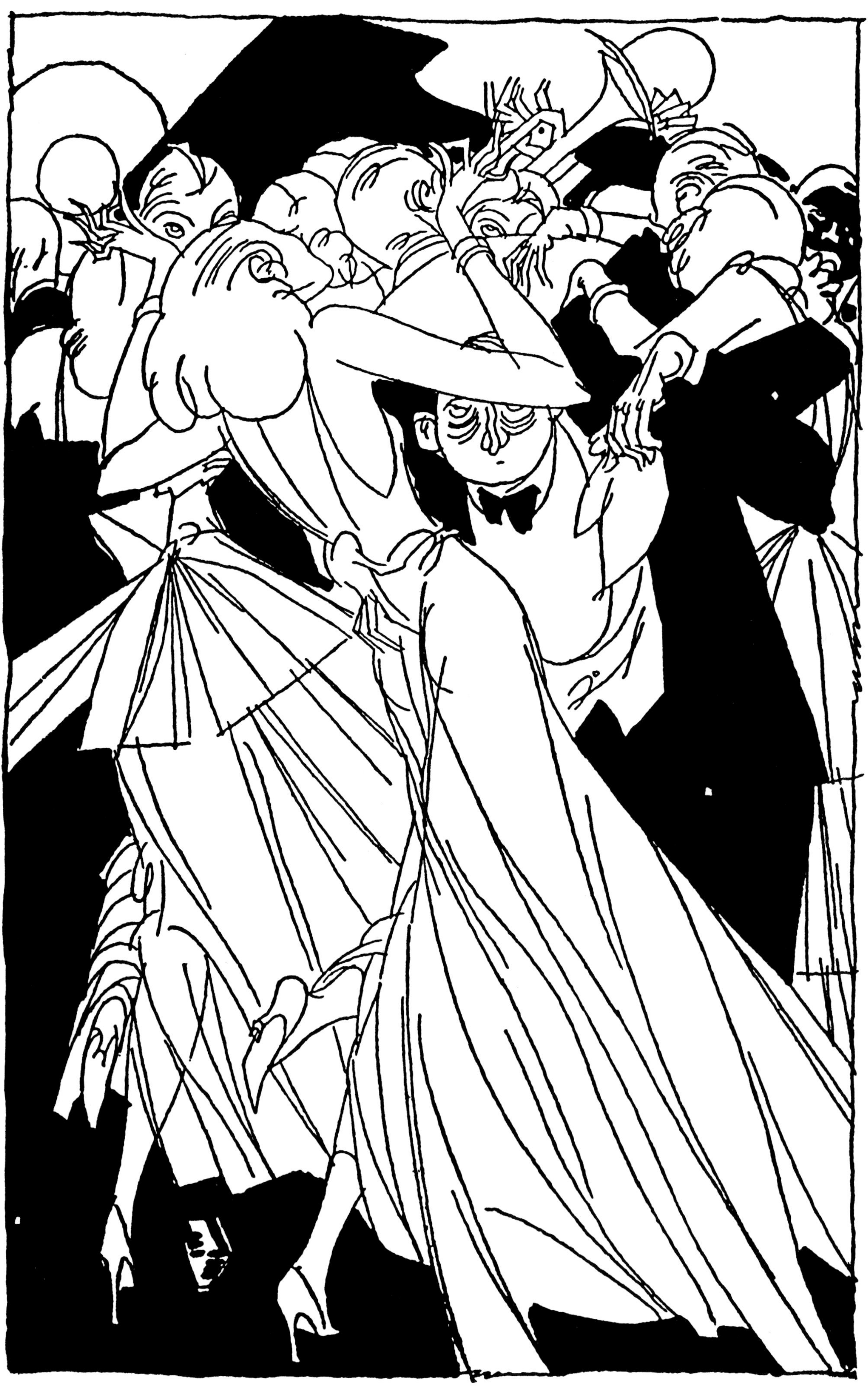

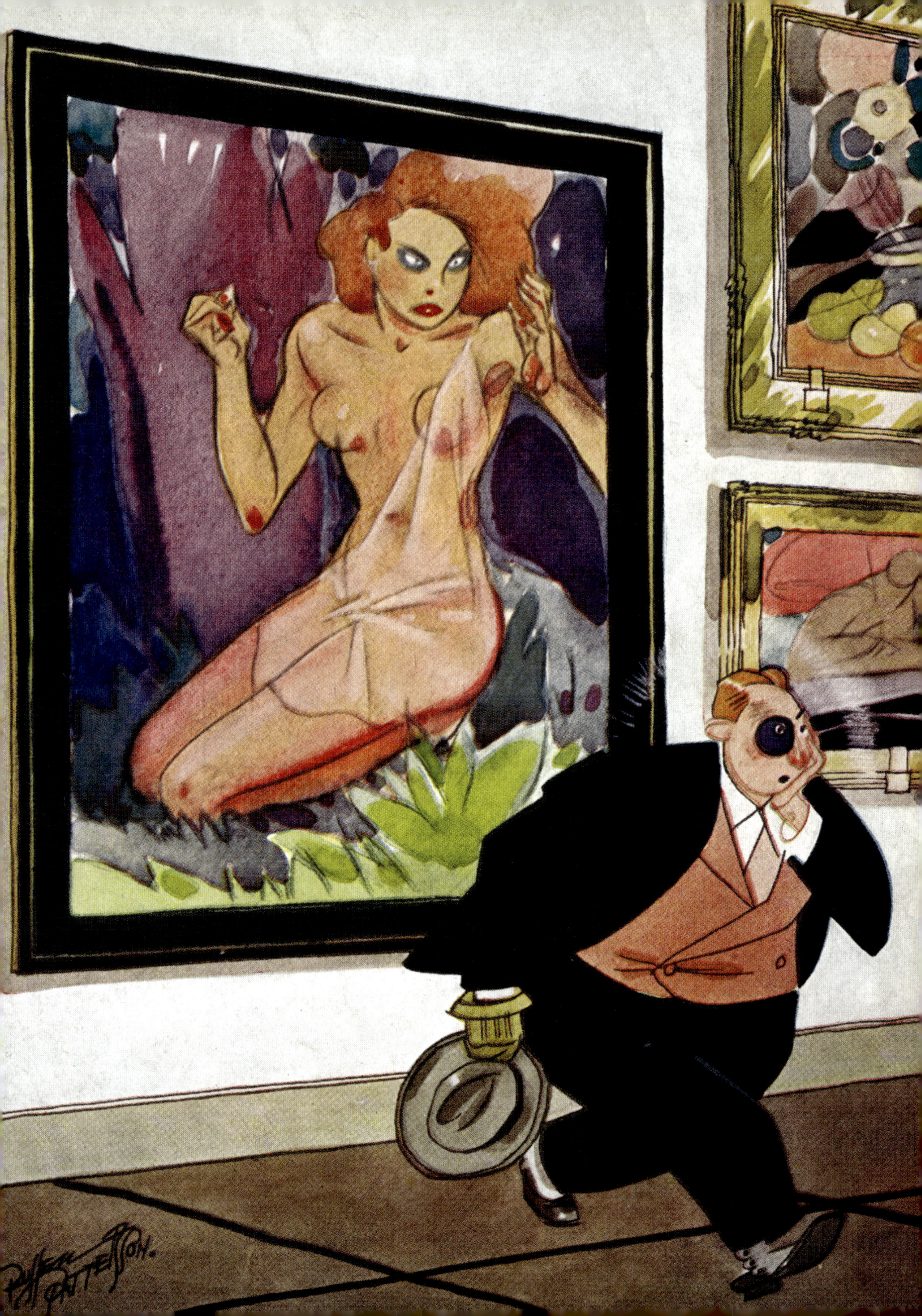
Russell Patterson.

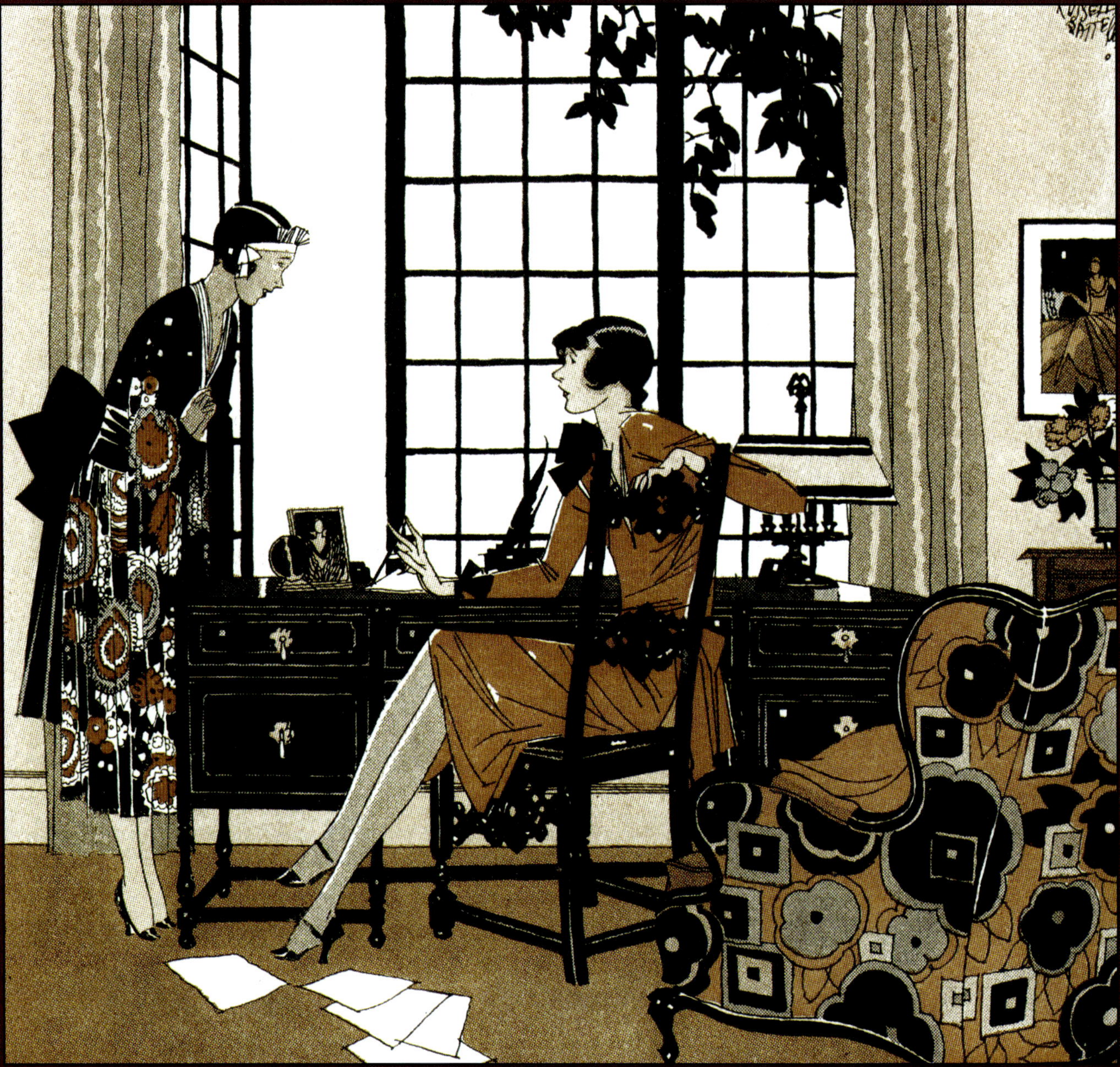

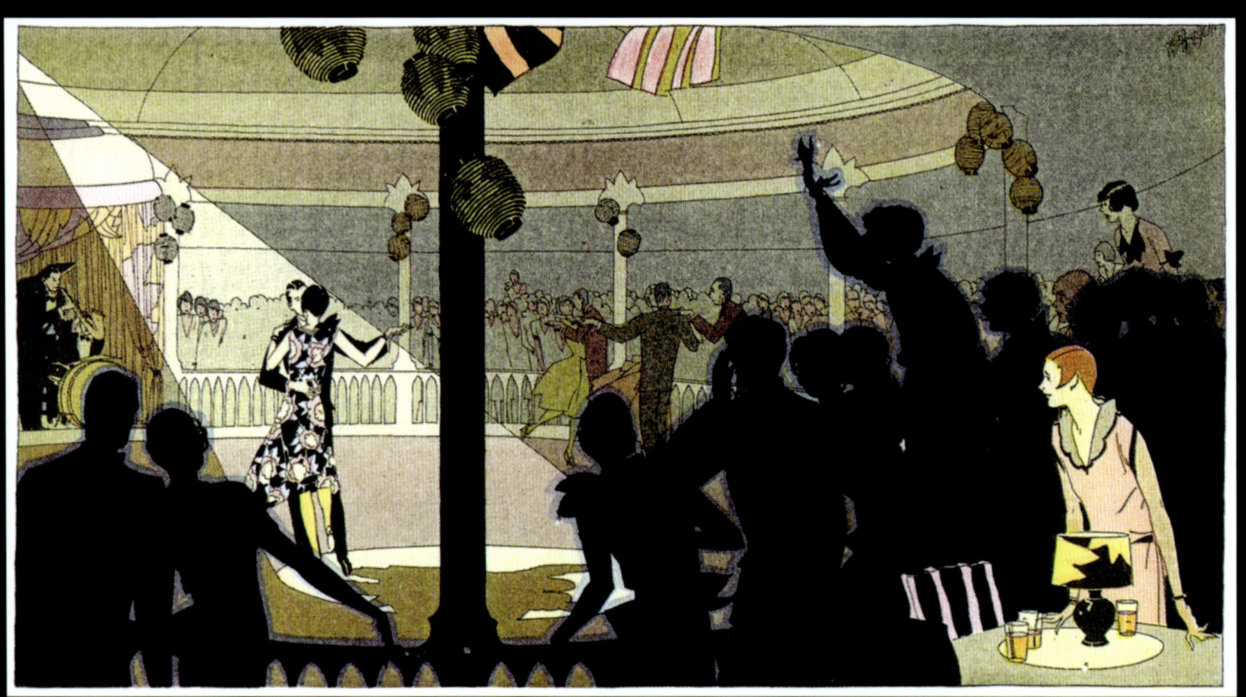

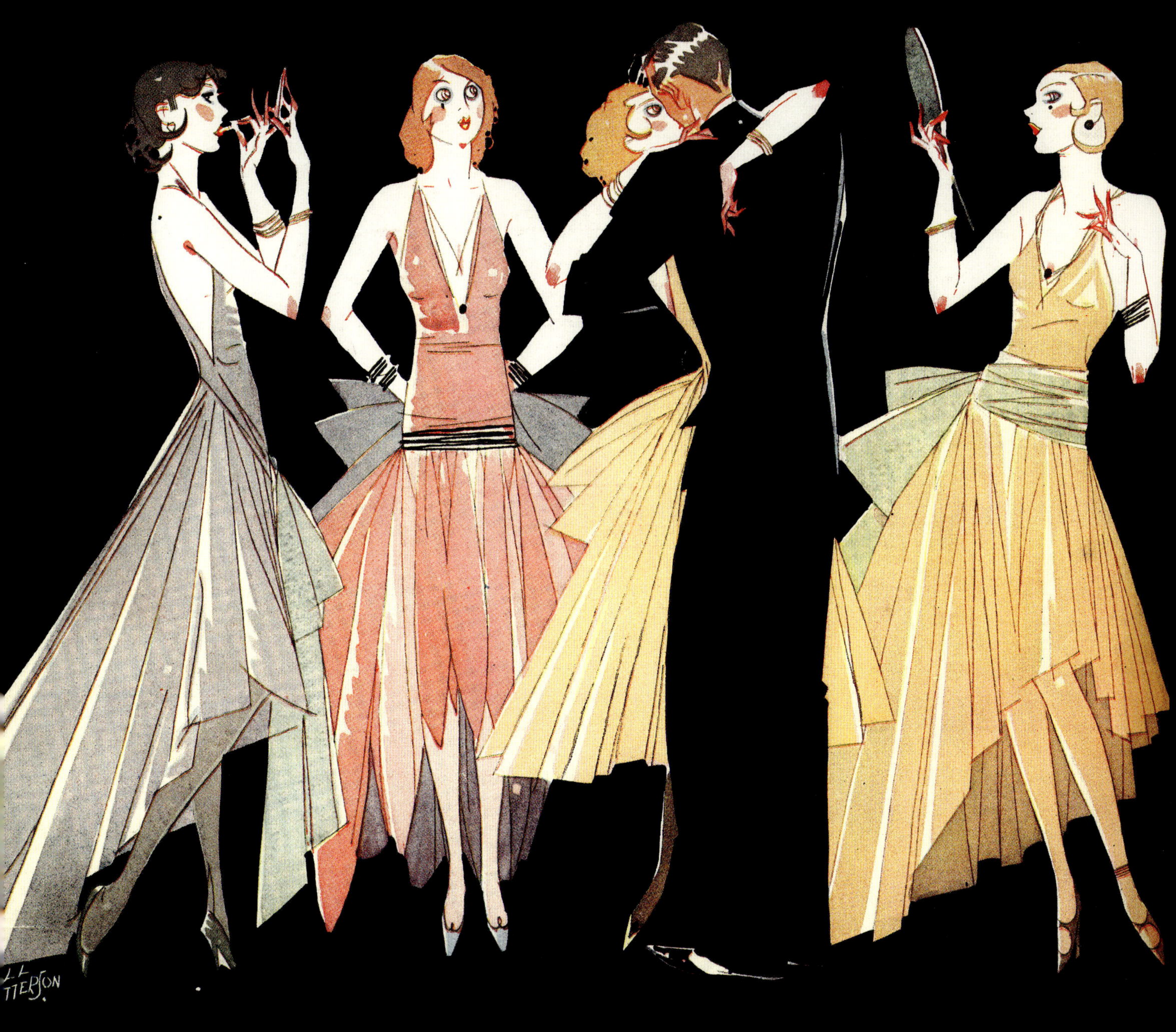

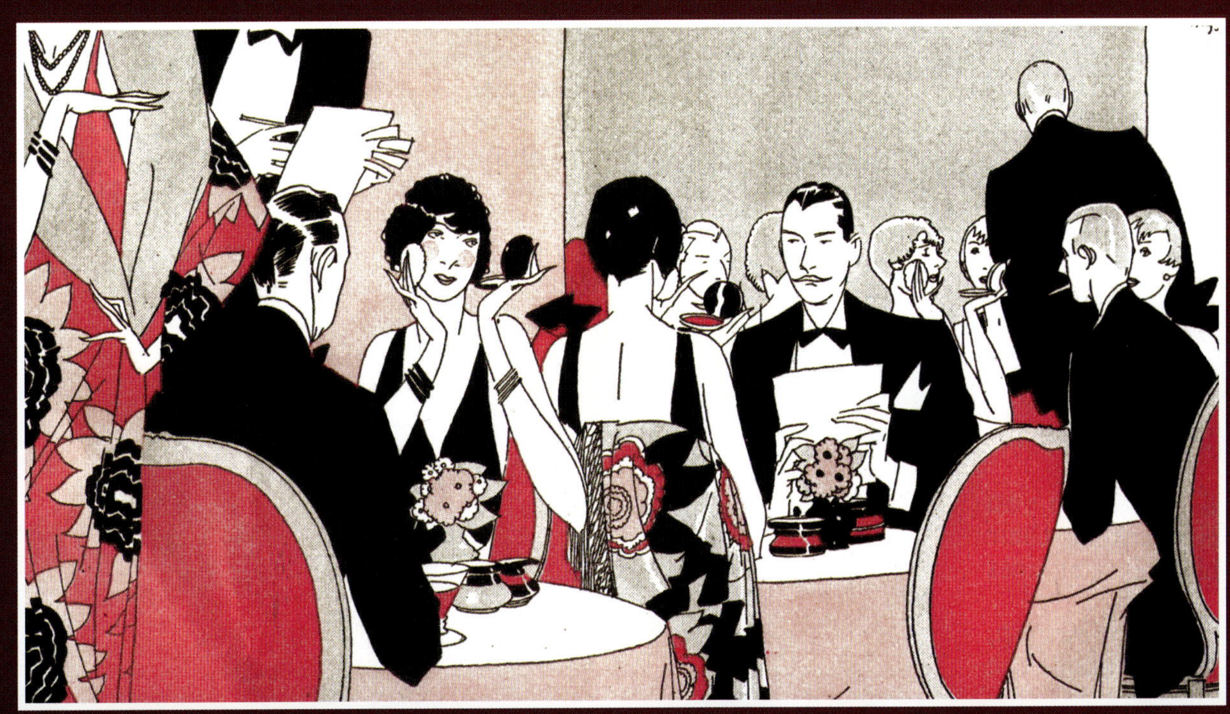

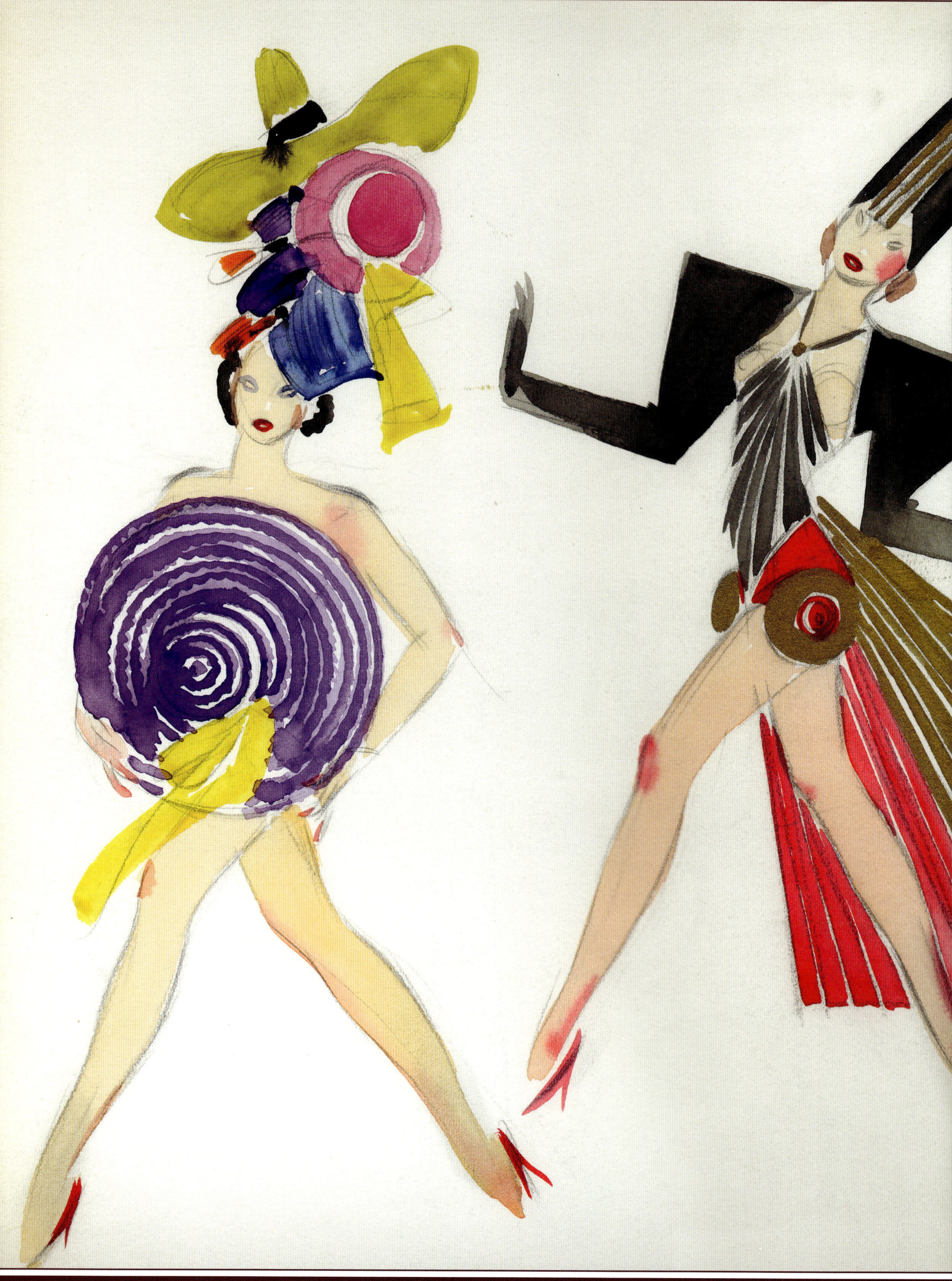

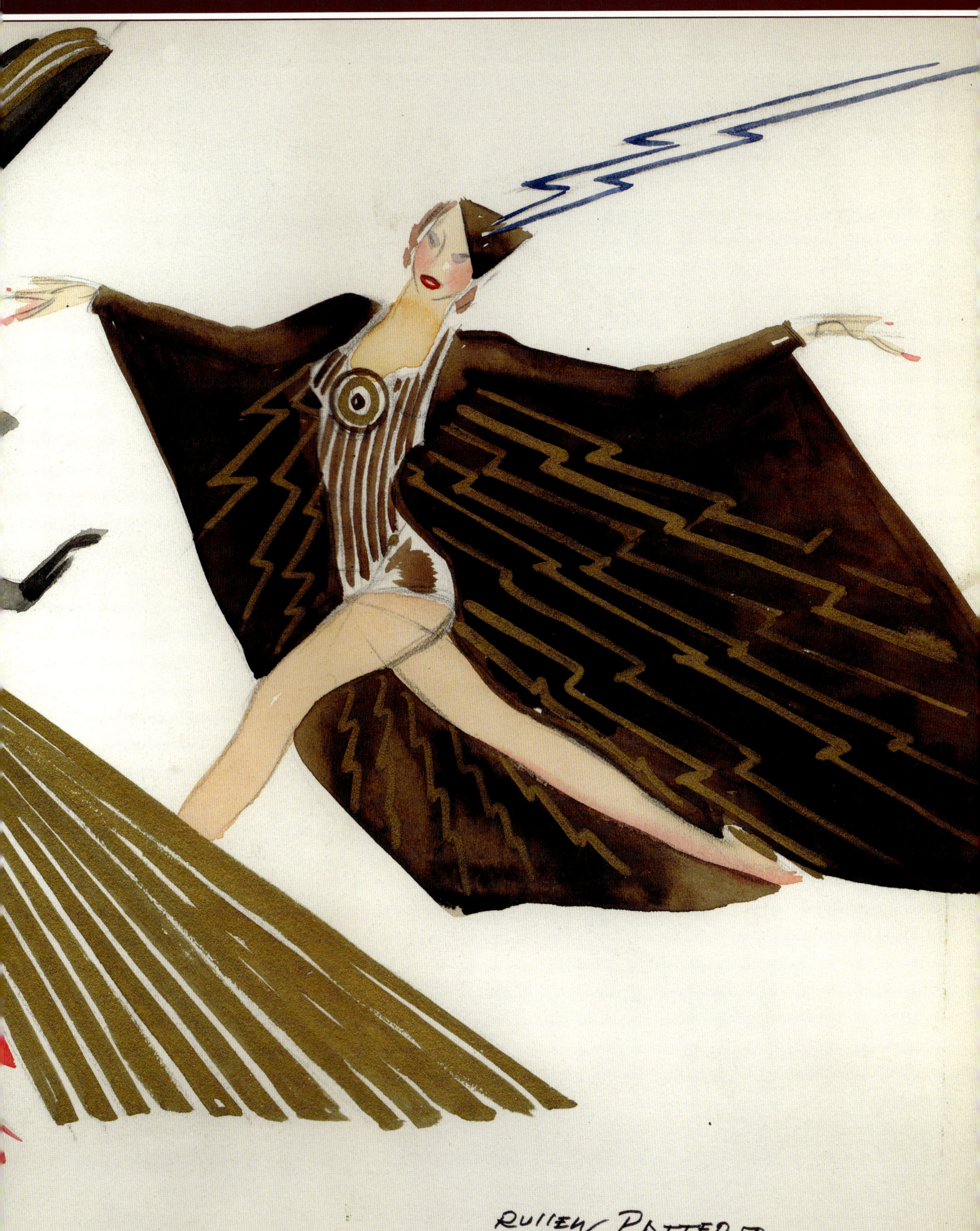
RUSSELL PATTERSON
FOR
"GIRL IN THE MAGAZINE A

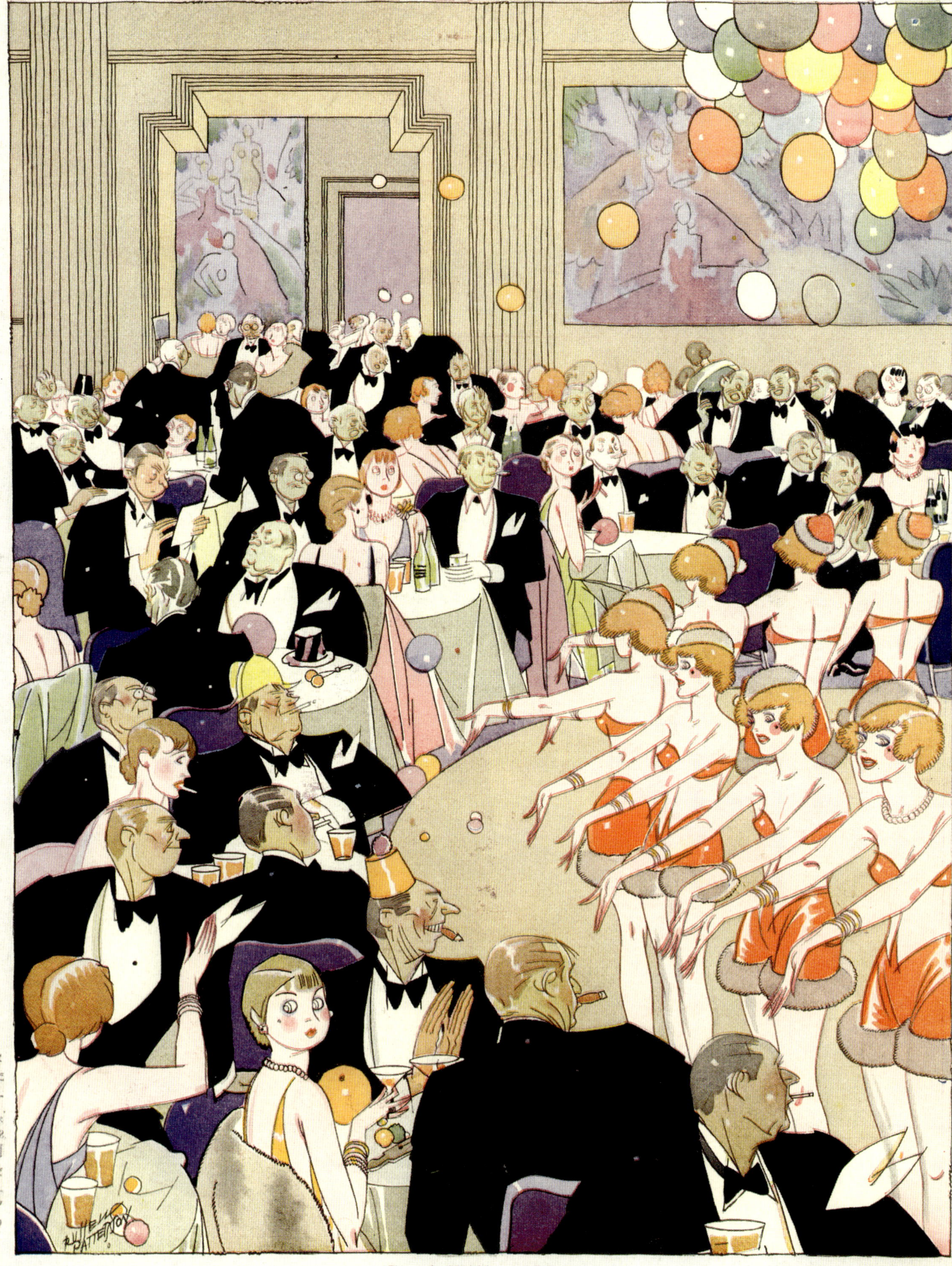

Good Will to Men

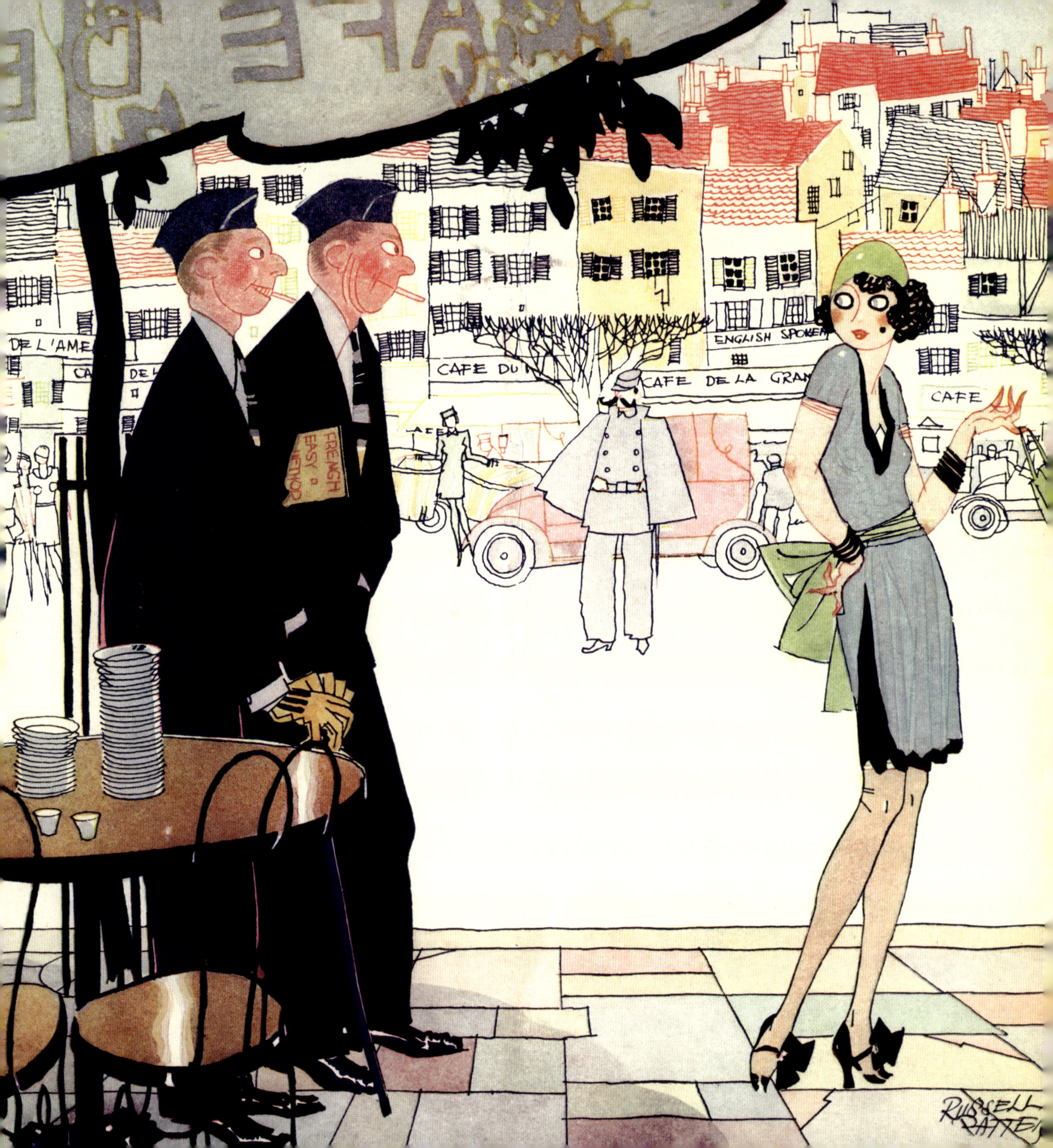
DE L'AME
CAFE DU
ENGLISH SPOKE
CAFE DE LA GRAN
CAFE
FRENCH EASY METHOD
RUSSELL PATTE

BALLYHOO

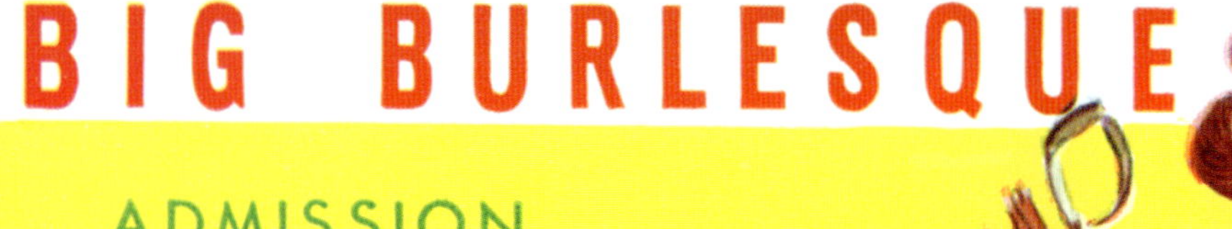

BIG BURLESQUE SHOW!

ADMISSION
15
CENTS

MAY

ZILCHSKY'S REVUE

50-GORGEOUS GIRLS-50

★ ★

SEE THE DARING

STRIP ACT!

A THOUSAND THRILLS!

A MILLION LAFFS!

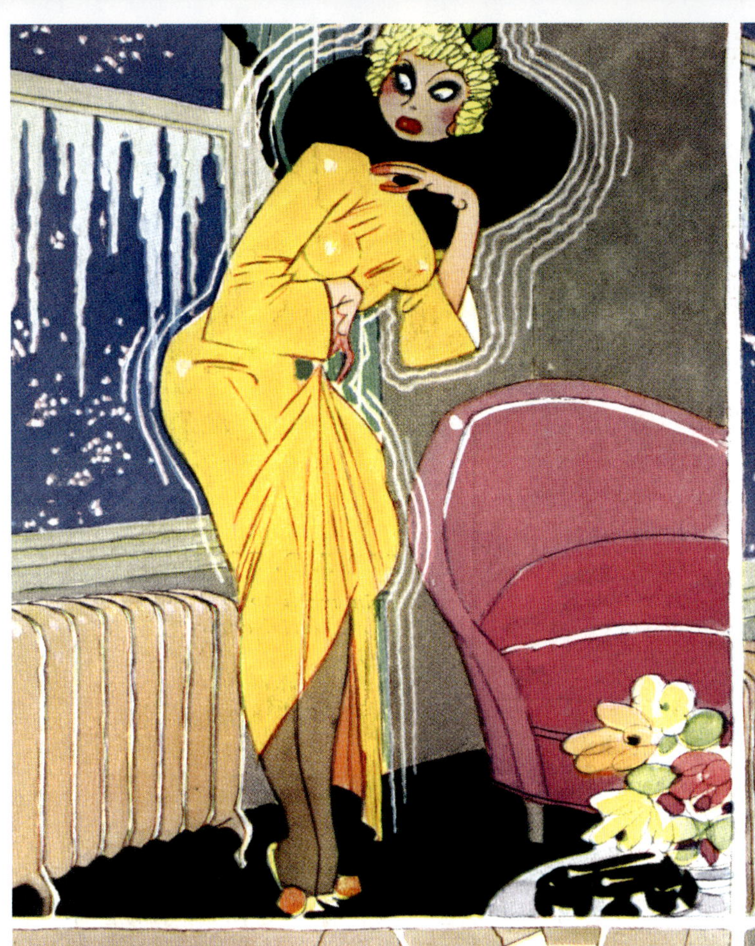
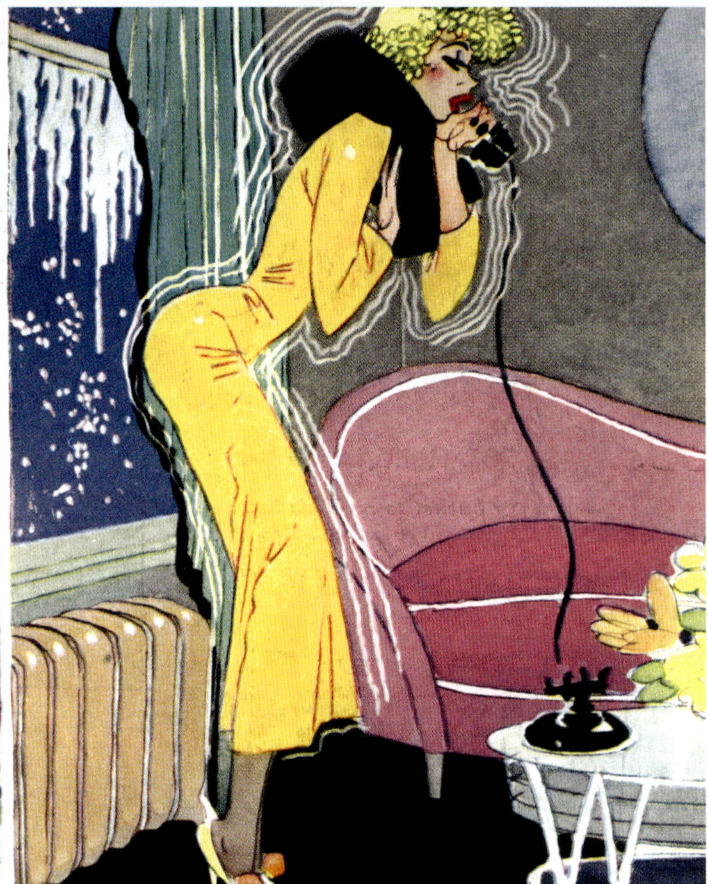
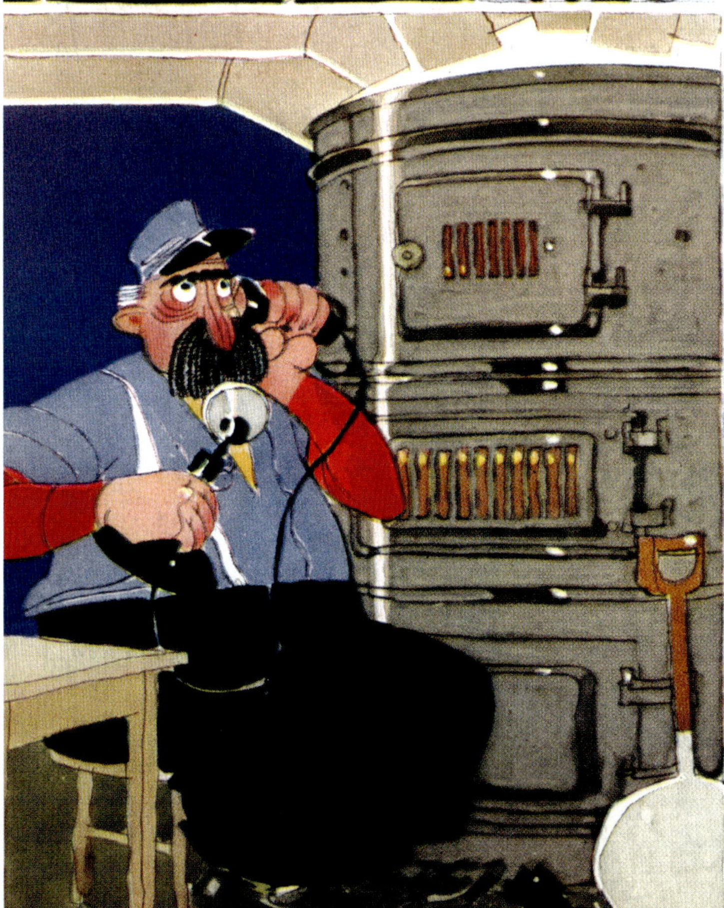
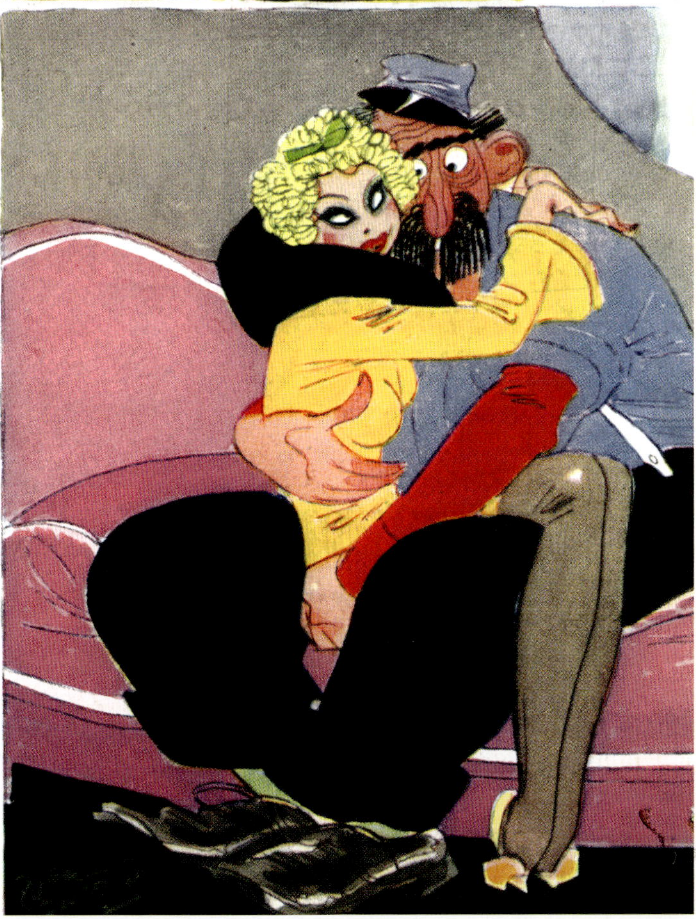

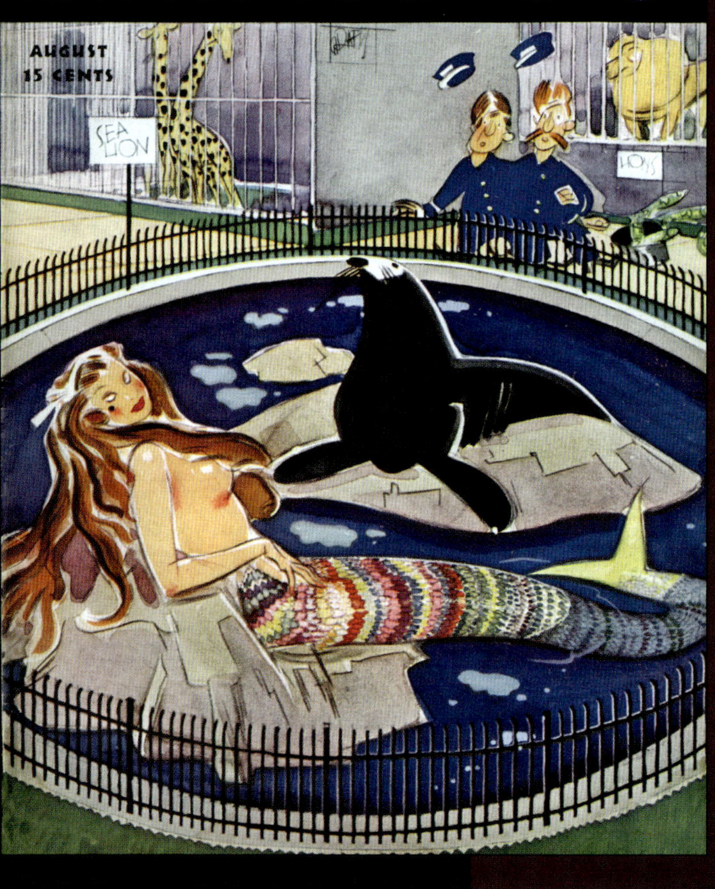
BALLYHOO
AUGUST
15 CENTS
SEA LION

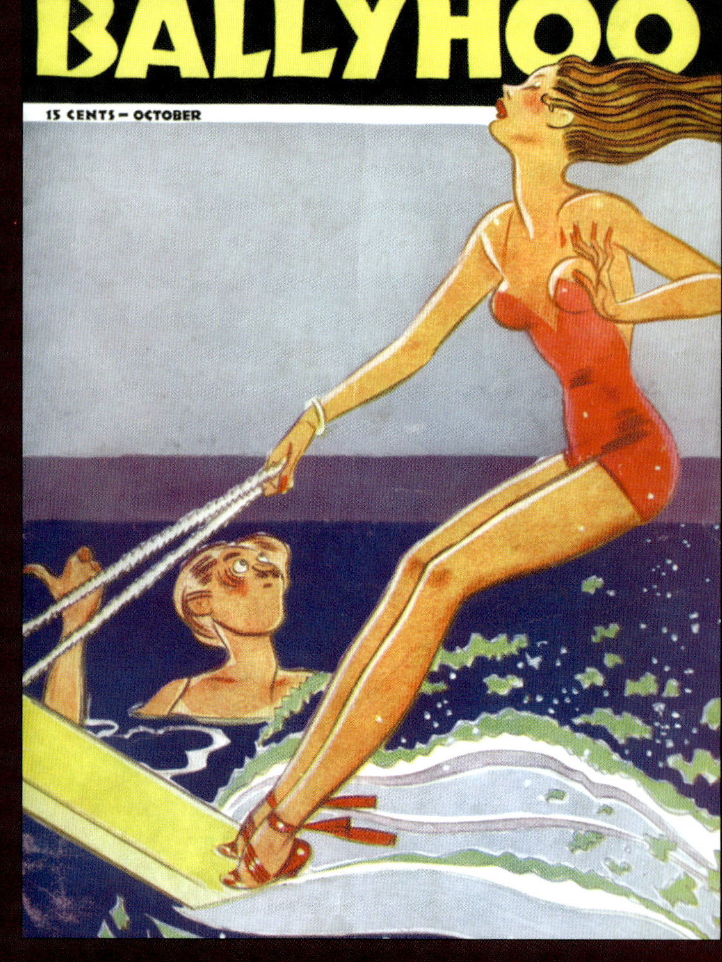
BALLYHOO
15 CENTS – OCTOBER

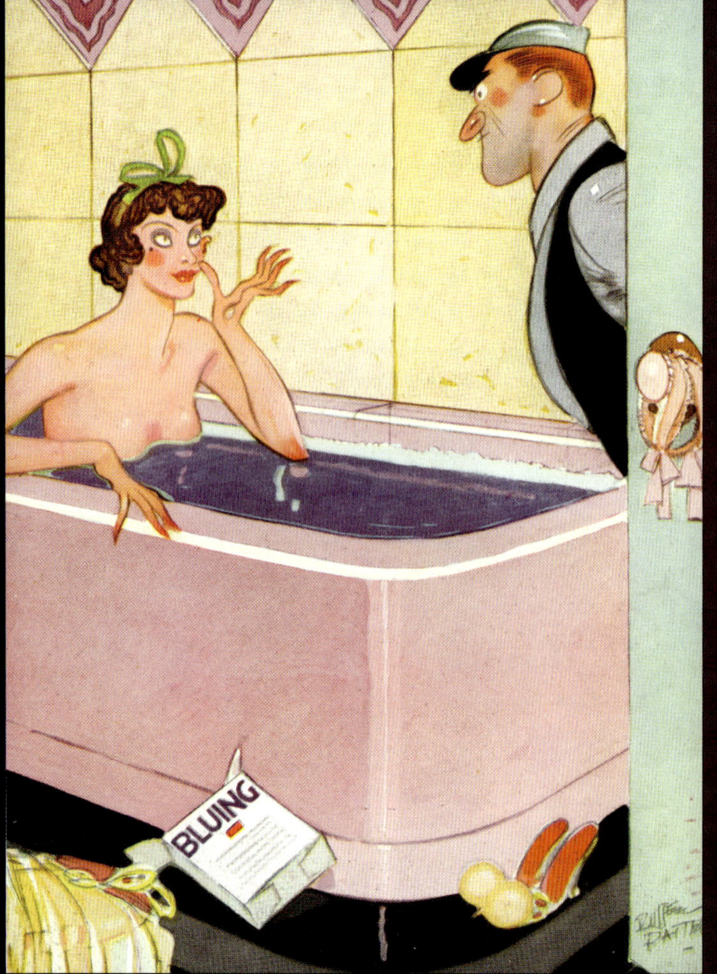
BLUING

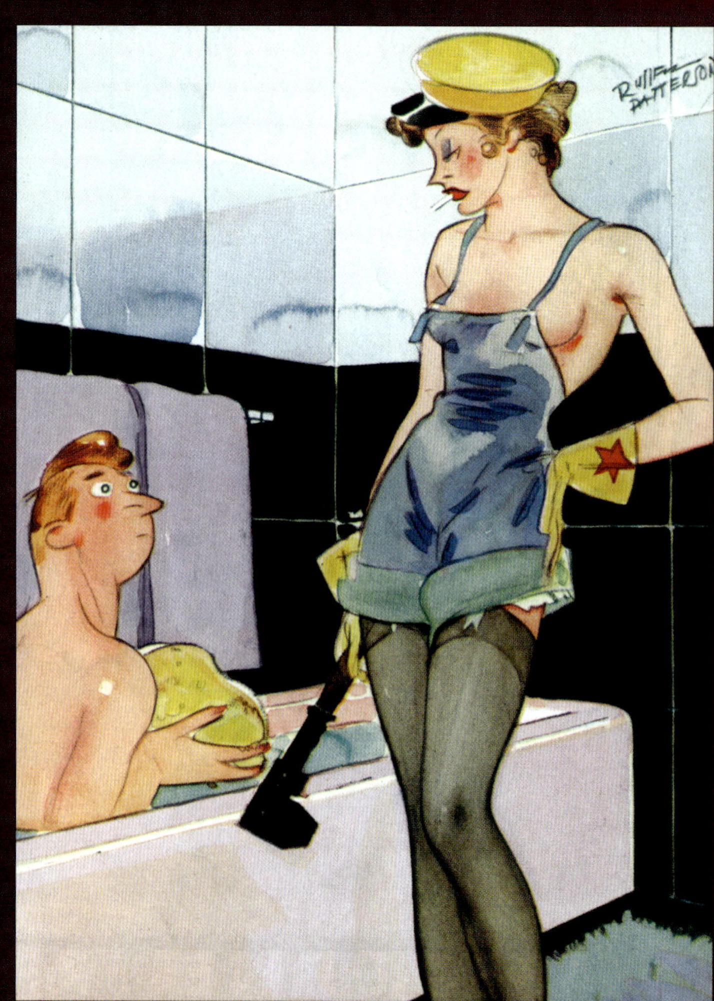
PATTERSON

BALLYHOO

HULA HULA NUMBER

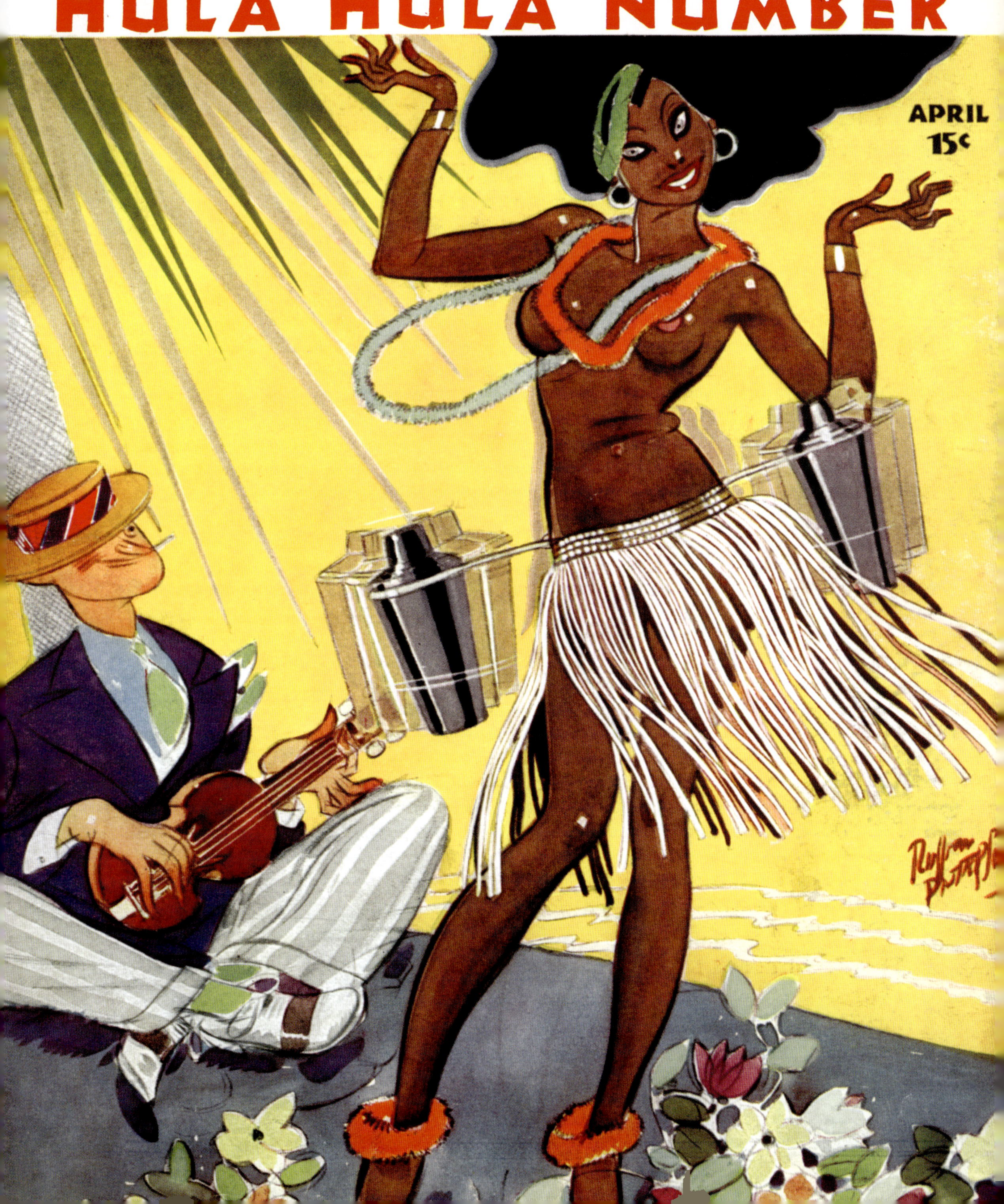

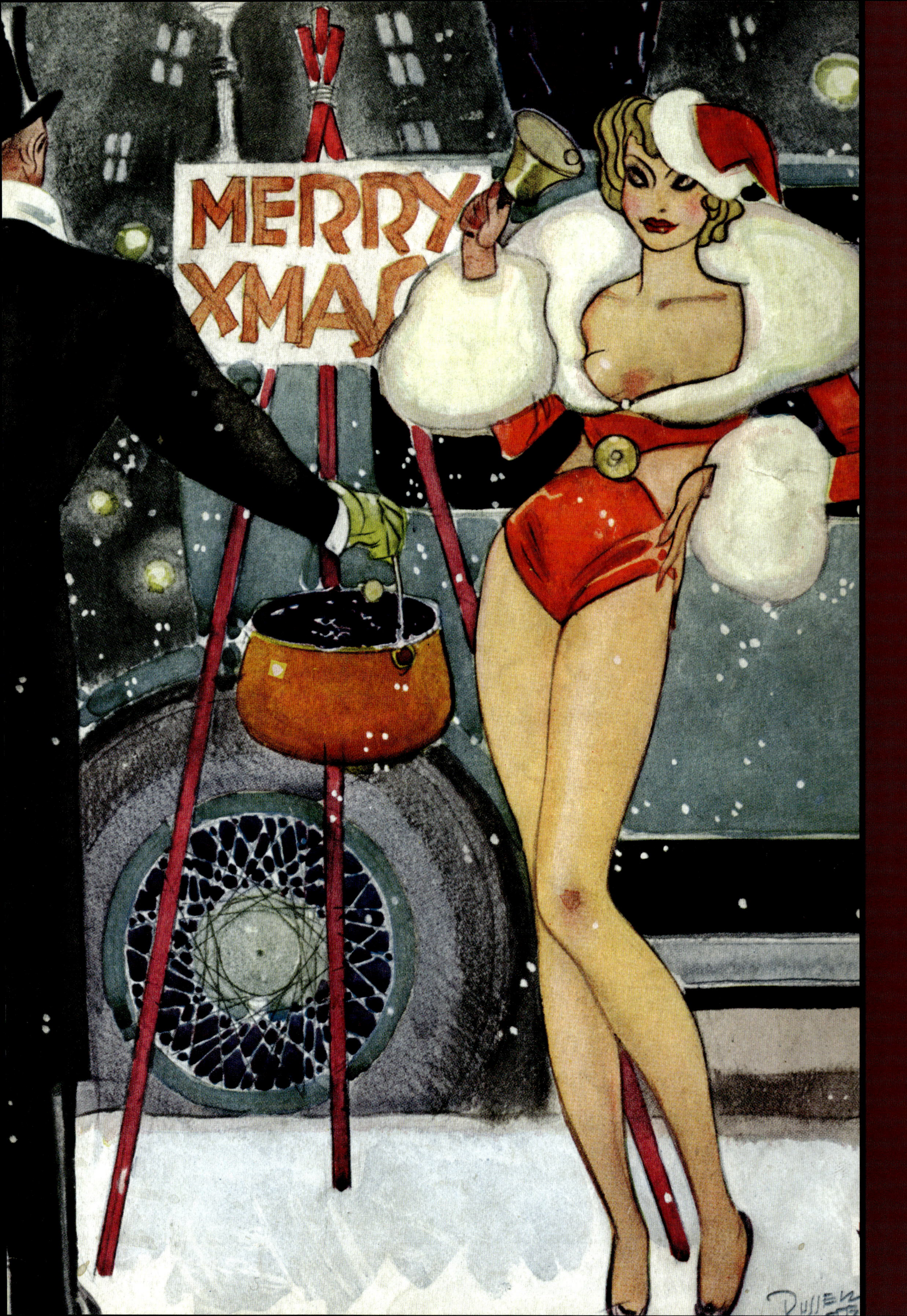
MERRY
XMAS

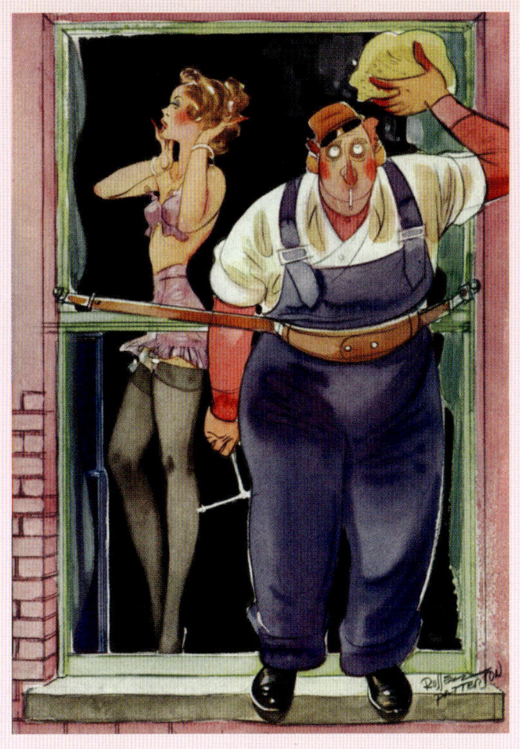

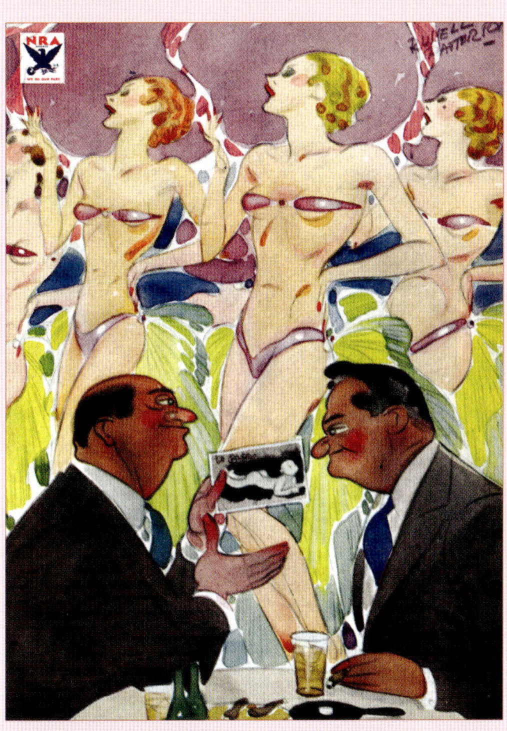

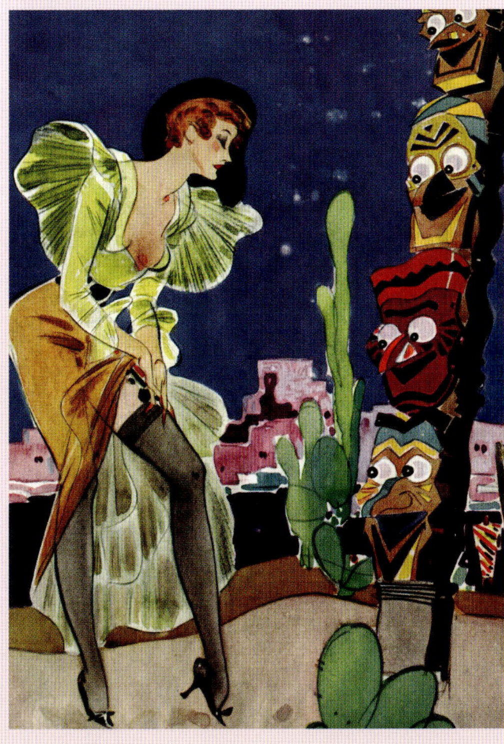

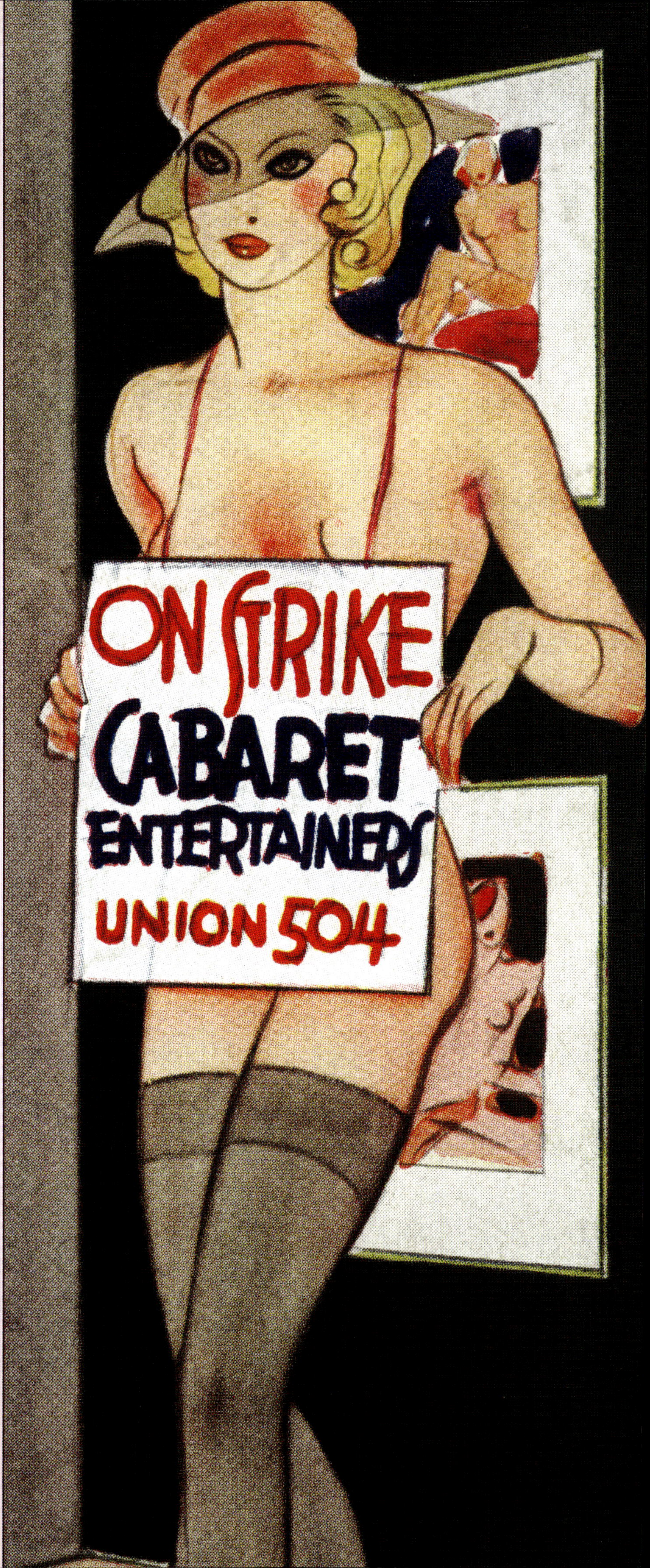

ON STRIKE
CABARET
ENTERTAINERS
UNION 504

College Humo

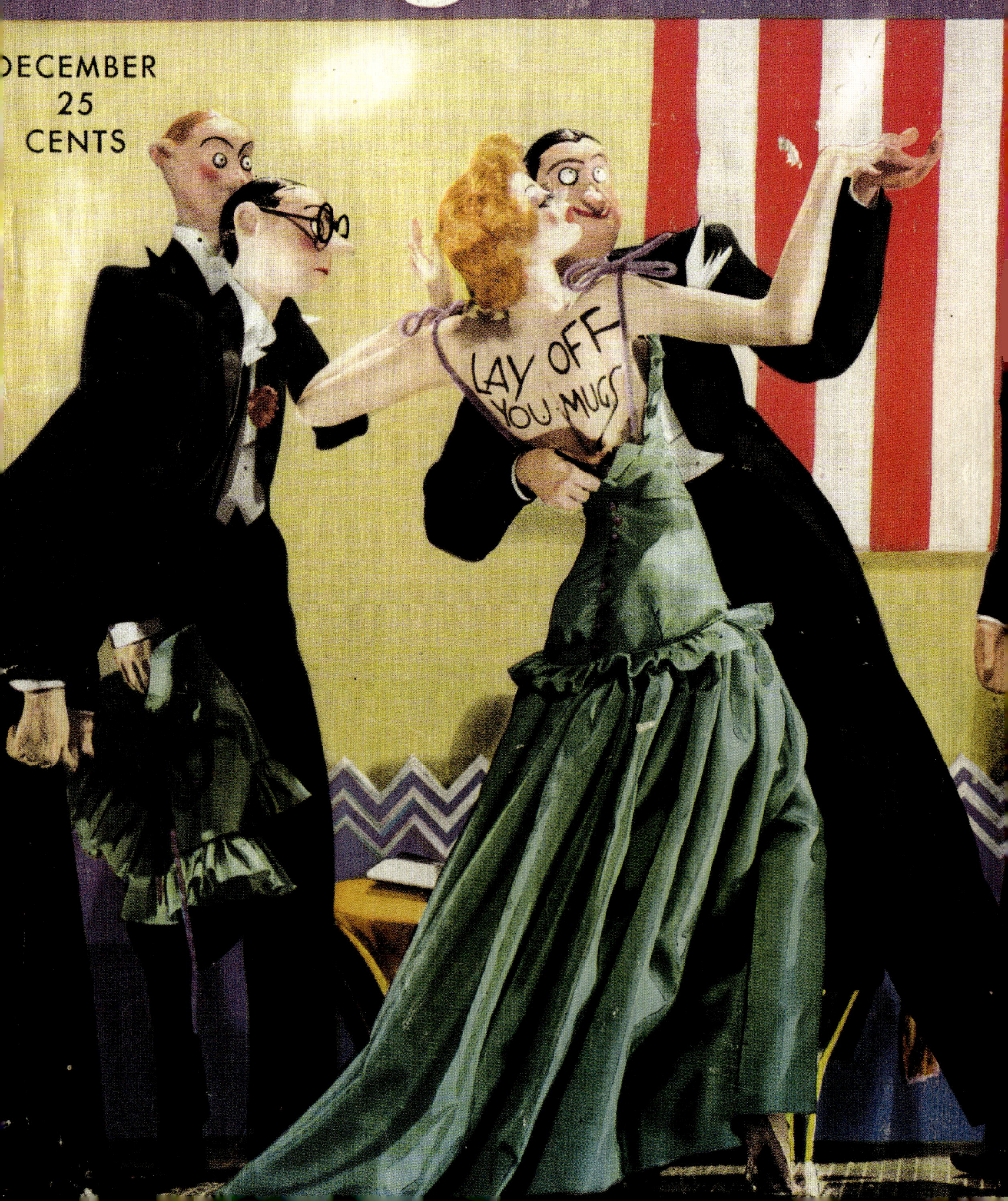

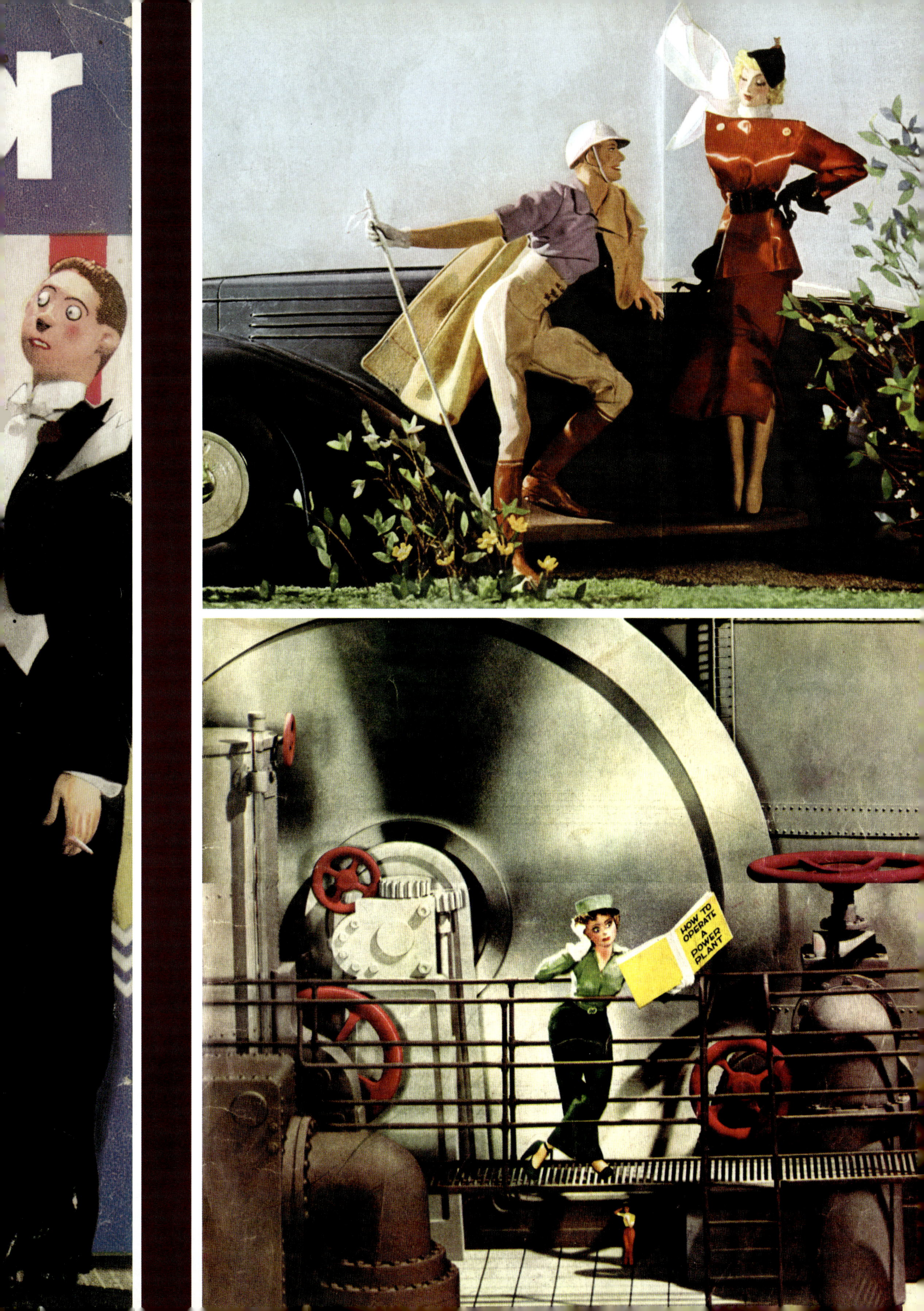
HOW TO OPERATE A POWER PLANT

Amusement
News

LIFE

Personalities
Sport

15 Cents

September 28 1928

ABLOID
URDER

TABLOID
AXE
VICTIM

TABLOID
SUICIDE

TABLOID
DEATH
CHAIR

TABLOID
HAMMER
SLAYER

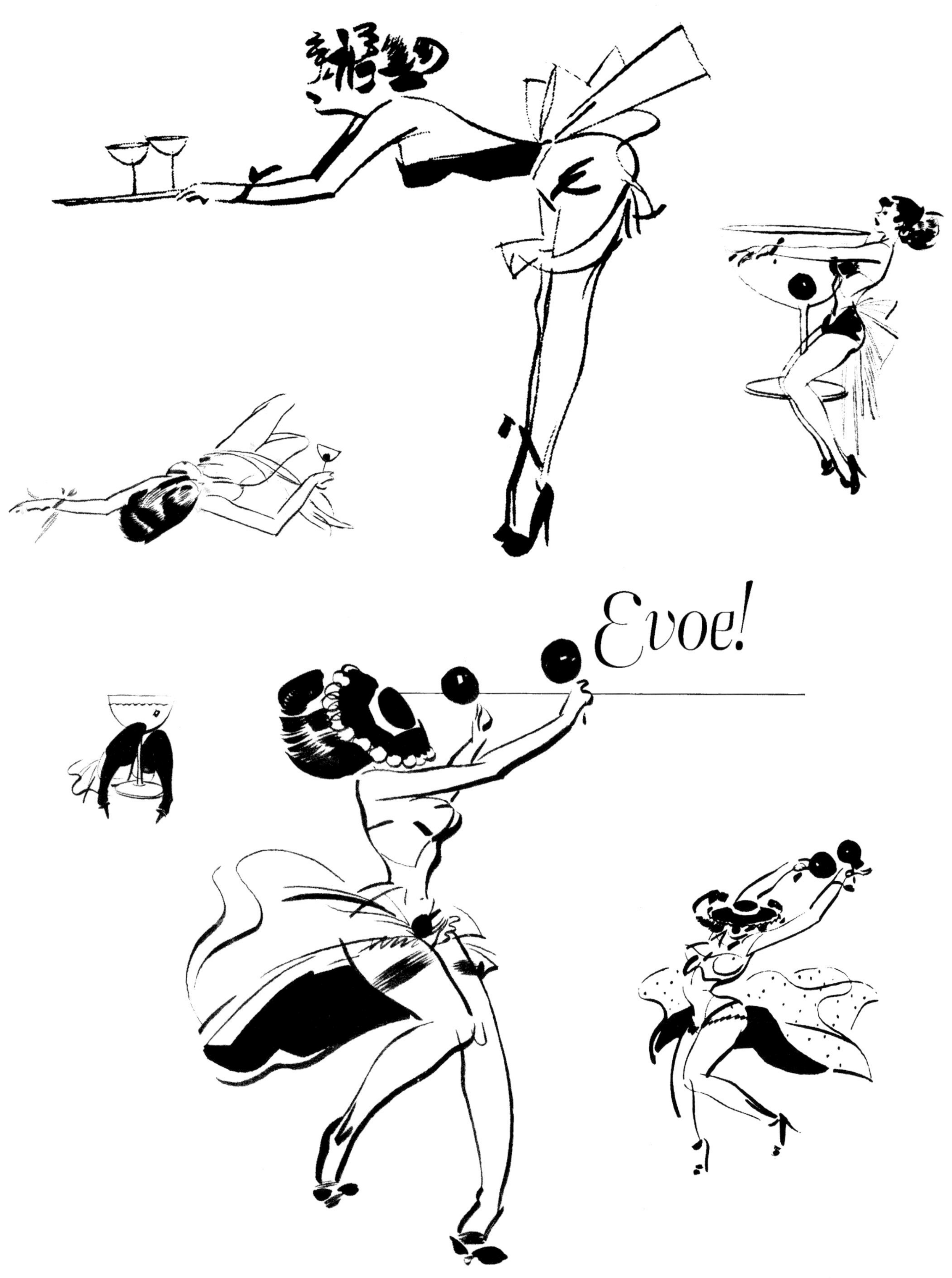

EVOE! —*Cry of the Bacchanals (cry of exhilaration at the feast of Bacchus, the pagan god of wine, drink, and merrymaking)*

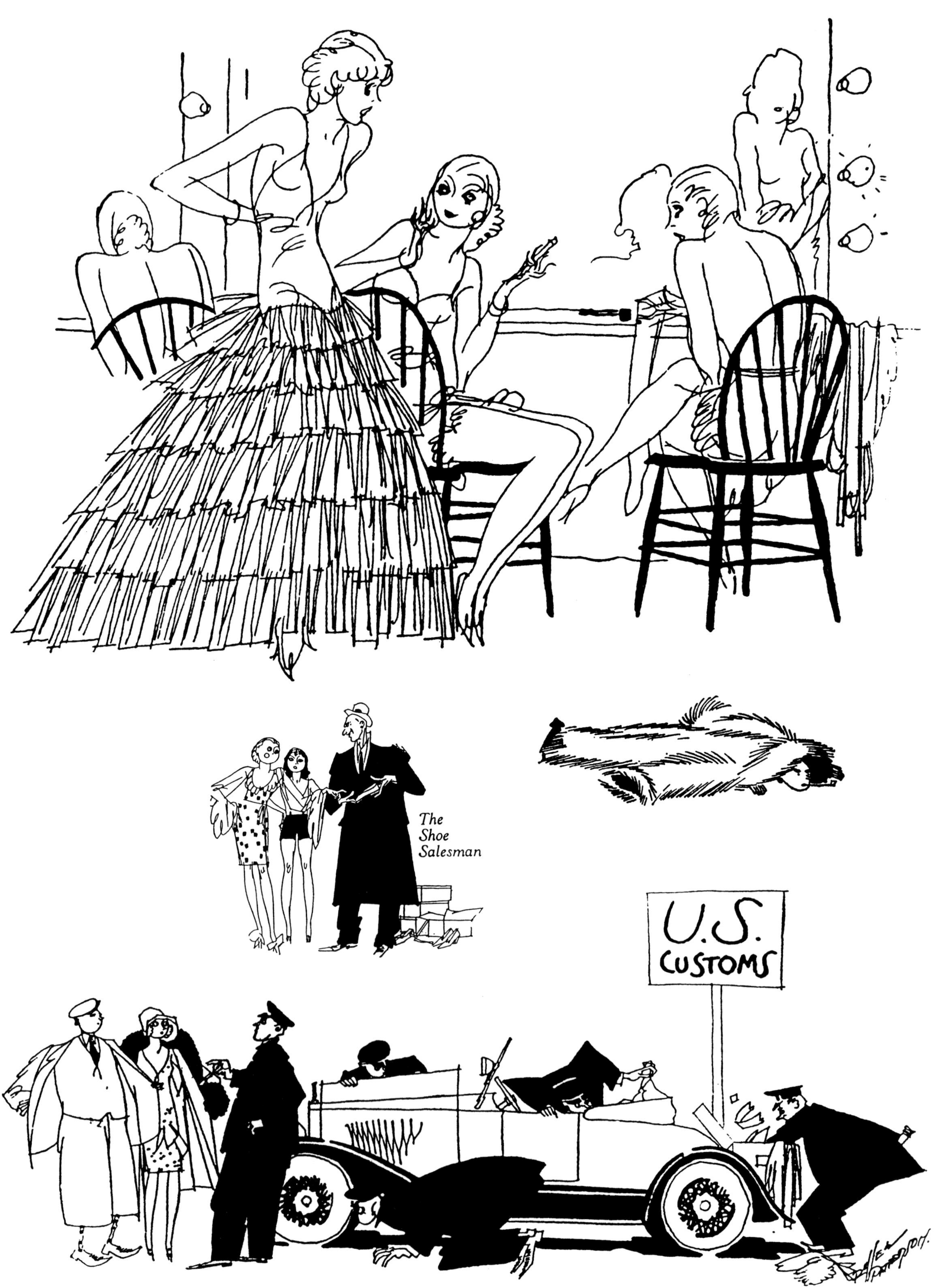
The Shoe Salesman
U.S. CUSTOMS

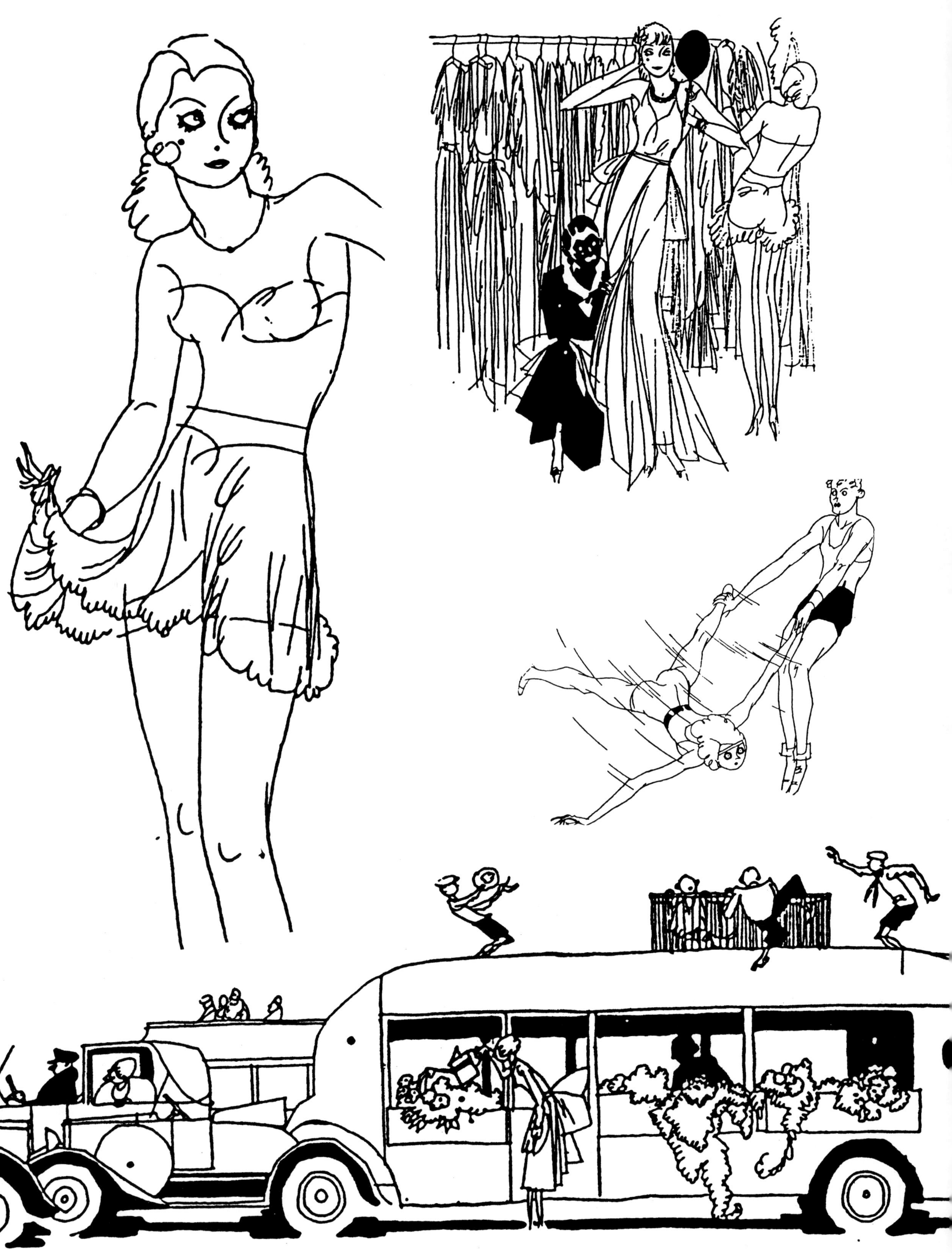

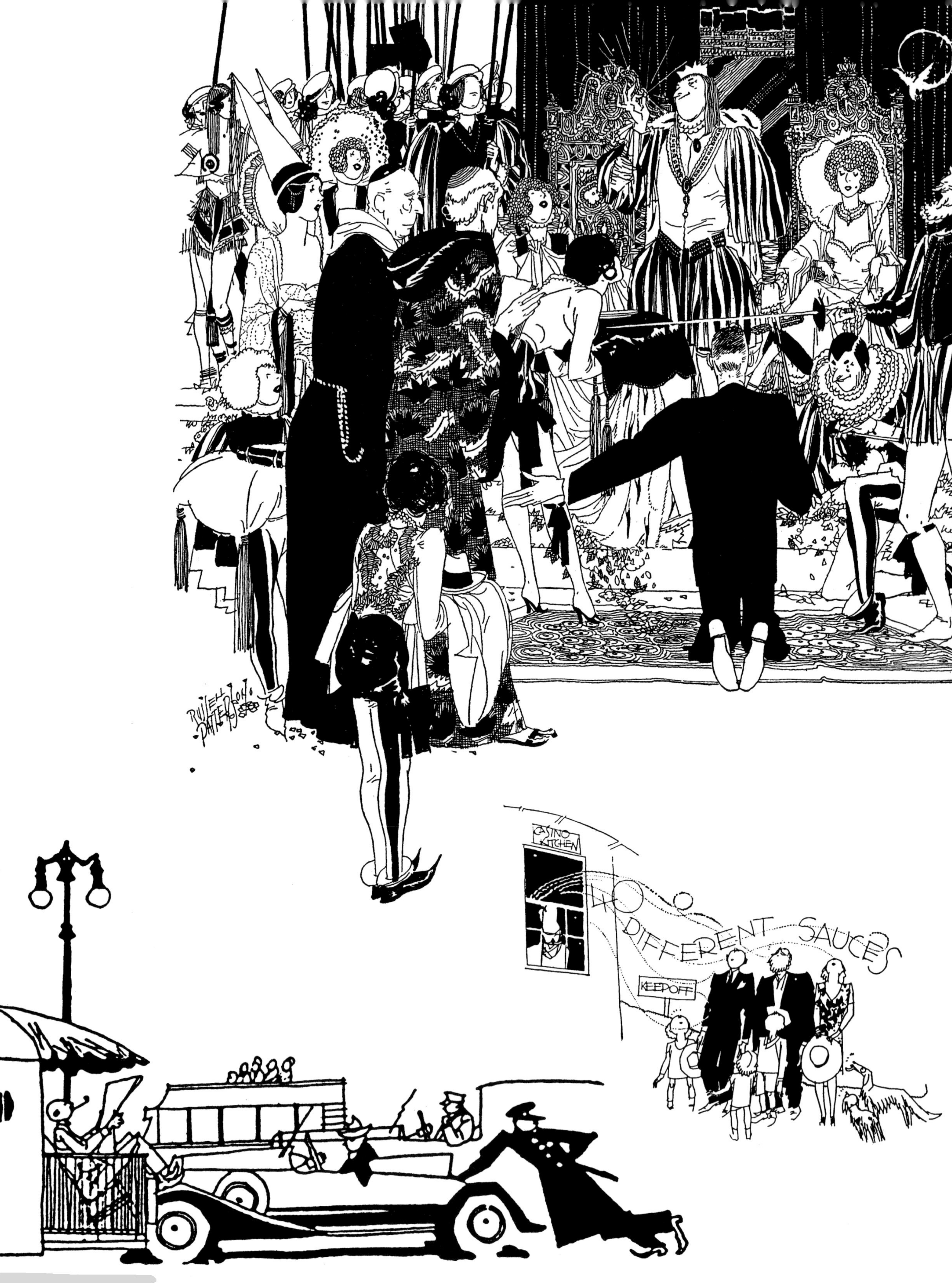
RUSSELL PATTERSON
CASINO KITCHEN
40 DIFFERENT SAUCES
KEEPOFF

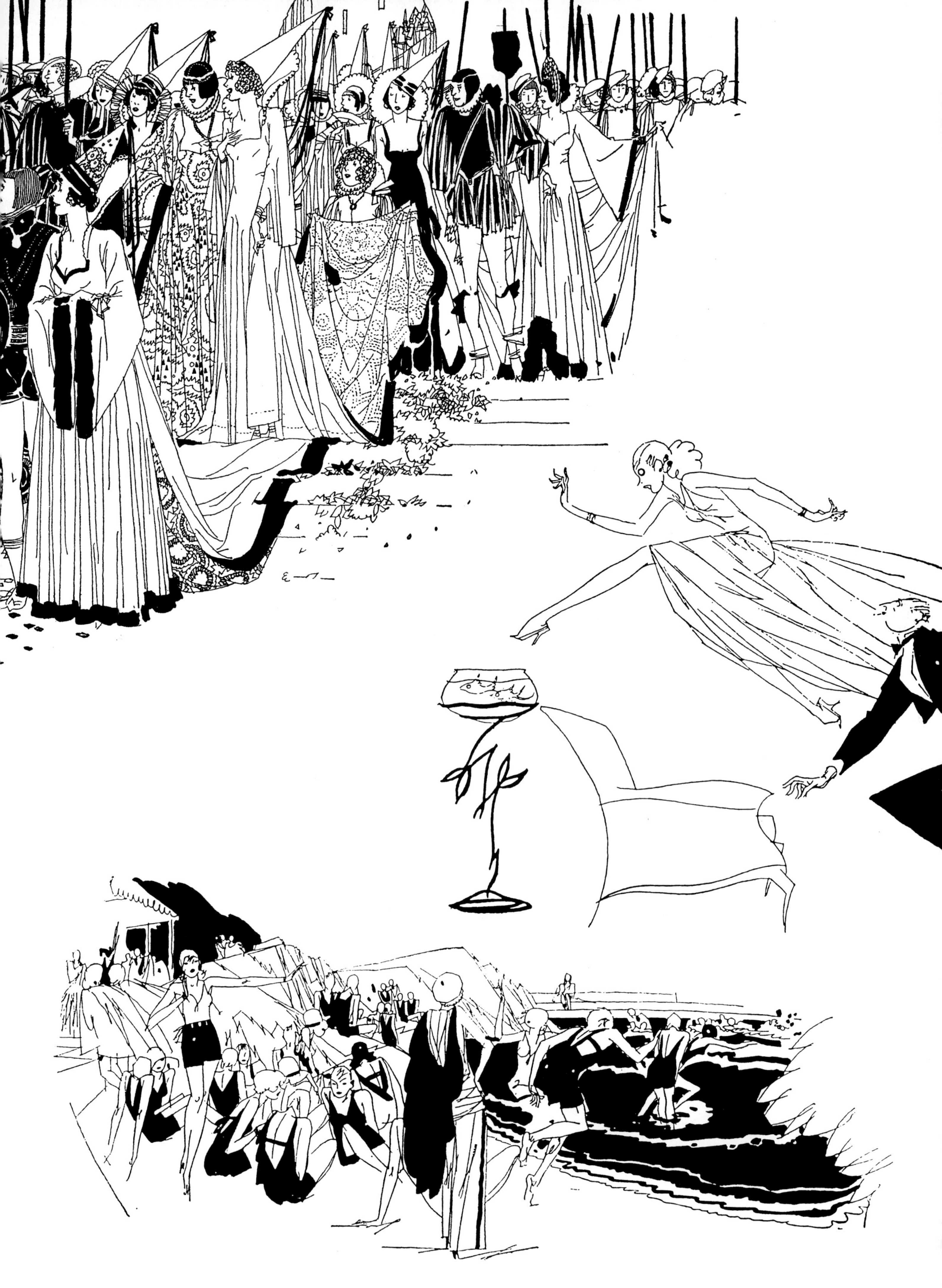

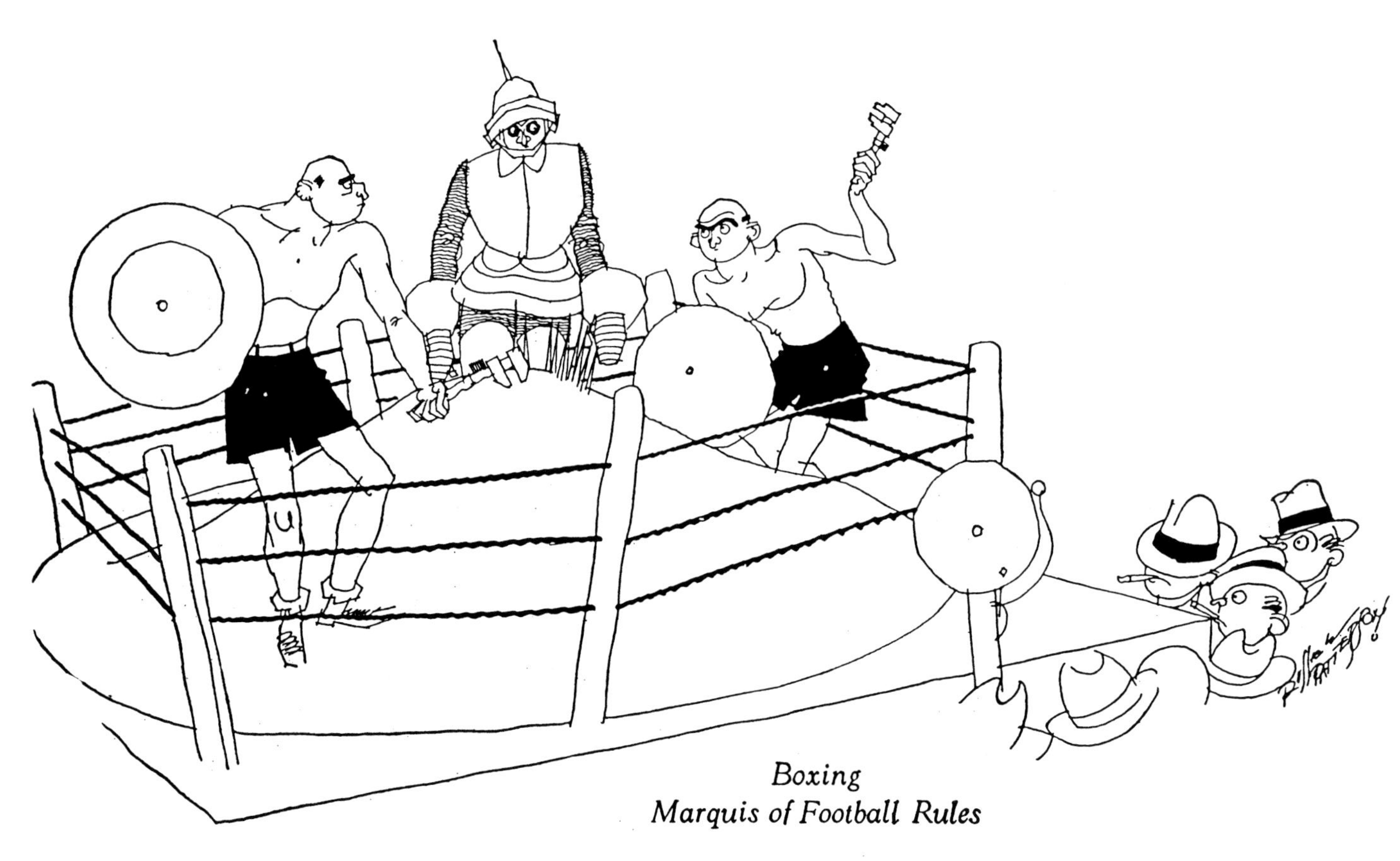

Boxing
Marquis of Football Rules

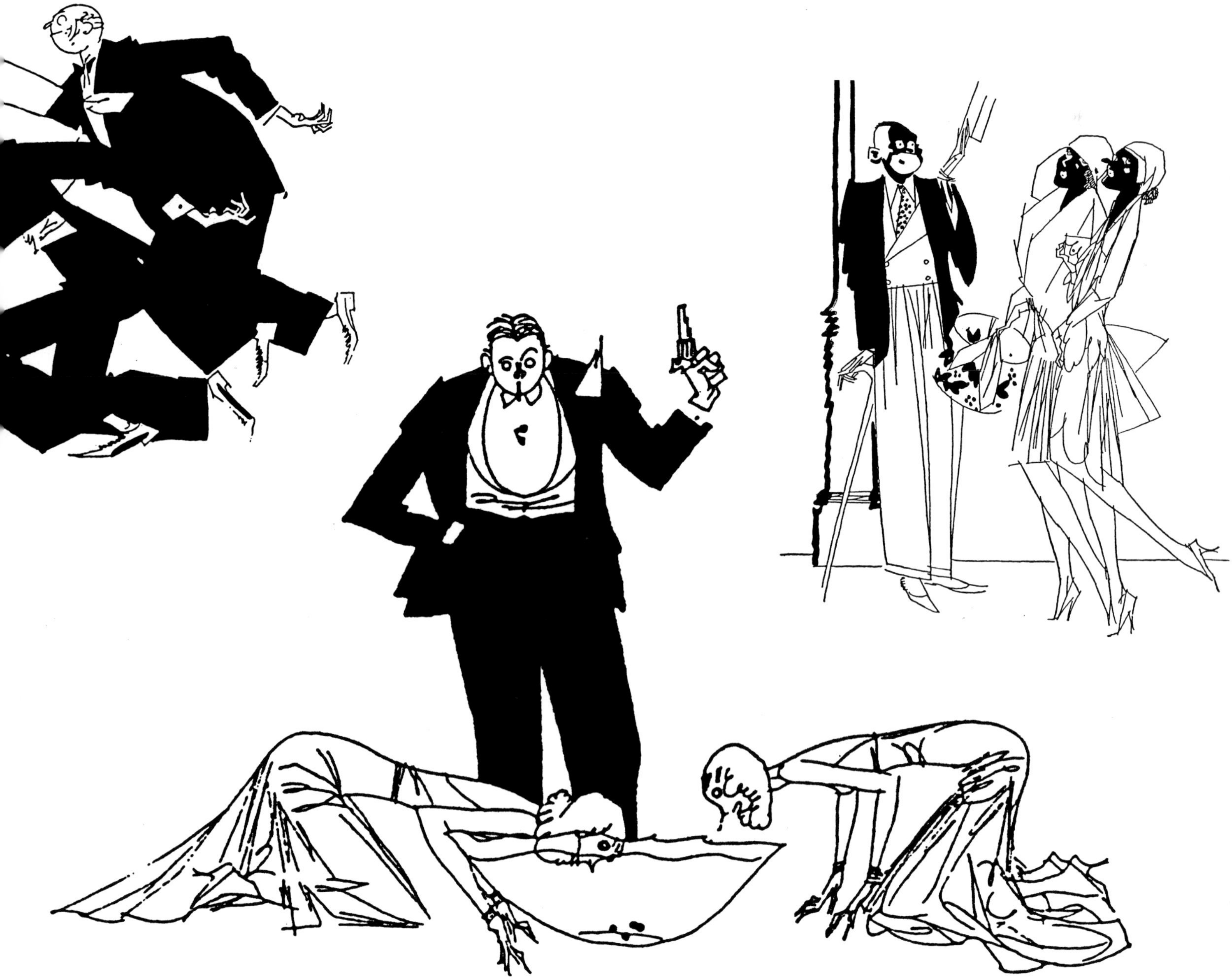

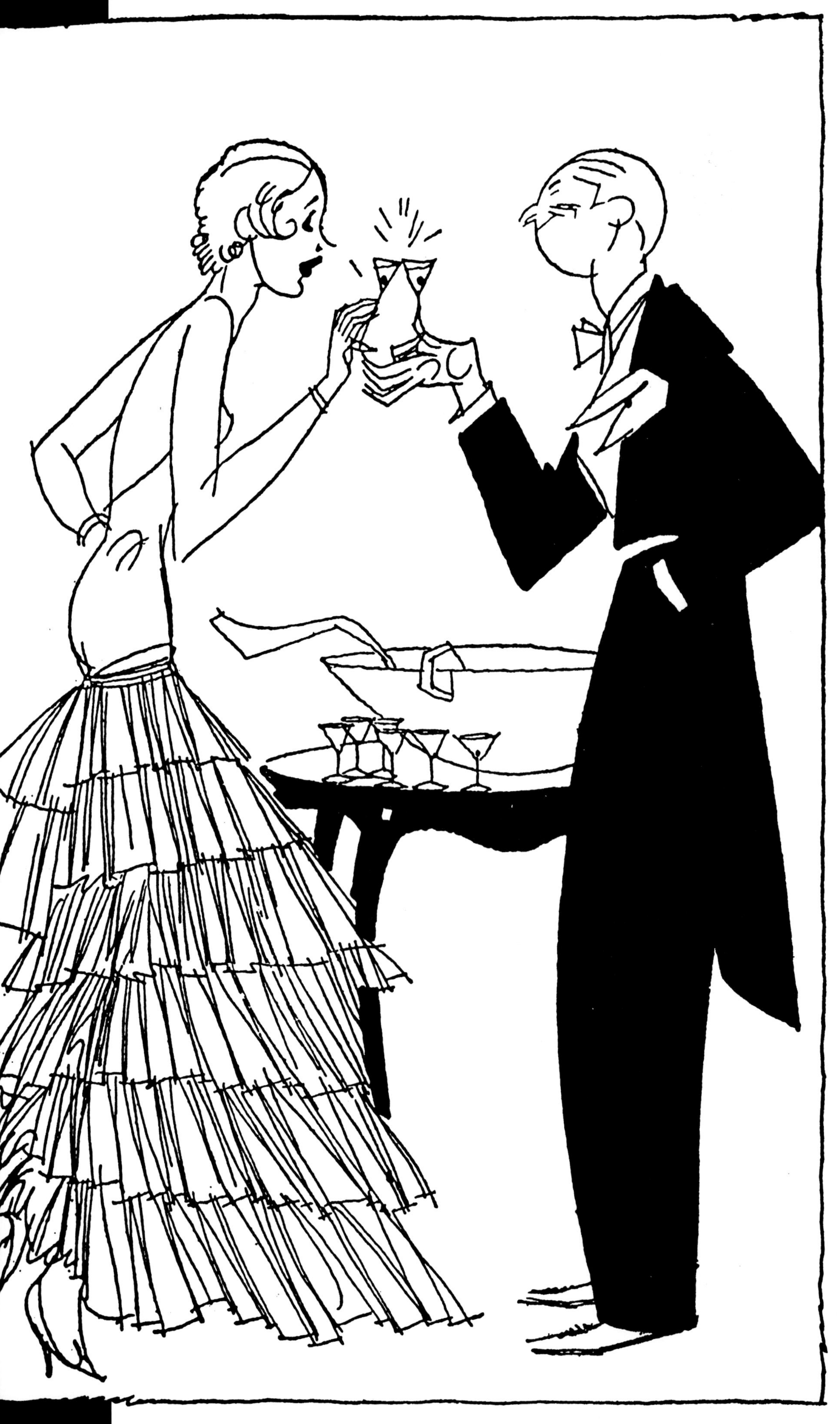

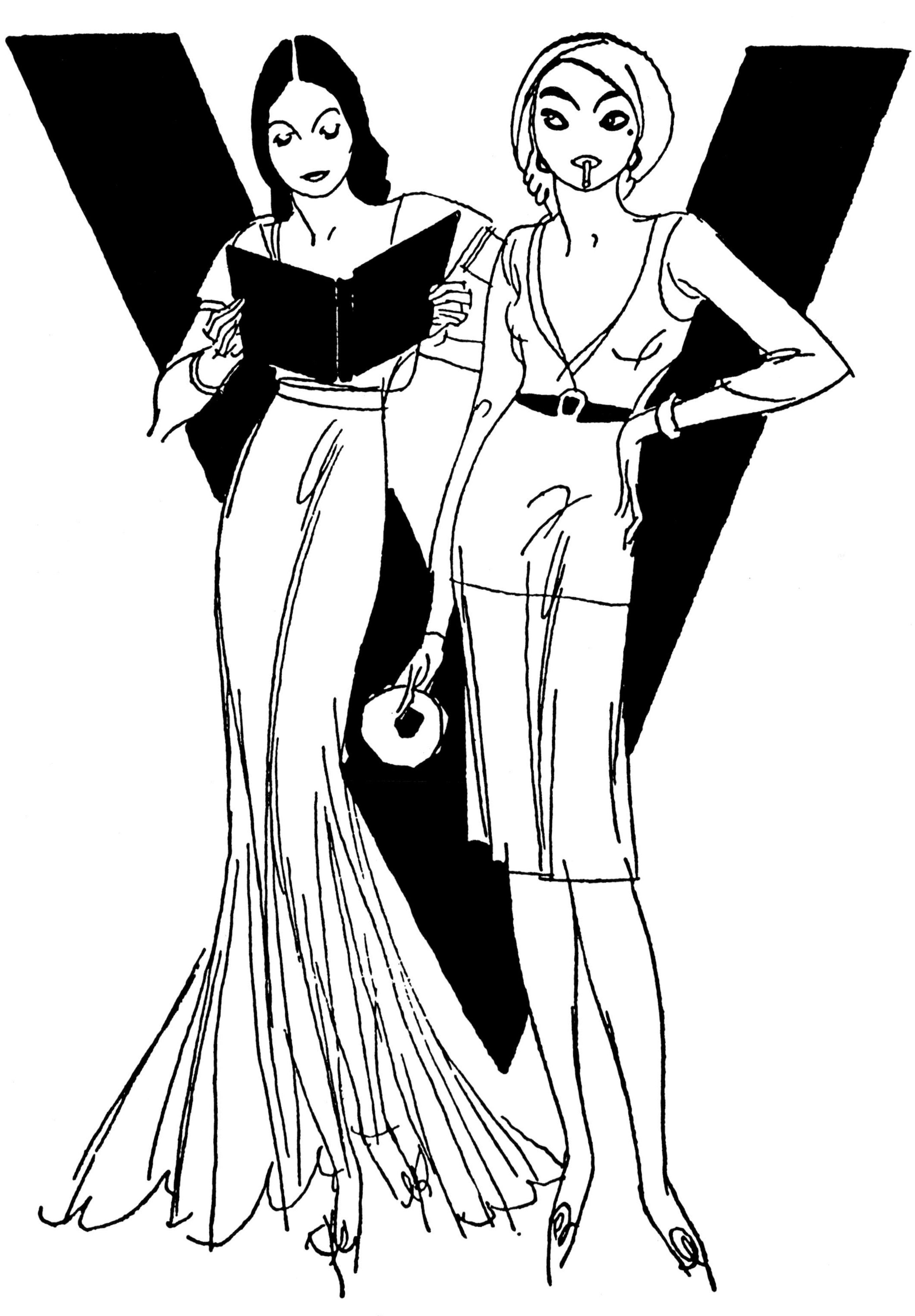

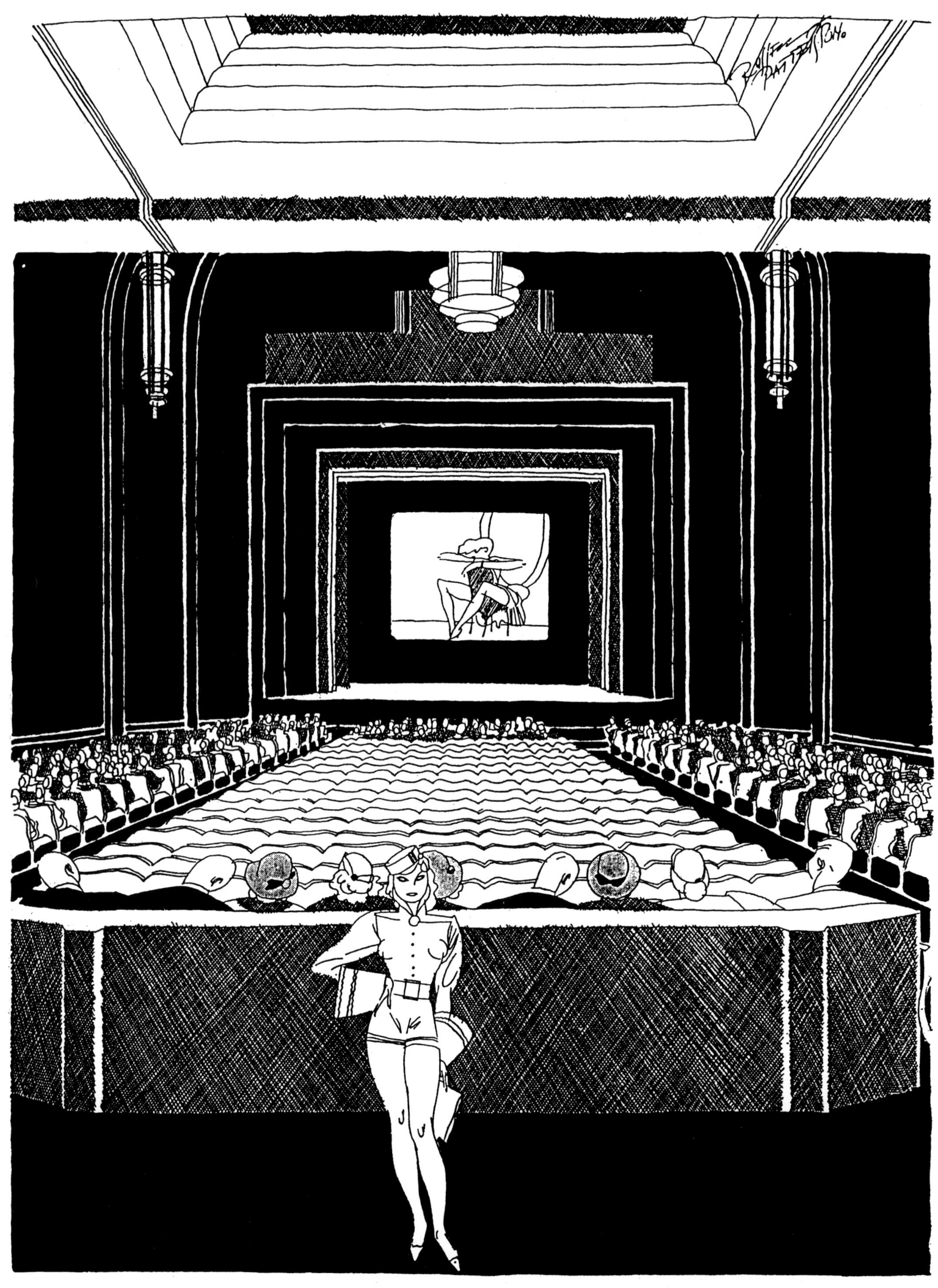

THE USHERETTE WHO MADE GOOD

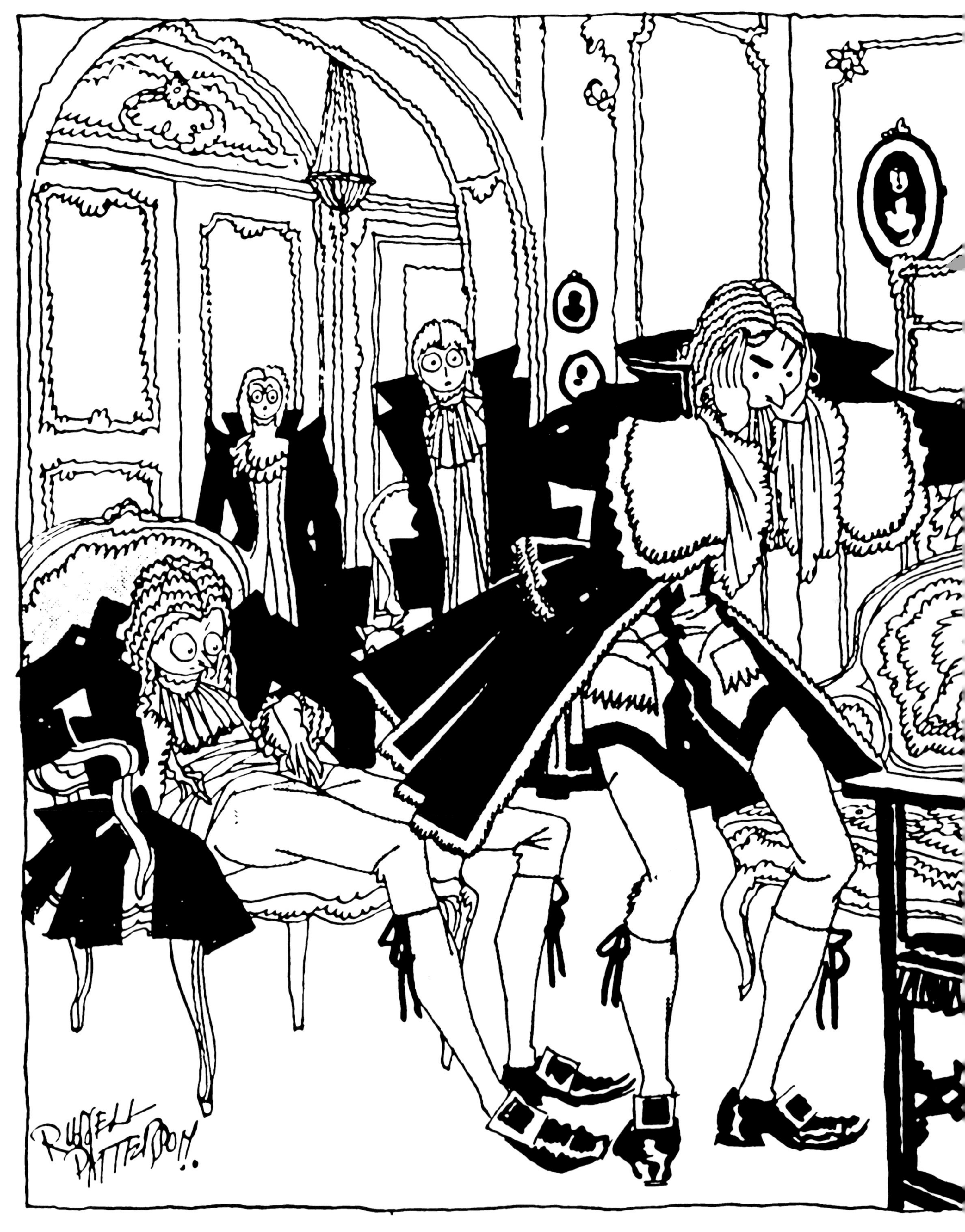

Confusion

Louis XIV Discovers that He Has Been

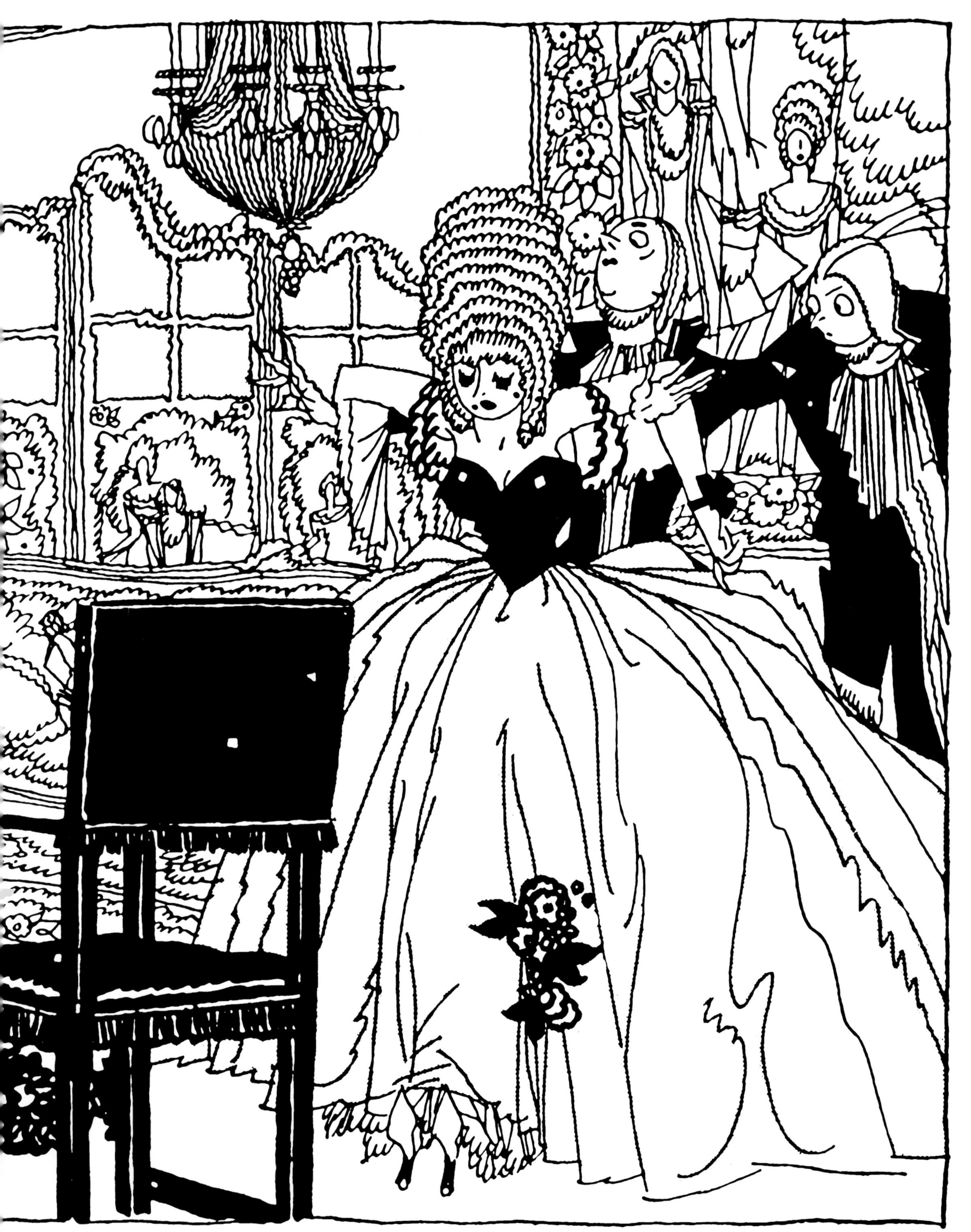

in Court

Given a Chair that is Not in His Period.

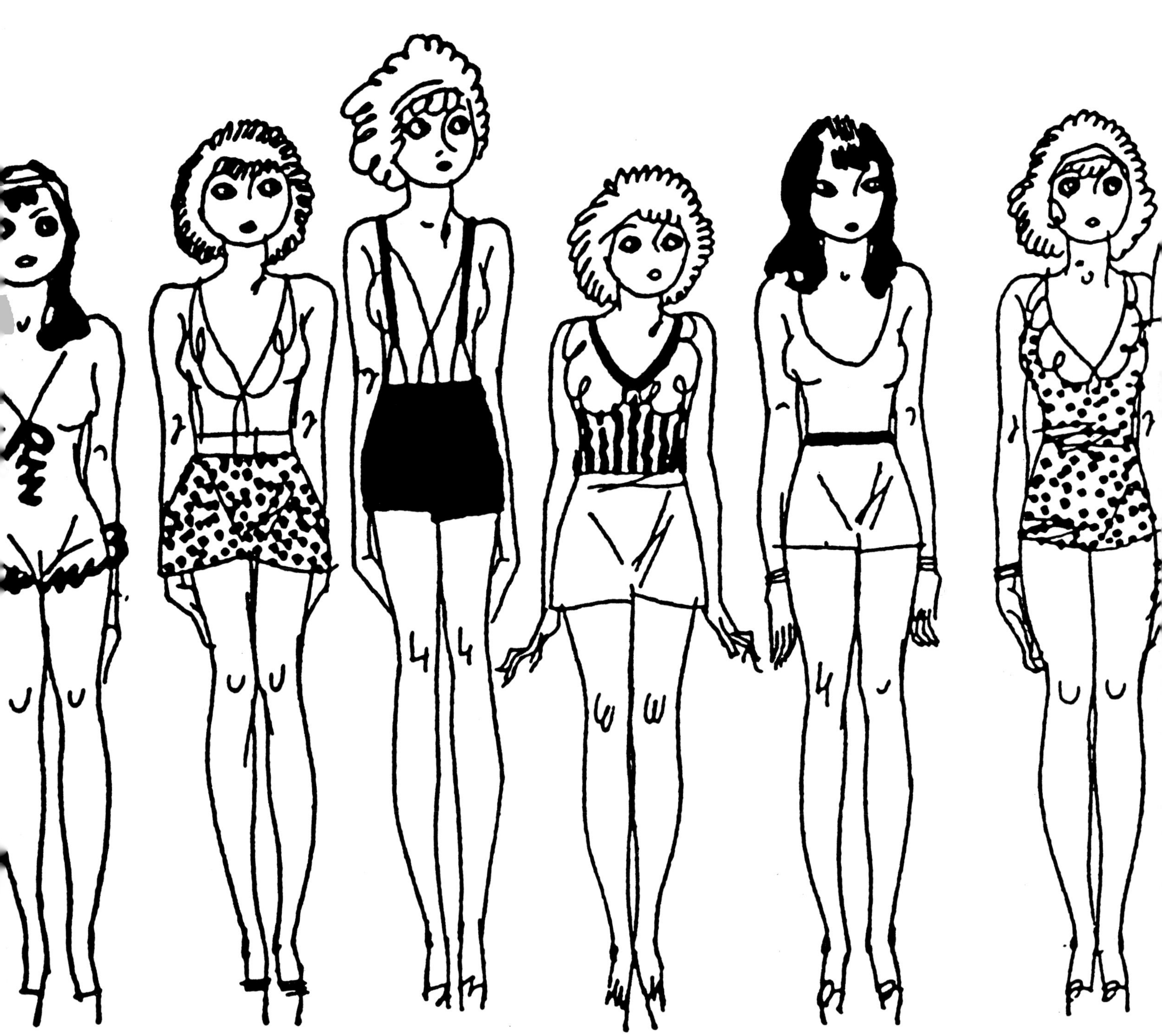

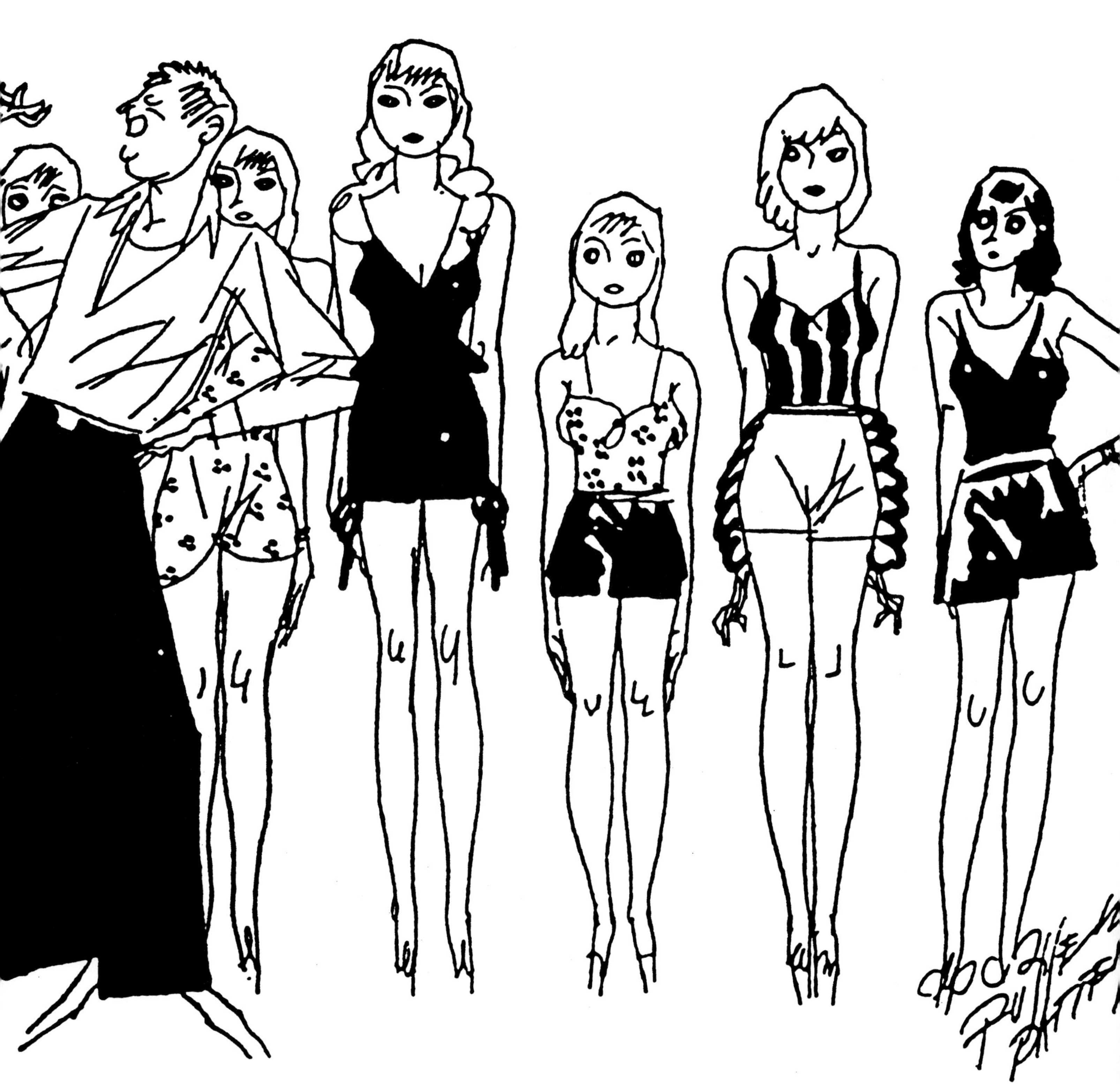

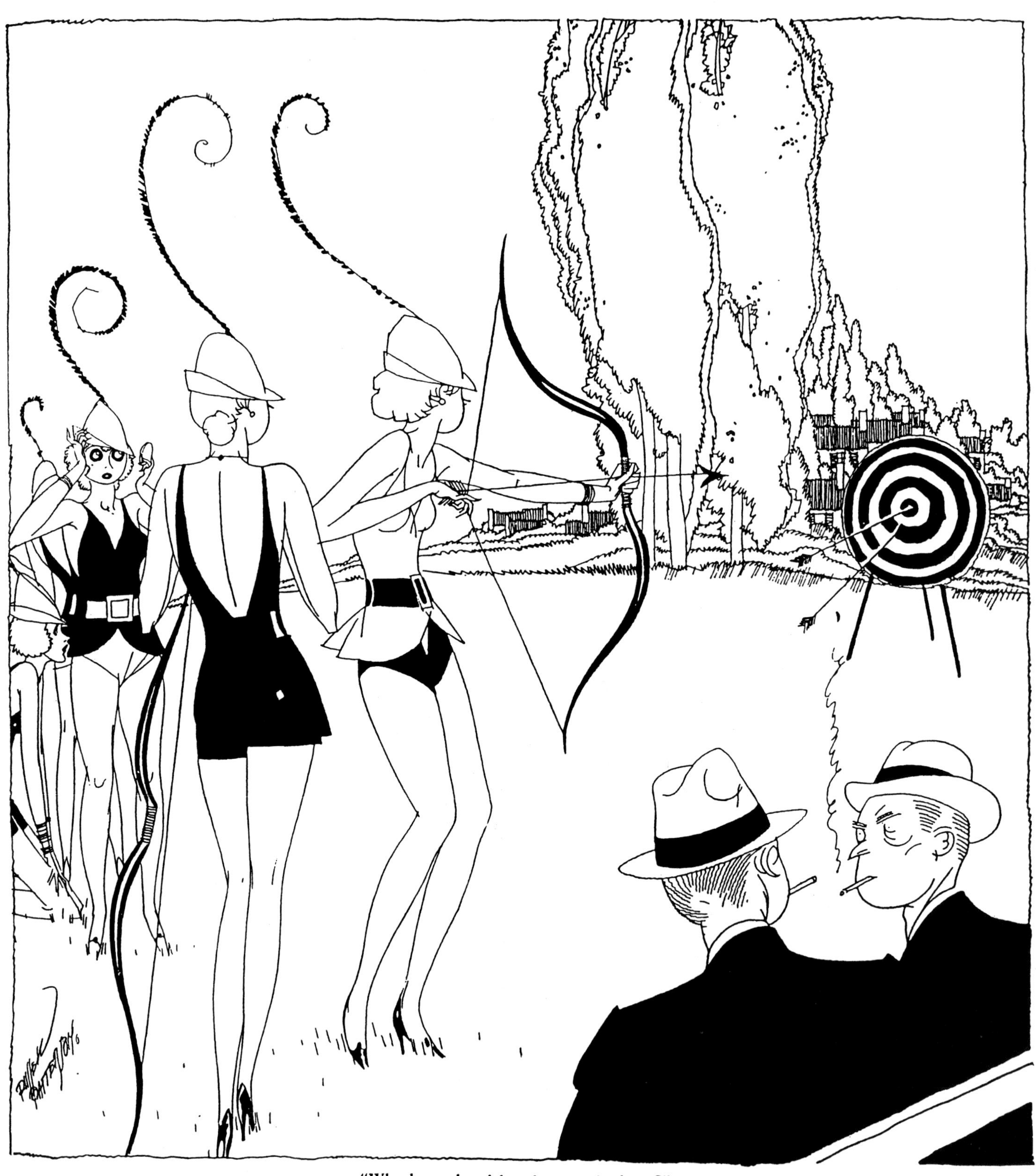

"Why have the girls taken up Archery?"
"They love the quaint mediæval costumes."

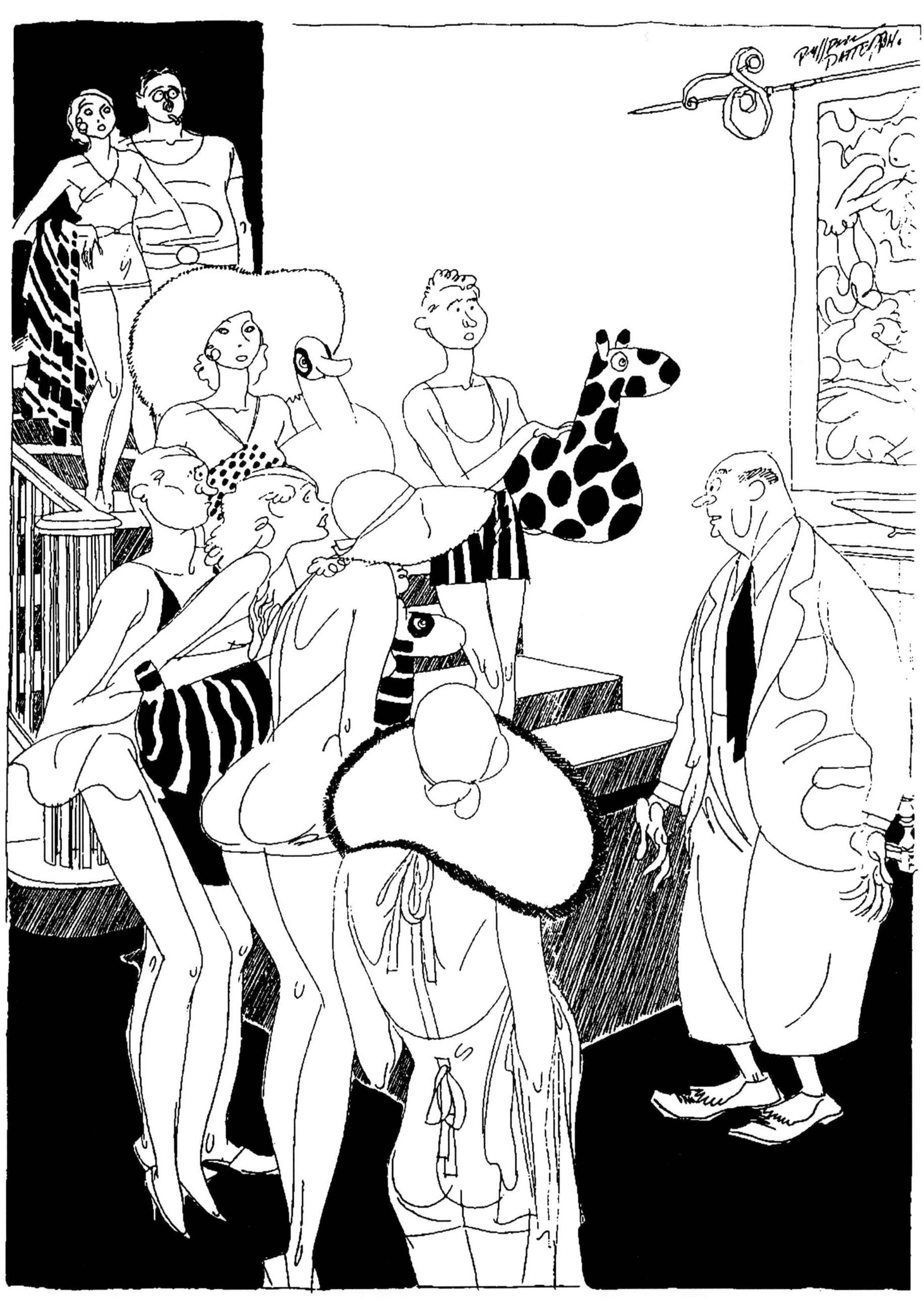

"Gosh, I was only kidding when I said we had a swimming pool."

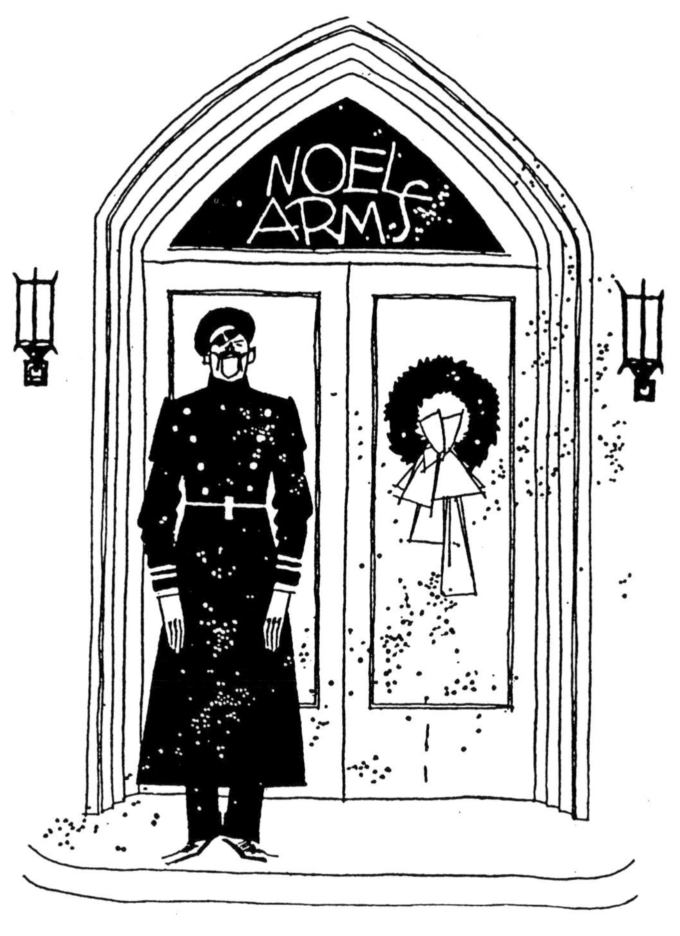
NOEL'S
ARMS

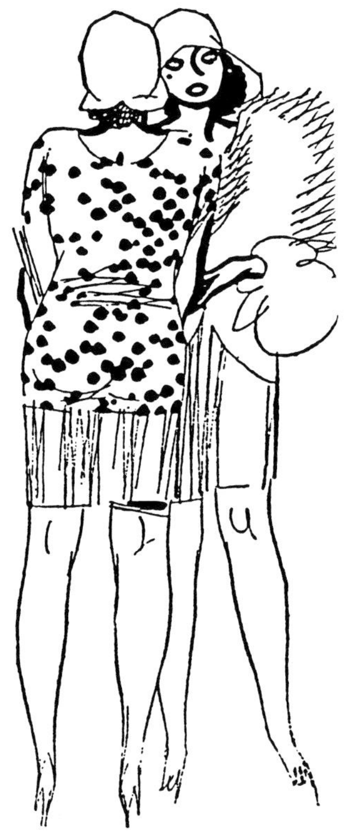

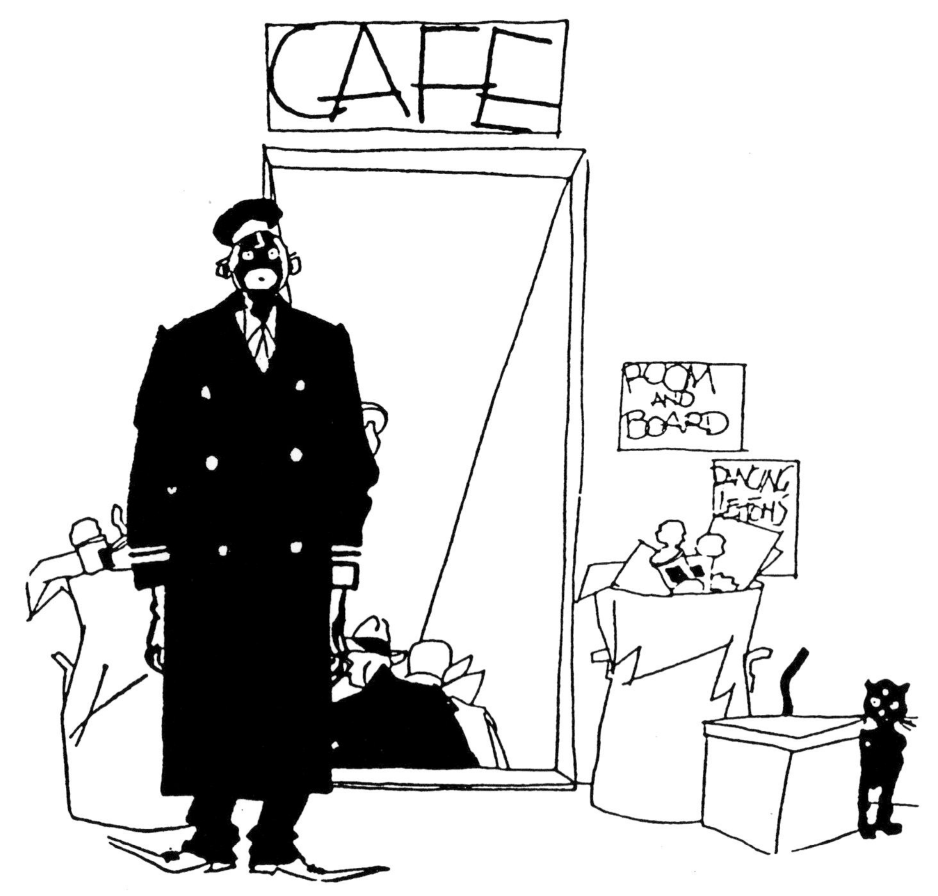
CAFE
ROOM AND BOARD
DANCING LESSONS

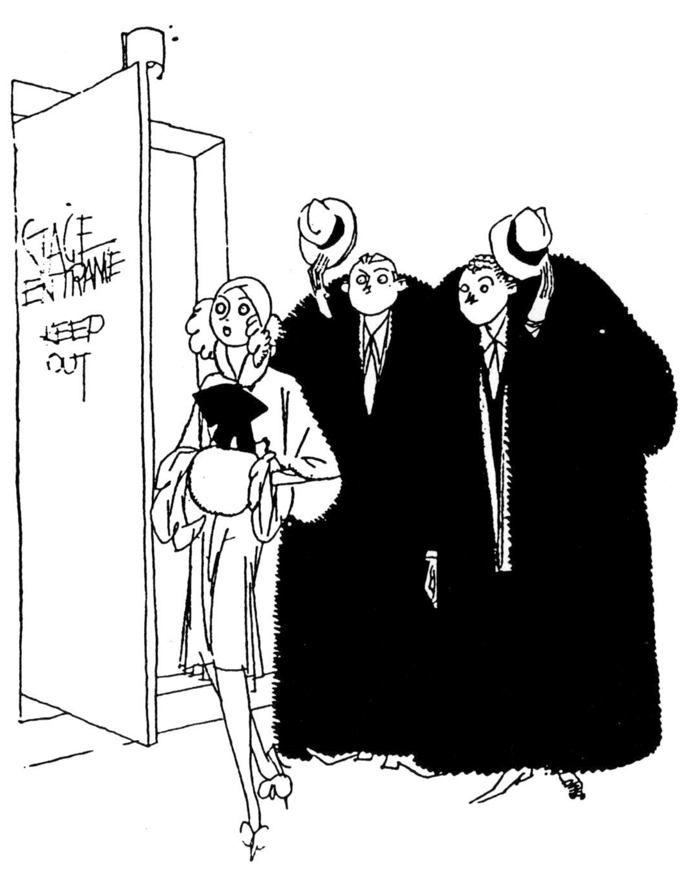
STAGE ENTRANCE
KEEP OUT

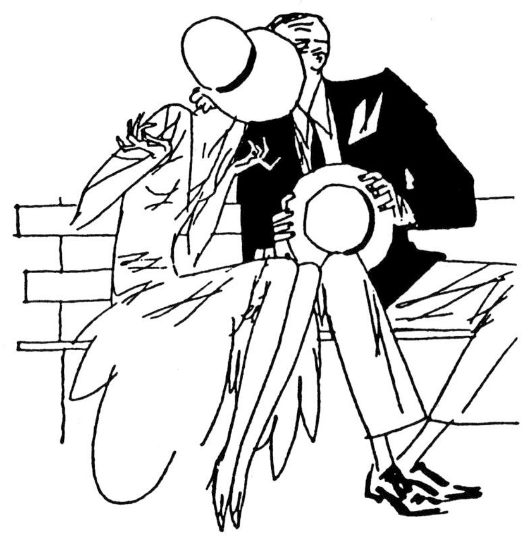

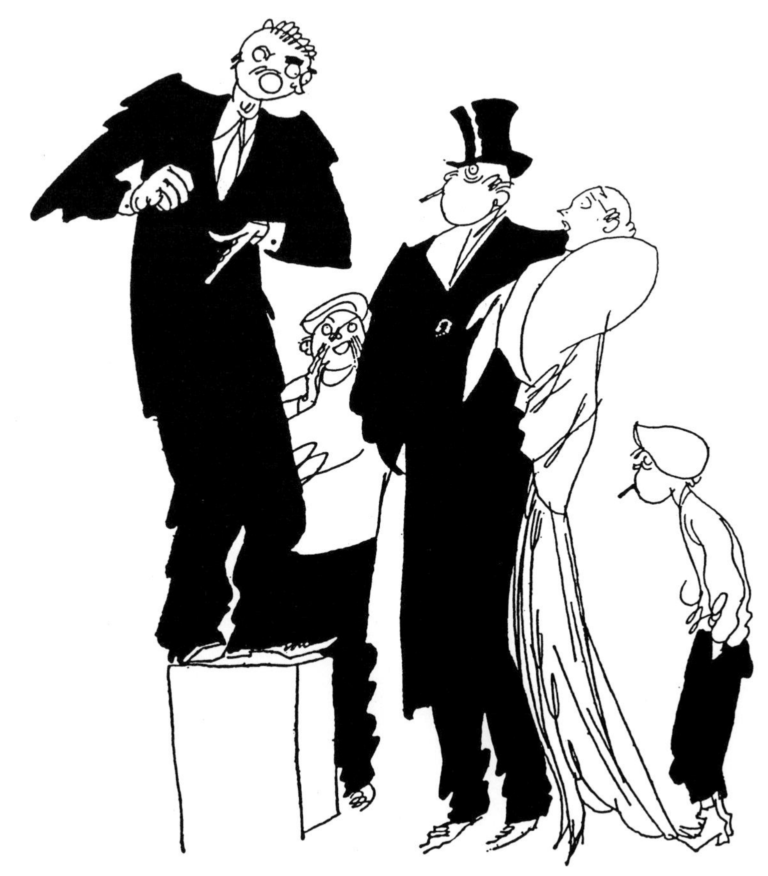

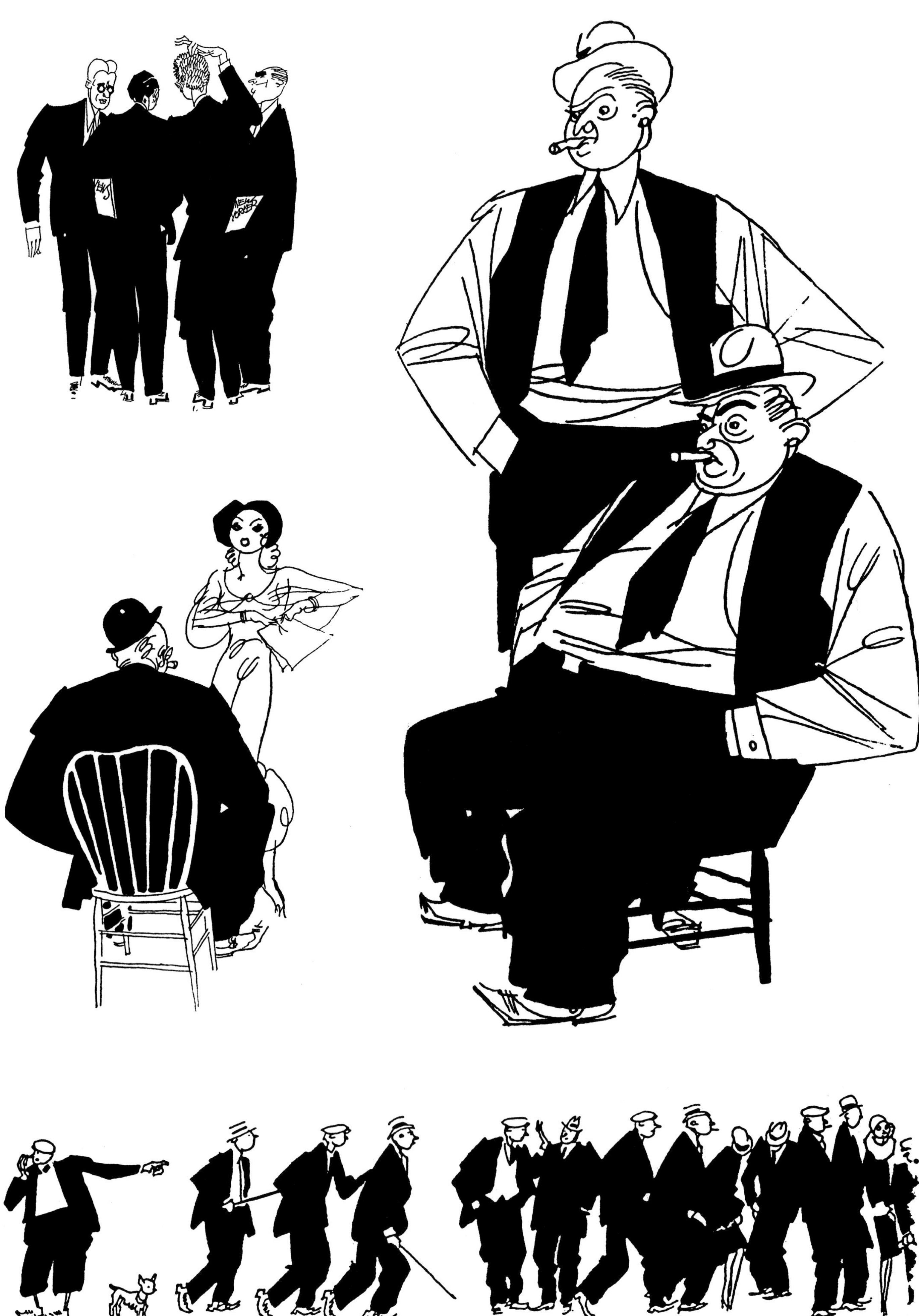

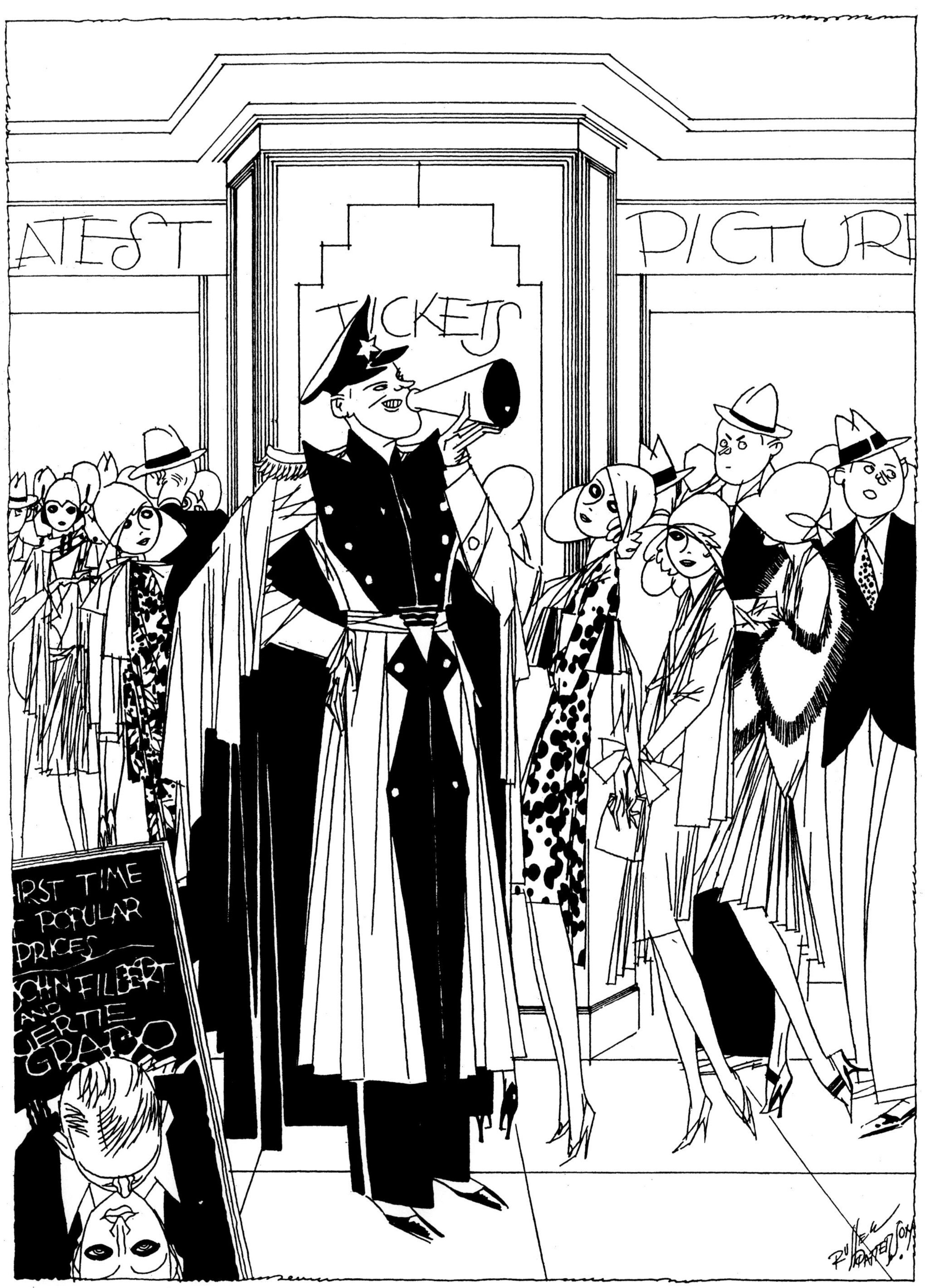

The **Former President of the Student Players Who Just Couldn't Give Up the Stage After Leaving College**

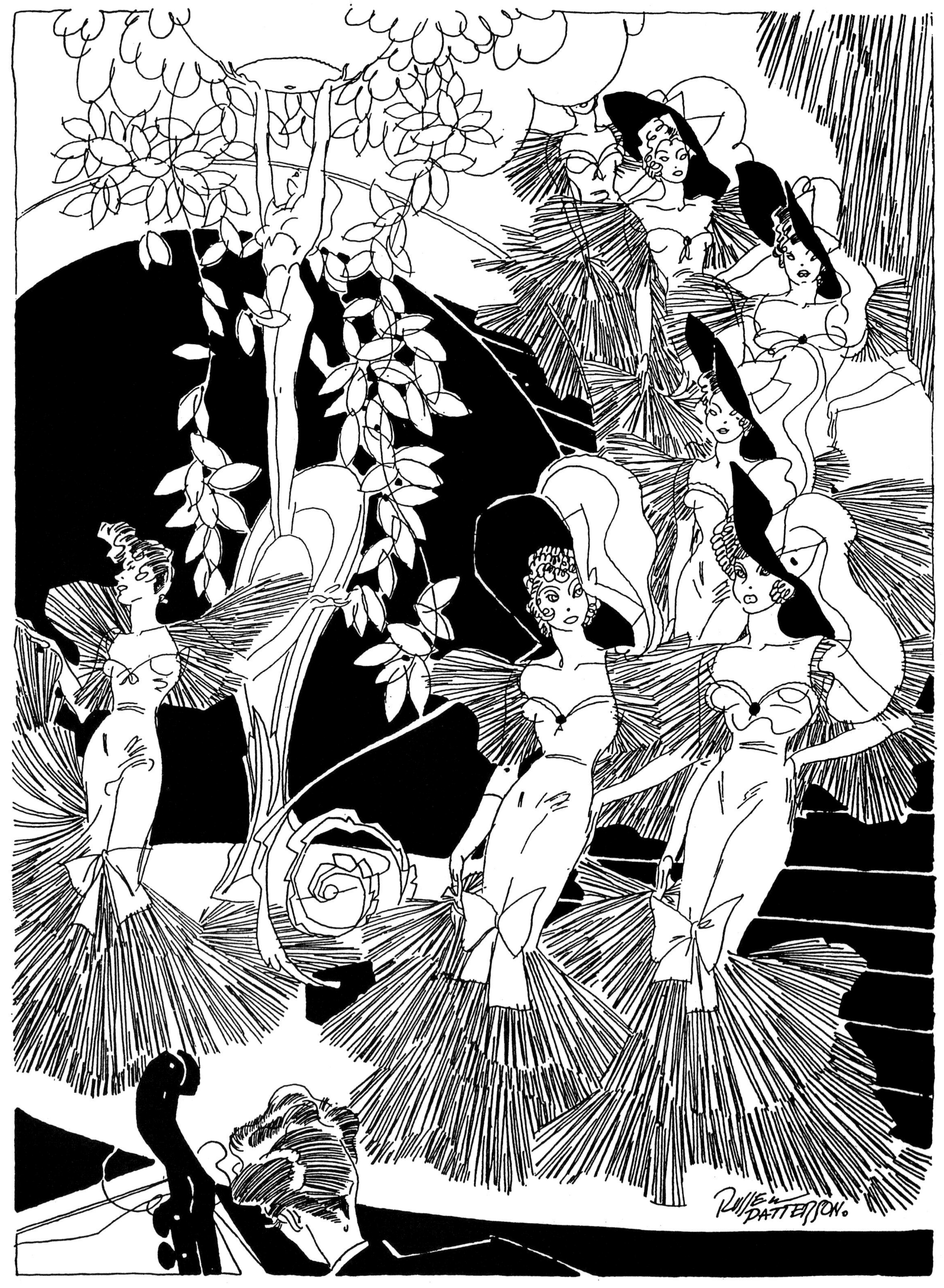
Russell Patterson

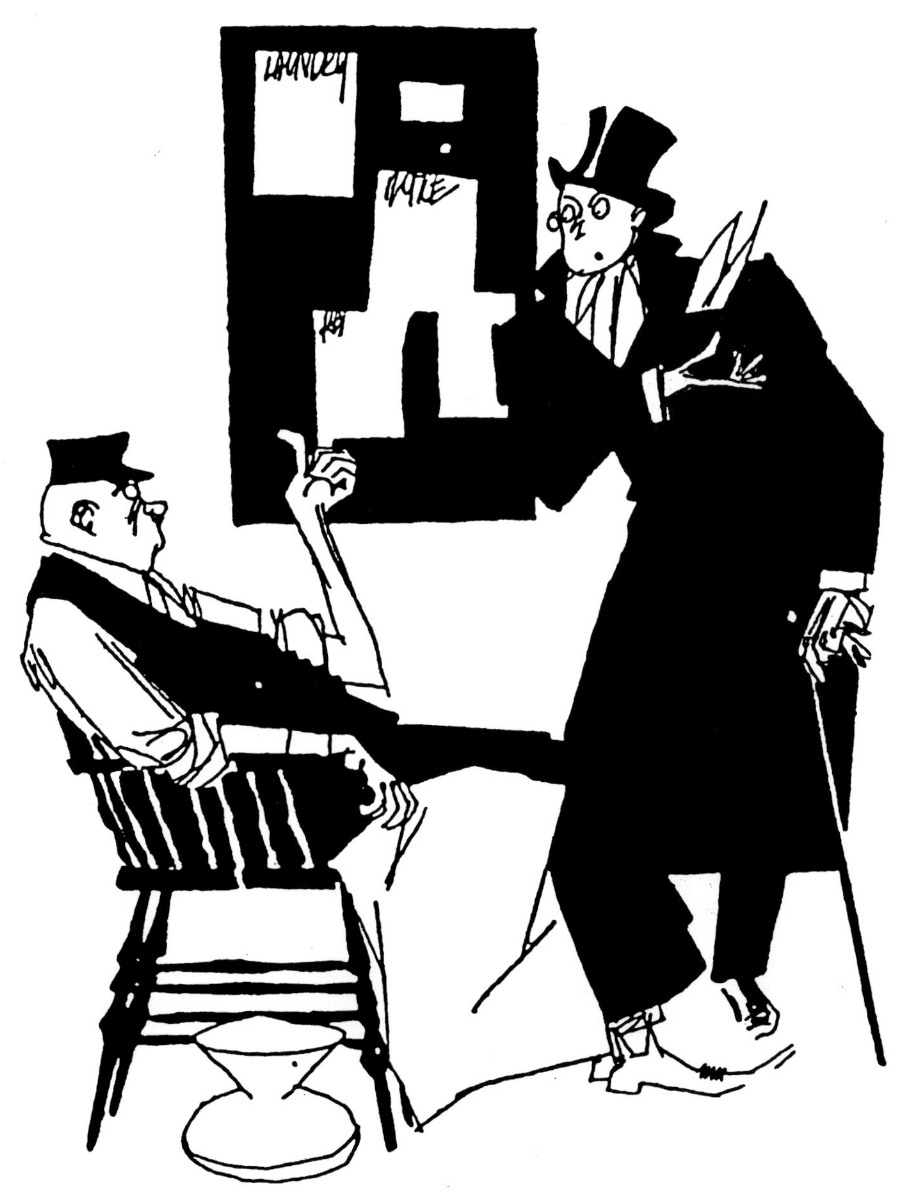
LAUNDRY

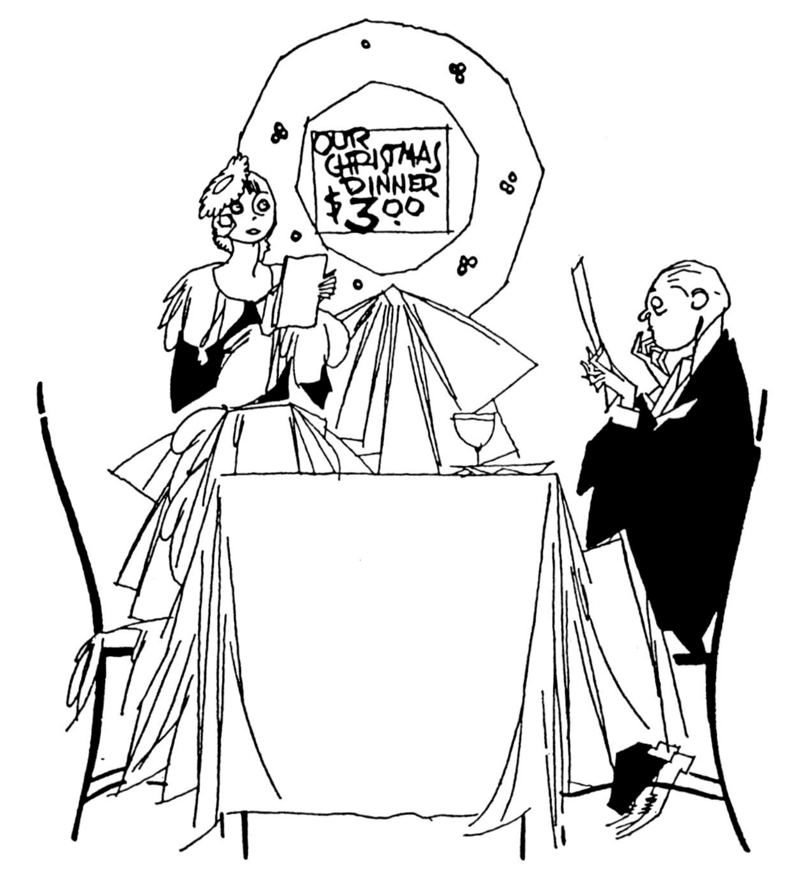
OUR CHRISTMAS DINNER $3.00

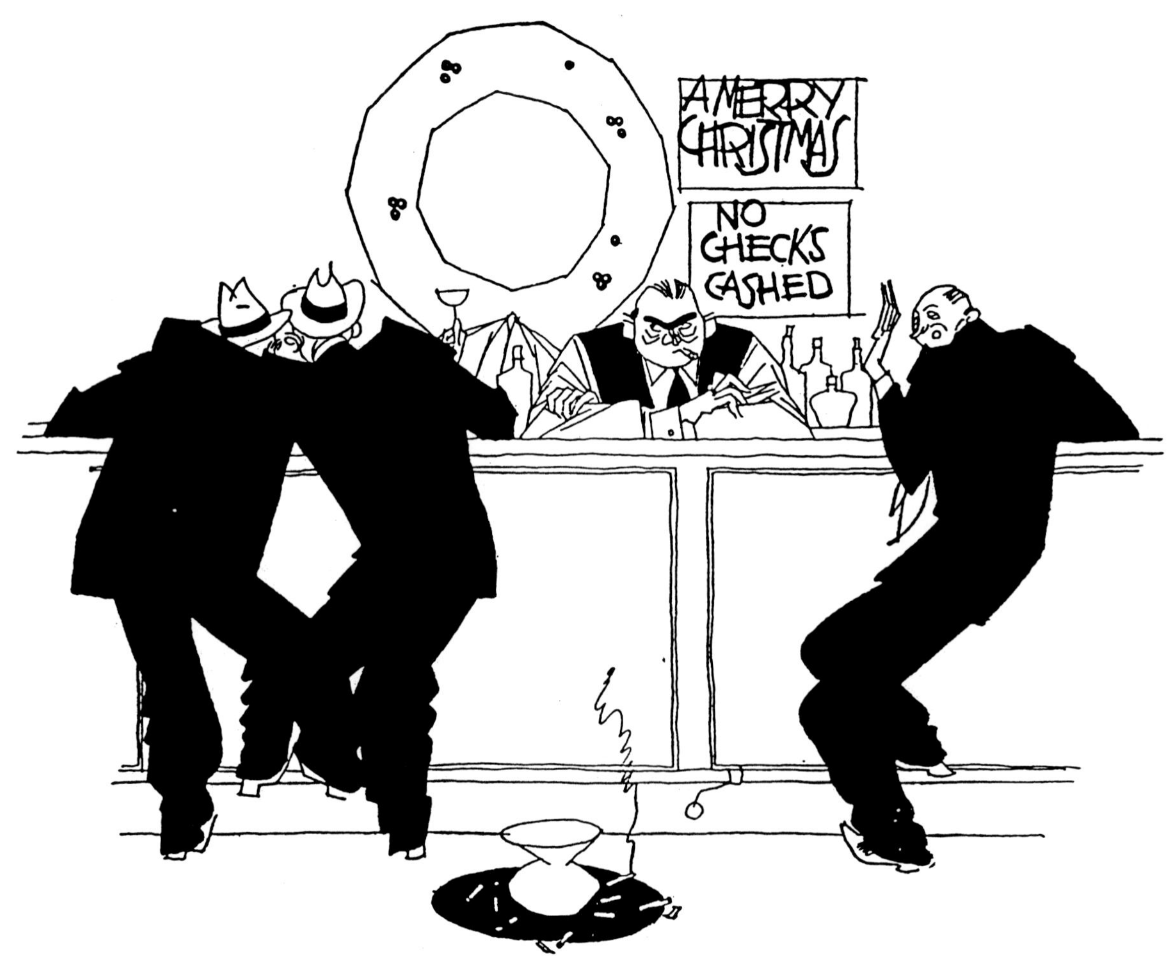
A MERRY CHRISTMAS
NO CHECKS CASHED

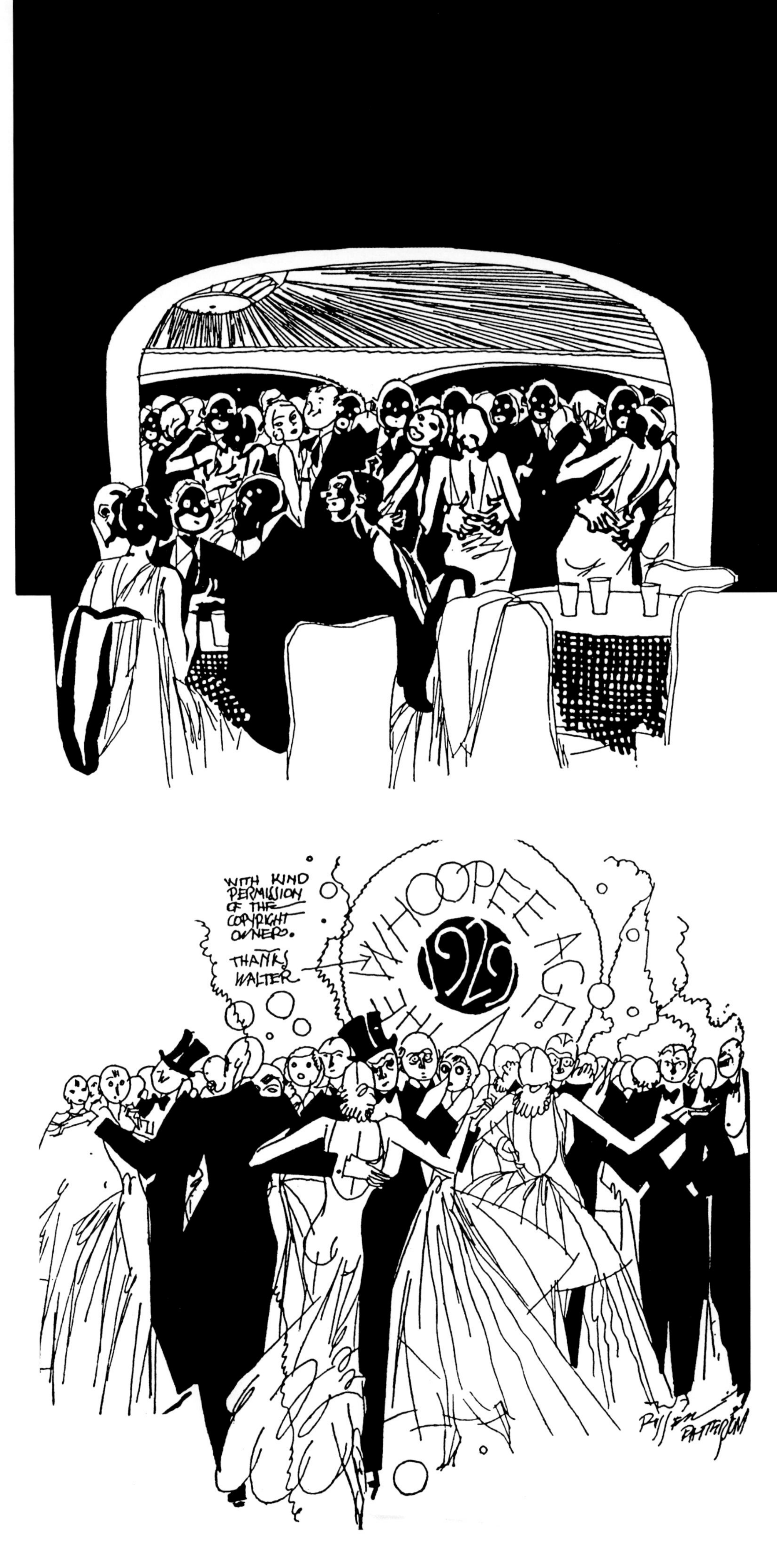
WITH KIND PERMISSION OF THE COPYRIGHT OWNERS.
THANKS WALTER
THE WHOOPEE AGE!
1925

THE PRETTY GIRL IN CARICATURE

as drawn by Russell Patterson

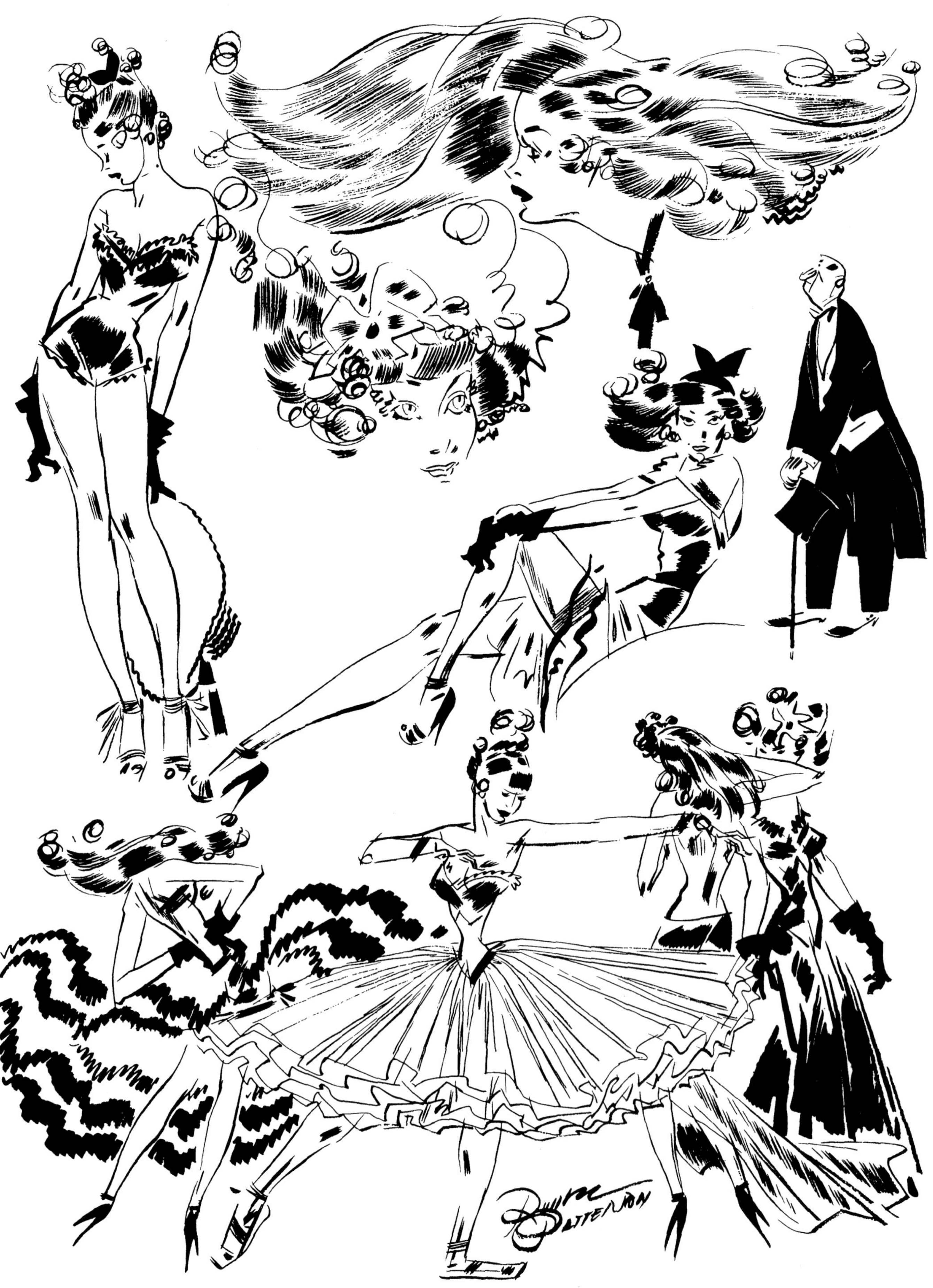

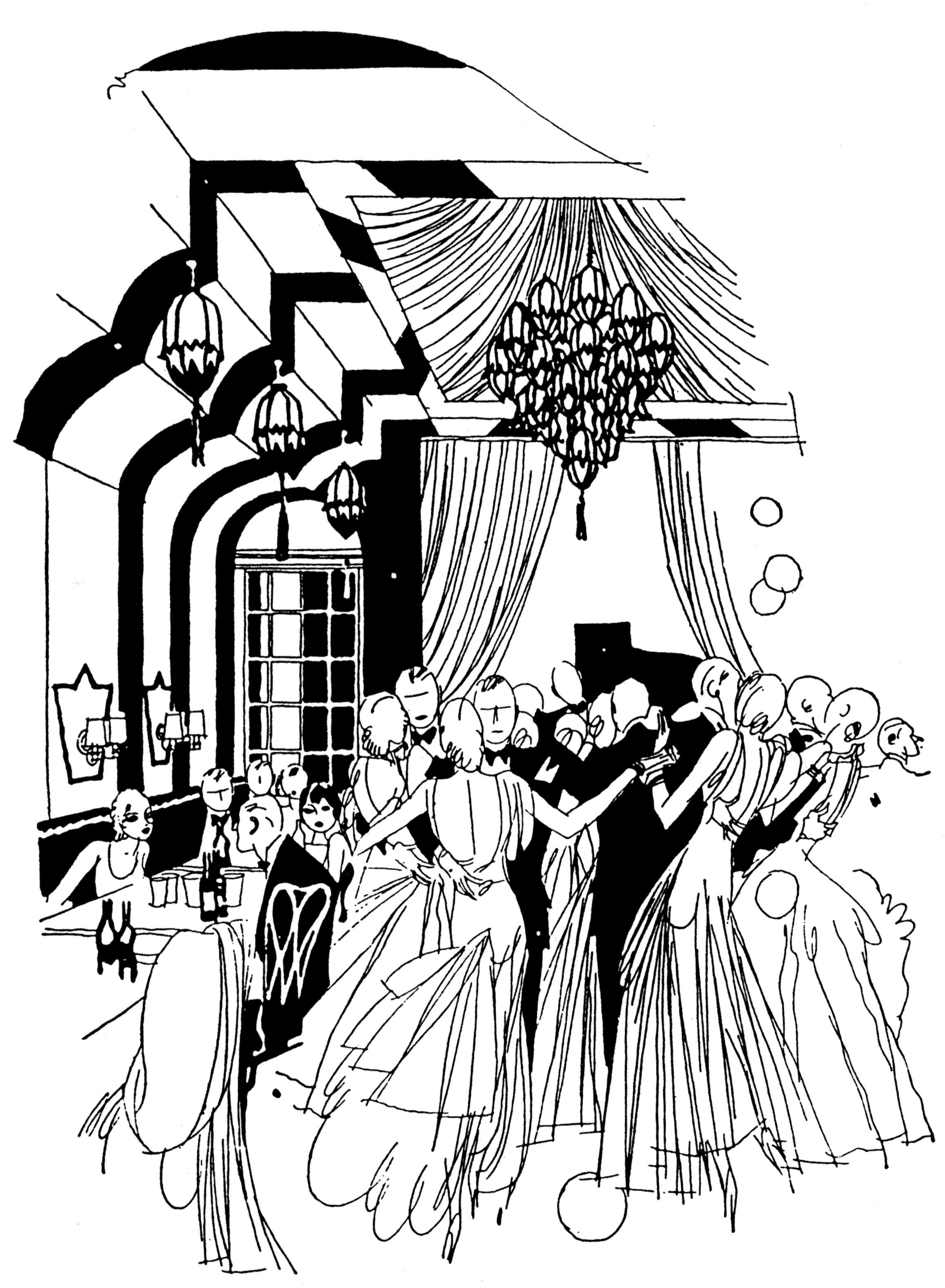

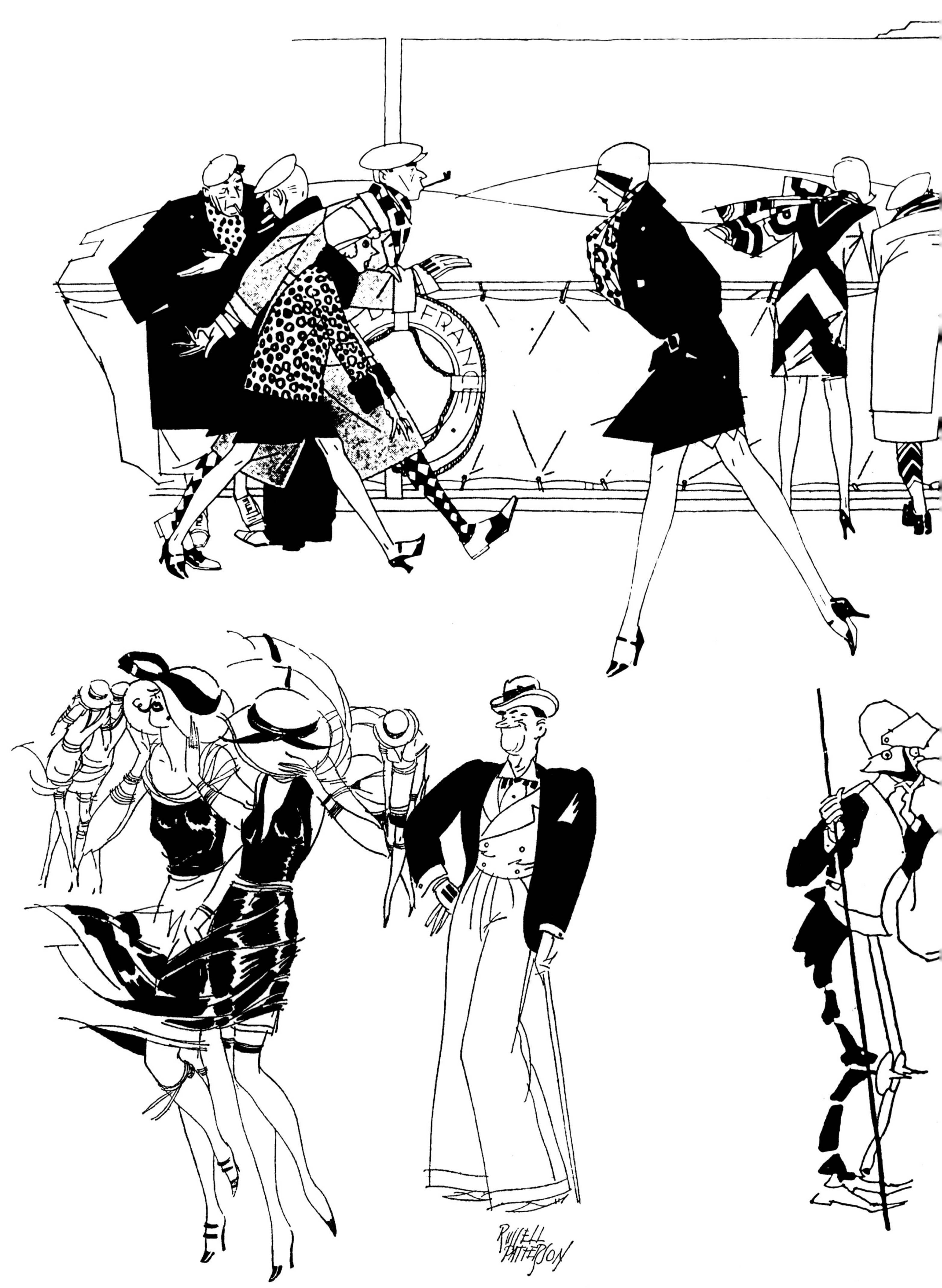
RUSSELL PATTERSON

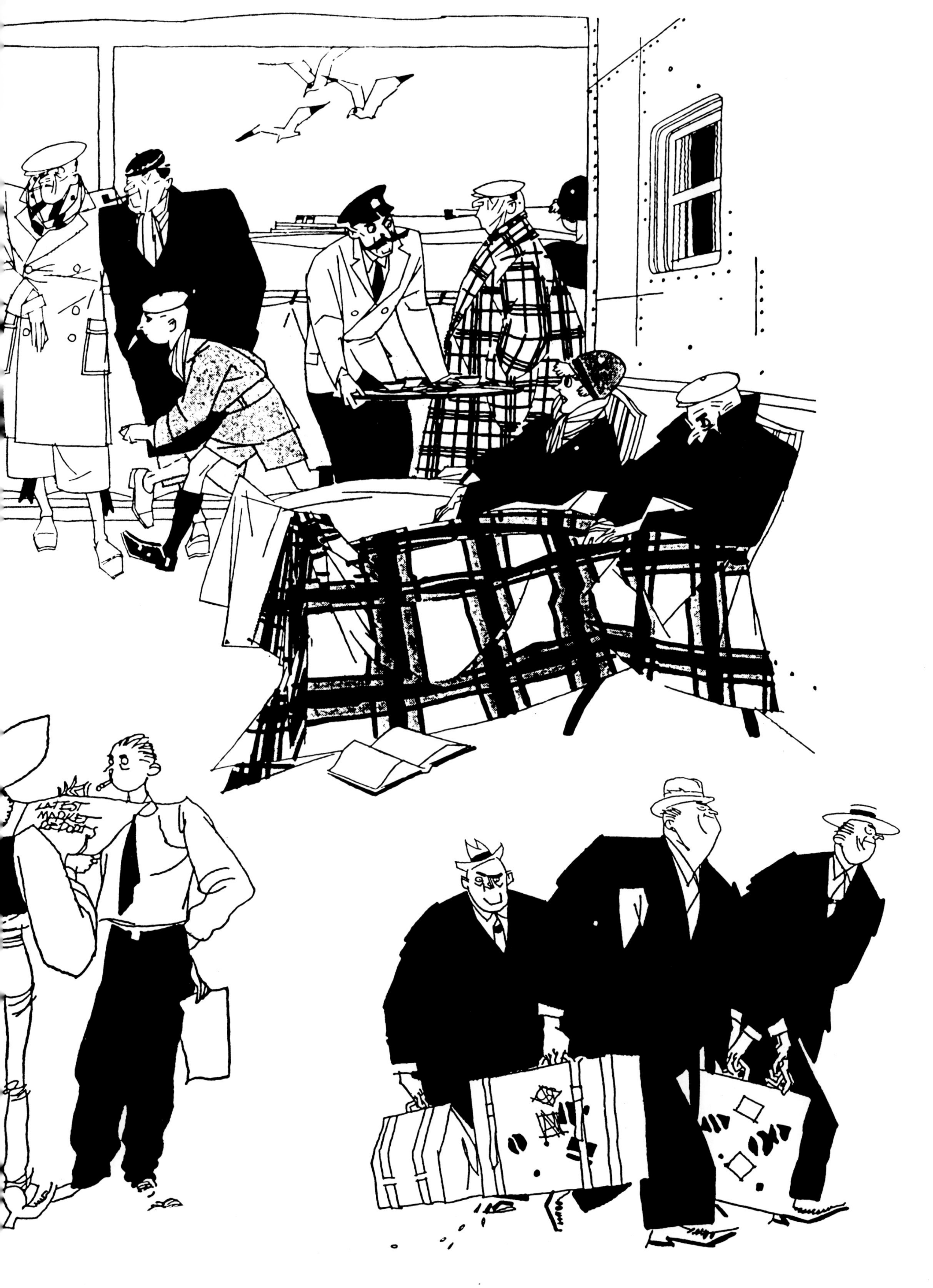
LATEST
MARKET

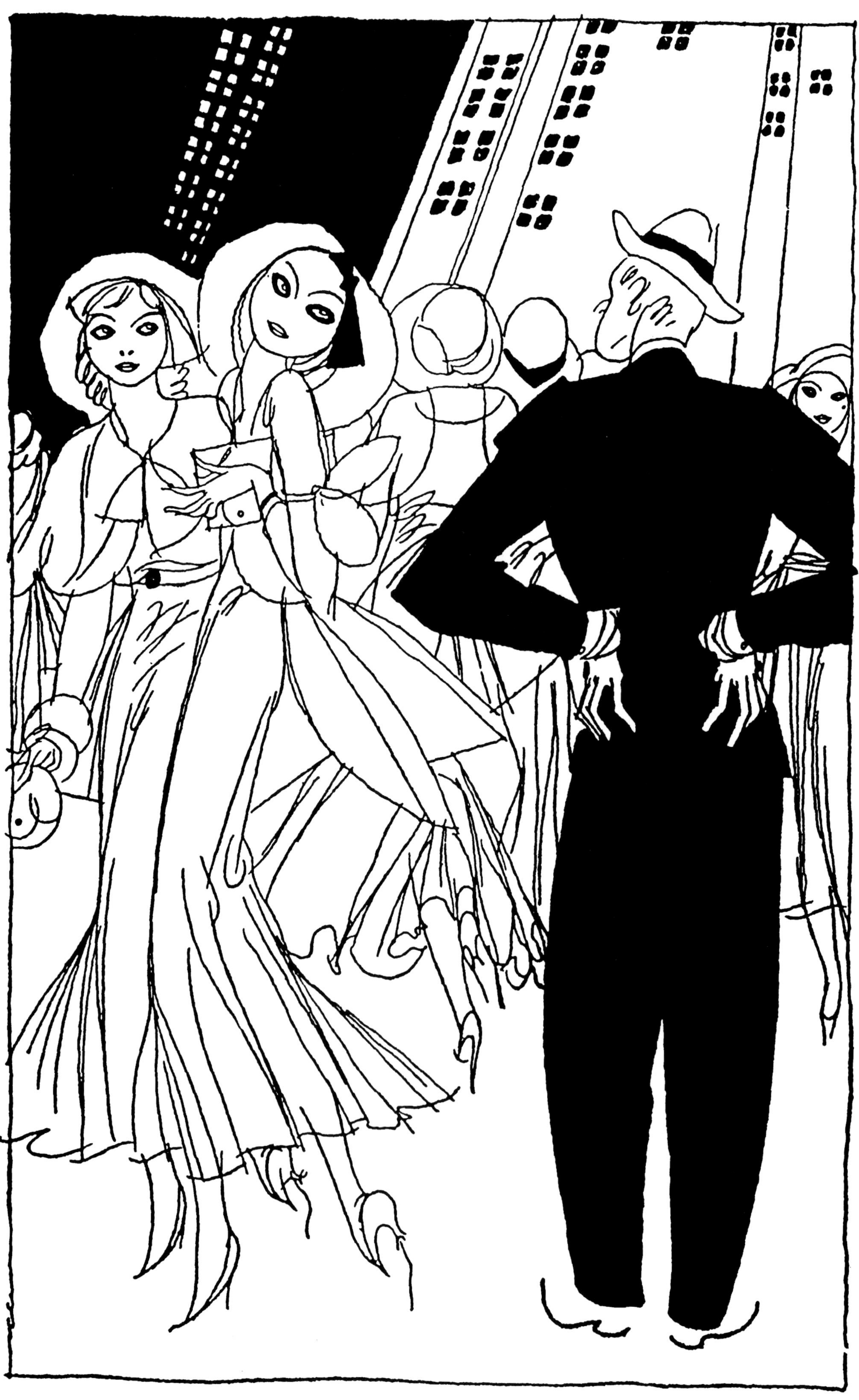

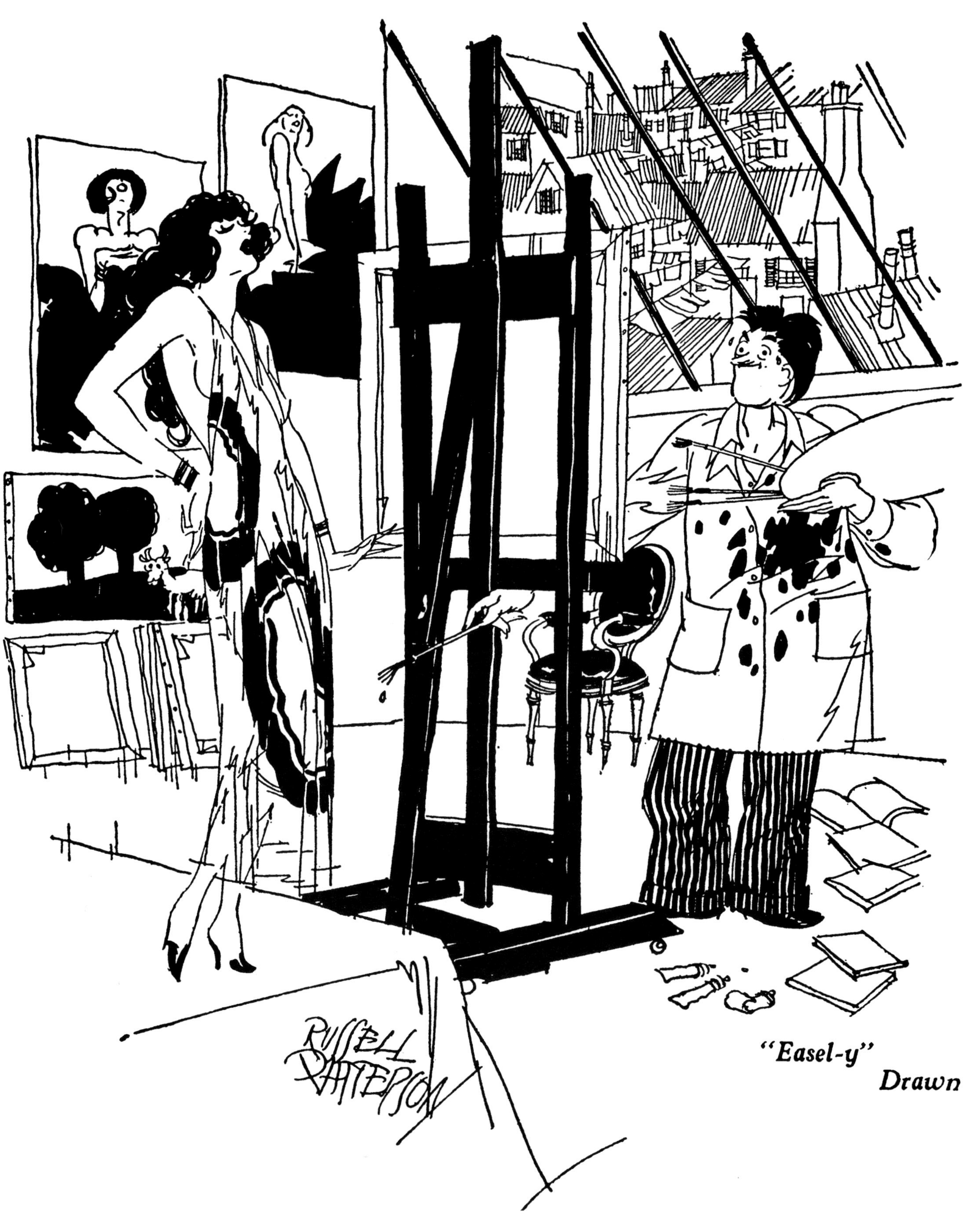

"Easel-y"
Drawn

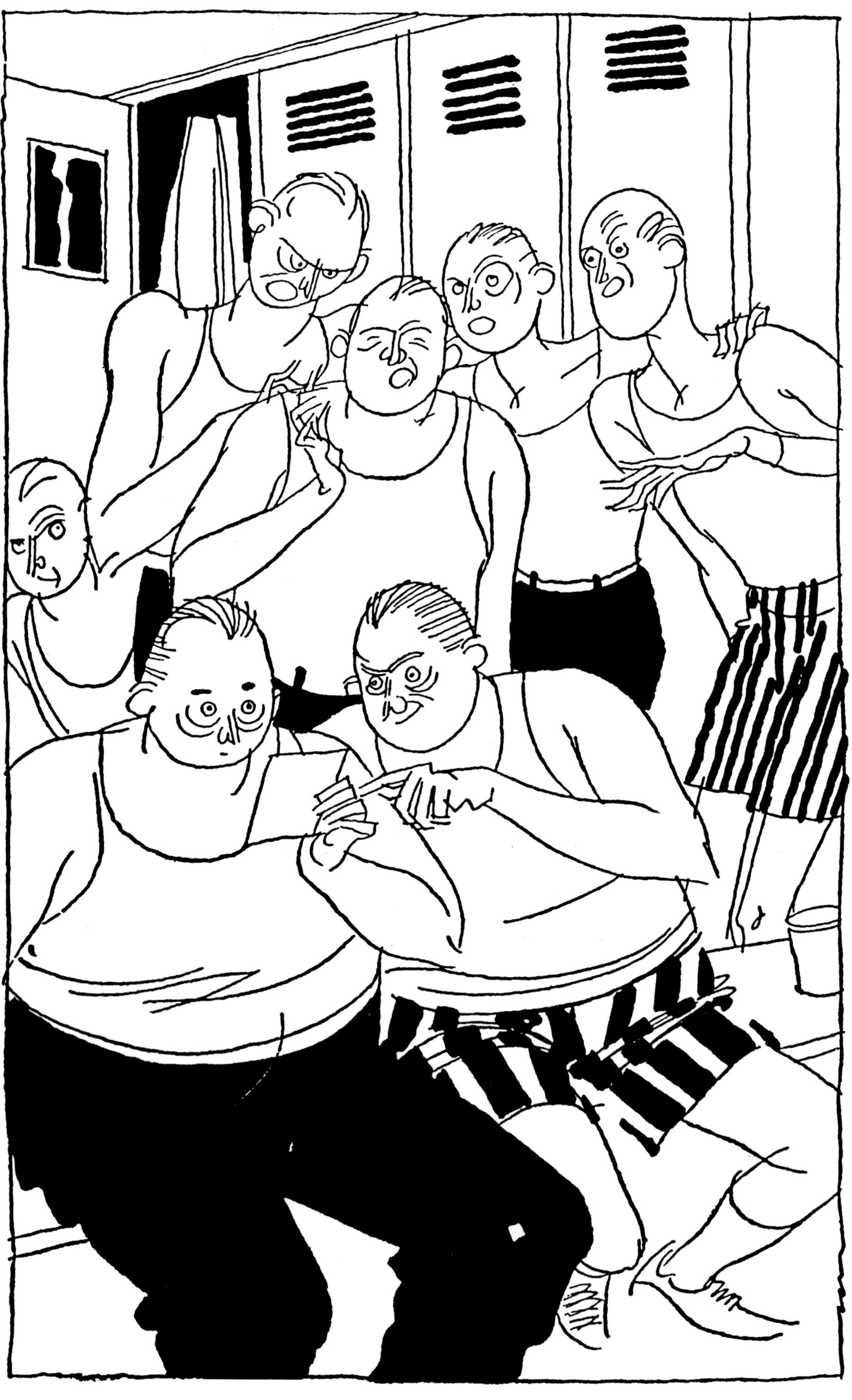

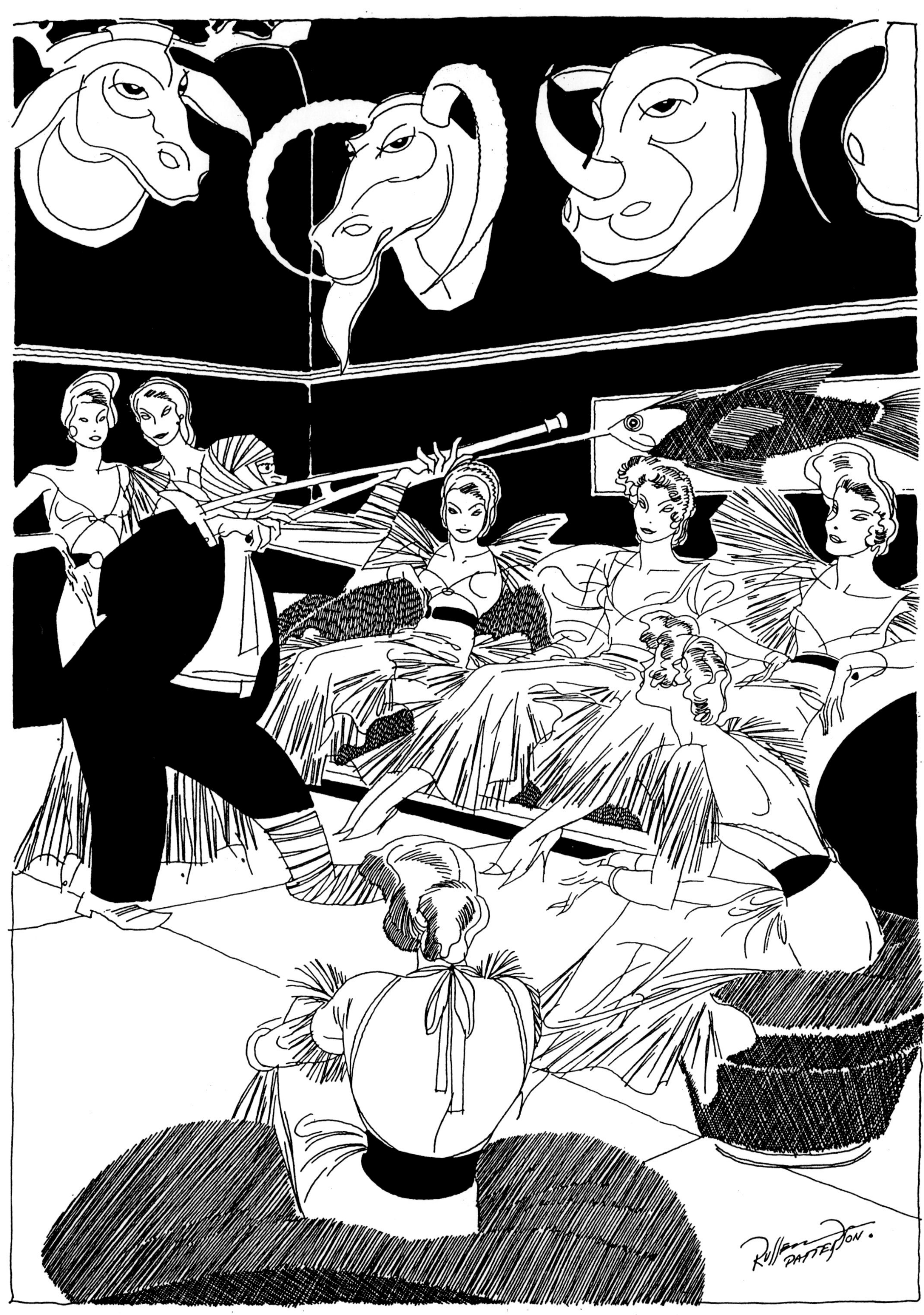

"I took steady aim and then 'click!'—the gun wasn't loaded!"

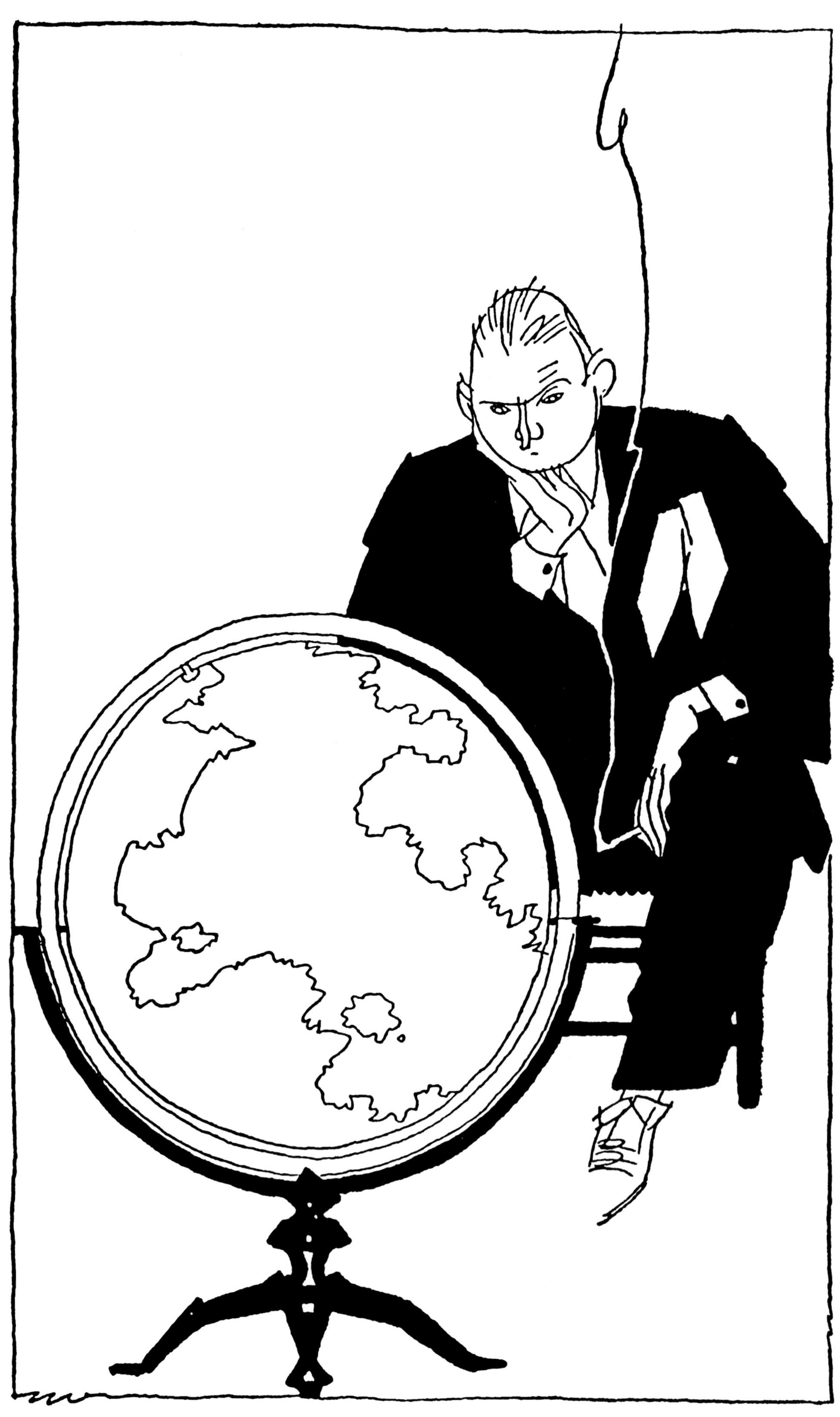

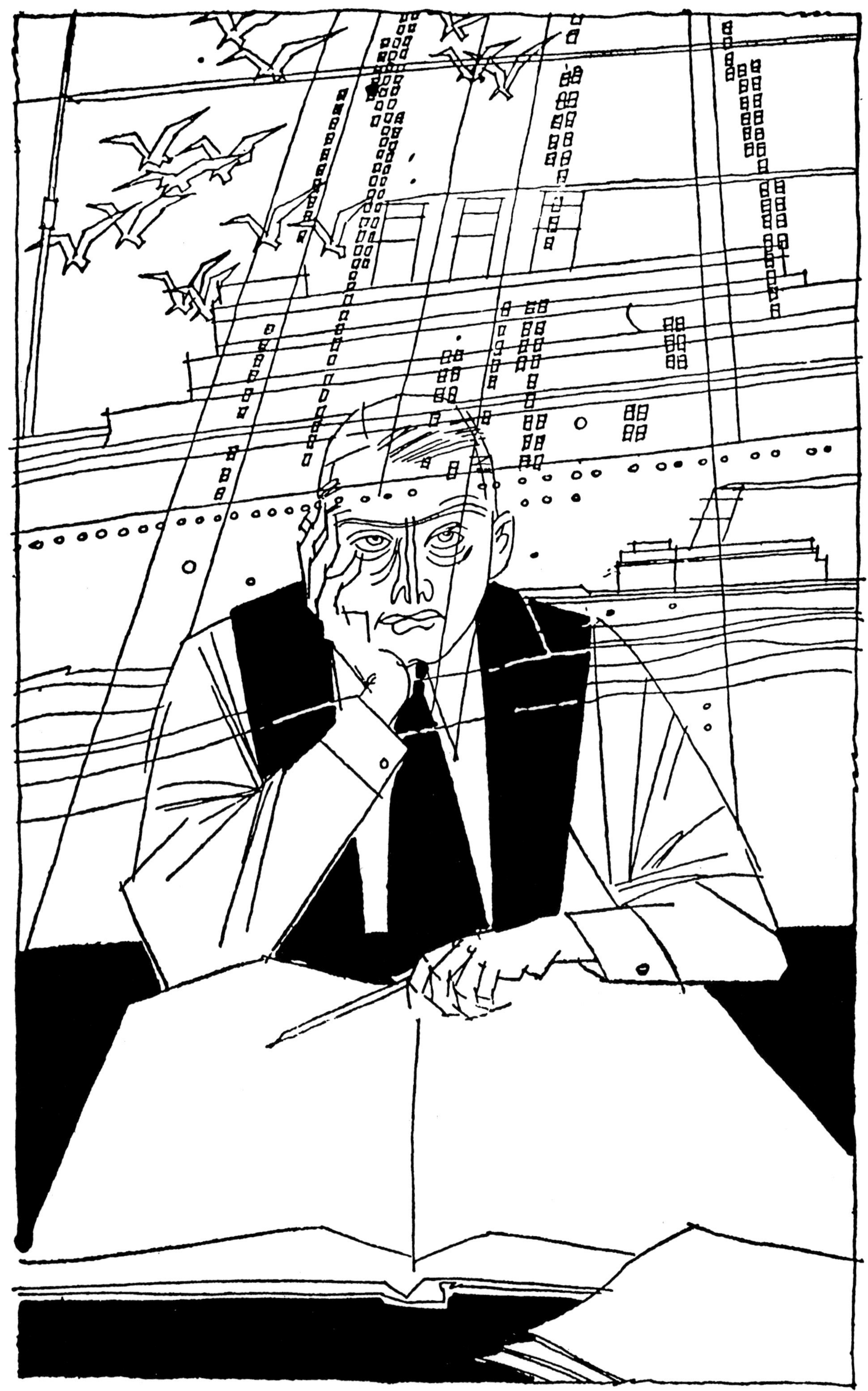

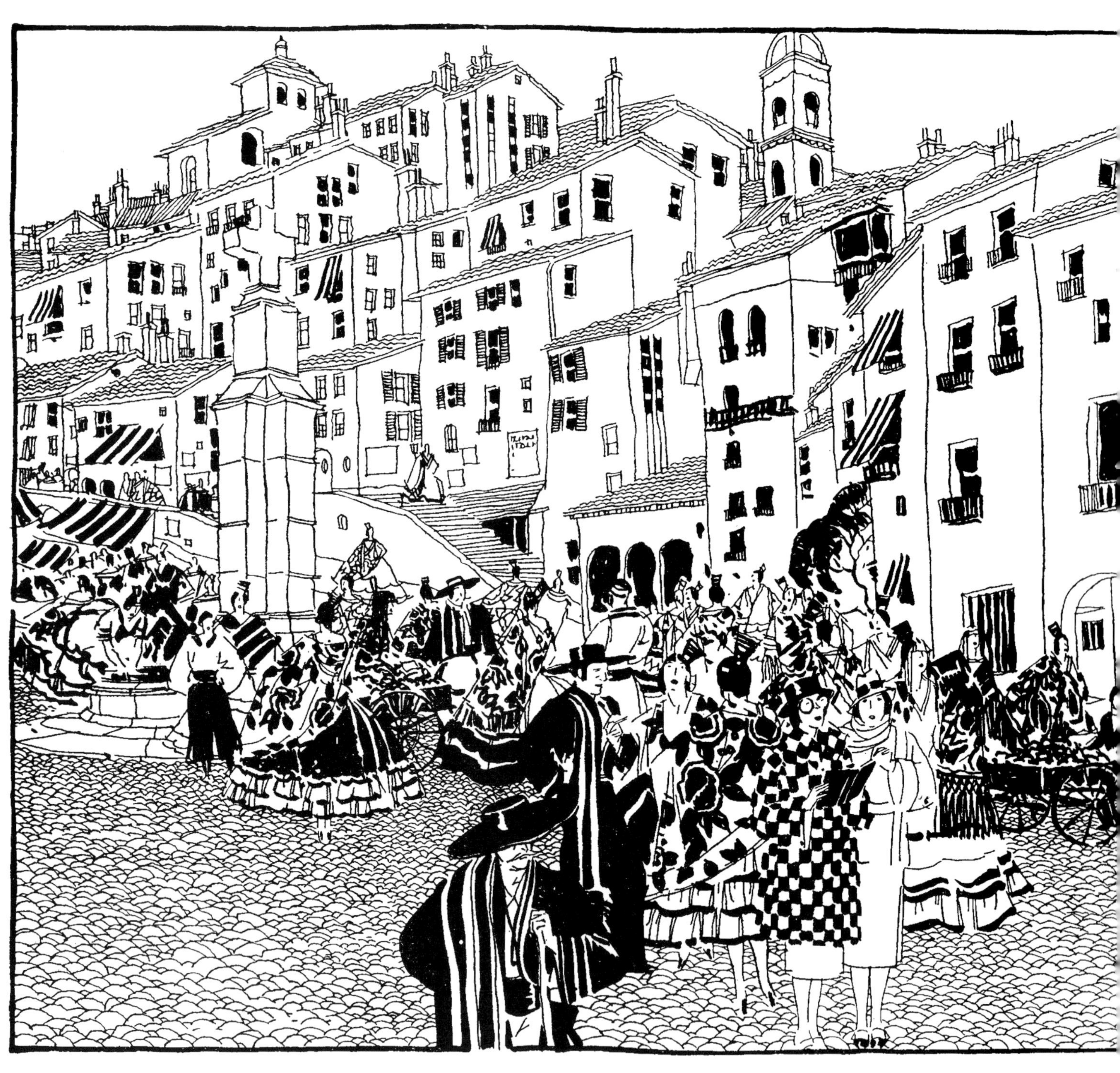

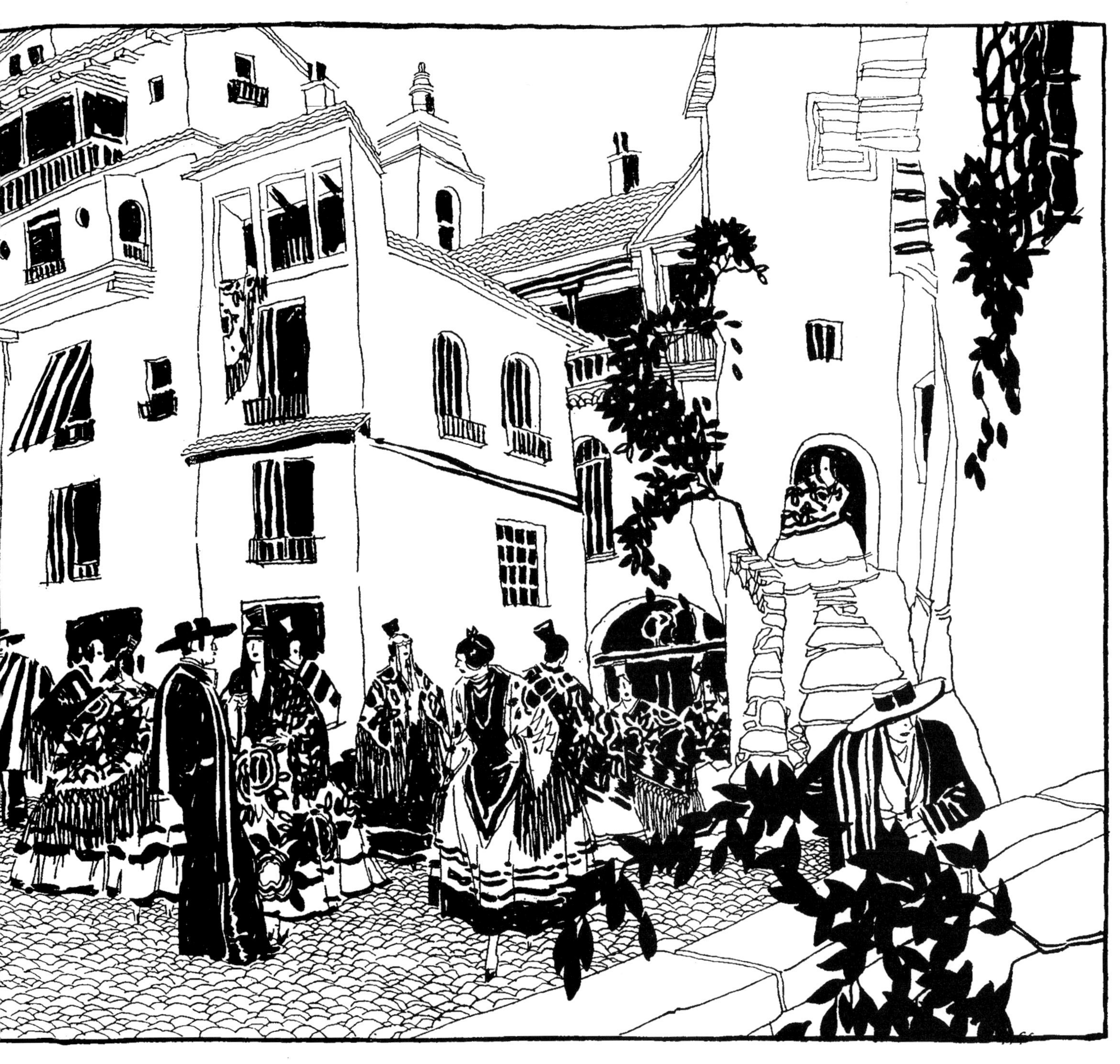

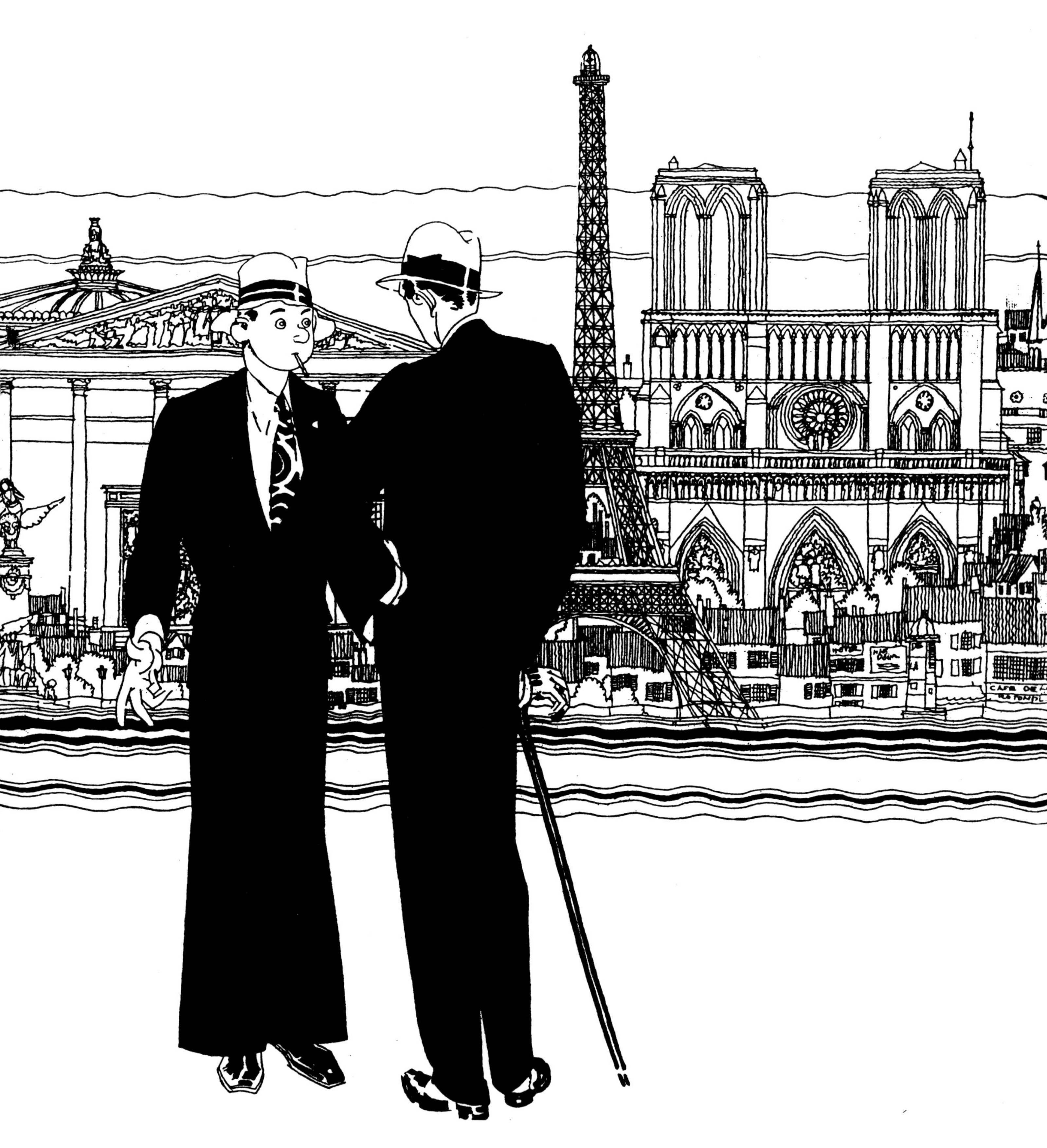

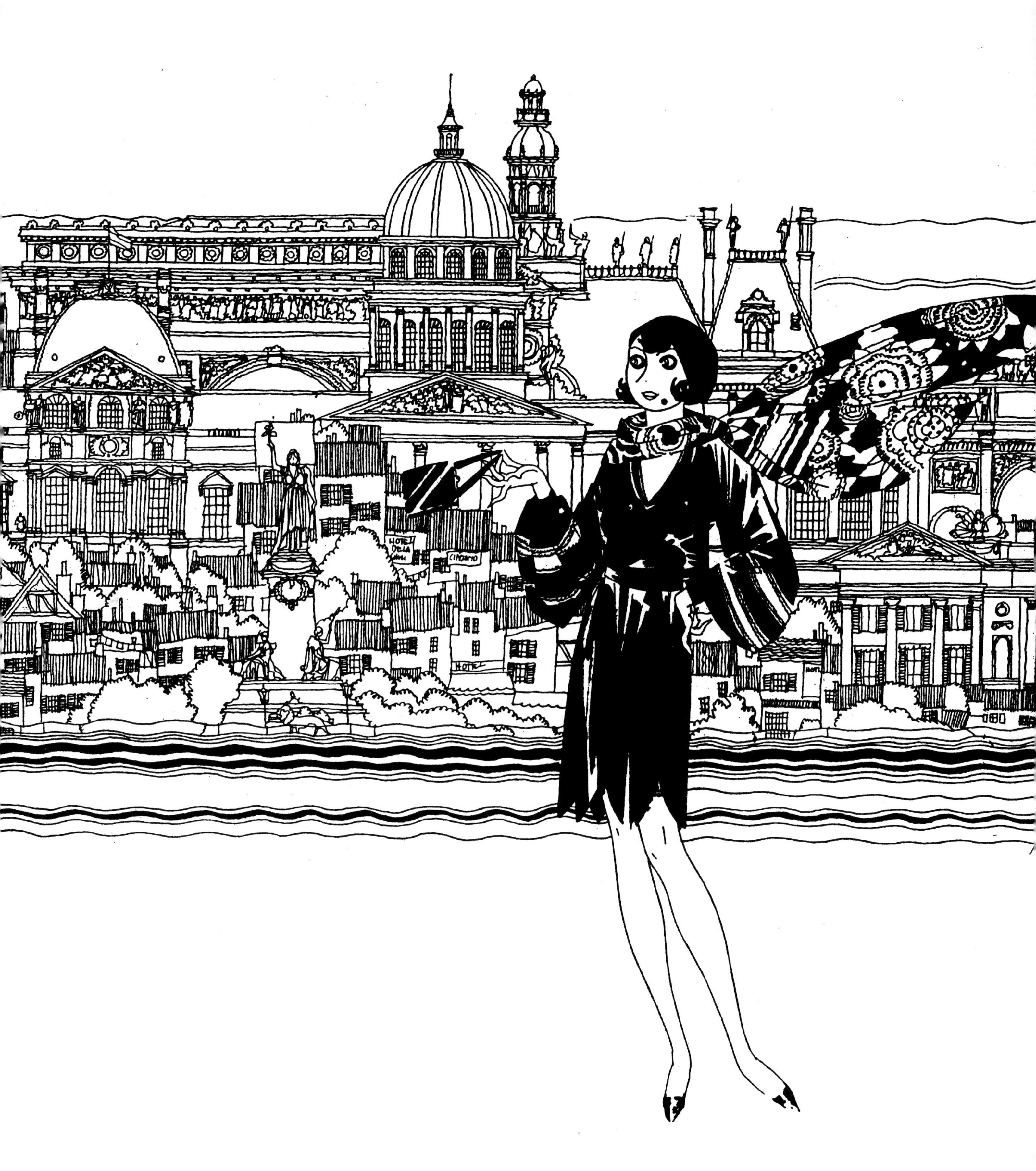

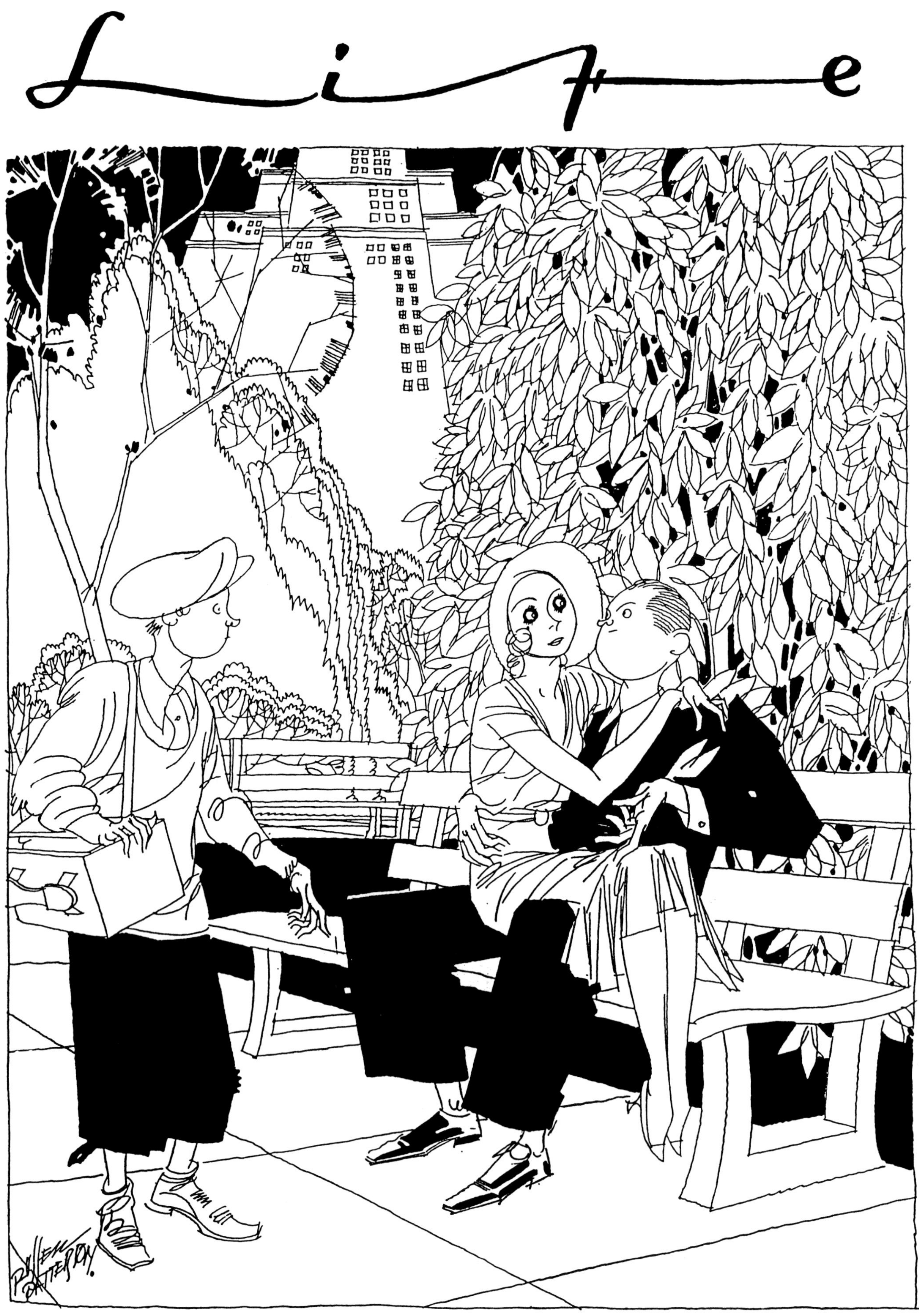

"Shine?"

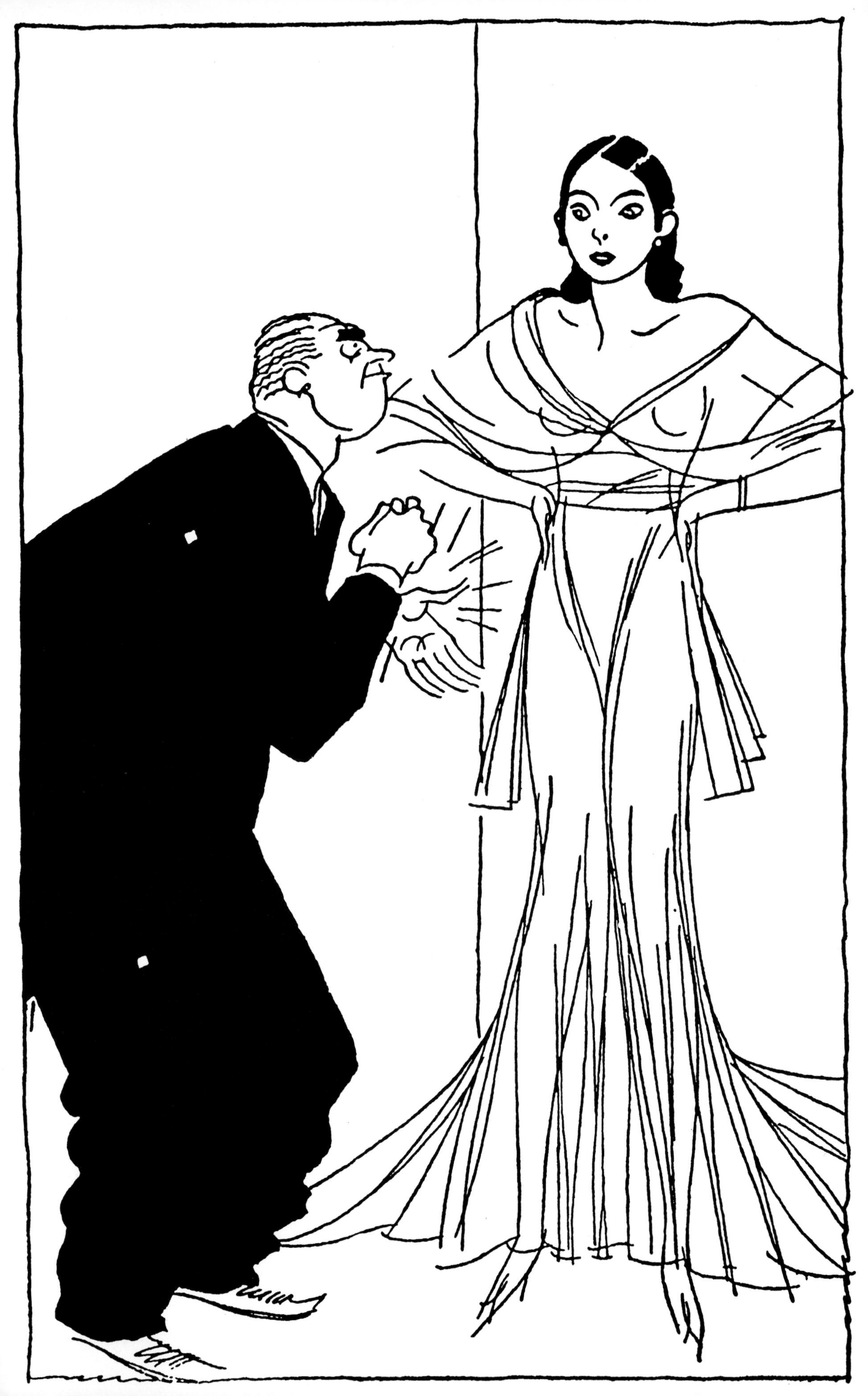

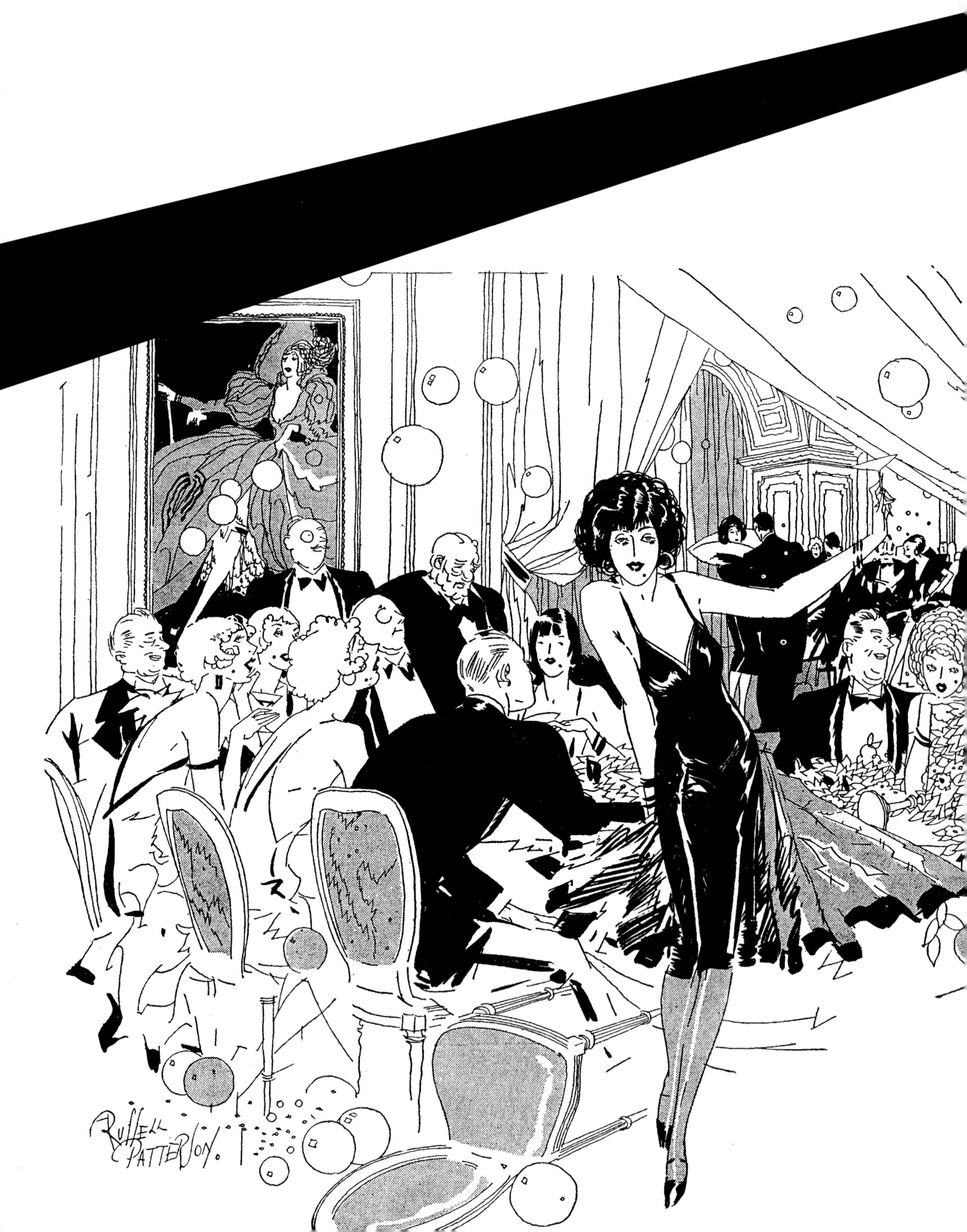
Russell Patterson.

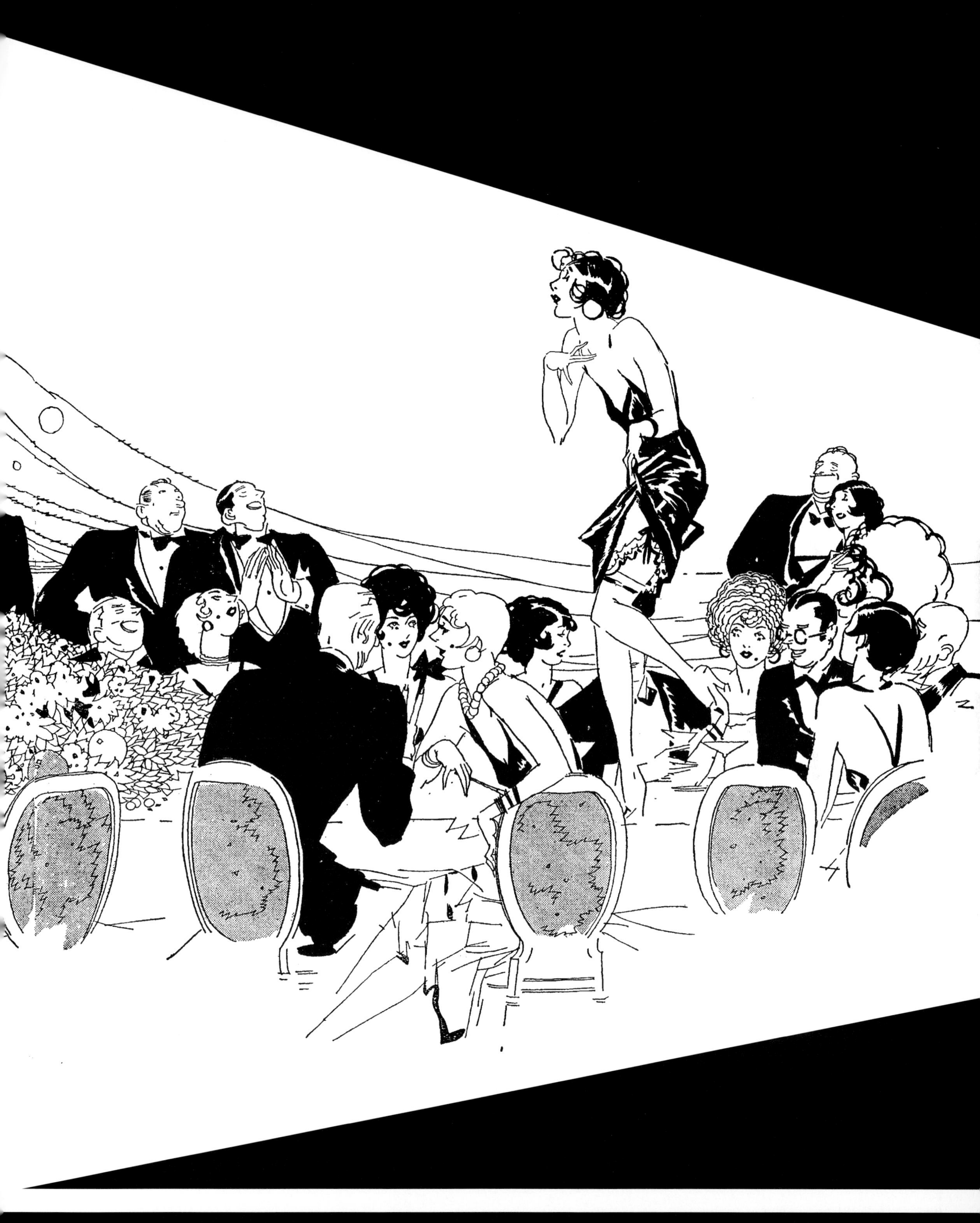

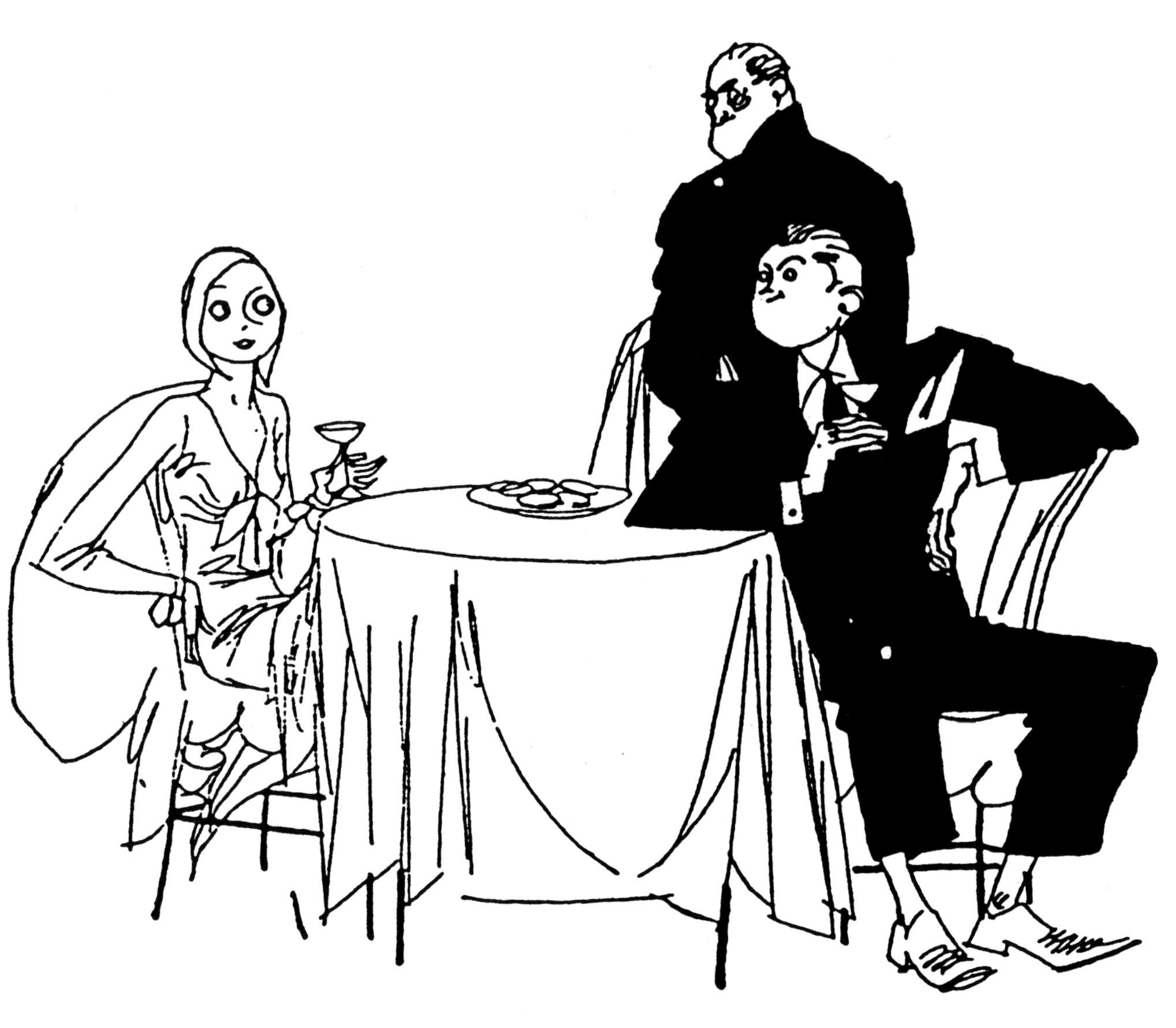

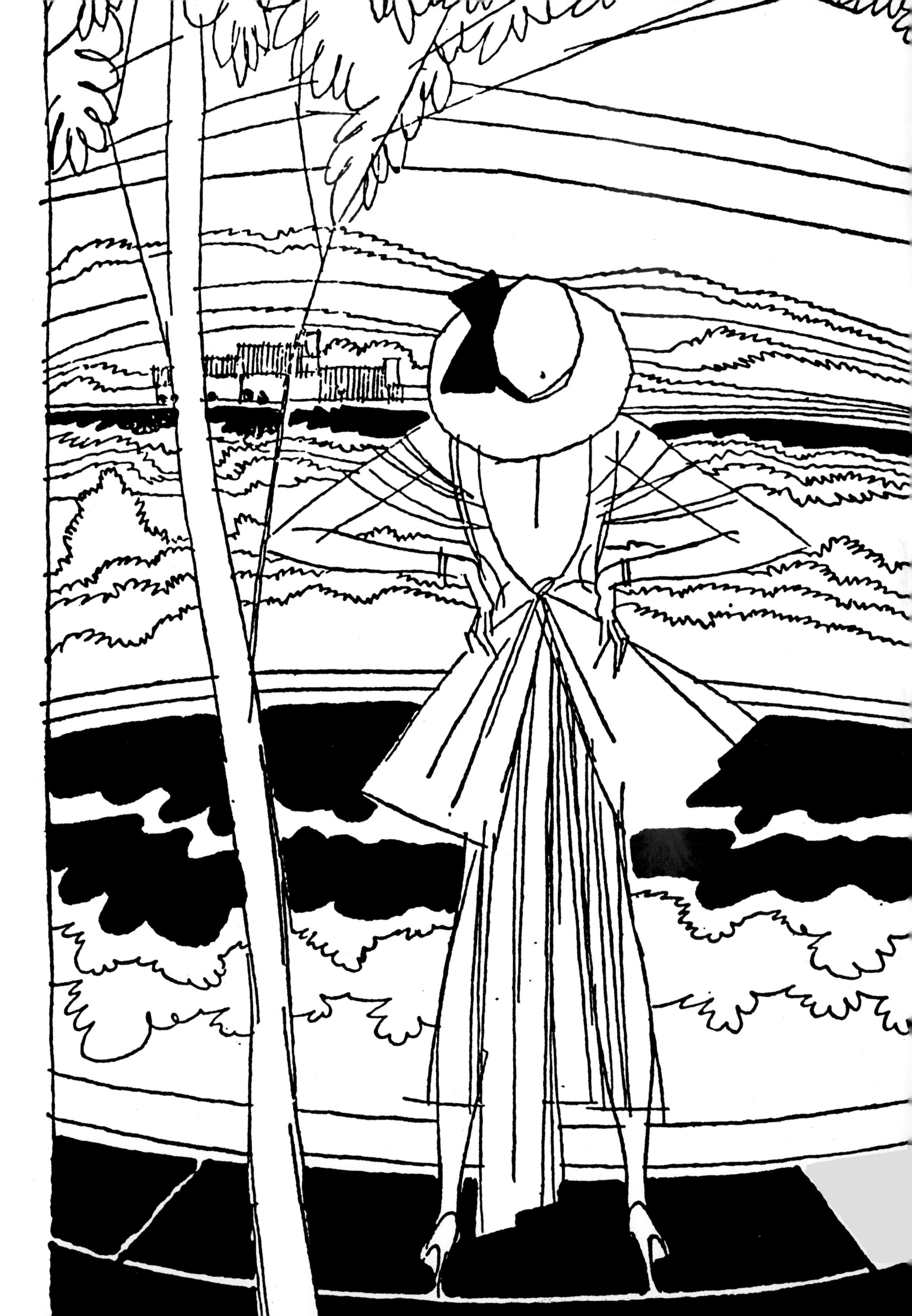

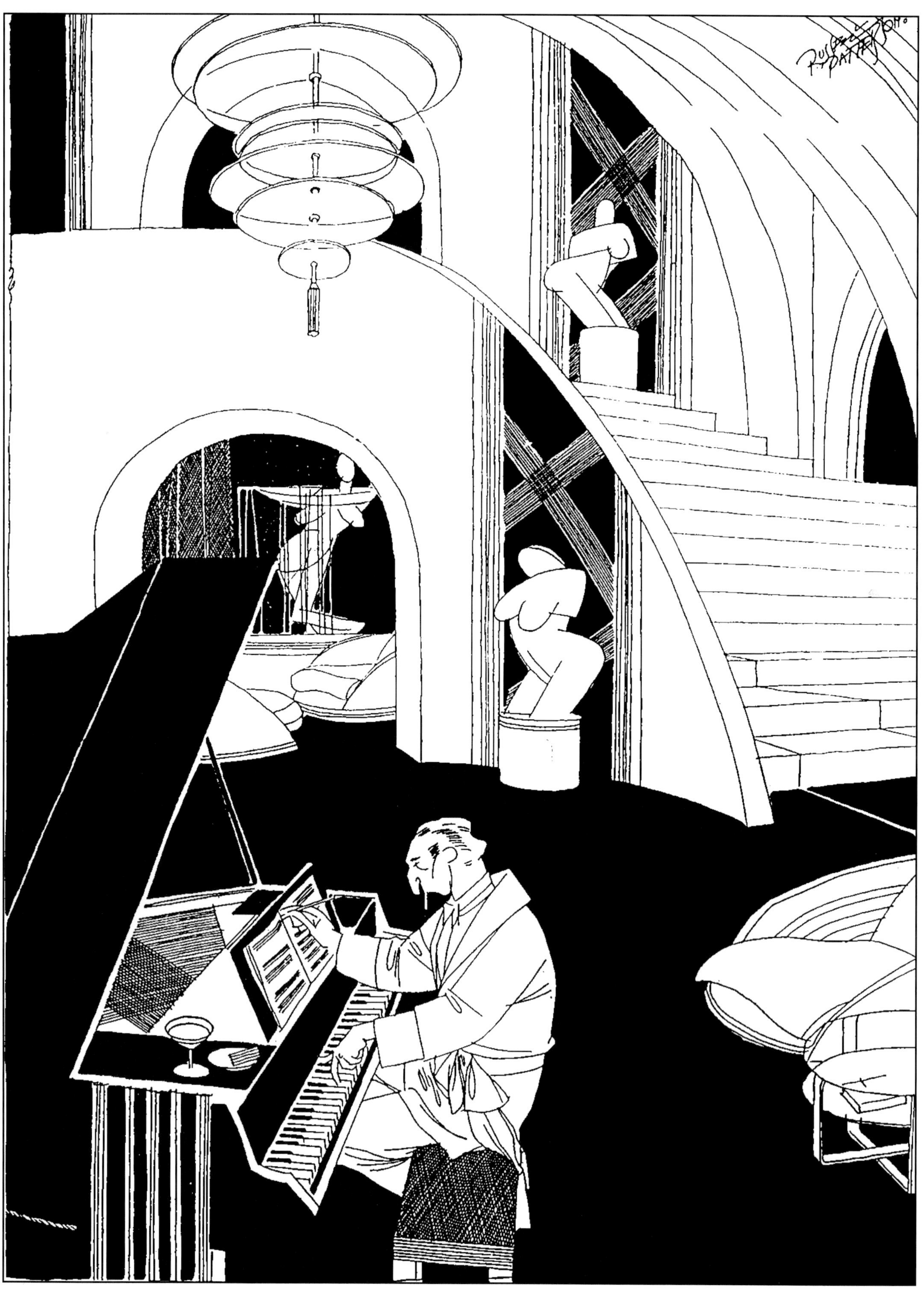

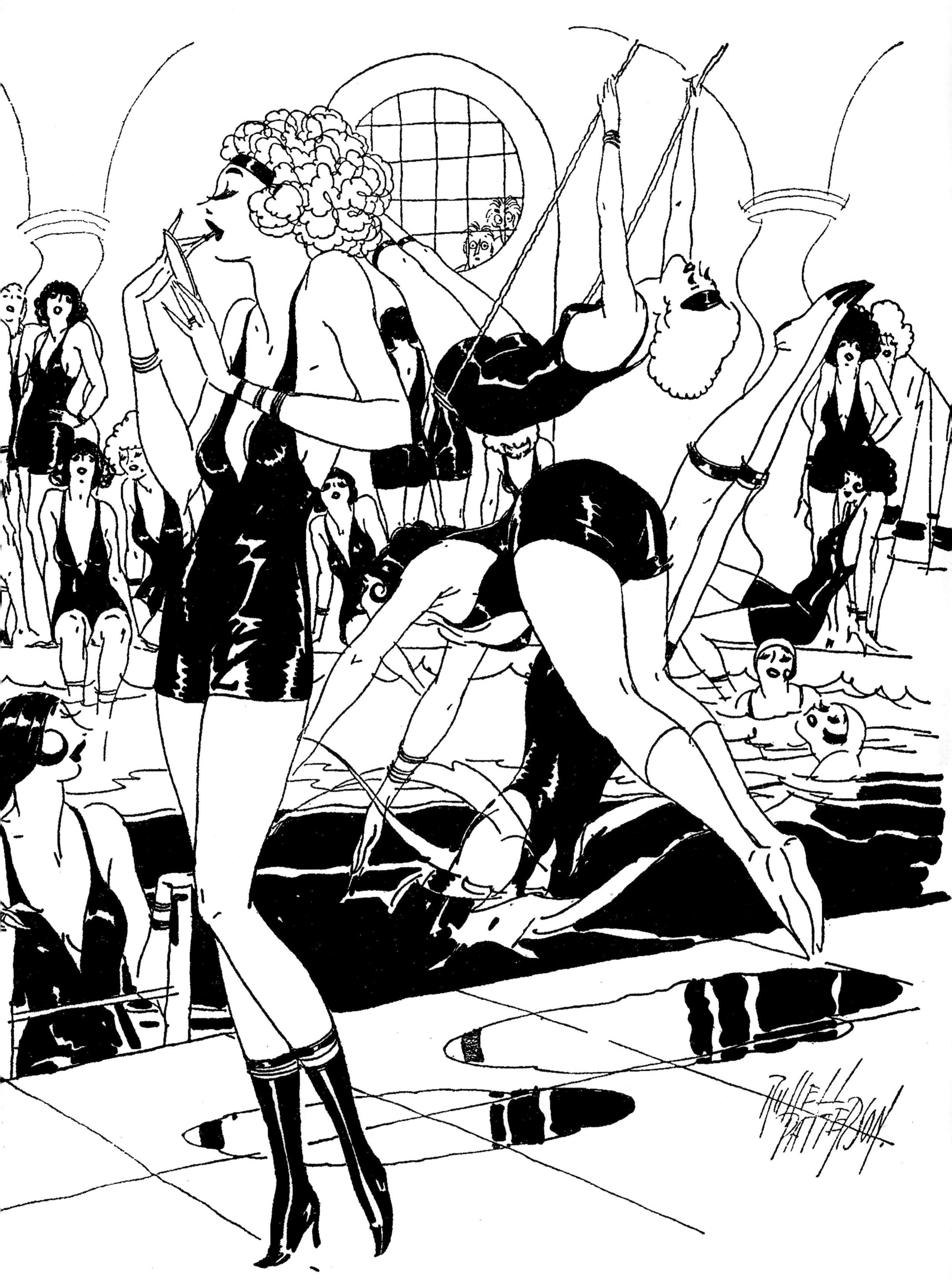

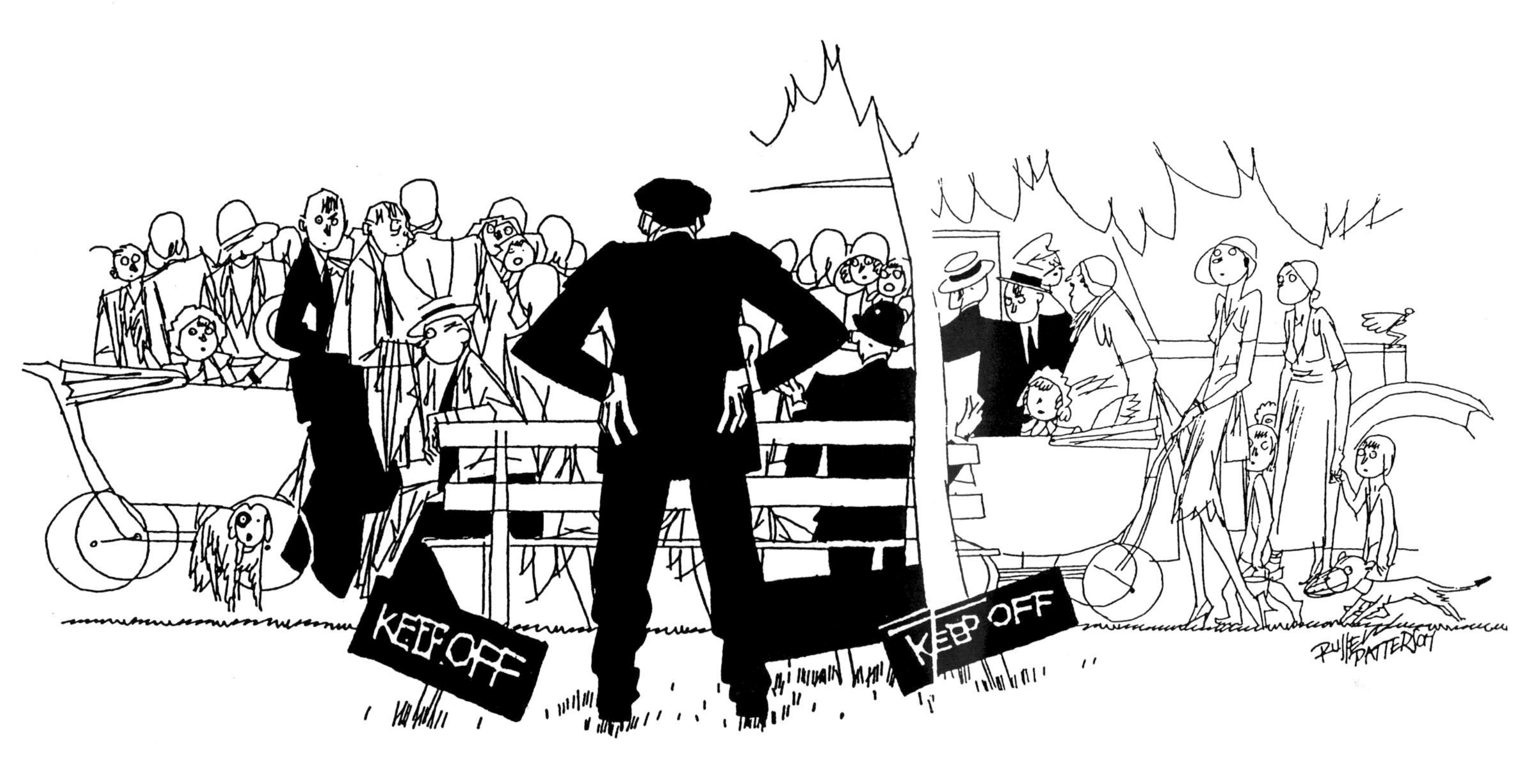
KEEP OFF
KEEP OFF
RUSSELL PATTERSON

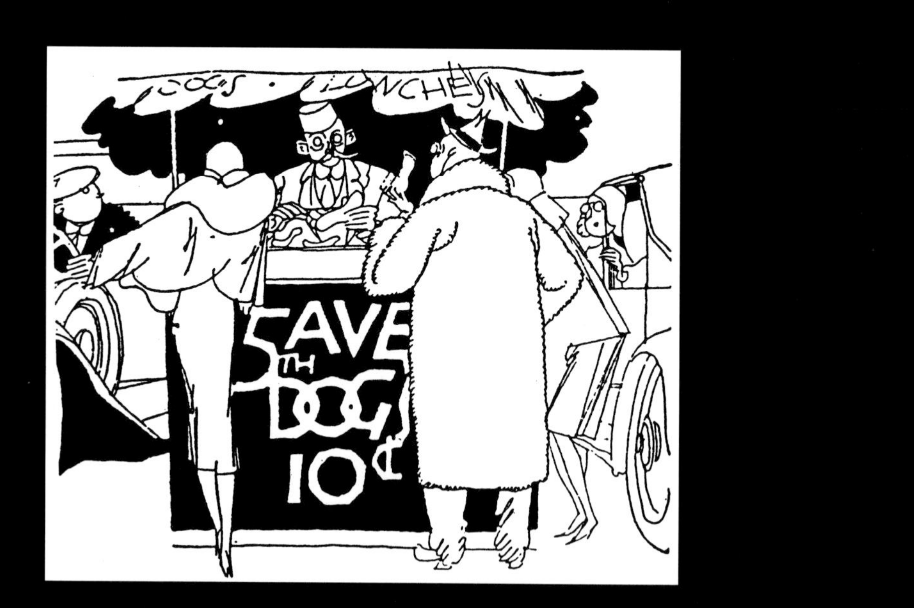

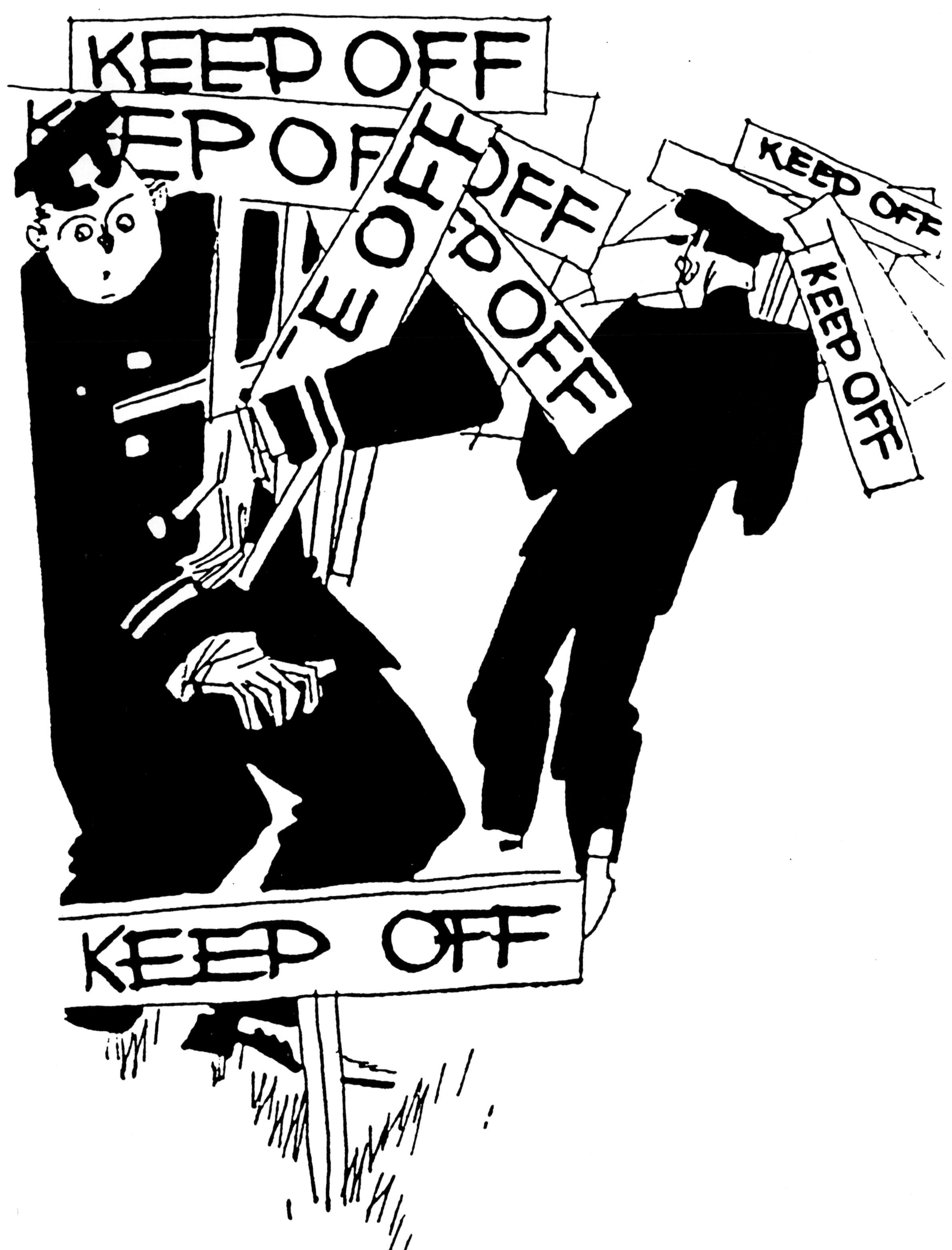
KEEP OFF
KEEP OFF
KEEP OFF
KEEP OFF

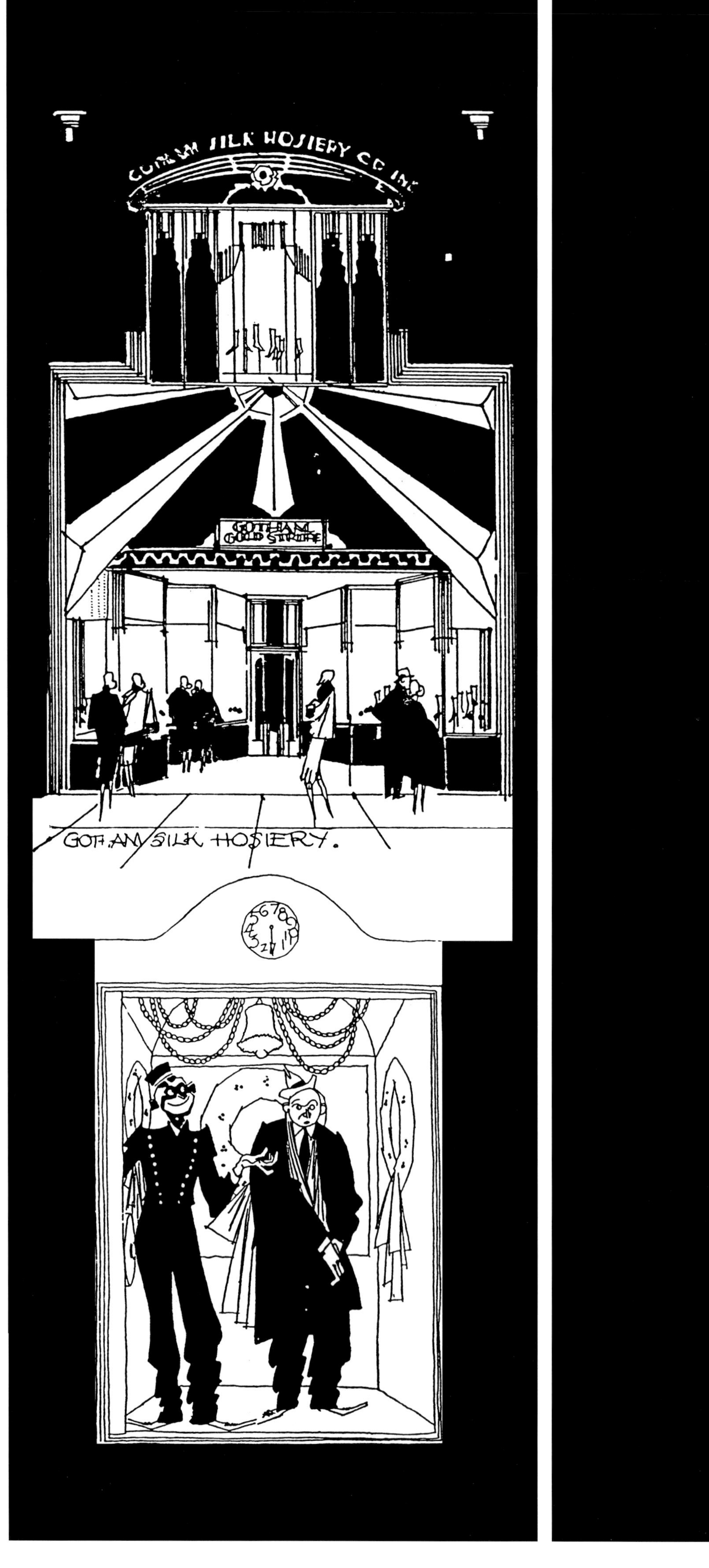
SILK HOSIERY CO INC
GOTHAM
GOLD STRIPE
GOTHAM SILK HOSIERY.

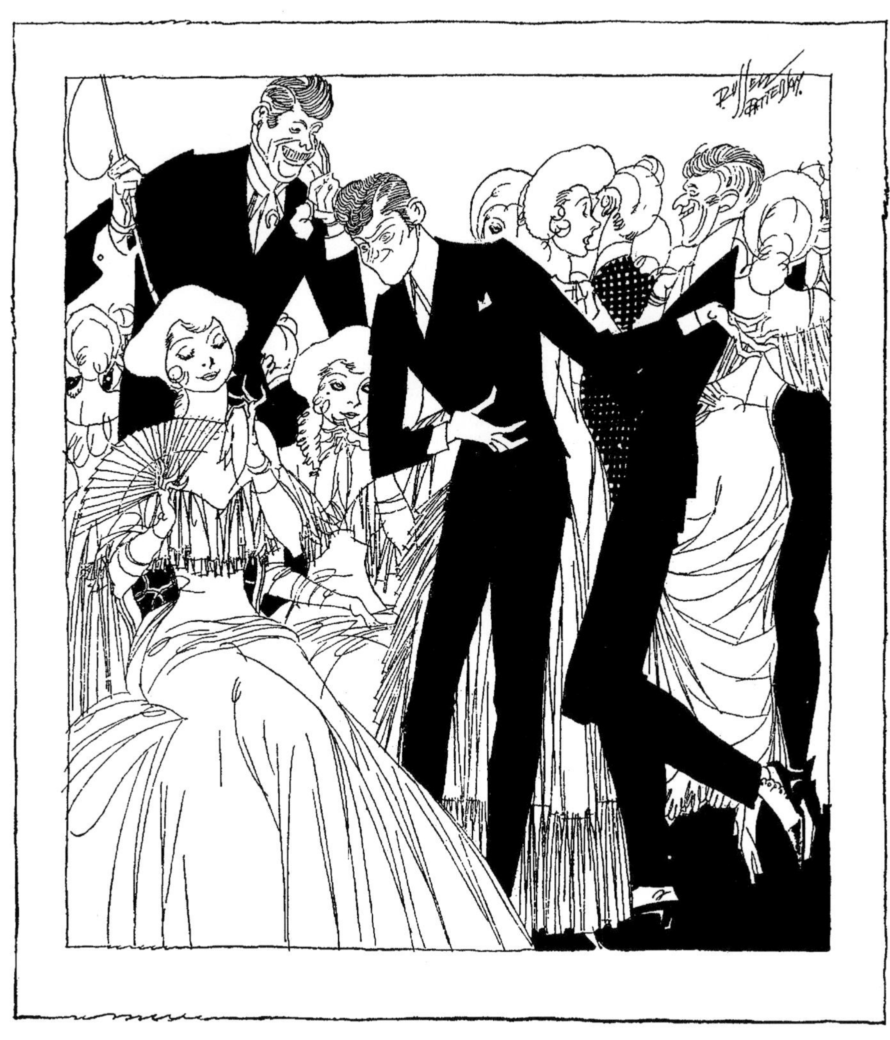

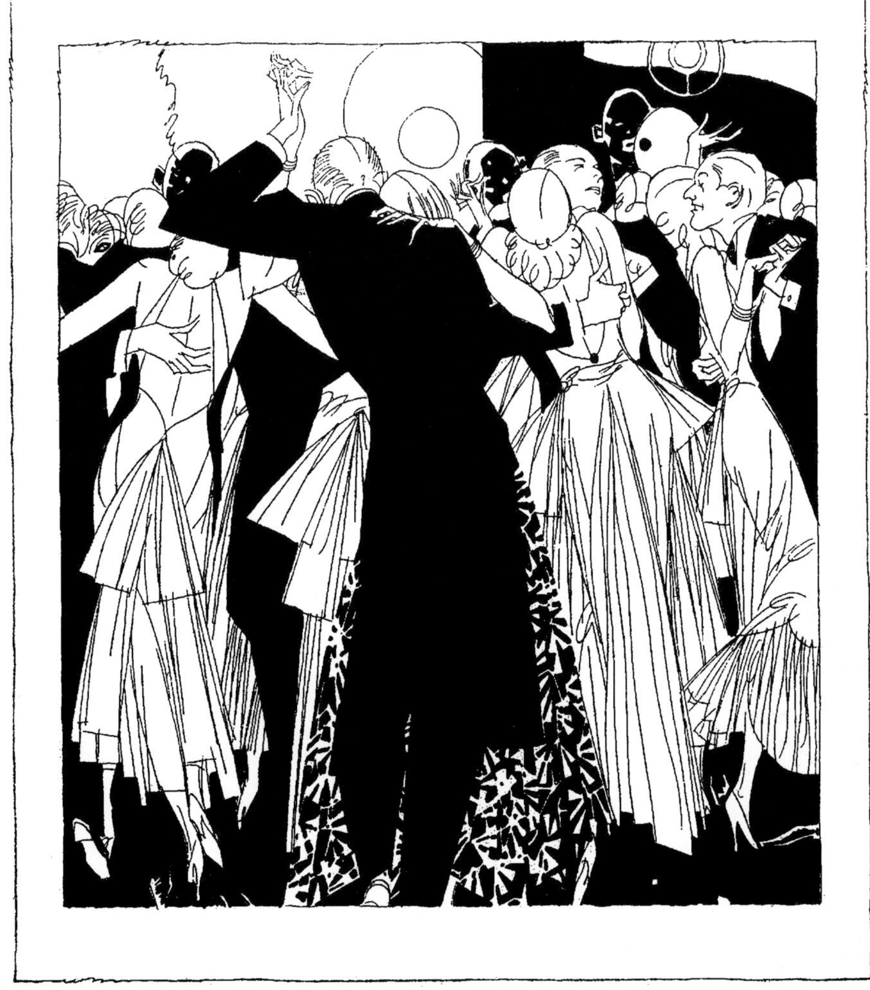

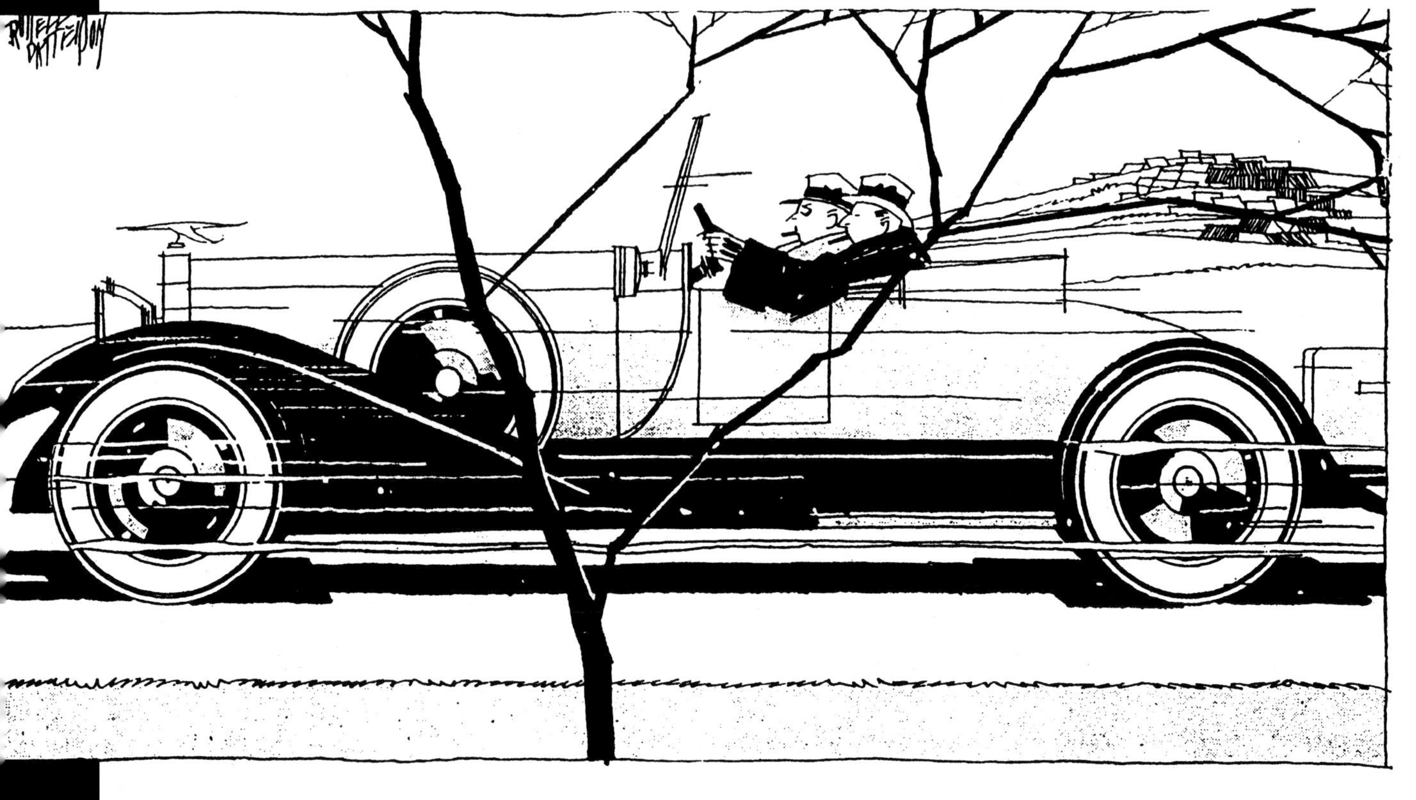

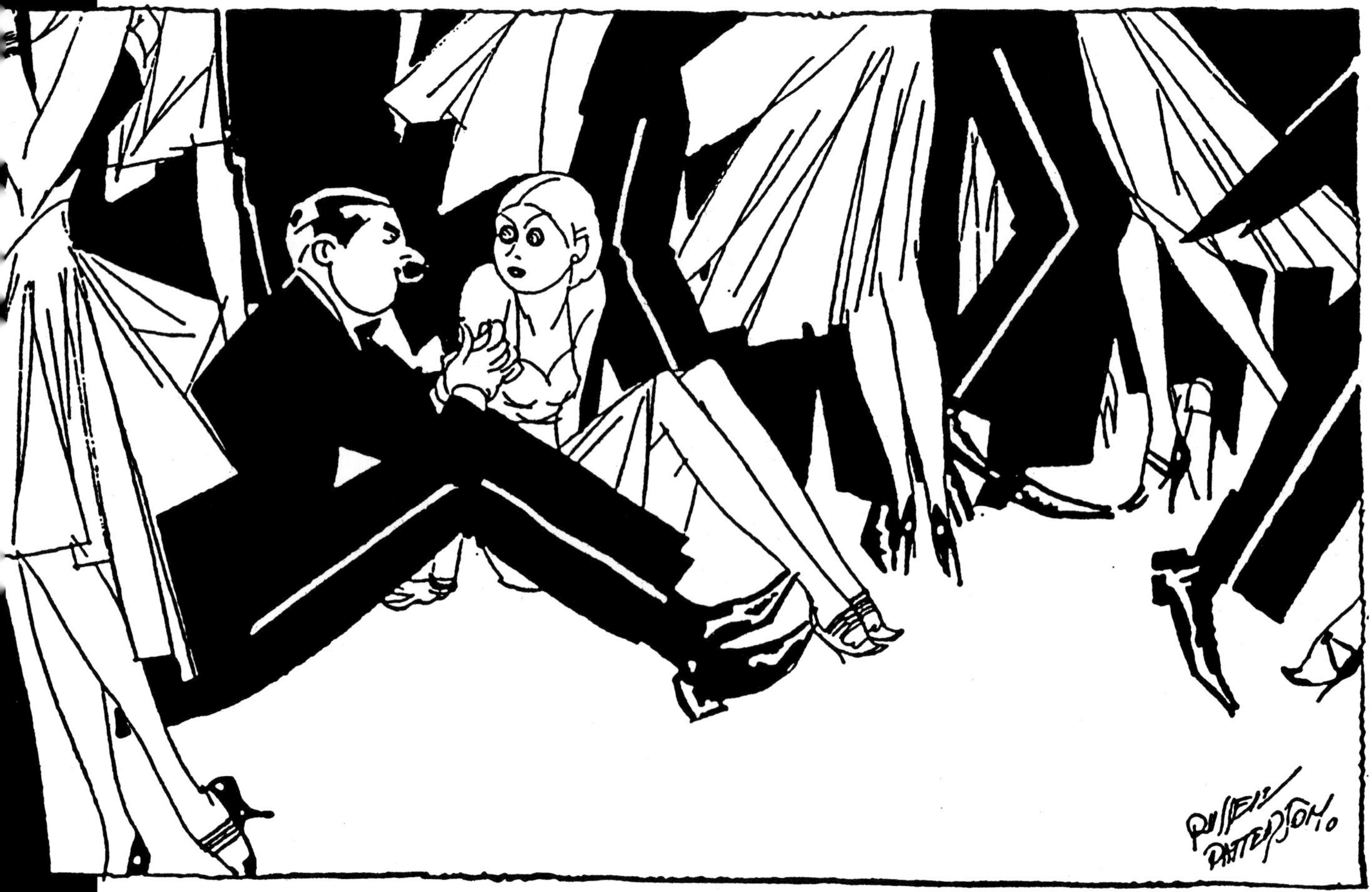

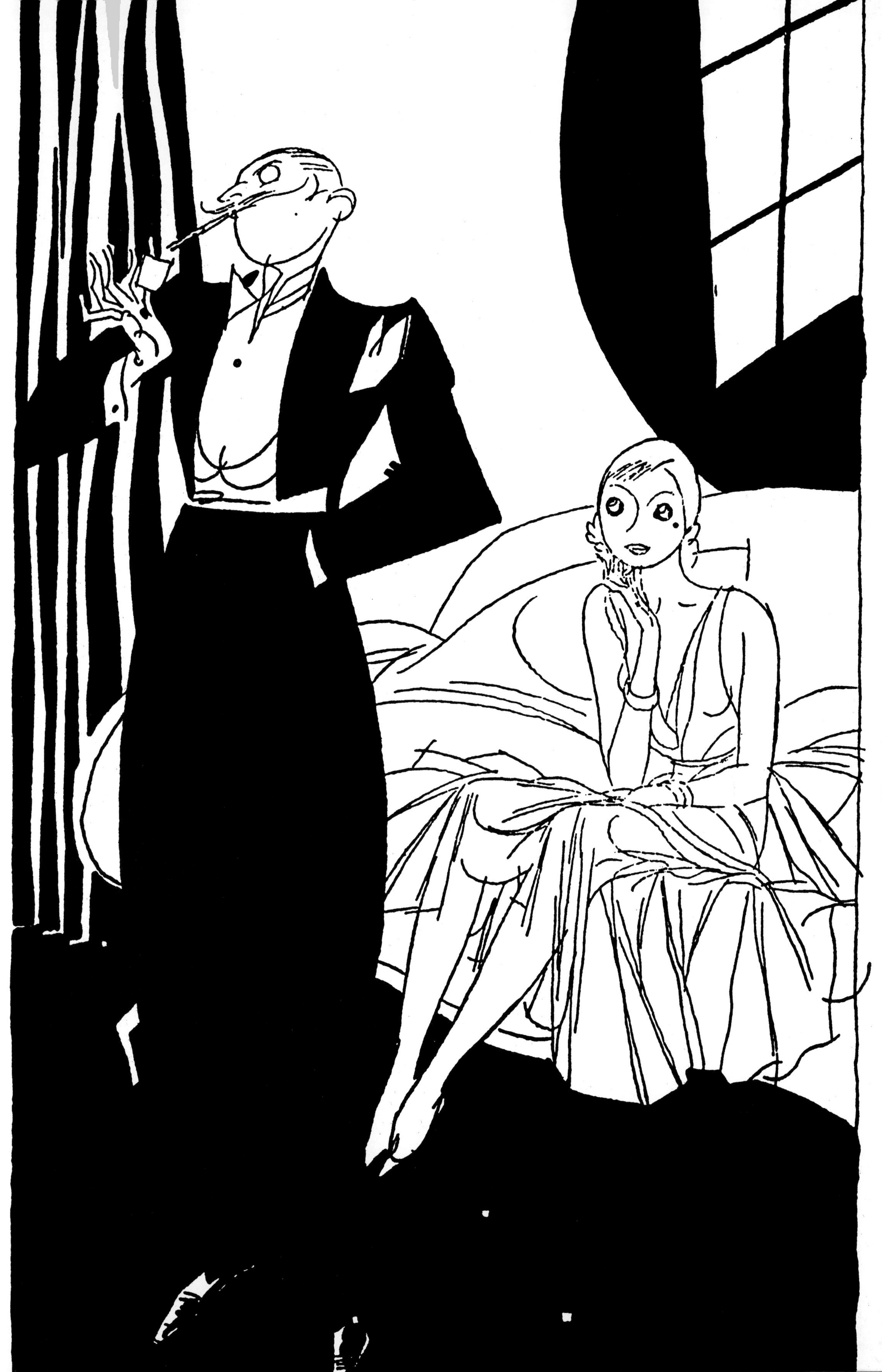

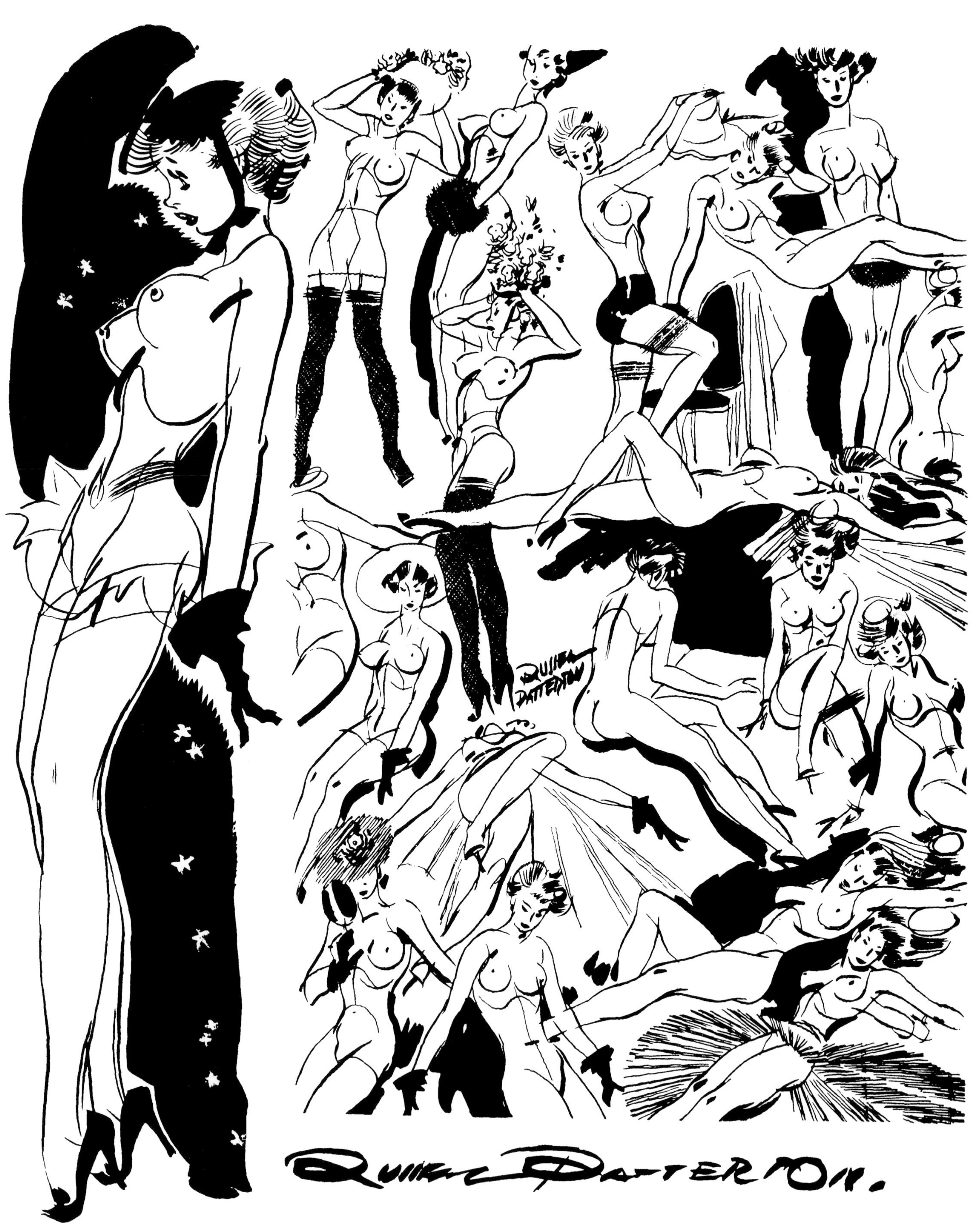

THE REUBEN AWARDS DINNER AND EVENING TONIGHT IS GIVEN IN HONOR OF THE MEMORY OF RUSSELL PATTERSON.

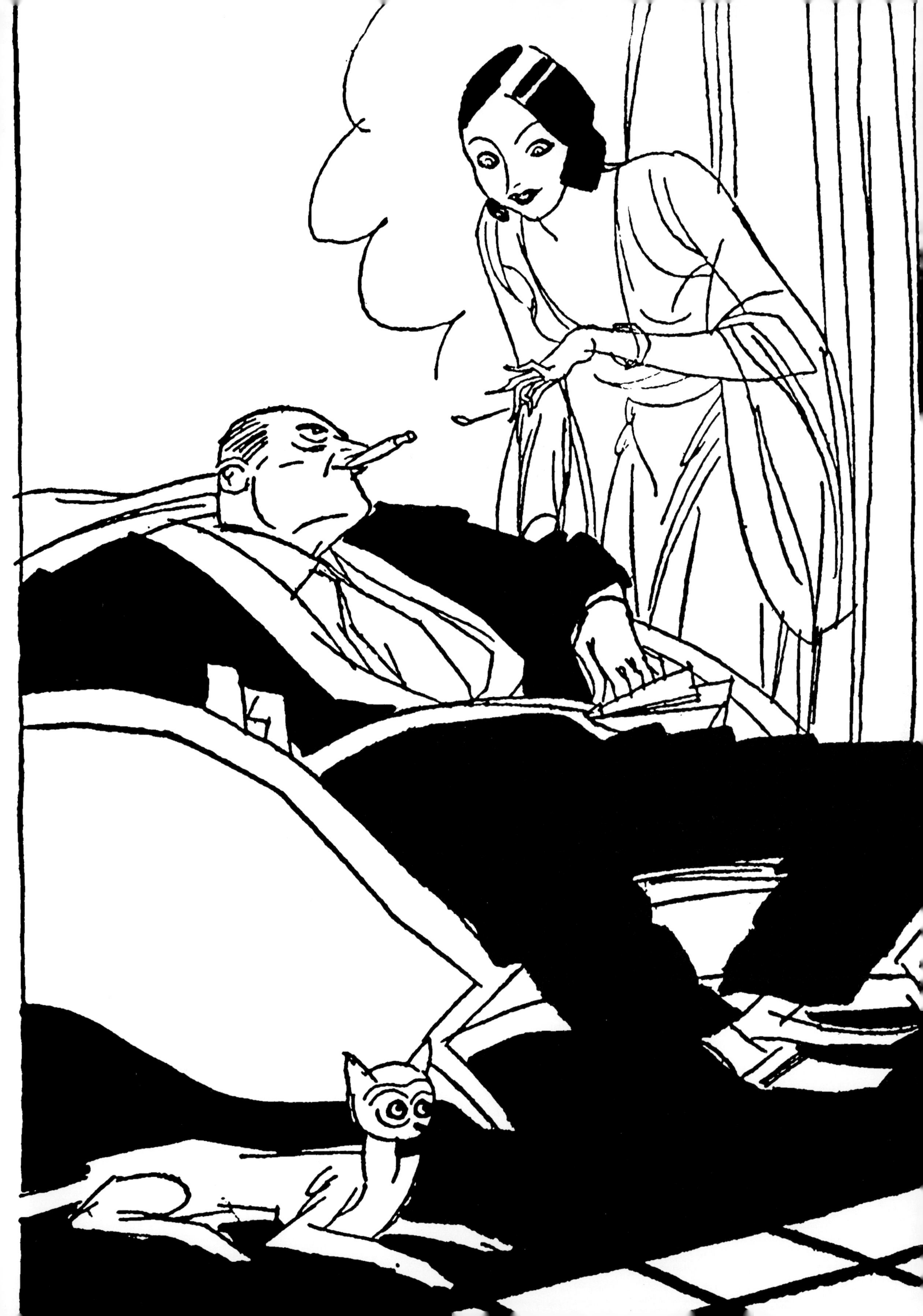

SHANE GLINES has a long resume working in the animation industry as a character designer for Spumco, Cartoon Network, Disney and Warner Bros., and is best know for his work on the *Batman*, *Superman* and *Batman Beyond* cartoons. More recently, he was the cover artist on the *Gotham Girls* mini-series and collaborated with Bruce Timm on the *Harley & Ivy* mini-series for DC Comics. He currently resides in Eugene, Oregon, where he is the proprietor of the vintage illustration archive www.cartoonretro.com.

ALEX CHUN is a longtime journalist living in Los Angeles. A former staff writer for the *Los Angeles Daily Journal*, his writing credits also include *Crain's Chicago Business*, *The Comics Journal* and *Comic Art Magazine*. He also edited a series of pin-up cartoon books for Fantagraphics, including *The Glamour Girls of Bill Ward*, *The Classic Pin-Up Art of Jack Cole* and *The Pin-Up Art of Dan DeCarlo*. In his spare time, he writes features for the *Los Angeles Times*, collects original cartoon pin-up art and maintains the website www.pinupcartoongallery.com.

ARMANDO MENDEZ lives and teaches writing in Los Angeles. Since 1999, he has written about comics, cartoon art, and Golden Age American illustration through his website *The Rules of Attraction* as well as articles on magazine illustrators, movie posters, and comic strips. Through his website and his association at comic conventions with his friend, bookseller Stuart Ng, he has enjoyed the companionship, generosity, and insight of comic art and illustration fans and professionals from all over the world.

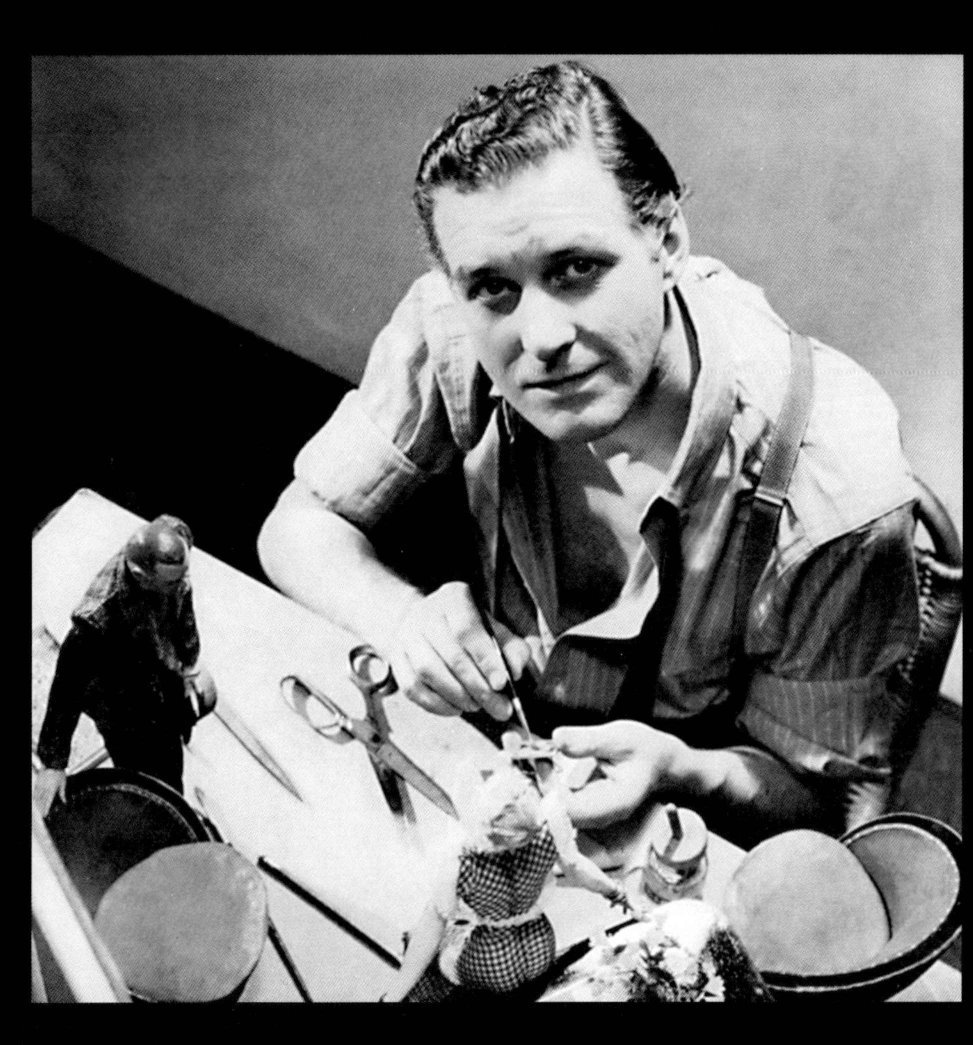

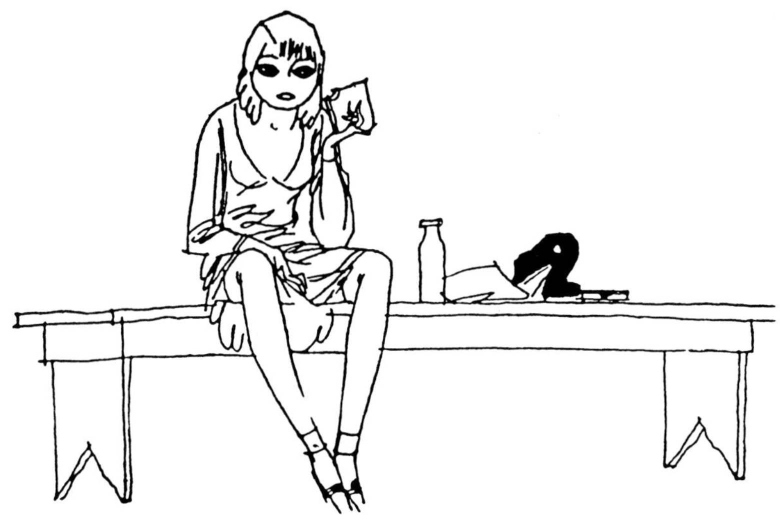